INDIAN DIASPORA
Contributions to their New Home

INDIAN DIASPORA
Contributions to their New Home

Ajay Dubey

Organisation for Diaspora Initiatives
New Delhi
in collaboration with

MD PUBLICATIONS PVT LTD
NEW DELHI
www.mdppl.com

Published by :

MD Publications Pvt Ltd
"MD House", 11, Darya Ganj,
New Delhi - 110 002
Phone : +91-11-45355555
E-mail : contact@mdppl.com
Website: www.mdppl.com

in collaboration with

Organisation for Diaspora Initiatives (www.odi.in)
New Delhi

ISBN: 978-81-7533-330-7

Published and Printed by Mr. Pranav Gupta on behalf of **MD Publications Pvt Ltd** at Times Press, New Delhi.

Notes on Contributors

Ajay Dubey

Professor, School of International Studies, Jawaharlal Nehru University, New Delhi and Editor in Chief, Diaspora Studies.

Amba Pandey

Researcher, South East Asian Studies Progremme, School of International Studies, Jawaharlal Nehru University, New Delhi.

Anand Kulkarni

Manager Policy, Department of Primary Industries, Government of Victoria, Melbourne.

Ashok Sharma

Visiting Scholar, Department of Political Science and Public Policy, The University of Waikato, Hamilton, New Zealand

Chit Dukhira

Eminent Scholar, Mauritius.

Jyoti Tyagi

Research Scholar, Centre for African Studies, School of International Studies, Jawaharlal Nehru University, New Delhi.

Kumar Mahabir

Anthropologist & Assistant Professor, School for Studies in Learning, Cognition and Education, University of Trinidad and Tobago (UTT), West Indies, Caribbean.

Lianboi Vaiphei

Assistant Professor, Department of Political Science, Indraprastha College for Women, Delhi University.

L. Vijayanathan

Senior Advisor, Royal Norwegian Embassy, New Delhi.

Pankaj Jha

Associate Fellow, Institute for Defence Studies and Analyses, New Delhi.

Prabodh Malhotra

Researcher, Centre for Strategic Economic Studies, Victoria University, Melbourne.

Prakash C. Jain

Professor, Centre for West Asian Studies, School of International Studies, Jawaharlal Nehru University, New Delhi.

Rajneesh Kumar Gupta

Research Fellow, Indian Institute of Foreign Trade (IIFT), New Delhi.

R.L. Chawla

Associate Professor, School of International Studies, Jawaharlal Nehru University, New Delhi.

Sadananda Sahoo

Lecturer, School of Interdisciplinary and Transdisciplinary Studies, Indira Gandhi National Open University, New Delhi.

Sasmita Mohanty

Research Scholar, Centre for African Studies, School of International Studies, Jawaharlal Nehru University, New Delhi.

Vidhan Pathak

Former Faculty, Department of Political Science & IR, Dire Dawa University, Ethiopia. Presently Post Doctoral Fellow at School of International Studies, Jawaharlal Nehru University, New Delhi.

PREFACE

Indians abroad are part of both classical and modern diaspora communities. The bulk of Indians, who during ancient times emigrated to Myanmar, China, and parts of South-East Asia and Central Asia as preachers and traders, were assimilated locally and became part of a latent or lost Indian diaspora. However, Indian migrants who relocated during colonial times have still retained their distinctiveness as Indian communities, manifesting varying degrees of identity. During the colonial period, almost all Indian migrants advanced up the socio-economic ladder within their respective, adopted countries. In many cases, their economic and professional growth had been quite outstanding and disproportionately higher than what their numbers would suggest. So, too, is the modern Indian diaspora that migrated after the Second World War, forming communities that are often prosperous, and economically, professionally and educationally highly developed.

The relatively advanced economic and professional position of Indians in the diaspora created an impression among local communities of Indian migrants as inward-looking and unwilling to make significant contributions to their newly adopted countries. Academic and research work on the Indian diasporas in the twentieth century remained largely focused on issues of discrimination perpetrated against them, efforts at integrating them into their host societies, and so on.

Since the mid-1990s, an about-turn in Indian foreign policy towards its diaspora has led to a pro-active association with its 'old' as well as 'new' diasporas. Unfortunately, this policy shift added further fuel to the mistaken belief of host communities, where Indian diasporas are located, that Indian migrants are just focused on their own advancement and interests; moreover, that they now intend to contribute actively to the growth of their mother country. This negative perception is amplified by a belief that while migrants did not contribute much earlier, they may now have an even less-focused commitment to the growth of their host countries. It is from this perspective that this work on the Indian diaspora examines the issues, extent, and dimensions of their contributions to their new home countries. In the context of the pro-active policy of the Indian government, its diaspora is less likely to respond positively if they are not confident of, and are not appreciated for, their contributions to their host countries. By focusing on these neglected aspects of the Indian diaspora, the book intends to initiate research, documentation, and novel assessments of the contributions made by the Indian diaspora to their newly adopted home countries.

Ajay Dubey
School of International Studies
Jawaharlal Nehru University, New Delhi

Introduction

The Indian overseas community, estimated at over 25 million, is spread across 196 countries. It includes the foreign citizens of Indian origin who are called People of Indian Origin (PIO), and Indian passport holders based in foreign countries known as Non-Resident Indians (NRI). This community comprises of various ethnic, linguistic and religious groups, which reflect the cultural and regional diversity of India. Migration patterns are varied in terms of historical context, causes and consequences, and Indians emigrated in different migration bursts and occupational capacities. During ancient times, they went as merchants and explorers from western India to Africa and the Middle East. From the eastern part of South India, they migrated to Burma, Indonesia and other countries in South-East Asia and the Far East, in the process also spreading the religion of Buddhism. A section of these people derived their livelihood from international trade and they maintained an international kinship and economic network with India; some South Indian rulers sent successful expeditions to the region, as well. However, these Indians are now, more or less, a lost diaspora.

The bulk of Indian migration took place during the colonial period. The previous small-scale movement of Indian people turned into a mass migration which, broadly speaking, took place in three distinct occupational capacities: (i) indentured workers in the sugar colonies of the Caribbean, Oceania, and Africa; (ii) under the *kangani/ maistry* system to Malaysia and Ceylon; and (iii) as 'free passenger' Indians. The free Indians (called Passenger Indians) went in small numbers as traders, money-lenders, and the like, to most places except a few in the Caribbean, widely spread in anglophone, francophone and lusophone territories. In the third phase, during the post-independence era, Indians migrated as highly skilled and skilled workers to the industrialised countries of Europe, North America, and Oceania, and as semi-skilled and unskilled workers to the Middle East. However, the latter were not allowed to obtain citizenship in their host countries. Over the years, the Indian diaspora grew in their host countries, gained in importance, and emerged as valuable assets for their new home and host countries.

The visibility and emergence of overseas Indians as a diasporic network coincided with the advent of globalisation. This network manifested itself in a diasporic web of a professionally advanced and economically affluent community originating from what was then a basically underdeveloped country. They were, by and large, well received by the indigenous communities in countries where they chose to settle down; they also grew comparatively faster and prospered more than other communities. This created the impression that the Indian diaspora largely focused inward on itself and were consumed by its own efforts, resulting in its more rapid advancement. Native and other communities felt that the Indian diaspora had exclusivist tendencies and was not adequately focused on the local society and host country, leading to the allegation that it was self-centred and only interested in its own betterment. This gave credence to the argument that Indian settlers have benefited a great deal in their new home, but did not contribute much to it. Therefore, there was no need for host governments to gear national policies to their advancement.

However, empirical studies show that Indian overseas communities contributed significantly to their host societies and countries. The present book is an attempt to examine the role of the Indian diaspora in, and the social, economic, cultural and political contributions it made to a particular host society. It emerges from the studies that whereas the older Indian diaspora contributed significantly in economic, cultural and political terms, the newer diaspora has made more visible contributions through its professional expertise in the economy and in the field of literature in its new home in Western Europe and North America. The presence of the newer diaspora in the latter also significantly contributed to promoting biiateral relations of countries in these regions with India. On the other hand, Indians in the Gulf region, due to their 'captive position' and high level of remittances to India, put that region and themselves in a high policy-priority position with the government of India. Therefore, this book – besides mapping out local achievements by Indian communities – attempts to tease out their contributions in promoting bilateral ties of their host countries with India. The book covers older, newer and captive NRI diasporas in anglophone, lusophone and francophone territories. Different chapters in the book have attempted to cover a representative range of cases from diverse geographical areas in the world.

Sadananda Sahoo in his well-researched article, 'Contribution of Indian Diaspora to Europe', has aptly remarked that there are several factors that determine the contribution of a diaspora community to the host society and that these include the composition of the diaspora group, the status of their residence in the host country, the politico-economic conditions of the host society, the 'coping-up' strategy, and so on. With these factors in mind, Sahoo has comprehensively discussed the contribution of the Indian diaspora in three European countries – Britain, France, and The Netherlands. The contribution of the Indian diaspora in Australia is analysed by Anand Kulkarni and Probodh Malhotra. Divided into five sections, the essay offers a detailed discussion of the contribution of Indians to the economic and social betterment of Australia, concentrating on more recent events and controversies, especially attacks on Indian students, and the implications these could have for the future role and influence of the Indian diaspora in that country.

The economic prosperity and professional achievements of Americans of Indian origin are well known, and there are clear trends pointing to the fact that Indians have recognised the importance of participation in the political process. This issue has been delved into by Ashok Sharma in his article, 'Indian American: Migrational Pattern, Professional Success, Cultural Emergence and their Political Activism'. According to him, throughout the 1990s and into the 2000s there has been an increasing trend towards the direct engagement of Indo-Americans in politics. Similarly, the influence of the Indo-Canadian community can be seen not only in Canadian society, generally speaking, but also in the domestic politics and foreign policy of Canada. In her article, Lianboi Vaipei presents the contribution of the Indian diaspora in Canada, a country of immigrants, as a beautiful journey. It discusses how Indian culture has influenced the social and cultural fabric of

Canadian society, and the contributions of Indians to Canadian politics and the economy. Ajay Dubey and Jyoti Tyagi in their well-presented article, 'Contribution of Indian Diaspora in Francophone', have made an attempt to throw light on a rather neglected area of Indian diaspora studies. *Francophonie*, as a broad regional and cultural-linguistic categorisation, consists of French-speaking countries worldwide and, overall, the francophone Indian diaspora constitutes more than five percent of the total Indian diaspora. This article presents a comprehensive discussion of the role and contribution of the Indian diaspora in a number of important francophone countries. It also raises the issue that Indian policy-makers have neglected the interests of Indians in these countries.

Another region of the world where Indians form a visible ethnic group is in the West Indies/Caribbean. Two articles have been included in this section. While Mahabir Kumar's article has taken a thematic approach based on categories like arts, sports, festivals, business, and so on, R. L. Chawla's article focuses on the economic role and contribution of the Indian diaspora in the Caribbean. Emphasising on the economic strength of the Indians in the Caribbean, Chawla states that the role of Indians from agricultural development in post colonial societies to managing modern corporate sector in a competitive urban environment can never be underestimated. According to Mahabir, in many ways the Indian community has brought India to the West Indies, with the introduction of Hinduism and Islam and has 'truly given new meaning' to the identity of being a West Indian.

A section on Africa starts off with a presentation by Rajneesh Kumar Gupta on East Africa. He discusses, in some detail, the contributions of the Indian diaspora in three key areas – the economy, politics, and culture – and then he goes on to show how PIOs, despite being a small minority, have made significant contributions to every strata of society. Indians have a long history of settlement in South Africa, and their contribution to the development of the country has been immense. Vidhan Pathak's article discusses this with a specific focus on the post-apartheid era, a period during which significant change has occurred directly affecting the Indian community. According to Pathak, this presents tremendous scope for South African Indians to get involved in, and contribute to, the development of the country. Sasmita Mohanty compares the contribution of the Indian diaspora in two very important, but unexplored, francophone and lusophone countries, Madagascar and Mozambique. The article shows how PIOs in Madagascar, while contributing immensely to the economy of Madagascar, have not been able to attain a socio-political status commensurate with their economic status. In stark contrast, PIOs in Mozambique are better educated and actively participate in the political and public life of the country. Another important country, but where Indians are in a majority, is Mauritius. Chit Dukhira's article traces the role and contributions of the Indian diaspora in a few prominent areas. These are politics, economy, education, oriental studies, and culture, print and visual media. However, he largely focuses on their political contributions, particularly with regard to constitutional reforms, voting rights and achievement of independence, in political sphere.

The contribution of the Indian diaspora in the Gulf region is aptly explored by P.C. Jain in an informative article, 'Contributing to the Success of Entrepreneurship: Indian Diaspora in United Arab Emirates'. In some detail he discusses the change in economic profile of Indians during the 1980s, and how Indian trading communities have become successful and thus contribute to the development of the United Arab Emirates (UAE).

Unlike other countries where PIOs have settled, the situation in Sri Lanka is rather complex as Sri Lankan Tamils have been struggling for the acknowledgement of their political rights and some of them have been engaged, until very recently, in sustained insurgency warfare against the government in Colombo. Nevertheless, Vijayanathan's article discusses the remarkable contribution and role of PIOs in Sri Lanka's economic growth and in achieving relative political stability. The article shows how the presence of PIOs is quite noticeable in various industries that make a significant contribution to the national income of the country. The article further analyses the key role of PIOs in national and regional politics. Pankaj Jha's article on the contribution of the Indian diaspora in Malaysia attempts to show how Indians have played a role in making a 'diversified Malaysia more harmonious and tolerant'. He stresses that there are fewer economic opportunities for ethnic Indians as opposed to those available to other ethnic groups. Though it has not reached its true potential, the Indian community is not at all a deprived community and participates in all levels of Malaysian life – political, economic, social, and cultural. The evolution of the position of Indo-Fijians, from their arrival in that Pacific island to the present, is discussed in an article by Amba Pandey. It traces their journey from the status of slaves to their current economic and political role, and explains how the Indian diaspora has helped Fiji to become an important nation in the South Pacific.

Throughout this volume, an attempt has been made to highlight the contributions of the Indian diaspora to their host countries. The articles included in the book provide valuable insights into the growth and development of Indians around the world, drawing attention to their economic, political and socio-cultural contributions to their host countries. As the Indian diaspora is increasing in significance, its reach and power is being acknowledged by the world. But what remains of crucial importance is that the contributions of Indians are acknowledged in their new home countries, and that they are seen not only as of intrinsic value to their home societies but also as indispensable human capital.

CONTENTS

1

Contribution of Indian Diaspora to Europe

Sadananda Sahoo

Introduction

Contribution of any community to the host society can be viewed in term of its manifest and latent consequences, which are often short term as well as long term. Certain contributions are visible or observable (manifest) in the socio-cultural and political arena and certain others are invisible but long term (latent). The process is not a simple rather it is a complex interplay of many factors. In this context, the contribution of Diaspora to the host society is a complex one.

Cultural evolutionists and sociologists find more evidence in the impact of migrant on host society. As migration is always selective and host society has the policy to welcome or not to welcome migrant group, it has a specific way to influence the host society as the composition of the migrant groups differs. This specific selection includes i.e. skills, gender, community, countries etc. For example, many countries prefer only professionals and not the unskilled. Certain countries and communities are preferred in some areas whereas others are not preferred.

There are several factors that determine the contribution to the host society, which include the composition of the diaspora group i.e., the profile of the diaspora that broadly are: education, skills, status of their stay in the host society, duration of stay, political-economic context they have settled in the host society, coping up strategy etc. An educated group will have better economic and political contribution than an uneducated group in any society. Similarly, a group which stays for longer time generally tends to acquire as well as influence the host culture in many ways.

Diasporic experiences and their contributions also vary according to the space available for the diasporic group to contribute. In certain countries, like USA, Diasporas are vibrant communities and play significant role in wide spectrum of socio-cultural, political and economic areas, where as, in certain other countries they have limited space as in the case of West Asia where strict laws do not allow migrant to play any role in the political and cultural sphere. So far as the European countries are concerned, many Diasporas have been experiencing differences based on the culture and policies of governments in power. There are differences between European countries in terms of accommodating the immigrants.

The current debate on the migration of talent is also having significant bearing on how we look at diaspora's contribution to the host country. A central element in contemporary regional development strategies is the ability for regions to attract and retain talented people. The underlying argument is that by attracting talented people, regions are better geared to meet the demand of competences of the knowledge economy and become more competitive. What is this talent? It is an endowment: natural abilities or qualities. A person who possesses unusual innate ability in some field or activity let it be any field of culture, entrepreneurship, scientific knowledge etc. Artists, statesmen, entrepreneurs, writers have a lot to offer to any society. This matters a lot to the socio-cultural, economic and political development of a country.

Before going to the contribution of Indian Diaspora to Europe, the article presents a broad contour of the Indian emigration. The article is divided into two sections, (I) about the Indian emigration in broad and the three European countries such as Britain, France and Netherlands in specific and (II) Contribution of Indian Diaspora in socio-economic, cultural and political fields.

To understand how the Indian diaspora contributed to the Europe, it is important to have an idea on the migration and composition of Indian diaspora in those countries. Let's have a cursory look at the formation of Indian diaspora as it shaped historically.

A brief history

The formation of Indian Diaspora is characterized by four broad patterns of overseas migration in terms of political economy:

- emigration that began in the 1830s to the British, French and Dutch colonies;
- emigration to the industrially developed countries during the post- World War II period;
- emigration to West Asia during 1970s and eighties; and
- emigration of software engineers and other professionals since mid nineteen eighties to developed countries.

Indian emigration in the first phase comprised of mostly indentured labour to European colonies to fill in the vacuum created by emancipation of African slaves in plantations, following the ban on the practice of slavery. Indenture labour was a new concept of plantation work on contract for a period of 3 to 5 years. The system of indenture labour was an ingenious invention of the British to keep their plantation economy thriving on labour under captivity and Hugh Tinker has very rightly described it as the new name for slavery.

The second wave of Indian emigration began during the middle of the 20th century to the developed countries like Britain, USA, Canada, Australia and New Zealand. Those who migrated during this phase hailed from urban middle class families and were well educated and professionally trained. They form the *New Diaspora* and maintain close ties with the places of their origin. This migration is also called "migration of talent" or "brain drain".

The third wave of emigration of the Indians to the West Asian countries is basically oriented to labour and servicing occupations on a contract basis. There were only 14,000 Indians in the Gulf in 1948 and 40,000 in 2001. Following the oil boom of the mid-1970s, the Middle East witnessed a massive induction of the South Asian workers. Here, the need for skilled South Asian workers, during the 1960s and early 1970s, has been eclipsed by the requirement for skilled labour since the 1980s. There are more than two million Indians in West Asia. The year 1973 experienced the beginning of the rapidly increasing demand for expatriate labour in oil exporting countries of the Gulf and North Africa, such as, Saudi Arabia, Kuwait, the United Arab Emirates, Bahrain, Qatar and Libya.

Migration of software engineers to the western countries, USA in particular, which occurred in a significant way during the last decade of the 20th century, forms the fourth wave of Indian emigration. They are considered to be the cream of India, trained in her premiere educational institutions such as IITs, IIMs and Universities. They are highly mobile and keep very close contact with India in terms of socio-economic interests.

Migration to Europe: United Kingdom, Netherlands and France

Migration to Europe is a complex phenomenon as compared to other waves of migration. There are direct and indirect migrations. Direct migration constitutes mostly those who migrated from India to the Europe. Indirect migrations are from the former colonies occupied by the Europe. There are also voluntary and involuntary migrations to Europe. Most of the migrants from India went as voluntary migrants where as People of Indian origin from many of the former colonies such as Uganda, Fiji, South Africa went to settle in various European countries as a result of ethnic problems in those former colonies.

United Kingdom

The United Kingdom has a large population of people of Indian origin (1.2 million in 2001) constituting 2.10 per cent of the country's population[1]. Two-thirds of Indians living in Europe are in the United Kingdom. The Indian population has been part of Britain for almost 300 years. During the period of the Raj, Indians were seamen, domestic servants, politicians, barristers, doctors and social celebrities (Visram 1986). Prior to the 1950s Indians in Britain were a middle-class group with a preponderance of doctors (Kondapi 1951), students [2] and international businessmen[3]. However, emigration to the United Kingdom started in the 1950s. Between 1955 and 1962, 146,300 Indian and Pakistani workers entered Britain, the timing of their migration being influenced by the varying fortunes of the UK's economy[4]. Those who migrated were construction or dockyard workers. During the early years of immigration, males outnumbered females, the ratio being 3:2 or 5:3 [5].

However in 1962, the British government imposed restrictions on unskilled labour migration, which fundamentally altered both the nature of South Asian migration and the permanence of resulting settlement. Migration was increasingly of (female) dependants and for marriage, and South Asian settlement became more permanent and family oriented.

During the 1960s and the 1970s large number of Indians immigrated to the UK from East Africa. One out of every four of the Indians and the Pakistanis in Britain has arrived via East Africa. In the late 1970s, there were more than 200,000 Asians from East Africa in Britain. Considerable East Asian migrants with capital started commercial enterprises in Britain. Britain also has a small number of East Indians from the Caribbean, Mauritius and South Africa.

The population of Asians living in Britain after the World War II was 7,000. During the next thirty years the Asian population grew a hundred folds. The number of immigrants was highest during the decade 1960-70. In all 196,395 Indians (107,190 males and 89,205 females) and 53,835 Kenyan Asians (28,900 males and 24,935 females) emigrated[6]. The size of the immigrants during the 1950s was small. About 47,500 persons from India (30,500 males and 17,000 females) and 14,500 from Pakistan (12,800 males and 1,700 females) immigrated to Britain during the 1950s[7]. The early migrants were mainly Sikhs. The later migrants were mainly Gujaratis and Punjabis. The Indians and the other Asians were absorbed mainly in the older labour intensive industries.

In the Indian community 57 per cent male workers were on manual work. The remainder of the Indians were found in a broad band of occupations: 6.6 per cent being employers or managers, 10.5 per cent being professional people, 18.9 per cent shop assistants and office workers, and 2.4 per cent serving in the armed forces[8]. A high proportion of Indian women also work in various industries.

Since the late 1960s, Indians are being employed in banks, department stores, insurance companies etc. Many Indian doctors are employed in hospitals. Their occupational distribution is now closer to that of the white British population. Indians are concentrated in the London Area and in the Southeast.

"The shift to a post-industrial society has strengthened the position of certain Asians who are clearly members of upwardly mobile and increasingly affluent 'new' class, which some commentators feel now exists. Other South Asians have not been so fortunate. They have seen their already weak position progressively undermined by social and economic change. For them, the post-industrial future is bleak, caught as they are on the wrong end of a new international division of labour in a country that does not care"[9].

The Netherlands

There is no proper documentation about the earliest emigration of Indians to the Netherlands. However, the contact between India and the Netherlands goes back to many centuries. The earliest reference of Indians arrival to Netherlands is found in a Dutch TV programme on Azad Hind Brigade, stationed in German-occupied Holland, which mentioned that a brigade of Sikhs arrived in German-occupied Holland in June, 1943. After 1600, the Dutch East India Company took over the spice trade from the Portuguese. There is no record showing that Indians visited or came to the Netherlands during that period. Hence, one can assume that the mass Indians immigration to the Netherlands is actually a post-World War II phenomenon. In the first phase, during the 1960s, 70s, and 80s, early Indian settlers came to the Netherlands mainly as students, researchers, or tourists. The next phase of Indian arrivals consisted of expatriates who came in with the advent of large Indian corporations to the Netherlands since the late 1980s-1990s.

At present, the Netherlands has the second largest population of people of Indian origin (PIOs) in Europe. There are two very distinct groups among the Indian community in the Netherlands - the PIOs from Suriname (whose roots are mainly in Uttar Pradesh and Bihar) and the non-resident Indians (NRIs). Those PIOs from Suriname migrated to the Netherlands when Suriname became independent in 1975. Before the independence of Suriname, the main motivation for Hindustanis to migrate to the Netherlands was the increased opportunities of higher education as compared to Suriname. In 1972, during the dictatorship of Idi Amin, a few hundred Indians migrated from Uganda to the Netherlands. In the recent past, PIOs from Afghanistan arrived in the Netherlands. There are also PIOs from Guyana, Malaysia, Mauritius and Trinidad. Besides the above, the Dutch have been adopting Indian children more or less on a regular basis. In recent years, we can find a fresh wave of Indians directly migrated to the Netherlands. Highly qualified professionals and entrepreneurs largely constitute the recent wave of Indians who came to seek their fortunes in the Netherlands. Many of them have retained Indian citizenship. They have gained considerable expertise in important spheres of economic and professional life.

The High Level Committee on Indian Diaspora estimated that the Indian diaspora population in Netherlands is about 217,000. Out of this, the Surinamese Indians (Sarnami Hindustanis as they often call themselves) are about 200,000 in number. There are about 15,000 NRIs and the remaining includes illegal immigrants. According to the Central Database of Statistics in Netherlands, at the end of the year 2005, there were 3,745 Indian passport holders and the number of people of Indian origin (first and second generation Indians), including Indians holding passports of other countries, was 13,800.

The Indian community was a prosperous business community on the eve of Independence. A series of incidents of assaults to life and property provoked the Indians to immigrate to The Netherlands. The increasing employment opportunities in The Netherlands were an incentive for them to migrate. More than one-third of the Surinamese of Indian origin took advantage of the Independence legislation and flew to The Netherlands in 1974-75 and later. Most of them are concentrated in the large cities of Amsterdam, The Hague and Rotterdam and are playing an important role in the economic and social life of the country. A small number of people immigrated to The Netherlands during the post Second World War period (about 3,500). They are mainly concentrated in educational institutions, medicine, law, business houses, hospitals and other service industries[10].

France

Following the Portuguese, British, and Dutch, the French also established trading bases in India. Their first establishment was in Pondicherry on the Coromandel Coast in southeastern India. Subsequent French settlements were Chandernagore in Bengal, northeastern India in 1688, Yanam in Andhra Pradesh in 1723, Mahe in 1725, and Karaikal in 1739. The French were constantly in conflict with the Dutch, and later on mainly with the British in India. At the height of French power in the mid-18th century, the French occupied most of southern India and the area lying in today's northern Andhra Pradesh and Orissa. Compared to British and Dutch, French area of control was very small. Due to this factor, French rulers could not take much of the Indian labour to their colonies as in the case of British.

Unlike UK, the detail statistics of Indian diaspora is not available in France as census on the basis of ethnicity or religions are banned in France. The High level Committee Report states that the total population of France is 58.8 million out of which PIOs are 55000 and NRIs are 10000. Thus, PIOs constitute around 0.110 per cent of the total population of France. Where as in U.K. the total population is 56.9 million, out of which PIOs and NRIs are approximately 1,200,000. Therefore, PIOs are around 2.109 per cent of the total population of the U.K. Indian immigrants in France are mostly from the former French colonies like Pondicherry, Karaikal etc. There is no general rule about their occupations but there are two kinds of Indian people in France: the first are those who came through their connection with former French colonies in India ("Comptoirs"), principally Yanam and to some extent Pondicherry and second, the smaller number of those who came for higher studies, professional or relational reasons (for example through marriage) from various parts of India mainly from Punjab.

The second wave of Indians in France was mostly Gujaratis, from former French colonies of Madagascar, Seychelles and Mauritius. In addition, a number of Persons of Indian Origin inhabit the French territories of Reunion Islands, Guadeloupe, and Martinique.

The third wave of Indian immigration to France is of skilled IT professionals. The number of Indian professionals in France has been growing in recent years, with many companies recruiting employees in India and moving them. Besides, a large number of Indian students are joining colleges for higher education in engineering and management studies and they too are often getting jobs in France.

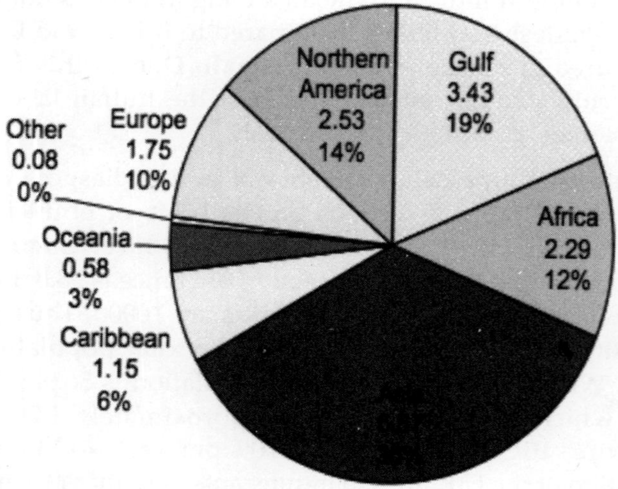

Indian Diaspora Population

Source: *High Level Committee on the Indian Diaspora (2002).*

Europe has about 10 per cent of the total Indian diaspora population. However, compared to the smaller number of European population this is not a very small number.

II

Contribution of Indian Diaspora to the Europe

Indian contribution to Europe goes back to the early civilization. Throughout the literature of Europe, tales of Indian origin can be discovered. European mathematics - and through them, the full range of European technical achievement-could hardly have existed without Indian numerals. But until the beginning of European colonization in Asia, India's contribution was usually filtered through other cultures.

Direct contact was only established with India after European expansion and the subsequent settlement of Indians in Europe after the colonization. Today, the Indian diaspora is international in its existence, and transnational in its activities. The internet, satellite television, global media conglomerates, Bollywood cinema, and popular culture all help define and bond as well as illuminate ruptures within this global community. Let us now highlight some of the contributions of the Indian Diaspora to Europe.

Britain

Compared to all other European countries, one of the most successful Indian diaspora is found in Britain. People of Indian Origin have been an integral part of the British Socio-Cultural and Economic landscape.

Politics

People from the Indian subcontinent have had a role in the politics of the United Kingdom, starting from the British educated Indians who struggled for independence as well as Indians who became Members of Parliament. Second- and third- generation British Asians have managed to become involved in politics at trade union, local and national level.

British Asians have also made an impact on the parliament of the United Kingdom. The first Asian Member of Parliament (MP) was Dadabhai Naoroji in 1892. He was quickly followed by fellow Parsis Mancherjee Bhownagree and Shapurji Saklatvala during the late 19th/early 20th centuries.

No other British Asian MP was elected until Keith Vaz was elected to the House of Commons in 1987. He was followed by others such as Piara habra, Niranjan Deva, Parmjit Dhanda, Swaraj Paul, Mohammad Sarwar (the first British Muslim MP), Khalid Mahmood and Parmjit Singh Gill. The first British-born Muslim to be elected to Parliament were Shahid Malik and Sadiq Khan in 2005, both of Asian descent.

Several British Asians have also been awarded peerages to sit in the House of Lords, including Lord Desai, Baroness Uddin (first Bangladeshi), Lord Alli, Lord Bilimoria, Lord Dholakia and Baroness Dunn (who, in a British English context is not Asian, but Oriental or Chinese).

Economy

UK represents diversity in ethnic communities and provides scope for their economic participation. The Indians have shown entrepreneurship and that contributes a lot towards to economic progress of UK.

British Asians generated a "staggering" £103bn a year to the UK economy, even though many arrived in this country penniless, homeless and unable to speak English.

A study by Joseph Rowntree Foundation (JRF), which is a British social policy research and development charity founded in 2007, found that British Indians have the lowest poverty rates among different ethnic groups in Britain second only to white British. Of different ethnic groups Bangladeshis (65 per cent), Pakistanis (55 per cent) and black Africans (45 per cent) had the highest rates; black Caribbeans (30 per cent), Indians (25 per cent), white other (25 per cent) and white British (20 per cent) had the lowest rates. According to BBC findings, the economic makeup in 2001 of Indian-born British Indians is as follows. 65.98 per cent of new immigrants were employed with 16.43 per cent being "low earners" (people earning less than £149.20 a week) and 18.13 per cent being 'high earners' (people earning more than £750 a week). By comparison settled Indian immigrants to the UK are actually slightly less likely to be in employment, 62.85 per cent in fact, the percentage of low and high earners for settled immigrants stood at 15.9 per cent and 7.88 per cent respectively. Therefore, on average, 64.42 per cent of Indian-born immigrants to the UK are employed. This figure is approximately 10 per cent lower than the rate of employment for British-born people (regardless of ethnicity), which stood at 73.49 per cent in 2001. It is also fair to say that there are economic differences within the British Indian population, for example, Hindu people are more likely to be wealthy than Sikh people.

A study by the Manchester-based Institute of Asian Professionals showed that Asians made up 2.5 per cent of the population, but accounted for 10 per cent of the country's economic output.

The institute published an Asian Power List, adding that the research came at a time when many Asians felt their lives were under "intense scrutiny."

Chairman Khalid Darr said: "The figures are quite staggering. Many on the list arrived on these shores without a penny to their name, and they have built multi-million pound business empires. Entrepreneurship, coupled with a wonderful work ethic, fuelled with a desire to better oneself, is a potent force driving the British Asian business community."

Socio-Cultural

Indian diaspora's contribution to the British culture is widespread and deep. The 1980s and 90s saw a renaissance of Indian writing in English many of whom are settled and lived most of their life in Britain. Much of the credit goes to these literary personas to make Indian culture familiar to the British society. Some of the most enduring figures in the literary field are Nobel Laureate V.S. Naipaul, Nirad C. Choudhuri, Salman Rushdie and Vikram Seth. These notable writers enriched the English language and literature further. Most of the writings reflected the Indian society and culture in varied form, thus, making the British and other western readers familiar with the rich Indian social life.

Diaspora becomes alive with the writings of these writers. Most of the writings of these diasporic writers are about India. A broad range of diasporic experience is found in the writings of V.S. Naipaul's novel, which narrate the diasporic journey. While Sulman Rushdie's acclaimed *Midnight's Children* (published in 1981) won the Booker Prize for Fiction, the James Tait won Black Memorial Prize (for fiction), an Arts Council Writers' Award and the English-Speaking Union Award, and in 1993 was judged to have been the "Booker of Bookers", the best novel to have won the Booker Prize for Fiction in the award's 25-year history. The novel narrates key events in the history of India through the story of pickle-factory worker Saleem Sinai, one of 1001 children born as India won independence from Britain in 1947. Many of his writings are about India and diasporic theme and hence familiarizing the social life of Indians to the British audiences.

Some of notable Indian entrepreneurs in Britain are L.N. Mittal who is considered to be the richest Indian in the world, Swaraj Paul, Nighat Awan, fellow curry queen Meena Pathak and Iqbal Ahmed, founder of East Manchester-based food processing company Seafood Marketing. Lakshmi N. Mittal who resides in Britain is currently Britain's richest man and the fifth richest man in the world. The Mittal family owns 43 per cent of Arcelor-Mittal, the world's largest steel manufacturer, which was known as Mittal Steel Company before the merger with Arcelor. He was listed in the *Forbes* List of Billionaires (2006) as the richest Indian and the fifth richest man in the world with an estimated fortune of $55.0 billion and, according to the Sunday Times Rich List 2006, is the richest in the UK, with a net worth of £29 billion. The *Financial Times* named Mittal its 2006 Person of the Year. In 2005, he was the third richest man in the world, according to *Forbes* List of billionaires (2005).

Besides ethnic music, Indian diaspora contributed to the music, which caters to the need of the multicultural population i.e., mostly fusion. The influence of Asian music has not only been from Asians living in the UK, but also from some UK artists that were starting using Asian instruments creating a new and dynamic sound that was a mixture of *sitars* and *tablas* with a more traditional rock-based Western instruments like the drums and guitars.

The influence on popular music has been a long standing one. Music producer, composer and song-writer Biddu produced and composed a number of music hits in the mid-1970s such as the smash hit Kung fu fighting for Carl Douglas and the 1 UK hit and worldwide smash I Love to Love (But My Baby Loves to Dance) for Tina Charles. Popular Punjab's Bhangra music has in addition become popular among many in the general British public. Some of the successful artists who made contribution to the mainstream British music through fusion are: Nitin Sawhney, Talvin Singh, Asian Dub

Foundation, Panjabi MC, Raghav, and the Rishi Rich Project (featuring Rishi Rich, Jay Sean and Juggy D).

Today numerous T.V. channels target at the million-strong Indian diaspora. This further not only provide access to the Indian culture for the Indian diaspora as well as to the British people. There are now channels in almost every language- Hindi, Gujarati, Punjabi, Bengali, Tamil, Malayalam, Kannada and Telugu. Out of all of the countries in the Indian diaspora, the UK is most likely to be the best at portraying Indian culture and life in the UK through television.

Long-running British soap operas, which had have all significant numbers of Indian characters includes *Coronation Street, East Enders, Emmerdale* and *Hollyoaks*. Indian characters are also found place in tele series such as *The Jewel in the Crown* and *Skins*. By far the most notable British Indian television shows are *Goodness Gracious Me* (though not running now) *The Kumars at No. 42*, a talk show that stars many famous British Indian actors including Sanjeev Bhaskar, Meera Syal, Indira Joshi and Vincent Ebrahim.

The resourcefulness of Indian diaspora is found almost in every spheres of social-cultural, economic and political life making them an integral part of the vibrant British society. Indian diaspora in Britain is a remarkable journey.

The Netherlands

Indian communities are slowly beginning to play active role in Netherlands. The state policies are often discouraging to have multicultural and freedom of political participation at the same level as in the case of United Kingdom.

Politics

Compared to United Kingdom the situation in politics in Netherlands is different. The politics is still the monopoly of Dutch people and there are no visible signs of multicultural presence in the politics. Major political institutions are the monarchy, the cabinet, the States General (parliament) and the judicial system. There are three other High Colleges of state, which stand on equal foot with parliament but have a less political role, of which the Council of State is the most important. Other levels of government are the municipalities, the water boards and the provinces. Although not mentioned in the constitution, political parties and the social partners organised in the Social Economic Council are important political institutions as well. Indians diaspora has no active presence in the political sphere in Netherlands. However, the Surinamese Indians are more active in political spheres than the direct migrants from India.

Dutch government remained reluctant to develop a policy for immigrant integration until 1970s. Though the situation is gradually changing today, the presence of colonial immigrants was considered a temporary phenomenon for long time. This was also manifest in the categorization of migrants as 'guest labourers' or 'international commuters'. Policies toward these temporary groups were mainly adhoc, aimed at participation in the economic sphere and retention of identity in the social-cultural sphere.

In the late 1970s and early 1980s, Dutch government developed an Ethnic Minorities Policy that had distinct multiculturalist traits. The policy problem was now reconceptualised in terms of participation and socio-cultural emancipation of ethnic or cultural minorities. Migrants were framed as "minorities" in Dutch society instead of temporary guests, and government decided to focus on those minorities whose position was characterized by an accumulation of cultural and socioeconomic difficulties and for whom the Dutch government felt a special historical responsibility[11].

Economy

There have been many success stories in the economic front. Mexx, the well-known fashion brand is a successful enterprise in Netherlands. Mexx was started by an Indian entrepreneur, Mr. Rattan Chadha, who had originally come to the Netherlands with very little capital. Today, Mexx is a multinational company with substantial annual turnover. There are many other similar examples. Mr. Lakhina, who is an entrepreneur and prominent member of the Indian community and the President of the Netherlands-India Chamber of Commerce and Trade (NICCT) says that the number of Indian millionaires as a proportion of the Indian community in the Netherlands would probably equal the number of Dutch millionaires per head of population here. The Netherlands is a place, which is clearly a business friendly nation, even to foreigners.

"Many Indians came to the Netherlands with little or no Dutch language skills, started working in Dutch companies, and quickly grew to occupy high positions in their professions", says Lakhina. Indian architects, lawyers, doctors, academicians and educationists have made their mark in Dutch society. They too came to the Netherlands with very limited resources. The Netherlands provided them with opportunities to set up business and these Indian professionals have been successful in making full use of the same, "And this trend continues even today", says Lakhina, and adds, "The Indian community in the Netherlands has done remarkably well in both the professional and business arena.

Socio-Cultural

The Netherlands is still an extreme representative of a "multicultural" vision of integration. The country allows immigrants easy access to formal social and political rights while at the same time facilitating expressions of foreigners' own cultural identity with the help of the state.

Broadly Indian presence adds to the socio-cultural mosaic of Netherlands. The Indian community in the Netherlands has also established a large number of temples, mosques and gurudwaras. Religious and cultural centers run by Mata Amritanandamayi, Anand Marg, Arya Samaj and ISKCON have branches throughout the Netherlands.

The socio-cultural contribution of Indian diaspora is visible in many spheres. There are a large number of (about

200) yoga schools in the Netherlands. Private cultural and religious organizations, numbering over two-dozen, teach classical Indian dance or music or both. Dutch institutions like the "Tritantrie Vidyapeeth", Royal Tropical Institute, the Netherlands India Association, RASA Utrecht, etc. organize Indian cultural programmes as well as film festivals in different cities.

The linguistic diversity is also another dimension added by the Indian diaspora to the society of Netherlands. The Surinamese Hindustani community has even managed to have parliamentary legislation passed providing for the teaching of Hindi in certain middle and high schools. There is also cooperation in the film and television sector. Royal Tropical Institute, Amsterdam regularly conducts special exhibitions, film festivals, and musical and other programmes to make the Dutch aware of the cultures of developing countries, including India. Indian musicians and dancers regularly perform at the Institute to packed audiences.

France

Although France is de facto a multicultural society, historically this interpretation has been contested. Multiculturalism in France is more as an ideological acceptance than in the real social practice. This is quite evident in their daily social life. The terms 'immigration' and 'immigrés' are still commonly used in contemporary political debates in France for ethnic minorities. The term is used not just for recent immigrants but also for men and women of ethnic origins who have spent all their life in France. Ironically, the term is used for the diasporas of African and Asian origins.

Indian diaspora is facing challenges of accommodation in the French society ever since it has settled there. Over the period, however, Indian community in France created their space, which reflected in many socio-cultural and economic spheres. The contribution of Indian diaspora is not very significant in many areas as compared to Britain and USA where the challenges and opportunities are favorable for diaspora communities to flourish as well as to contribute positively.

Politics

The government of France is a unique hybrid of presidential and parliamentary systems that reflect rich political traditions and culture- the conflictual political culture of France currently is somewhat more consensual than in the past. Due to the strong cultural orientation even in politics diaspora communities are still not very active in the French politics.

The theme of inward immigration was economics, but immigration from the African continent transformed into a political issue from the 1960s onwards. The immigration of the 1960s was increasing the immigrant population and this gave rise to issues of difference amongst the French population. The French Governments were aware of this and they acted to contain the situation by banning inward immigration.

French scholars and political actors have consistently argued that in France political and social institutions have historically transformed immigrants into Frenchmen, while in the United States, similar institutions have legitimated "American 'pluricultural' model". Indian diaspora in France is relatively not playing active role in socio-cultural and economic arena due to the fact that French society is still not open to the diversity.

Economy

Diasporas in general played an important role in the development of France. For the French, immigration originated from within Europe and Africa. The overriding theme of inward immigration to France was economics and specifically labours. France in its early development (1850-1870) was concerned with building its empire and hence it imported labours from other countries. This continued till the World War II. The Post War period in France saw a change in terms of French immigration policy. Its policy took on a more selective nature and it selected European workers over African workers. The French Government aimed to limit the influence of immigrants upon French society by concentrating their policy upon European workers. The matter of economics undermined French Post War immigration policy, which in turn saw more inward immigration from the African continent.

France is of the advance economy even though it has extensive government ownership and intervention to one that relies more on market mechanisms. The government in the process of partially or fully privatized many large companies, banks, and insurers. The economy demands international labour force. The labour force participation in France is in agriculture 4.1 per cent, industry 24.4 per cent and in services 71.5 per cent. Most of the recent Indian diasporas are into the service sectors. Apart from the IT skilled professionals who contribute to the new economy in the France, there are individual success stories too.

There are some diasporic individual success stories in France too. Gope Hathiramani a Sindhi businessman who owns a plush crystalware shop at the upmarket Rue de Rivoli in Paris is known to be the richest Indian there. Even though in recent years there are number of Indian professionals found in France, as a community they have not present itself as a well-organized group of professionals. The recent effort by the Indian Professional Association in France is to bring together professionals of Indian origin in France to promote professional and social interaction to share individual experiences for mutual benefit and to provide a forum for exchange of interdisciplinary knowledge by organizing meetings, seminars and conferences with Indian and French experts.

Socio-Cultural

Whereas American culture posits the notion of the "melting-pot" and cultural diversity, the expression "French culture" tends to refer implicitly to a specific geographical entity. However, in recent years France is encountering many diasporic cultures and hence France represents a multicultural society in the making. The cultural and social evolution that France has experienced during the three last decades in relation to the recognition of cultural diversity of its citizens has turned out due to diverse new historic circumstances, which did not exist in the past. Different statistical French sources confirm that the number of French citizens of foreign origin is very high. Like any other diaspora living in France, the cultural presence of the Indian diaspora in France is not very significant.

Conclusion

There are some differences when we talk about Indian diaspora in USA in comparison to Europe. Favell has argued (1999) that European states are not "nations of immigrants" like the USA, Canada or Australia, where "indigenous" populations are minute and dwarfed (where not exterminated) by voluntary or forced migrants from elsewhere. There are also differences within the European countries and the diaspora's participation and contribution to the host society varies according to the available socio-cultural and political and economic situation of the country.

Contrary to what was predicted in the 1970s, international migration did not slacken, but intensified, with ever greater numbers of migrants and refugees drawn from an ever-increasing range sending societies seeking entry to an ever-widening range of countries of reception. It has been suggested, however, that whereas past migrants settled in the countries of reception, in this "new age of migration"[12], they retain significant, continuing ties with countries of origin.

There are also complex issue that involves transnationalism. Transmigration entails manifold socio-economic, political and cultural linkages across boundaries, raises questions about identity (and identification), and rights and entitlements, and problematises 'bounded conceptualizations of race, class, ethnicity, and nationalism. Thus, the continuing interaction between diaspora and the host country has already given new space or civilizational existence.

Endnotes

1. Government of India, 2001. *Report of the High Level Committee on the Indian Diaspora,* New Delhi: Indian Council of World Affairs, pp.xvii-xx.
2. Kanitkar, H. 1972. 'An Indian Elite in Britain', *New Community,* vol.1, pp.378-83
3. Desai, R. 1963. *Indian Immigrants in Britain,* London: Oxford University Press.
4. Robinson, Vughan. 1990. 'Boom and Gloom: The Success and Failure of South Asians in Britain', in Colin Clarke et al.eds., *South Asians Overseas,* Cambridge: Cambridge University Press.
5. Tinker, Hugh. 1977. *The Banyan Tree: Overseas Emigrants from India, Pakistan and Bangladesh,* London: Oxford University Press, p.165
6. *Ibid,* p.169
7. *Ibid,* p.167.
8. *Ibid,* p.176.
9. Robinson, Vughan, Op.Cit., p.194.
10. Mahavir, Vasant. 1993. 'Community of Non-Resident Indians and People of Indian Origin in the Netherlands', in Jagat K Motwani.eds. *Global Indian Diaspora: Yesterday, Today and Tomorrow,* New York: Global Organisation of People of Indian Origin, p.417.
11. Rath, J. 2001. 'Research on Immigrant Ethnic Minorities in the Netherlands'in Ratcliffe eds. *The Politics of Social Science Research. Race, Ethnicity and Social Change,* New York: Palgrave.
12. Castles, S. and Miller, M. J. 1998. *The Age of Migration: International Population Movements in the Modern World,* Second Edition, London: Macmillan.

2

Indians in Australia: Contributions, Controversies and Challenges

Anand Kulkarni and Prabodh Malhotra

Introduction

Australia is a nation of immigrants. However, the contribution of Australia's indigenous aborigines to enrich the landscape of Australian society is also well recognized. Australia's culturally diverse population comprises migrants from more than 100 countries, who have made significant contributions to Australia, economically, socially and culturally. In March 2009, Australia's population reached 21.8 million, recording a growth of 2.1 per cent over a 12-month period (or an increase of 439,100 people), a growth figure not reached since the post-war migration of 1950s and 1960s.[1] The latest growth compares with a rate of 1.2 per cent five years ago. Overseas migration accounted for 63 per cent (or 278,200) of this recent increase. Australia has the world's highest foreign-born population (24.6 per cent) compared with Canada at 19.2 per cent and the United States at 11.7 per cent.[2]

Migrants play a significant role in Australia's economic activity because of their working age at the time of arrival. In a recent report, Access Economics (2008) estimates that only 9 per cent of migrants in 2006-07 were aged over 45 years compared with 38 per cent of the general population. Typical migrants (particularly in the skilled category) are aged between 20 and 40 years. At this age, their contribution to taxation revenue is far greater than their call on government expenses. Access Economics estimates the annual benefits of the 2006-07 migrants intake at A$536 million in the first year, which grows to A$1.34 billion by year 2026-2027 at 2007-08 prices. As we shall see, Indian migrants are making key contributions to the economic and social betterment of Australia.

Section 2 of this chapter provides a brief overview of Indian migration to Australia from a historical perspective. Section 3, the focus of the chapter, examines in detail the economic, socio-cultural, political and institutional contribution of the Indian diaspora, concentrating on more recent times. Section 4 looks at more recent controversies, especially the attacks on Indian students, and the extent to which such controversies can and do influence the ongoing contribution of the Indian diaspora in Australia. Section 5 provides some concluding remarks. Throughout this chapter, as appropriate, the challenges confronting the Indian diaspora in Australia are identified, which will have implications for the future role and functions of the diaspora in this country.

Indians in Australia

Indians have held a long standing affinity with Australia. The first Indian is believed to have come to Australia as part of Captain Cook's ship. Between 1800 and 1860 a small group of Indians arrived in Australia as labourers for the British Colonial authorities. In the latter part of the 19th century, Sikhs and Muslims from Punjab also settled in Australia as labourers and traders.[3] These early settlers from India took part in the rush for gold in the Victorian fields at Bendigo and Ballarat. A significant number of Indians ran camel trains before roads and other infrastructures were developed in Australia. Strangely enough, these Indians were not identified as Indians, but known as Afghans, who played a vital role in keeping the communication and supply lines open between

Melbourne and the center of Australia.[4] The train *Ghan Express* from Adelaide to Darwin is named after those Indians.

According to the High Commission of India in Australia (2009), the number of Indians in Australia was less than 7000 in the early 1900s and this number remained stable until WWII. The influx of Indian professionals such as doctors began to increase from the 1960s. However, the 'White Australia' policy significantly hampered the migration from Non-European countries including India. This controversial policy was gradually dismantled and the final vestiges of the policy were removed in 1973.[5] Since the mid 1980's, other professionals such as information technology (IT) experts have joined the Indian diaspora in Australia. More recently, non-professionals (e.g. business migrants) from India as well as Indians from other countries have also relocated to Australia. In addition, a large number of Indian students have come to Australia in recent years (discussed later in the chapter).

Broadly speaking, Indians in Australia comprise three major groups; namely, Punjabis, Kannadis (IT professionals from Bangalore) and the Fijian-Indians, who fled Fiji after the military coup.[6] A distinction between the major groups of Indians in Australia can be also made on the basis of the location of their settlement, which generally forms the basis of their contribution to different economic sectors. While the first arrivals, primarily Punjabis, mostly settled in the rural area and engaged in the agricultural sector, professionals under the skilled migration program mostly settled in the capital cities i.e. Sydney, Melbourne and Brisbane.[7] The Fiji-Indians also mostly settled in urban Australia. As at June 30 2008, the total number of Indians permanently residing in Australia is estimated at 239,000, which, in relative terms, is around 1 per cent of Australia's population.[8] However, the ABS counts Indians as only those whose country of birth is marked as India. Thus, the total number of "Indians living in Australia" may be greater, because many Indians have come from countries such as Fiji, Sri Lanka, UK, Africa and Malaysia rather than India.[9]

Contribution of Indian Diaspora to Australia

This section examines the contribution of the Indian diaspora to Australia, particularly focusing on the last decade or so because more than 40 per cent of the Indians in Australia arrived after 2000.[10] This section is divided into the sub-themes of economic, social and cultural, and political and institutional contributions of the Indian diaspora to Australia.

Economic Contribution

Within the sphere of economic contribution, there are three elements that are most significant: skilled migration; international students; and business and entrepreneurs.

Skilled Migration

Australia's immigration system is a multi-category programme designed to customize migrant intake to meet Australia's requirements. Under the programme, the major categories include skilled, family and refugees. In recent years, Australia's permanent immigration intake has increasingly emphasized the skilled component. For example, in 1995-96, Australia issued 24,100 permanent visas under the skilled category compared with 108,450 in 2007-08. The latter figure equates to more than two skilled visas for every family visa issued in 2007-2008.

In 1995-96, a total of 56,700 family visas were granted compared with 24,100 skilled visas noted above.[11] Australia's permanent immigration programme reflects its intention of building its stock of skilled human resources. However, in order to address Australia's long term interests, the programme recently introduced provisions for temporary migration. For example, in 2007-08, around 418,000 business visit visas were granted that allow visitors up to 2-3 months business related trips to Australia. Additionally, in 2007-08 Australian employers also sponsored 110,570 skilled workers to work and live in Australia on a temporary basis for up to 4 years. This was because these employers were unable to fill the skill shortages from within the domestic labour market.[12]

Table 1 shows the total permanent migrant intake and skilled migrant intake for years 1998-99 and 2008-09 with the key source countries. A number of observations can be made in the table. First, while Australia's total migration less than doubled from 81,820 in 1998-1999 to 150,217 in 2008-2009, the skilled migration increased more significantly from 34,000 to 87,245 over the same time. Second, the growth of Indian migrants in absolute as well as in relative terms particularly skilled migrants, was higher than for any other country in the same study years. Third, in 2008-09, the share of skilled migrants from India was the second largest of all countries behind the UK. In 1998-99, India ranked 5th in the skilled migrant category behind the UK, South Africa, China and Indonesia. Fourth, while India's share of total permanent migration grew from 3.8 per cent in 1998-99 to 12.8 per cent in 2008-09, the increase of its share from 5.9 per cent to 17 per cent in skilled migration is quite significant.[13] The Organisation for Economic Co-operation and Development (OECD 2009) suggests that between 1998 and 2007, the *growth* of Indians migrating to Australia was amongst the highest when compared to the growth of Indian migration to Canada, Germany, New Zealand, United Kingdom and the United States.[14] However, in absolute numbers, Indian migration to Australia is below migration to some of these other OECD countries.

The above noted increase of Indian migrants has contributed to Australia in a variety of ways. The recent growth means that one in six skilled migrants in 2008-09 came from India, which suggests a growing role and prominence of Indians in addressing the economic and skills needs of Australia. Based on Access Economics[15] noted earlier, the economic contribution of skilled Indians who migrated in 2006-07 can be estimated at A$41 million for the first year. Their contribution would be expected to reach A$101 million in 2026-27 at 2007-08 prices. Nevertheless, the contribution of Indians in Australia goes beyond just the direct economic benefits as the following examples demonstrate.

A recent Australian Bureau of Statistics study suggests that the India born Australian residents are more likely to have tertiary qualifications (Bachelor Degrees, Post Graduate Degrees, graduate diplomas), compared to Chinese born, those born elsewhere and the total population.[16] This is because the Indian value system places fundamental importance on education and the pursuit of education goes beyond education for education's sake. Under the Indian culture, there seems to be a correlation between education and the meeting of family responsibility as well as the attainment of social status, which could be the result of unlocking the shackles of the traditional caste system.[17]

Another study suggests that around 30 per cent of employed Indian-born are professionals, relatively high paid and have highly skilled jobs. This figure compares with 21.8 per cent for Chinese born and 19.0 per cent for Australian born. However, the latter two countries are more strongly represented in the managerial category.[18]

These data relating to educational attainment and occupation shows that Indian born people in Australia are contributing strongly to Australia's knowledge economy, in which human capital formation such as education, training, skills development and research promote national competitive advantage.

Research indicates that investment in human capital is vital to productivity growth, promoting technological change and diffusion, and even contributing to greater social cohesion. Fuente and Ciccone argue that the returns from investments in human capital are possibly more significant and enduring than investments from physical capital.[19] In fact, a number of studies emphasize the importance of education, training and skills formation for productivity, technological progress and economic growth (see for example, Productivity Commission (2002) and Kreuger & Lindahl (2001))[20]. Recent studies identify research and development (R&D), innovation, and human capital formation, as the drivers of competitiveness for nations, including emerging economies[21]. Joint research ventures between India and Australia are also emerging.

The importance of the international mobility of skilled labour, including especially science and technology personnel, in driving competitive advantage for those nations, which attract and retained skilled labour, must be emphasized.[22] This is consistent with the studies outlined above. With its large, relatively young and skilled workforce, India is a most attractive source of labour. The growth of skilled Indian migrants to Australia was noted earlier in the chapter, as a key contributor to Australia's economic and skills needs, including addressing skills shortages in this country. A study estimates that more than half of India's population is less than 25 years of age.[23] Notwithstanding the questions on the quality of, and access to, India's education and training system, and its own skills need, India has the potential to have a surplus workforce to meet the needs of other countries[24]. Australia is likely to continue to be one of the beneficiaries of this.

Indian Students in Australia

Australia's education sector attracts a large number of students from many countries, contributing significantly to Australia's exports. The growing contribution and importance of Indian students in Australia is reflected in a variety of ways. Firstly is the direct contribution of Indian students to Australian education exports. In 2008, education exports contributed $15.5 billion to Australia's economy, of which, Indian students accounted for around $2.4 billion or 15.5 per cent.[25] In recent years, the number of Indian students in Australia has grown more rapidly than students from any other country (see Table 2). Table 2 shows that after China, India is the second largest contributor to Australia's education exports.

Enrolment data for the year to date August 2009, as shown in Figure 1, shows 109,356 Indian students in Australia compared with 137,431 students from China.[26] However, Reuters India suggests that in May 2009, there were 93,000 Indian students in Australia.[27] The enrolment data could differ from the actual number of students because they can enrol into more than one stream of education. In relative terms, India's share of all overseas student enrolments in 2009 was 19.3 per cent compared with China at 24.2 per cent. However, China's share of 31.5 per cent in the higher education enrolments is much more robust than India's share of 13.6 per cent. Indian enrolments dominate in the vocational education and training (VET) sector, where students train in trades such as automotive, cookery and hair dressing. Here India has a 34.2 per cent share of total VET enrolments compared to China at 14.4 per cent.[28]

Secondly, overseas students are a major focus of Australia's migration programme, because they have the propensity to stay back and permanently settle in Australia. Indian students are an important contributor in this. The Indian students in Australia are considered as "migrants in-transition". According to Hawthorne, more than half of the skilled Indian migrants were former international students living in Australia.[29] The recent changes to Australia's skilled migration policy make it easier for overseas students to apply for permanent residence (PR) upon completion of their studies. Research shows a direct relationship between the courses offered by Australia's education industry and its skilled migration programmes. For example, Tsukamoto argues that 66 per cent of Indian and 38 per cent of Chinese students are choosing to stay in Australia after they finish their study.[30] Taking the approximate figure of 93,000 Indian students in Australia and applying Tsukamoto estimates would suggest that around 55,000 of these Indian students would be applying for permanent residency, and if granted, they would join Australia's skilled (as well as non-and semi-skilled) workforce for the next 20-30 years. A study for IDP international, an international education recruitment firm, also supports the Hawthorne and Tsukamoto arguments. This study, based on a survey of Australian tertiary educated international graduates, reveals that Indian and Chinese graduates are more likely to have permanent residency in Australia, have worked in Australia and intend to work in Australia, compared to graduates from other nationalities.[31]

Thirdly, a key contribution by Indian students (and other international students) is that they are an important element of global knowledge flows, and broader economic and social links through alumni, professional and personal networks. Through business, trade and investment, and in the scientific and social arenas, these linkages benefit both India and Australia. According to recent work, the old premise of "brain drain" is being challenged by "brain circulation".[32] Return migration and continuous movements between countries benefit both sending and receiving countries, particularly in the knowledge economy, where people to people contacts around the world are important in acquiring and sharing new ideas and promoting collaborative ventures, including in key science and technology projects.[33]

Business and Entrepreneurship

Indian businesses, either owned by the diaspora in this country, or with Indian diaspora in senior positions in local companies, are making a very substantial contribution to the economic growth and prosperity of Australia.

For example, a number of Indian companies, including Information Technology companies such as Mphasis and Infosys, have a significant presence in Australia, while Indian Foreign Direct Investment (FDI) in Australia was worth $69 million in 2008.[34] Another Indian consortium is set to invest some $63 million through an Australian based venture, which would be India's largest Greenfield investment in the eastern seaboard of Australia, aimed at producing and exporting oils and biodiesel.[35]

More broadly, the bilateral trade has also grown significantly in recent years. Australian merchandise exports to India recorded $13,525 million in 2008 suggesting a year-on-year growth of 46 per cent between 2003 and 2008. In the same year, Australian imports of Indian merchandise were valued at $1831 million and the yearly growth rate was 26 per cent.[36]

In the services sector in 2008, the education related travel and personal travel, excluding education, dominated

Australian exports (largely tourism-$197 million). Personal travel, excluding education also dominated Australia's services imports in 2008 ($304 million) and computer and information services ($85 million).[37]

Indian Diaspora in Australia is highly entrepreneurial. For example, an Indian owned and run business, *Panachee,* is located in Chadstone, Melbourne, Australia's largest and exclusive shopping mall. Panachee is unique in providing a "one stop shopping" experience relating to pre-and post-natal goods and services. Believed to be a world first, this new business model sells fashion apparel, books and toys as well as pharmacy items. This innovative approach combines the sales of high quality goods and services, with convenience and time saving benefits for expectant mothers.[38]

A different yet equally innovative example of Indian business in Australia is the recent establishment of *Tiffins,* which is based on the Anglo-Indian concept of Tiffin as a light lunch that originated in Mumbai.[39] Office workers in Mumbai receive freshly heated meals from relatives in dishes stacked one on top of the other in steel containers that are delivered through a complex network of people on bicycles. The Australian variation of Tiffin provides meals for office workers delivered by three wheel cycles, in authentic Tiffin-like containers. Unlike the original Indian model, the Australian variant is essentially a mobile restaurant, in which relatively inexpensive orders are placed on line and delivered to offices in the central business district of Melbourne (and also increasingly outer suburbs). This unique lunch time experience earned Tiffin an important business award in 2009.[40]

The Australia-India Business Council (AIBC), which also has State and Territory Divisions, is an important vehicle for promoting business and economic links between the two countries. Established in 1986, the AIBC provides, among other things, business matching services, information on business contacts in both countries and helps to facilitate trade missions. The AIBC comprises representatives of Indian business leaders in Australia, and reinforces the valuable contribution of the Indian business diaspora in promoting trade and business opportunities in Australia as well as India.[41]

Social and Cultural Contribution

The Indian diaspora's contribution to Australia extends beyond just the economic domain.

A glance at India's media in Australia reveals the impact and contributions of Indians to this country beyond skilled migration. There are at least a dozen Indian newspapers published in Australia. In addition, there are radio programmes in different Indian languages across capital cities. The recent increase in Indian migration has had a profound effect on the Australian life style. For example, there are presently 1349 Yoga centres across Australia and more than 1100 Indian restaurants and take-aways currently listed in the Australian Yellow Pages.[42] It should be also noted that not all businesses list in the Yellow Pages. Hence, the actual number of India related businesses would certainly be higher. In contrast, there were fewer than 40 Indian restaurants in the whole of Australia in 1980. Now, there are also a large number of Indian grocery stores in all capital cities. In addition, a significant number of mainstream supermarkets such as Coles and Safeway have significantly increased their stock of Indian food items such as frozen *samosas,* as well as spices and groceries. The number of Indian fashion stores around Australia is also quite significant. All this has given Australians a choice in many aspects of their life style.

Bollywood, and its associated activities, have made a major impact on Australia. Apart from the regular screening of Bollywood productions in Australian cinemas, a number of Bollywood dance schools provide instruction and entertainment and thus enrich Australia's diverse cultural base. The links between the Indian and Australian film industries go back many decades. However, this relationship was strengthened in the late 1990's when Feroz Khan undertook filming in Australia for 40 days. More recently in 2006 and 2007, three Bollywood blockbusters were filmed in Australia. "Love story 2050" was shot in Adelaide, "Hey Baby" filmed in NSW and "Chak De India" in Melbourne.[43] The movie "Victory" based on a cricket hero's story, was filmed in part in Melbourne in 2008 drawing on, amongst others, Australian cricket stars.[44]

In addition, world renowned Indian artists have established classical dance schools in Australia. These schools reflect India's diversity and traditions of excellence in classical dance such as Mohiniattam and Bharatnatyam. Importantly in Australia, these schools also fuse traditional Indian dances with Western dances as well as indigenous cultural dances.[45]

Many Indian businesses here contribute not only to greater wealth and job creation in this country, but also exhibit strong social conscience. For example, Indian businesses have donated generously following the bushfire tragedy in many parts of Australia in the summer of 2008-2009. The breadth and depth of the relationship of Indian diaspora is nicely summed up by Melissa Parke, the West Australian Member of Federal Parliament in the following quote "Australia's relationship with India goes beyond the oft cited notion of cricket, curry and the Commonwealth".[46] Coincidently, both countries share the same public holiday on the 26th of January, which marks Australia Day and India's Republic Day.

India's increasing influence in Australia is also evident in the fact that two of India's main festivals are now publicly celebrated. Thousands of people including a significant number of Australians participate in the annual festivals of Holi and Diwali in most capital cities. These events are often co-sponsored by Indian community organizations and government agencies, at which the presence of ministers, members of parliament and other government representatives highlight the importance of Indian events.

Another indication of India's growing influence in Australia, including the pro-active contribution of the Indian diaspora, is the establishment of the Australia-India Institute at the University of Melbourne in September 2009. According to Julia Gillard, Deputy Prime Minister of Australia, this institute is a three way partnership between the University of Melbourne, La Trobe University and the University of New South Wales, that would be expected to support research, teaching and the holding of conferences. The aims of this institute include strengthening and sustaining bilateral relationships between Australia and India, with a key focus to enhance Australia's understanding of India, its culture, its place in the world and future prospects.[47]

Political and Institutional Contribution

In this sub-section we consider briefly the contribution made by Indians in Australia in key institutions for public policy decision making, and political and social influence in Australia.

It must be said that compared to other places such as the U.K and the U.S, that the Indian influence in the political-institutional sphere has been relatively limited. In this sense, the Indian diaspora's contribution in Australia is representative of what we call nascent diaspora engagement compared to deep diaspora engagement in the U.K and U.S. We contend that the integration of the Indian diaspora in the U.K and U.S is more widespread, pervasive and fundamental so as to allow for significant contributions by the Indian diaspora in those countries in the public policy decision making arenas.

For example, except for at the local government level, there are no members of Parliament at State or Federal level from the Indian Diaspora in Australia. In the UK, in the early part of this decade, Indians had significant national political representation with 4 elected members of the National Parliament and 11 members of the House of Lords. At the local government level, there were more than 250 Indian Councillors in the UK.[48] In the US, Bobby Jindal of Indian origin is the Governor of Loiusana, and Ms Nikki Randhawa

Haley is in the race to become Governor of South Carolina, and if successful would become the first Indian American woman to hold such a high office.[49] Moreover, some key posts in the Obama administration are also occupied by people of Indian origin, including, for example, the Chief Information Officer, Vivek Kundra. Integration at the political level would be vital in extending the Indian influence into the key policy decision making apparatus in Australia and for lasting contributions to the wider community.

Secondly, the Indian presence in institutions for law and order, such as the judiciary and police force, is almost non-existent. Admittedly, people from other Asian countries are equally absent from these institutions. According to the 2006 census, there were only 19 Indians in the Victoria police.[50] Perhaps the apparent misunderstandings of the Indian students and police, as discussed later, could have been avoided, or at least ameliorated, with more police of Indian origin. Finally, people of Indian origin are also absent from Australia's mainstream media. Indians, by becoming more integrated into mainstream media, would not only further promote India's contribution to Australia but also draw the attention of the general population to concerns of Indians living in Australia.[51]

The relatively limited contribution of the Indian diaspora to Australia in these arenas reflects possibly a number of factors. Indian interests in Australia have been much more pronounced in the academic, professional and business fields. Further, it can be argued that opportunities for Indian participation in these institutions have been limited. Finally, and more broadly, it can be suggested that the relationship between the two countries has not yet reached a level of maturity (or scale of migration from India to Australia compared to Indians migrating to the U.K and U.S) to accommodate extensive representation in key political and associated institutions.

However, the Indian diaspora does make a contribution in quasi-political institutions, such as advisory bodies to

Governments in Australia. For example, an Indian has been appointed as a Commissioner for the Victorian Multicultural Commission, a key Victorian Government body to promote cultural diversity in the State of Victoria.

Further, the Indian diaspora plays a role in the work of the Australia-India Council (AIC), an advisory body set up by the Federal Government in 1992 to help develop and promote awareness of the relationship between the two countries in the economic, educational, social and cultural spheres.[52]

Controversies

There have been certain controversies of late, which need to be raised as they may adversely impact on the ongoing and significant contribution of the Indian diaspora in Australia. Attacks on Indian students could have a significant impact on Indian students' enrolments. A recent study of potential Indian students by IDP indicates a decline of around 80 per cent in appointments at IDP offices in the wake of attacks on students[53], which could lead to a drop of 50 per cent in enrolments next year, although things are likely to improve after that.[54] There are potentially a number of flows on effects from the attacks on students. Apart from a possible drop off in future enrolments, existing Indian students here may be tempted to leave prematurely, thus, further adversely affecting Australia's export income and the potential source of skilled labour for Australia. Further, and more broadly, the controversy and negative press associated with attacks on students may engender negative perceptions amongst the wider community regarding the Indian diaspora in Australia, and towards India more generally. This may constrain the ability of the Indian diaspora to maintain its existing activities and fulfil its immense potential economic, social and cultural contributions. However, it should be noted that another IDP survey of 1130 Indian students (out of a broader survey of 6000 students from a range of countries) found that 26 per cent ranked Australia as the number one destination for safety (UK 20 per cent, Canada 20 per cent, New Zealand 13 per cent and US 15 per cent) as well as number one on best Government policies to protect international students.[55] This surprising result, arguably, may reflect Australia's long standing reputation as a safe destination amongst visitors, rather than simply responses to recent activities. According to the IDP, it may also reflect private opinions of students diverging from broader public opinions as represented in the media.[56]

The media commentary in both countries, and the so-called live coverage on the Indian TV, the screening of angry Indian students in Australia, including holding student rallies and bringing the traffic to a stand still in the central business district of Melbourne, and the talk of possible retaliatory violence by Indian students, has overstated the extent and magnitude of the attacks against Indian students. However, it can be conceded that at least some of the attacks have had racial connotations.

It should be noted that a significant range of measures and the swiftness of response demonstrate how seriously the various government agencies and the Indian community here have taken the issue. This is reflected in a number of ways at Federal and State levels including: High level Ministerial Delegations to and from India; the establishment in Australia of a special national taskforce to co-ordinate action in response to violence against Indian students; increased police surveillance and patrolling in trouble spots; information to students on accommodation, safety and employment matters in Australia; and various other State Government initiatives to reinforce the welcoming attitude to Indian students in Australia, and promote more effective links between Indian students and the local community.[57]

Looking ahead, there are challenges in not allowing certain incidents to jeopardise the long standing goodwill between the two countries, and the pivotal role of the Indian diaspora in shaping positive attitudes of both countries to each other.

Despite the recent initiatives outlined above to address the attacks on Indian students, more will be needed. In particular, we suggest the following.

- Calm is needed on all sides to approach the issue in

a more measured fashion;

- It will be important to build a long term national, concerted and co-ordinated effort in Australia rather than a fragmented knee jerk response;
- Engagement across all sections of the Australian community will be important, not just in particular locations or directed to particular groups; and
- More preparation will need to be done pre-arrival and post arrival in Australia to ensure that Indian students can integrate more effectively and easily into the mainstream Australian community.

The Indian diaspora as a whole faces key challenges in assisting in efforts to moderate tensions. Through its strong reputation and its deep and wide connections into the local Australian community, the Indian diaspora overall has an important role to play in promoting goodwill on both sides. For example, we contend that inclusive events, orchestrated by the Indian diaspora, such as Diwali (as mentioned previously), highlight the contribution of Indian culture to Australia and will go some way to smoothing over strained relations. Another suggestion we make is to celebrate the common symbolic day of 26th January (Indian Republic Day and Australia Day), through various events and the launching of joint economic, social and cultural projects between the Indian diaspora and broader Australian community.

Concluding remarks

Currently, around 240,000 Indians permanently live in Australia, which is a substantial increase from less than 7,000 Indians in Australia a century ago. A significant proportion of Indian migrants belong to professionals, highly paid or highly skilled categories. The Indian migrants have greatly contributed to Australia in a range of spheres. While Indians have contributed considerably at the economic, social and cultural level, the Indian contribution to Australia's knowledge economy is particularly significant, because Indians tend to have high levels of education.

Around 100,000 students from India are enrolled into various courses in Australia. While the vast majority of Indian students are enrolled into vocational education and training (VET) courses such as cookery and hair dressing, around 14 per cent of them account for higher education. This is because there is a direct connection between the VET courses offered and Australia's migration intake programme, which provide an easy transition from student to migrant status.

Following the attacks on Indian students early 2009, various government agencies have developed a framework designed to provide adequate safety for overseas students in general and the Indian students in particular. A range of new measures at the macro as well as at the micro level have been introduced. These measures range from the establishment of high-level inter-government bodies to police patrols in identified areas. However, more preparatory work would need to be undertaken at the pre-and post-arrival stages in order to facilitate a seamless integration of students into the mainstream Australian society.

There are challenges ahead facing the Indians in Australia, despite the already many achievements and substantial contribution of the Indian diaspora in a variety of fields. One of these key challenges will be to make an effective transition from nascent Diaspora engagement to deep Diaspora engagement. While Indian entrepreneurs are making their mark in Australia's business landscape, it is important for Indians to integrate more effectively into the key institutions of Australia's decision-making apparatus. In the long run, Indians also need to ensure sufficient participation in the law and order agencies, which would increase the understanding of Indian values and its culture among Australians and *vice-a versa*. Through this, the Indian contribution to Australia in all of its spheres can be further widened and deepened. It will also be very important for the Indian diaspora to utilise its networks and connections with the local community to re-build relationships in the wake of recent tensions.

Table 1: Total Migration and Total Skilled Migration (1998-1999 and 2008-2009)

Country of birth	Total Migration 1998-99	2008-09	Average Annual Growth(%)	Total Skilled 1998-99	2008-09	Average Annual Growth(%)
UK	10409	24835	13.9	6430	19047	19.6
India	3111	19278	52	2055	14609	61.1
China (excluding Taiwan and SARS)	7765	17982	13.2	2939	10133	24.5
South Africa	6153	8523	3.9	5495	7389	3.4
Philippines	4173	6920	6.6	1321	3899	19.5
Sri Lanka	1233	4334	25.2	470	2941	52.6
Malaysia	1586	4158	16.2	1012	3353	23.1
Iraq	2353	4148	7.6	34	104	20.6
Korea (South)	1230	3276	16.6	608	2543	31.8
Vietnam	2977	3033	0.2	82	387	37.2
USA	1661	2150	2.9	478	786	6.4
Indonesia	3213	2140	-3.3	2266	925	-5.9
Others	22571	33483	4.8	7192	14814	10.6
Total	81820	150217	8.4	34651	87245	15.2

Source: Department of Immigration and Citizenship (DIAC)-2 (2009).

Note: Data here includes both persons who arrived during the reference period as migrants and persons who arrived as temporary entrants, and were later granted permanent migration. Data on non-visaed permanent arrivals from New Zealand are not included in the Table.

Table 2 : Australia's exports of education related services by top 5 nationalities ($m)

	2006	2007	2008	% increase: 2006-2008
China	2,358	2,738	3,421	45.1
India	1,086	1,618	2, 389	120
Republic of Korea	826	964	1,076	30.3
Malaysia	617	670	753	22.0
Thailand	428	498	603	40.9

Source: Australian Education International-1 2009.

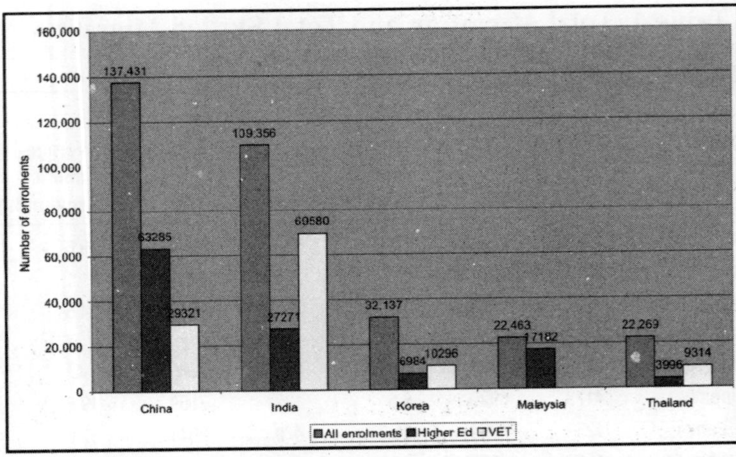

Graph 1: Top Five Countries in Student Enrolments in Australia Year to Date August 2009

Source: Australian Education International-2 2009.

Note: VET figures for Malaysia are not available.

Endnotes

1. Australian Bureau of Statistics (ABS)-1. 2009. *Australia Continues to Experience High Population Growth*, Australian Demographic Statistics. Canberra: Australian Government.

2. Hawthorne, Lesleyanne-1. 2007. 'Labour market outcomes for migrant professionals: Canada and Australia comparison', Citizen and Canada, Government of Canada, Ottawa.

3. High Commission of India in Australia (The). 2009. 'Indian Community in Australia', http://www.hcindia-au.org/indian_in_australia.html. Accessed on 5 November 2009.

4. Jain, Surinder. 2009. 'Evolving History of Indian Arrival in Australia', http://indians.australians.com/INDIAN-ARRIVAL-IN-AUSTRALIA.htm. Accessed on 21 September 2009.

5. Department of Immigration and Citizenship (DIAC)-1. 2009. '*Abolition of White Australia Policy*', Fact Sheet – 8, Australian Government, Canberra, http://www.immi.gov.au/media/fact-sheets/08abolition.htm. Accessed on 6 November 2009.

6. Voight-Graf, Carmen. 2005. 'The construction of transnational spaces by Indian migrants in Australia', *Journal of Ethnic and Migration Studies,* vol. 31, no. 2, pp. 365-384.

7. Jain, Surinder. 2009. 'Evolving History of Indian Arrival in Australia', http://indians.australians.com/ INDIAN-ARRIVAL-IN-AUSTRALIA.htm. Accessed on 21 September 2009.

8. Australian Bureau of Statistics (ABS)-2. 2009. *Migration 2007-2008,* Australian Government, Canberra.

9. Department of Immigration and Multicultural Affairs (DIMA). 2000. *Multicultural Australia: The India-born Community,* Australian Government, Canberra.

10. Australian Bureau of Statistics (ABS)-2. 2009. *Migration 2007-2008,* Australian Government, Canberra.

11. Australian Bureau of Statistics (ABS)-3. 2009. *Perspectives on Skilled Migrants,* Australian Government, Canberra, April.

12. Ibid.

13. Department of Immigration and Citizenship (DIAC)-2. 2009. *'Settlement Database Top 20 Countries by Migration Stream',* Tailored settlement reports, Australian Government, Canberra, data extracted on 9 October 2009.

14. OECD. 2009. 'International Migration Database: OECD Stat Extracts', Organisation for Economic Co-operation and Development, Paris, http://stats.oecd.org/index.aspx?lang=eng. Accessed on 30 October 2009.

15. Access Economics. 2008. *Migrants Fiscal Impact Model: 2008 Update,* Department of Immigration and Citizenship, Canberra.

16. Australian Bureau of Statistics (ABS)-4. 2009. *Australian Social Trends Expanding Links with China and India,* Australian Government, Canberra.

17. Faria, Ana I. 2001. The future of Indian ethnicity in Australia: An educational and cultural perspective, *International Education Journal,* Educational Research Conference 2001 Special Issue, vol. 2, no. 4, pp. 134-143.

18. Australian Bureau of Statistics (ABS). 2008. *Perspectives on Migrants: People Born in China and India,* Canberra: Australian Government.

19. Fuente, Angel dl and Ciccone Antonio. 2003. *'Human Capital in a Global and Knowledge-Based Economy: Assessment at EU Country level'*, Part 2, Employment and Social Affairs, Employment and European Social Fund, European Commission, Directorate-General for Employment and Social Affairs, Brussels, April.

20. Krueger, Alan B and Lindahl, Mikael. 2001. 'Education for Growth: Why and for Whom?', *Journal of Economic Literature*, vol. 39, no. 4, pp. 1101-36.

20. Productivity Commission. 2002. *'Skill and Australia's Productivity Surge'*, Australian Government, Canberra.

21. Committee on Prospering in the Global Economy of the 21st Century. 2007. *An Agenda for American Science and Technology Rising Above the Gathering Storm: Energizing and Employing Americans for a Brighter Economic Future*, National Academy of Sciences, National Academy of Engineering and Institute of Medicine of the National Academies, The National Academies Press, Washington D.C.

21. OECD-1. 2008. *'Science, Technology and Industry Outlook'*, Organisation for Economic Co-operation and Development, Paris.

22. OECD-2. 2008. *'The Global Competition For Talent: Mobility of the Highly Skilled'*, Organisation for Economic Co-operation and Development, Paris.

23. Leadbeater, Charles and Wilsdon, James. 2007. *The Atlas of Ideas: How Asian Innovation can Benefit us All*, London: Demos.

24. Manpower. 2008. *'India's Borderless Workforce: A Manpower White Paper'*, Developed in Collaboration with Laveeesh Bhandari and Payal Malik, Indicus Analytics, New Delhi.

25. Australian Educational International-1. 2009. *Research Snapshot*, Australian Government, Canberra, June.

26. Australian Educational International-2. 2009. *International Student Enrolment Data Tables* 7a, 9a, 10a, Australian Government, Canberra.

27. Reuters India. 2009. 'Indian Students Protest in Australia against Attacks', 7 June, http://in.reuters.com/article/topNews/idINIndia-40139420090607. Accessed on 2 November 2009.

28. Australian Educational International-2. 2009. *International Student Enrolment Data Tables* 7a, 9a, 10a, Australian Government, Canberra.

29. Hawthorne, Lesleyanne -2. 2007. Outcomes: Language, employment and further study, Canberra, Australia Educational International, Australian Government, Canberra.

30. Tsukamoto, K. 2009. 'The Interconnections between Australia's International Education Industry and its Skilled Migration Programs' in J Fegan and M H Field, eds, *Education Across Borders: Politics, Policy and Legislative Action,* Dordrecht: Springer.

31. Banks, Melissa and Alan Olsen, eds. 2008. *Outcomes of and Impacts of International Education: From International Students to Australian Graduates: The Journey of a Lifetime,* Canberra: IDP Education.

32. Banks, Melissa and Alan Olsen, eds. 2008. *Outcomes of and Impacts of International Education: From International Students to Australian Graduates: The Journey of a Lifetime,* Canberra: IDP Education.

32. Ibid.

33. Bound, Kirsten. 2007. *'India: The Uneven Innovator - The Atlas of Ideas: Mapping the New Geography of Science'*, London: Demos.

33. Day, Natalie and Stilgoe, Jack. 2009. *Knowledge Nomads: Why Science Needs Migration,* London: Demos.

34. Department of Foreign Affairs (DFAT). 2009. *'India Fact Sheets'*, Australian Government, Canberra.

35. *G'day India-1*. 2009. 'Indian Consortium Invests $63 million in Australia', vol. 3, no. 30.

36. Department of Foreign Affairs (DFAT). 2009. *'India Fact Sheets'*, Australian Government, Canberra.

37. Ibid.

38. *Bharat Times*. 2009. 'World First Maternity Concept Store Launched in Chadstone', September.

39. Tiffins. 2009. 'About us', http://www.tiffins.com.au. Accessed on 16 October 2009.

40. Business 3000 Winners. 2009. Category: Encouragement Award, http://www.b3000.org.au/winners-2009. Accessed on 29 October 2009.

41. Australia India Business Council. 2009. 'What We Do', http://www.aibc.org.au/Profile/What_We_Do, Accessed on 12 April 2009.

42. Yellow Pages-1. 2009. 'Restaurants Indian – All States', http://www.yellowpages.com.au/. Accessed on 2 November 2009.

43. Bollywood in Australia. 2009. 'India-Australia Film Relations: A Brief', http://bollywoodinaustralia.com/. Accessed on 9 October 2009.

44. Huxley, John. 2008. 'Bollywood Film Makers Turn Sport into Art', *The Age*, 9 January.

45. Australia Dancing. 2009. 'Indian Dance in Australia', http://www.australiadancing.org/subjects/3821.html. Accessed on 9 October 2009.

45. A program of the Natya Sudha Dance School in Melbourne in 2007 combined Mohiniattam dance from Kerala with Australian Aboroginal dance. Author attended this performance.

45. Singh, Gurmukh. 2009. 'I Am in the Race to Become Governor: Indian American Woman', *G'day India*, vol. 3, no. 28.

46. Parke, Melissa. 2009. 'More to Relation with Indian than Curry and Cricket', *Daily Telegraph,* 18 August, http://www.dailytelegraph.com.au/news/breaking-news/more-to-relationship-with-india-than-cricket-and-curry/story-e6freuyi-1225763324890. Accessed on 12 October 2009.

47. Gillard, Julia. 2009. 'Australia India Institute to Strengthen International Ties', http;//www/dewr.gov.au/Ministers/Gillard/ MediaReleases / Pages / Article 090807_12. Accessed on 9 October 2009.

48. Report of High Level Committee on Indian Diaspora, 2001. *'The Indian Diaspora'*, Ministry of External Affairs, Government of India, New Delhi.

49. Singh, Gurmukh. 2009. 'I Am in the Race to Become Governor: Indian American Woman', *G'day India*, vol. 3, no. 28.

50. *Indian Voice.* 2009. 'Can a Mono-cultural Police Force Gain the Trust of a Multicultural Community?' July.

51. Jabbal, Preeti. 2009. 'Making it in a Man's World' News Makers

in Oz media' Interview with Sushi Das of The Age, *Indian Link*, September.

52. AIC- Department of Foreign Affairs and Trade (DFAT). 2009. 'About the Australia-India Council' http://www.dfat.gov.au/aic/aic_intro.html. Accessed on 12 April 2009.

53. *G'day India*-2. 2009. 'Australia in Panic as Indian Students Back out', vol. 3, no. 28.

54. Das, Sushi. 2009. 'Students Rate Australia Safest', *The Age*, 13 October.

55. IDP international, 2009. 'Australia Still Number One for Safety Survey', presentation to international education conference, 12 October, http://www.aiec.idp.com/medi_releases.aspx. Accessed on 29 October 2009.

56. Das, Sushi. 2009. 'Students Rate Australia Safest', *The Age*, 13 October.

57. Banham, Cynthia and Gilmore, Heath. 2009. 'Rudd forms Indian Violence Taskforce' *Sydney Morning Herald*, June 3.

57. Brumby, J. 2009. 'Strengthening Relationships with India', *Beyond India*, October.

57. *G'day India*-3. 2009. 'State Premier Writes to Indian Students', vol. 3, no. 29.

57. Venu Gopal, R. 2009. 'Danny-guide for International Students', *Bharat Times*, October.

3

Indian Americans: Migrational Pattern, Professional Success, Cultural Emergence and their Political Activism

Ashok Sharma

Migration of people from India to different parts of the world is not a new phenomenon. They migrated to different regions of the world as and when they had the opportunity to do so. Today when we look at the demographic map of the world there is hardly any country where there are no people of India origin. According to estimates, there are over 20 million PIOs and some six million non-resident Indians living in the various parts of the world, particularly in the Gulf countries, Africa, West Indies, South and South-east Asia, Australia, Europe, and North America. In some countries, they comprise a considerable percentage of the total population (viz, Mauritius, Singapore, Fizi, etc.) while in others they belong to a microscopic minority.

Theoretically speaking, human beings leave their place of origin for a variety of reasons, such as environmental deterioration, political and religious persecution, economic hardship, search for a better life, and sense of adventure. Migration pattern of Indians can be put into three categories.

In ancient times Indian migration was characterised by

cultural expansionism. Saints and seers moved into different directions with deep knowledge of philosophy and the rich Indian cultural heritage and for the spread of religious messages, particularly that of Buddhism. Second phase of migration took place during the British rule, which was in the form of indentured labour to colonies especially the British colonies. Human cargo found their way to Africa, Mauritius, the Caribbian region, Fiji and South East Asia. This was one of the most exploitive and inhuman movement of people as it was forced migration. Third phase, which is contemporary plus started in post-independent era, particularly in the second half of the 20th century. This can be characterized as voluntary migration as the people migrated for better economic opportunities and standard of living. This phase is also known as "Brain Drain" wave because most of the migrants have been highly skilled professionals, such as, doctors, engineers, technicians and lawyers.

The United States, Canada and United Kingdom were ahead of other countries as the destination of Indian migrants in the third phase of history of migration. The United States, a country of immigrants, witnessed a significant number of Indian immigration. The US is like a melting pot in which all ethnic groups get assimilated into one homogeneous American culture and at the same time retain their own socio-cultural identities. Indians, who migrated in large numbers after passage of Immigration Act of 1965, are though not in large numbers, have, nonetheless, occupied a prominent place in the American life. They have assimilated in the larger American culture and retained their own identity as well. Today, they are held to be a model minority in the American melting pot.

For a long time, the Indian community in the US did not actively participate in the political processes and activities to voice their opinion. Their political activism was insignificant in comparison to other ethnic groups. However, the situation changed in the late 1980s and early 1990s. More and more number of Indian Americans began to show their interests in local political activities. Increased population with the changing migrational pattern and professional and material success of Indian American community has resulted into the increasing participation in the US political process. Commensurate to their achievements in different walks of life they are now actively participating in the US politics. This overall rising profile of Indian Americans has also resulted in their cultural emergence and influence in American socio-cultural life. Thus, what emerges from the above is an overview of Indian Diaspora in the United States. This article looks into the migrational and settlement pattern of Indian Diaspora in the United States. Focusing on economic and professional status of Indian Americans this paper takes an account of their contribution towards cultural, economic, professional and political life in the United States. Finally, before concluding, this article looks into the political activism and lobbying done for betterment of US-India relations that has emerged as one of the major achievements of Indian American community.

To deal above, this article is divided into five sections. The first section deals with migrational pattern of Indians in the United States, which covers pre-1965 phase as well as post-1965 phase. This division is significant as in pre-1965 phase the Indian American community were unskilled, mostly agricultural labourers and in post-1965 phase, the immigrants were skilled and educated, consisting of professional class doctors, engineers, academicians, etc. Second section looks into the settlement pattern of Indian community in the United States. Unlike other Asian ethnic groups, who are mostly ghettoized and concentrated in one area, the Indian Americans are evenly distributed throughout America and has contributed to its "Melting Pot" culture. Third part deals with professional and economic advancement of Indian Americans and their contribution in these fields in America. As an ethnic group their economic and professional success is much ahead of other ethnic groups. Fourth section explores their cultural contribution in their adopted land in the field of food, culture, entertainment, religion etc. Fifth section looks into their political participation and lobbying efforts for betterment of US-India relations, which has increased immensely in recent years. Their political clout is quite visible in their lobbying effort for smooth passage of Indo-US nuclear deal, which augurs well for both the countries strategically as well as commercially.

Migrational Pattern of Indian Americans

It is not an exaggeration to call the United States of America a land of immigrants. The history of that country is a history of waves of migration. People have settled there from all known civilizations of the world. In the 17th Century, the English Puritans settled in the New England States, even as the Spanish settled in Florida. Early in the 19th century came the great flood of Irish and German immigrants- 2 million Irish and 1.5 million Germans came to America between 1815 and 1860. The next wave brought 10 million Western European- English, Dutch, Swedes and Norwegians to American shores between 1880 and 1890. The third wave was even bigger: 16 million from 1890 the 1914. Most of these newcomers were Eastern and Southern Europeans - Sicilians, Greeks, Poles, Czeches, Italians and Russians' Jews.[1]

While the US has continued to be the primary destination of immigrants, Asian influx replaced the European in the 20th century. Koreans, Filipinos and Vietnamese began to join an already substantial Asian population consisting mainly of Chinese and Japanese. A sizeable section of the Asian migrants is of Indian origin popularly known as Indian-Americans, who are not only a growing community in the US, their achievements and professional success of late have become matters of envy to other Asian Americans, if not to other Americans at large. During various phases in modern history, diverse groups of India came to the United States for many different purposes: students, scholars, diplomats, political activists, religious leaders, merchants, visitors, professionals, sojourners, immigrants, and refugees.

For the convenience of analysis, the migration of Indians to the US can be broadly divided into two phases (i) the early immigrants till mid-sixties; (ii) the post-1965 immigrants, when stricter and detailed immigration laws were passed by the US Congress.

Immigration Act of 1965 passed during President Lyndon Johnson's administration, brought drastic changes in immigration policy and reversed a half century old policy of discrimination against Asian immigrants. This Act deleted ethnicity and race as a factor of elimination; removed the restrictive Asian quota under the 1921 law; abolished the national origins quota system (as was fixed in 1924); removed the "Barred Zone"provisions of the 1917 law; set a ceiling of 170,000 immigrant visa annually for the nations of Eastern Hemisphere (with a ceiling of 29,000 for any one nation) and 120,000 for the countries of Western Hemisphere , and set up seven preference categories, favouring the entry of professionals and skilled workers which the U.S. needed most.[2]

India has become one of the major beneficiaries of the 1965 Immigration Act. This act facilitated the way for thousands of Indians to immigrate to the US, to have their economic desires fulfiled and also helped them to form a distinct ethnic community of their own. Now immigrants entered from almost every Asian Country, the majority, however emigrated from China, India, the Philippines, Korea and Vietnam. The number of Indians gradually increased in 1965 onwards and the trend in Indian immigration took a new turn, with Indians from Caribbean Islands, British Commonwealth countries, European countries, and about 70,000 Indian refugees from business and professional classes, expelled by Idi Amin regime in Uganda in the early 1970s, entering the US under a special clause.[3]

Table 1 : Number of Indian Immigrants to the U.S. (1966-75)

Year	No. of Immigrants
1966	2458
1967	2642
1968	4682
1969	5963
1970	10114
1971	14310
1972	16926
1973	12256
1974	11863
1975	14939
Total	**96153**

Table 1 indicates that from 1966 to 1975 altogether 96,153 Indians imigrated to the U.S. and surprisingly the number was highest in 1972 when Indo-US relations became very strained in the wake of 1971 Indo-Pakistan war that led to the birth of Bangladesh. By 1979, the seven leading exporters of manpower to America were all from the third world and India ranked sixth after Mexico, the Philippines, China (including Taiwan and Hong Kong). In the 1980 census, the Indian American Community accounted for 387,223. In five year i.e., from 1976 to 1980 a total of 291,070 had immigrated to the US. The 1990 U.S. Census recorded the number of Indian-Americans at 815,447 and between the 1980 and 1990 census, the annual growth rate of the community was 8.5 per cent.[4]

According to the estimate of the Population Reference Bureau, the Indian American Population has grown by 103 per cent in 1980-90, a growth rate second only to Chinese. Among Asian American ethnic groups and by 55 per cent in 1990-97, second only to Vietnamese. The Indian American Population number 1.215 million in 1997, making it the third largest Asian American ethnic group in the U.S. after the Chinese and the Filipino Americans, leaving behind the Japanese.[5] Given the Census of 1990, of all the Asian Population, the Asian Indians ranked fourth after the Chinese (1, 645,472).[6]

Table 2 : Number of Indian Immigrants to the U.S. (1981-1991)

Year	Number
1981	21522
1982	21738
1983	25451
1984	24964
1985	26026
1986	26227
1987	27803
1988	26268
1989	31175
1990	30667

The Filipinos (1,406,770) and the Japanese (842,562) but outnumbered the Koreans, the Vietnamese, and others. While the Asian represented 2.92 per cent, the Indians represented 0.33 of the total U.S. population of 248, 709, 873 in 1990, and comprised 11.21 per cent of total Asian population and pacific Islander population of 7,273, 662 (1990).

As far as South Asian countries are concerned Indian immigration to the U.S. is far ahead of its neighbours. But Pakistan, Bangladesh and Sri Lanka's immigration pattern shows that their percentage have been increasing in 1970-1990 (see table 3).

Table 3 : Immigrants from India and Other South Asian Countries, 1970-1990

Year	Total	India		Pakistan		Bangladesh		Sri Lanka	
1970	11884	10114	85.1	1528	12.9			226	1.9
1975	19297	15773	81.7	2620	13.6	404	2.1	432	2.2
1980	27912	22608	81.0	4265	15.3	532	1.9	397	1.4
1985	33469	26026	77.8	5744	17.2	1146	3.4	553	1.6
1989	42112	31175	74.0	8000	19.0	2180	5.2	757	1.8
1990	42624	30667	72.0	9729	22.8	1252	2.9	976	2.3

Source: Immigration and Naturalization Service (1965-1977, 1978-1989; Statistical Year Book, 1990).

According to the U.S. Census 2000, the Indian American population stands at 1678, 765 out of a total US population of 281,421,906. Between 1990 and 2000 the overall population growth rate for Indian Americans was 105.87 per cent, which is the single largest growth among the Asian American Community, which stand at 7.6 per cent. According to 2000 Census, Indian Americans are the 3rd largest ethnic group among the Asian American Community after the Chinese American and the Filipino American. According to 2000 US census Asian American Community grew at a rate of 48.26 from 1990-2000. Above ten million Asian Americans constitute 3.6 per cent of the U.S. population, while Indian Americans represent 0.6 per cent of the U.S. population and 16.4 per cent Asian American population.[7]

GRAPHS ON CENSUS 2000

GRAPH –I

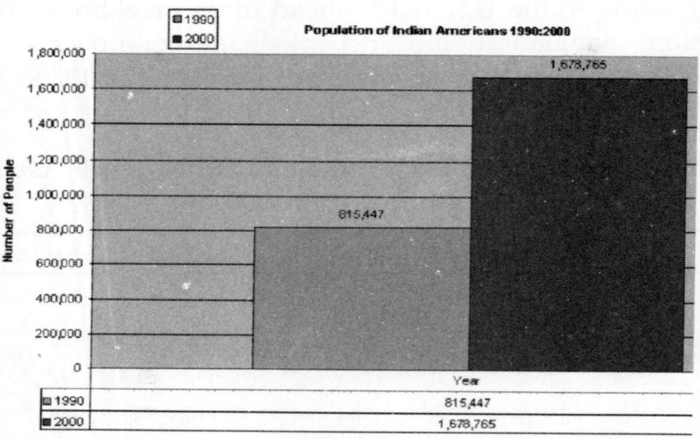

GRAPH- II

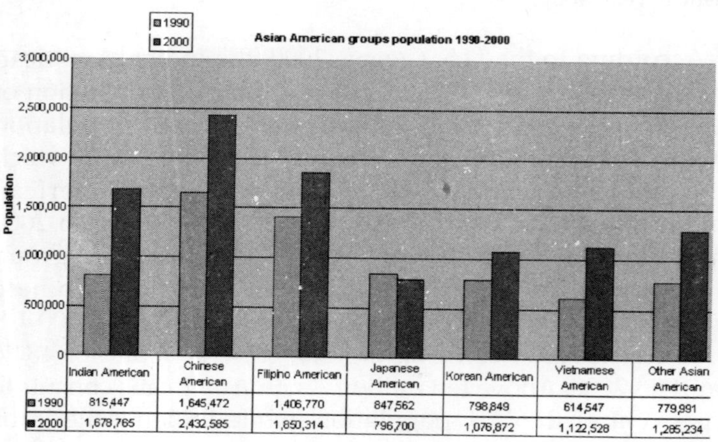

GRAPH- III

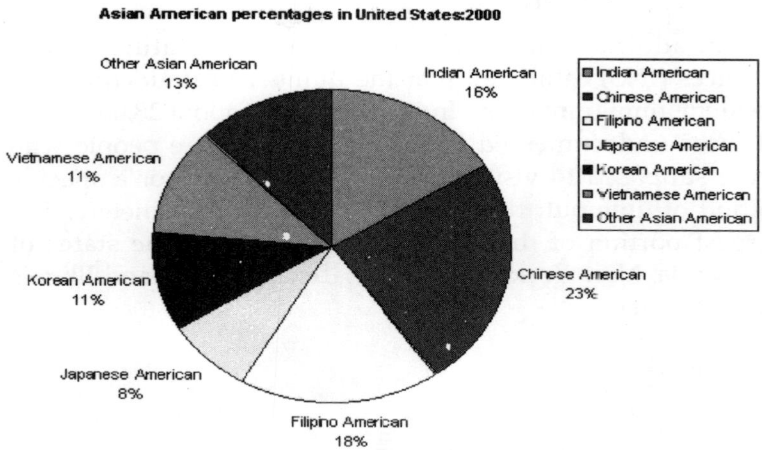

Source: http://www.iacfpa.org/census2K/census.htm.

The increase in the Indian American population from 1990 to 2000 is two fold. According to the India Abroad Center for Political Awareness' (IACPA) interpretation, a key factor that accounts for the rising numbers in the Indian American Community is the influx of H-1B Visa holders and their families (spouses and children) who have helped stimulate economic growth at unprecedented rates in the last several years. The number of H-1B visas issued to these from India jumped from 2,697 in 1990 to 15,228 in 1995 to 55,047 in 2000, according to figures from the State Department. IACPA sees that this sharp rise in the number of H-1B visa holder has fueled the growth in the Indian American community. This has particularly occurred between from 1997 to 2000, when considering the Indian American population was 1.215 million in 1997, according to an estimate given by professor Sharon Lee of Portland State University. Some growth in the Indian American Community can also be attributed to immigrants being admitted between 1990-2000 with number varying between 30,000 and 45,000 from India annually achieving permanent residence, as noted in materials from the immigration, and naturalization services (INS). The number of Indian Americans population is roughly equivalent to that of the state of Nebraska.[8]

In addition, the U.S. Immigration and Naturalization Services (INS) estimated that the number of undocumented resident immigrants from India in 1992 was about 28,000. Most of those undocumented Indian immigration are people who were supposed to visit the United States only for a specific period of time but then decided to remain indefinetely. The largest portion of these immigrants reside in the states of California, New York, New Jersey, Texas, Florida and Illinois in that order.

GRAPH -IV

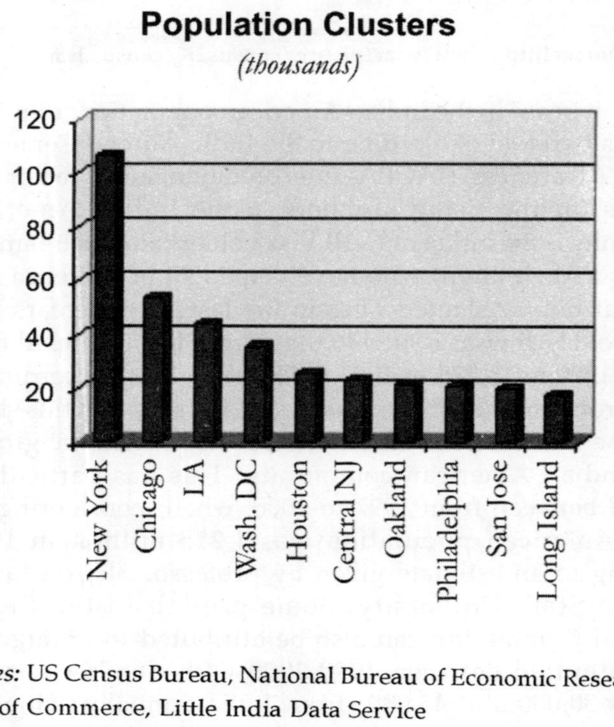

Sources: US Census Bureau, National Bureau of Economic Research, US Dept. of Commerce, Little India Data Service

The Indian American Community in the United States has experienced a remarkable transformation from its modest beginings. They left their homelands to settle in America in the hope of better economic opportunites and a better lifestyle. But at the same time it is also true that the U.S. desired, welcomed and hosted them in its national interests, economic and otherwise. The early immigrants catered to the American needs for labourers and in post 1965 phase skilled workers, engineers, doctors, scientists, educationists, software computer experts, information and technology experts, contributed to other sectors of American life and society.

Settlement Patterns of Indian Americans

The Indian American population today is more or less evenly distributed throughout America, although the early Indian immigration, like other Asian immigration showed a kind of ethnic concentration in the American West Coast, especially in California. Early Indian immigrants were ghettoised because they had many common traits, such as, agrarian orientation, illiteracy, poor knowledge of English and willingness to get married to non-Indians, especially poor Hispanic. They generally belonged to North West region of India, and most of them belonged to Sikh Community. They were dependent on each other.[9]

In post-1965 phase, Indian Americans are remarkably widely distributed as compared to other Asian Groups. This is obvious from the residential patterns of Indian Americans that shows they have been staying only in the West Coast region of America. In fact for Indian Americans, proximity to other Indians seems to be on low priority and desirability of a given residential area on grounds such as property, value and location are on a high priority. The Table 4 shows that nearly 20 per cent of Indian Americans have settled in California and only 3 per cent reside in other West Coast states. By contrast the largest proportion 35 per cent of Indian Americans have settled in the North-East and mostly in two States, New York and New Jersey.

Table 4 : Distribution of Indian Americans by Region and Major States in 1980 and 1990

	1980		1990		Increase	
	N	Per cent	N	Per cent	N	Per cent
U.S. Total	361531	100.0	815447	100.0	453916	125.6
West	71992	19.9	188608	23.1	116616	162.0
California	57901	16.0	159973	19.6	102072	176.3
Midwest	85175	23.6	146211	17.9	61036	71.7
Illinois	35749	9.9	64200	7.8	28.452	79.6
Michigan	14690	4.1	23845	2.9	9155	62.3
Ohio	13106	3.6	20848	2.6	7742	59.1
Northeast	120758	33.4	285103	35.0	164345	136.1
New York	60505	16.7	140985	17.3	80480	133.0
Pennsylvania	15212	4.2	28386	3.5	13184	86.7
New Jersy	29510	8.2	79440	9.7	49930	169.2
South	83606	23.1	195525	24.0	111919	133.9
Texas	22231	6.1	55795	6.8	33564	151.0
Florida	9144	2.5	31457	3.9	22313	244.0
Virginia	8483	2.3	20494	2.5	12011	141.6
Maryland	13705	3.8	28330	3.5	14625	106.7

Source: U.S. Bureau of the Census (1983,Table 62, 1993a, Table 253)

The New York- New Jersey, home to more than 30 per cent of Indian Americans, can be considered the capital of Indian Americans in the U.S. The high concentration of Indian immigrants in New York and New Jersey is due to the fact that these two states absorbed a large number of Indian immigrant medical professionals in the late 1960s and the early 1970s, following the pattern of chain migration, many other Indian immigrants settled in these two states. A good number of Indians have also settled in such states as Illinios, Texas and Florida.

In fact, large Indian American community exist in every state of the US, the five largest states— California, Texas, New

York, New Jersey and Illinois, is home to Indian American populations of over 60,000 each. Washington D.C. metropolitan areas has a community of over 50,000 people. Indian Americans are the largest of Asian American ethnic groups in New Jersey, the second largest (after the Chinese Americans) in New York and Maryland, and (after Filipinos) in Illinois, and the third largest (after Vietnamese and Chinese) in Texas.[10] For the statewise distribution of the Indian American community in the U.S. refer to Table 4.

One can find Indian grocery stores and other ethnically oriented business flourishing in Flushing and Jackson Hights (in the Queen Borough of New York City) in Edison and Iselin (in Central New Jersy), and on Devon Street (in Chicago). However, they have not established India town in any city comparable to China town in many cities and Koreatown in Los Angeles. In post-1965 phase, Indians have been able to create symbolic communities. They have settled around workplaces, such as high technology firms, hospitals, universities, and hotels/motels in or around metropolitan areas or along state highways. They have also developed places of worship, stores and other services around their residences.[11] Selection of the residences of the Indians rest on pragmatic criterias such as access to work, proximity to the best schools in their neighbourhoods for their children's education, property values, and proximity to relatives and friends.

Residential patterns of Indian Americans shows that they have not formed a little India or Indiatown as ecological ghettos. Unlike Chinese Americans (they have China town in many cities) and Korean Americans (they have formed Koreatown in Los Angeles) the recent Indian Americans and also Filipino Americans have not established ethnic ghettos.

Chinese immigrants in San Francisco, New York City, Los Angeles and other cities established segragated communities known as Chinatowns. Chinese created Chinatowns somewhat involuntarily in response to racial oppression and violence against them, in late 19th century. Because of the convenience of employment in ethnic business, ethnic food and language a large number of recent immigrants from China have resided in Chinatowns. Consequently, a significant proportion of Chinese Americans in each major Chinese Community still live in Chinatown. In the same manner, Korean in Los Angeles have also established an ethnic ghetto named Koreatown, which is the only officially recognised Korean enclave in the U.S.[12]

Although Indian Americans are highly represented in suburban residential areas, they have not formed ethnic concentration leading to ghettoization of the community. There are number of reasons for this. First, the Indian Americans, though apparently homogeneous to the outsiders, but in reality they lack cultural homogenity and are divided on the basis of religion, language and region of origin. Secondly, Indian Americans are characterised by higher educational and occupational levels than other Asian immigrants. Immigrants from middle class and professional background generally do not need an ethnic ghetto. Thirdly, their fluency in English language enable them to comfortably live with other Americans. Yet another reason may have to do with Hindus and Hinduism. Hinduism, unlike Christianity or Islam is not a congregational religion. Moreover, Hindu temples have significant influences in language based group identification.[13] However, the lack of ethnic concentration should not be taken as if there is no pan-Indian American organizations. Residential pattern of Indian Americans have not negatively affected their political activism and related lobbying activities.

Professional Success of Indian Americans

Indian Diaspora in the US popularly known as Indian Americans, with a population of around two million, have made their presence felt in every walk of life in United States. They are well placed in the education and economic fields and this speaks of their achievement, which is ahead of most of the ethnic groups.

Indian population in the US recorded a phenomenal growth of 105.87 per cent in the past decade, the highest among all Asian origin groups, according to the US Census Bureau 2000. It increased by more than two-fold in 2000, growing to 1,678,765 or 0.6 per cent of the total US population from 815,447 or 0.3 per cent of the total population in 1990 beating the figures posted by the Chinese, Filipinos, Japanese, Koreans, Vietnamese and "Other Asian" (including Pakistanis, Bangladeshis, Sri Lankans) categories.

According to the latest survey of the US Census Bureau, Indian population in the United States grew from almost 1,678,000 in 2000 to 2,319,000 in 2005: a growth rate of 38 per cent, the highest for any Asian American community, and among the fastest growing ethnic group in the United States after Hispanic Americans. At present, they are third largest Asian American group in US after the Chinese and the Filipinos. They constitute 0.8 per cent of the total US Population.

Indian Americans have left their mark as academicians, entrepreneurs, doctors, lawyers, engineers and financiers. They have attained a high level of education with more than 87 per cent completing high school, at least 62 per cent having some college education and as much as 58 per cent over the age of 25 holding a bachelor's degree or higher. 72.3 per cent of Indian Americans constitute the work force of which 43.6 per cent are employed in managerial and professional specialties.[14]

Of all the immigrant groups in the U.S., the Indians' Americans are in the highest income group. In the words of former President R. M. Nixon ".... the average Indian immigrant to the U.S. has higher income than average American."[15] Their per capita income is $17,777.00, that is, higher as compared with a national per capita income of $14,143.00. Their poverty rate is only 9.7 per cent, lower than the national average 13 per cent and annual buying power is around $20 billion annually in US.

They have made excellent progress in the field of science, technology, medicine and academia. Over 5000 faculty members in Universities and 30,000 Indian-American medical doctors, forming single medical ethnic group, are present in US. They command over 50 per cent of the economy in the lodging sector owning around 12,500 hotels, with a total market value of their properties estimated at $31b.

Their latest area has been in the fields of computer technology and software sector. 1/4 of programmers are Indian and 1/3 of the wages paid in the entire IT industry goes to Indian InfoTech technicians working in the U.S.A. About 300,000 Indian Americans work in technology firms in Silicon Valley accounting for more than 15 per cent of high-tech startups in that region. Their median income in that region is estimated to be $125,000 (average $200,000) a year. In 2002, there were over 223,000 Indian Americans owned firms in the U.S., employing more than 610,000 workers, and generating more than $88 billion in revenue.

The image of wealthy Indian Americans gets puffy boost following latest estimates from the investment firm Merrill Lynch that there are 200,000 millionaires of Indian Origin in the U.S., which means that one in every nine Indians in the U.S. is a millionaire, considering their total population around 1.8 million. For the record, the United States has an estimated 2.1 millionaires, which is less than one per cent of its population compared to the nearly 10 per cent of Indian Americans making it the wealthiest immigrant in U.S.[16]

The economic advancement and entrepreneurship of Indian Americans further gets reflected from the fact that in recent years the United States has seen Indian as heads of major U.S. companies — Sanjay Jha of Motorola Mobile company and PepsiCo Inc.'s Indra Nooyi are among about a dozen current CEOs. The professional status and economic advancement of Indian Americans have facilitated cultural emergence and political activism of Indians in American socio-political arena.

Retaining Indianness and Cultural Contribution

Indians are the richest ethnic community in the United States and have proved their mettle in different walks of life in a multicultural society like America. Not only they have very well assimilated in the American society but also they have retained their Indianness, family values and contributed towards spreading Indian culture in the United States too.

The influence of Yoga and Ayurveda on Americans is another mark, which Indians in the United States have left in US. Yoga has become immensely popular in the United States and people are not only practicing it but they are earning by teaching yoga in America. Yoga is already a multi-billion dollar industry in the USA, with 18 million American practitioners, with revenues of $27 billion per year revenues (from classes, videos, books, conferences, retreats) and over 10,000 studios/teachers. Over 98 per cent of yoga teachers and students in USA are non-Indians. America's yoga centres are potential retail outlets for Indian culture. Ayurveda rakes in $2 billion a year and is part of the high growth international market for plant medicines. Although spread of Yoga and ayurveda can not be entirely attributed to Indian Americans but certainly they have tried to promote their culture and the credit goes to them also.[17]

But when it comes to retaining Indianness in strict sense of family values and culture, it can be aptly illustrated in the professional success of Indian Americans. The success in different walks of life of Indian Americans in comparison to other ethnic community and Native Americans is very much attributed to the family values and structure, which Indians have been able to retain in the United States. Indians in America help their kith and kins by helping each other and this has helped in small business. Indian families are closely knit. Parents and elder members of the family make sacrifices for their children and brothers help brothers. Indian grocery stores, motels and hotels and other businesses usually are the product of pooling together of extended family resources. This is absent in other communities. For Indian Americans this is a common practice for parents or parents-in-law to arrive for lengthy stays, or for nieces, nephews or the children of cousins to be informally adopted into U.S. households for the duration of their college-going years, as they are in India. The open expansiveness of the Indian family may not be its most unique feature, but it is one of the most enduring and admirable features. The children of the Indian Americans can look forward to their parents to be involved in their lives, to pay college tuition and living expenses, to assist them find marriage partners, help them set up new homes and assist them with new babies. For example in Queens, N.Y., entire villages from Punjab state in India have re-established themselves and maintain their traditional family values.[18]

The belief that close contact with relatives should be cultivated is shared by most Indian families, where the definition of a relative is broad, and includes not only immediate and distant blood relatives, but friends from the same town/village/city and so on. When contact with immediate relatives is not possible to maintain, surrogate familial relations are assiduously developed. New immigrants to the community are often given material and emotional support; at celebratory or other events like deaths, it is this circle that serves as the immediate family.

However, the challenges for the Indian Americans are how to imbibe and inculcate Indian values, norms and culture. This is most disturbing for the first generation of Indian immigrants as home and family figure significantly in their definition of Indian consciousness. There are difference of opinion among Indian Americans on the idea of Indianness and how it can be imbibed into the new generation. However, generally traditional music and dance, religious and ceremonial practice, regional food-joints, ethnic clothing or ornamentation, popular culture, films, media, and special summer camps are helpful in cultivating Indianness.

Also the Indian families are finding it difficult to absorb dominant norms, like the nuclear family. They find it tough to reconcile these changing norms and end up differentiating between work life and home life. As a result, they follow the prevalent work ethics of the US at workplace and maintain their Indianness at home. Women's role is pivotal in putting up and retaining extended family structures, and in the socialization of their U.S. born children. By maintaining religious tradition and extended family structure women often find themselves under stress. Also at times maintaining Indianness at times leads to sticking to the older, static and rigid image of India as the outlook of Indians long settled in the U.S. have become static in time, even as India has progressed and changed. Finally, despite all the odds Indian community has survived, flourished and retained their Indianness in multicultural America and contributing towards popular American food, entertainment and religious culture.

Food

Indians have introduced Indian cuisine to the United States, and it has become established as a popular cuisine in the country, with hundreds of Indian food-joints nationwide. After the Immigration Act of 1965 with the increase in the Indian population in the United States and with it the prevalence of Indian cuisine, especially in San Francisco, Los Angeles, Chicago, the New York City neighborhoods of Murray Hill, Jackson Heights and East 6th Street, and in Edison, NJ. All-you-can-eat buffets with several standard dishes are typical in some Indian restaurants in the United States. At present, there are many Indian markets and stores in United States. Some of biggest Indian markets are in Silicon Valley, Chicago, New York City, the Philadelphia metropolitan area, and Edison, New Jersey. Areas with a significant Indian market presence also include Devon Avenue neighborhood/ market in Chicago and Pioneer Blvd. in the Los Angeles region. Other predominantly Indian neighborhoods are Journal Square in Jersey City, New Jersey, Jackson Heights in Queens, New York, Hilcroft Avenue in Houston, Texas and the SE Maynard Road/Chatham Square area in Cary, North Carolina.[19]

Recreation and Entertainment

Indian Americans have preserved their likings in the field of entertainment too. There are Hindi radio stations in areas with high Indian populations, including Radio Humsafar, Radio Salaam Namaste, FunAsia Radio. There are also Tamil radio stations in the United States.[20]

Several cable and satellite providers offer Indian channels: Asianet, Sun TV, Star TV, TV Asia, Zee TV, Sony TV, NDTV and Gemini. Others have offered Indian content for subscription, such as the Cricket World Cup.

Many metropolitan areas with high Indian-American populations now have movie theatres specialized for showing Indian movies (primarily Hindi/Bollywood and in the South Indian languages of Tamil and Telugu. Silicon Valley, for example has two such multiplexes: one in Fremont and one in San Jose).

The Dallas - Ft.Worth Metroplex has a "Desi" Multiplex called Amar Akbar Anthony in the Richardson township. The area also has a movie theatre that plays Indian movies, FunAsia. In 2006, the first 24 x 7 Desi F.M. station in North America was launched, Radio Salaam Namaste 104.9 FM, in the Dallas area. A similar multiplex, featuring Indian film exclusively on two screens (and other international films on four additional screens) opened in 2002 in Cary, N.C.. In July 2005, MTV premiered a spin-off network called MTV Desi which targets Indian Americans.[21]

Cultural emergence of Indian Americans and their contribution to popular American mainstream culture is now being noticed and visible in Hollywood movies and Television shows. For instance, director Manoj Night Shyamlan, two time academy award nominated Indian American Filmmaker and scriptwriter, got international fame when he directed and scripted "The Sixth Sense". Based on the lives of slumdwellers of Mumbai, the movie *Slumdog Millionaire* is a big hit around the world, but particularly in the U.S., having just won eight Academy Awards and grossing over $120 million dollars in North America symbolizes the cultural emergence and influence of India and Indian Americans in popular-mainstream American culture.

Model and cooking author Padma Lakshmi's "Top Chef" TV season and then became the celebrity face for many products, Anoop Desai, dubbed "Noop Dogg," drew fans with his singing on "American Idol," and Aziz Ansari was in TV's medical comedy "Scrubs" before moving to a regular role in the upcoming comedy series "Parks and Recreation". Indian Americans have shown their presence felt in the field of TV journalism too. For instance, Fareed Zakaria, editor of Newsweek International and Sanjay Gupta, a neurosurgeon and medical correspondent, have their own weekend shows on CNN. Indian music and themes are gradually occupying its place in popular American culture. Indian dance and music as a fusion with genres such as hip-hop, house, and reggae, and in such forms it has become a pop sensation in the United States as well as United Kingdom.

Religion

Communities of Hindus, Buddhists, Zoroastrians, Sikhs, Jains, Muslims, and Christians from India have established their religions in the country. As of 2000, the American Hindu population was around a million, if all are taken as Indian origin, this would make around 62.5 per cent of Indian Americans (1.6 million in 2000) as Hindu.[22] There are many Hindu temples across the United States. ISKCON, Swaminarayan Sampraday, BAPS Sanstha, Chinmaya Mission, and Swadhyay Pariwar are well-established in the US.

There are many Indian Christian churches across the US; Syro-Malabar Catholic Church, Syro-Malankara Catholic Church, Knanaya catholic, Indian Orthodox Church, Mar Thoma Church (reformed orthodox), Malankara Syriac Orthodox Church, Knanaya eastern orthodox, Church of South India, The Pentecostal Mission, India Pentecostal Church of God, and there are also a number of Indian Christians in mainstream American churches. Among Indian Muslims the prominent organizations include the Indian Muslim Council - USA.[23] A large percentage of American Muslims are of Indian origin. Most Indian Muslims, however, are affiliated with larger mainstream Muslim population of the US. The large Parsi community is represented by the Federation of Zoroastrian Associations of North America.[24]

Swami Vivekananda brought Hinduism to the West at the 1893 Parliament of the World's Religions.[25]. The Vedanta

Society has been important in subsequent Parliaments. Today, Hinduism is among the fastest-growing religions in the United States and many Hindu temples, most of them built by Indian Americans have emerged in different cities and towns of America. Hindu philosophy and spirituality has greatly influenced American life. More than 18 million Americans are now practicing some form of Yoga. In particular, Kriya Yoga was introduced to America by Paramahansa Yogananda. In addition, A.C Bhaktivedanta Swami Prabhupada initiated a popular ISKCON also known as Hare Krishna movement while preaching Bhakti yoga. Rajan Zed, Hindu chaplain, delivered the first Hindu prayer in United States Senate in 2007.

On 14th October 2009, the US President Barack Obama celebrated Diwali by lighting the ceremonial lamp at the White House amidst chanting of Vedic mantras, seeking world peace, tranquility and happiness. This was the first time that any U.S. president attended and celebrated Diwali at the White House, giving official recognition to this festival celebrated by many Hindus. This marks the latest cultural influence India and Indian Americans in the United States.

Political Participation and Lobbying for US-India Relations

The professional and material success has not made Indian American community complacent rather it has led to the increasing awareness among Indians to participate in the political process and voice their opinion. Commensurate to their achievements in different walks of life they are now actively participating in U.S. politics. They have realized that without this they can neither protect their rights as a minority nor safeguard their interests or ensure their security against other competitive or less privileged groups. Their political activism can be divided into two phases: 1.Pre-1965 Phase & 2.Post-1965 Phase.

1. Pre-1965 Phase

As regards the pre-1965 phase, while 19th century need not be taken into account due negligible number of Indians in U.S. the pre Indian independence phase too was not very impressive due to their political activities were restricted to protest against restrictive U.S. immigration and naturalization laws. While issues like individual rights and issues of justice and redress were important to Indian Americans, they were concerned for India's independence, as they had to suffer the humiliation and discrimination. In pre-1965 phase their political involvement was restricted to the activities of the Ghadar party dedicated to overthrow British rule in India and Komgata Maru incident of 1914. Because of their non-citizenship status they had to participate in the American political process from outside the system. India league of America founded by J.J. Singh (also lobbied for Indian citizenship Act of 1946), the National Committees for India's Friends, the Indian Welfare and other groups of Indian businessmen and intellectuals lobbied for issues concerning Indians in US and also put India's case for independence effectively before liberal American audiences.[26]

The declaration of India's independence and the passage of Citizenship Act of 1946 encouraged the Indians to influence the political process from within. It was reflected soon when Dilip Singh Saund was elected as a judge of a justice court in 1953 and elected to the U.S. House of Representatives in 1956. He was also appointed to the House Foreign Affairs Committee. In fact, Indian Americans had realized that while it was important to fight for minority rights, it was also equally important to identify with largest national issues so as to make their presence felt in a democracy.

2. Post-1965 Phase

Indian Americans were politically involved throughout 1970s and 1980s and their political activism revolved around the issues like racial discrimination and for minority rights. In fact, sense of representation, urge to protect the community's interest and sense of ethnic security and identity marked the pattern of their political activism during these two decades.

The lobbying by American Indian Association (AIA) to preserve the minority status of Indians while allowing them a distinct identity led to the 1980 Census Bureau classify Indians in U.S. as Asian Indians.[27] The attack on Indian women who put cosmetic dot on their foreheads between their eyebrows in 1986-87 by a group of Americans calling themselves *Dotbusters* particularly in New Jersey; taunts and violence on Indian males by Whites, African Americans and Hispanics; and also the murder of Nawaz Modi, an Indian American, by a Hispanic youth forced the Indian Americans to seriously ponder over the situation. They organized marches, meetings and sit-ins to halt further attacks and their efforts led to the reexamination of the police by the New Jersey State Attorney Generals office in March in 1988.[28]

In employment sector they had to face the Glass Ceiling Act, meaning which they were not getting the kind of status and rewards received by Whites for the similar accomplishments also effectively shutting out large number of Asians from the top level of management and organization.[29] Also the American Association of Physicians of Indian Origin claimed that Indians educated in foreign medical schools, were denied opportunities for licensing, residences and staffing privileges. These entire incidences reflected the resentments against the prosperity of Indian Americans in economic and professional fields. The Indians responded against these incidents with protests, sit-ins, organizing meetings and marches against these crimes.

Finally in 1990s, after years of sitting on the political sidelines, the Indian-American community came to realize that their safety and prosperity would not be long lasting unless they actively participate in U.S. politics. As a result, Indian Americans as an ethnic group have sought to protect their interests through forming over 1000 Indian-American organizations across the country.[30] This period saw the entry of Indian immigrants in information technology field enhancing the economic profile of Indian Americans, which was already good and have more voting power that led Indian-

Americans to become increasingly involved in the political system of the United States.

Their political activism, which was insignificant in comparison to other ethnic groups, is changing now. More and more numbers of Indian Americans began to show interests in domestic politics. Today they have India Caucus in both House and Senate and the organizations like IAFPE, IACPA, USINPAC, etc., are lobbying for their cause. They are actively taking part in election process either by contesting or by activities like fund raising for the candidates.

After D. S. Saund, the Indian presence in Congress was nowhere to be seen with no elect officials for forty years. The year 1994 marked the resurgence of such a presence. For instance, Peter Mathews an Indian by race and origin, ran for a Congressional seat from California in 1994 as a Democrat, although he lost in the same year, Ram Uppulari and Kunwar Sunil Singh Dhillon sought tickets for contesting Congressional election of 1994 from the State of Tennessee and Maryland respectively but they were not able to defeat their rivals from their own parties. Also some Indian Americans contested state legislative election, like Kanak Dutt from legislature of New Jersey state and Ram Higorani from Connecticut on Democratic party but could not win the election.[31]

Indian-Americans have traditionally exercised the most political influence in comparison with direct politics through their campaign contributions, and are actively involved in fundraising efforts for political candidates on the federal, state and local levels. In recent years, they have begun taking a more direct role in politics, as well as continuing to help through their financial contributions. Perhaps the highest profile effort to play a direct role in politics is by Kumar Barve, a US born Indian American, a Delegate for several terms in the Maryland assembly; State representative Upendra Chivukula in New Jersey; and Satveer Choudhary who became the youngest Senator of Minnesota. Dr. Ven Challa ran for the Republican seat in North Carolina.[32]

Several Indian-Americans have held the position of mayor. Examples are Bala K. Srinivas in Hollywood Park, Texas, John Abraham in Teaneck, New Jersey, and Arun Jhaveri in Burien, Washington. Like these leaders, more and more Indian-Americans have the courage, ambition and resources to pursue election for public office. The Clinton Administration also appointed Indian-Americans to various levels of government.

The November 2002 election saw more than 25 Indian American candidates bid for political office at the local, state and federal level. Five of them succeeded Kumar Barve, Senator Satveer Chaudhary retained their seats and Democrat Swati Dandekar made history in her maiden bid for a seat in the Iowa State Assembly. At the grassroots level, Uma Sengupta had a successful bid to the Assembly District of Queens in New York and Leela Rai became the trustee of the Yuba Community College District in Sutter County, California. The latest example of Indians involvement in direct politics is of Bobby Jindal contesting for Louisiana gubernatorial post, on a Republican ticket and Kamala Hariss victory as a district attorney of San Francisco.[33] Bobby Jindal is at present a member of the US Congress from Louisiana.

The trends of Indians playing direct role in US politics continued to show a positive sign in the US election 2004. Chiranjiv Kathuria made the bid for the Republican nomination for the US senate seat in Illinois. Rohit Khanna , Peter Mathews, Ayesha Nariman and Arjinderpal Singh tried for Democratic nominations from their Congressional districts. They lost but they received good percentage of votes. Bobby Piyush Jindal, Tim Philips and Inam ur-Rehman ran for the Republican Party nomination from their Congressional districts. But the only success at the national level after Dalip Saund is Bobby Piyush Jindal from the first Congressional District of Louisiana in the US election 2004. At the state level Ash Bhatt (D), Chonchol Gupta (R), Swati Dandekar (D), Sreenivasa Dandamudi (D) and Nikki Randhawa Haley (R) made their presence felt. But only success was Swati Dandekar, who was re-elected in the 36th State House district of Iowa[34]. In Mid-US Election 2006 Indians have shown an active participation into politics by fund-raising activities and contesting direct election.

Indian-Americans are working at all levels of the political spectrum, and their efforts, particularly in grassroots movements, are growing. Their political activities involved fund raising activities for political candidates on the federal, state and local levels. They have contributed to both the parties and their contribution has increased in recent years. Although no total tally exists, campaign finance records show four top Indian donors alone gave nearly $850,000 during the decade to many races and donations went to both the parties. In 1992 election they raised $4million and in 2000 Presidential election Indian Americans contribution was $7million.[35]

The Indian American community's ability to raise money attracted politicians from both sides in the US election 2004. Their lobbying efforts through these fund raising efforts and involvement in electioneering process was noticed by both parties. Both President Bush and Kerry took note of the Indian American community's political potential and they have had their share of vote.

The Indian Americans have shown an active participation for a better US-India relation. Congressional Caucus on India and Indian Americans in US Congress was formed with a dual mission of being an advocate for the concerns and needs of the Indian American Community and to promote better Indo-US ties. The Caucus members like Frank Pallone, S. Brown, Ackerman, Stephen Solaraz, Jim McDermott, Ed Royce, Joe Wilson and Crowley have been vocal for Indian Americans and India on many important issues such as terrorism, foreign aid, Kashmir, commercial ties, etc. They have countered India's opponent's activities in Congress and administration, and educated Congress members on the issues concerning India so that the Congress could in turn then question the administration and influence policy making.[36] Formation of Friends of India Group in US Senate under the co-chairmanship of John Cornyn and Hillary Clinton dedicated to address a single country is another example of growing political clout of India and Indian Americans in the US.

The recent Henry J. Hyde US-India Peaceful Nuclear Cooperation Act is another example of growing clout and increasing political participation of Indian Diaspora in the United States. Since July 2005 Indian Americans have been lobbying with US-India Business Council and India Caucus members for the successful passage of the Indo-US Nuclear agreement in the US Congress.[37] They countered non-proliferations lobby in the US Congress and adversaries of India in the US Congress at every stage of the Indo-US nuclear bill.

Indian Americans did intense lobbying in final stage especially when it was being tabled before the Senate and House of Representative for voting to become an Act. They realized that an easy passage of the agreement is not possible, so one could witness various pro-nuclear lobbying activities by the affluent Indian Americans.

Although Republicans had the required majority in the US Congress and the deal was being backed by the Bush administration, there were deeply entrenched actors within the US State Department and the non-proliferation lobby that opposed the US decision to make India an exception to nuclear regulations. Anti Indo-US nuclear lobby groups and nonproliferation activists like David Albright, prominent Republicans like Indiana's Dan Burton and California's Dana Rohrabacher resisted the deal. Pakistan and China also made their best efforts to block it in Congress.

The lobbying against Indo-US nuclear deal, meant to address India's looming energy crisis, energizing Indian Americans. Their intensive drive to support the nuclear pact included heavy spending on lobbying, campaign contributions and public relations to persuade Congress to approve the deal. They hired lobbyists, organized fund-raisers, and inundated Capitol Hill with briefings, phone calls and petitions. They organized meetings with prominent members of Congress to muster support for the deal and lobbied members of the Foreign Relations Committees in both houses to get the bill on the floor of the house. Indian Americans and the Indian government had been actively lobbying for Henry Hyde's support for the pact.

For many Indian Americans this contentious battle in Congress was a unique opportunity to demonstrate their growing political influence in their adopted country. Looking at the divisions within the India Caucus in Congress over the intrinsic worth of the deal, Indian Americans, along with leading India Caucus members Garry Ackerman, Frank Pallone, John Cornyn and Indian American organizations like USINPAC, IACPA, IAFPE lobbied to ensure that the 39 members of the India Caucus in the Senate and more than 180 members of the Caucus in the House of Representatives vote for the deal.[38]

India reached out to the 43 member Black Caucus and 20 member Hispanic Caucus to expand its legislative support. The Black Caucus has been wary of India's closeness to the Republican administration and Jewish groups. There exists a traditional antipathy between African Americans and Jewish Americans. India's vote against the Iranian nuclear programme strengthened support from the powerful American Israel Public Affairs Committee (AIPAC) and US-India Political Action Committee (USINPAC) to collaborate on countering terrorism, security, sale of high tech weapons etc.

Much of the lobbying focused on lawmakers from the New York metropolitan region, with its heavy concentration of Indian-Americans. USINPAC organized a fundraiser month for Senator Hillary Clinton, co-chairwoman of the Senate's 39-member India Caucus. Most members of the India Caucus are Democrats, but many of them had shown reluctance in supporting the bill, since they take the nuclear non-proliferation agenda very seriously. The support of Hillary Clinton and her husband, Bill Clinton, former President and a prominent Democratic leader, who seriously pursued non-proliferation policies, ensured the support of a majority of the Democrats for the nuclear pact. In this Indian Americans lobby proved fruitful.[39]

In addition, the United States -India Business Council (USIBC) and Indian American Friendship Council was also involved in lobbying for the nuclear deal. USIBC worked with Patton Boggs, one of the leading and most expensive lobbying firms in Washington, DC. Patton Boggs, reportedly hired by the Indian government at a cost of $1.3 million, joined Barbour, Griffith & Rogers, headed by Robert Blackwill (former US ambassador to India) and the Venable Law firm, to launch a concerted lobbying campaign to convince US Congressmen that approving the necessary changes in US non-proliferation law is essential for the strategic partnership between US and India. The Indian government also retained former Senator Birch Bayh of Indiana to help in its lobbying efforts.[40]

In fact, the passage of the Indo-US deal in the Congress could not have been possible without the intense lobbying by Indian Americans backed by the Indian government, business interest groups and the Bush administration.

Conclusion

Even if the predominant pattern has been one of political inactivity, there are clear trends in opposite direction. The trends show that Indians have recognized the importance of political participation. Throughout 1990s and 2000 onwards there have been increasing trend of their direct role in politics. Their economic prosperity, educational achievements, and professional accomplishments and their status of one of leading player in Information Technology have made them awaken. Finally, the professional success of Indian Americans has resulted into their increasing influence in American socio-political-cultural life. Commensurate to their contribution and success in the professional field, the Indian American community is showing their clout in political arena too. Hoping to translate their growing economic prosperity the new groups of Indian Americans are inspiring the budding politician under the banner of Indian American Leadership Initiative (IALI) and Washington Leadership Program (WLP) of IACPA.

They are now organizing, participating, lobbying Capitol Hill, collecting campaign funds — and U.S. politicians are paying attention. Finally, the era of Indian Americans political apathy is over and now they not only make powerful statement with the pocket bucks but also a great political statement. All these initiatives and developments are encouraging.

However, when compared to other ethnic communities, like Jews, Hispanics Indian Americans are still marginal in mainstream politics. Despite the recent surge, elected officials are few, and their voting bloc small. Political knowledge of US govt. at different levels, organized and institutional activism at grassroots level, singular and united effort, coalition building with other communities, increasing political contribution, and inspiring the new generation to enter in politics through internship programs can lead to better prospects for Indian Americans in direct politics.

Endnotes

1. Goel, Madan Lal . 'Asian Americans', http:// www.uwf.edu/govt/goel.html.
2. Fisher, Maxine P. 1980. *The Indian in the New York City: A Study of Immigrants from India*, Columbia: Columbia University Press, pp.19-20. Also see, http://www.indianembassy.org.html.
3. Sheth, Manju. 1995. 'Asian Indian Americans' in Pyong Gap Min. eds. *Asian Americans, Contemporary Trends and Issues*, London: Sage Publications, pp.172-173.
4. The US Department of Commerce-Economic and Statistics Administration, Bureau of Census, 1990. *Census of the Population: Asian and Pacific Islands in the U.S.*, Washington, D.C.
5. 'India-US Relations', *A Report of the U.S. Embassy to India, 1999.*
6. U.S. Immigration and Naturalization Service: *Annual Report*, 1990.

7. 'The Indian American Community in the United States', *Report of Embassy of India in Washington D.C.*, 2003.
8. http:/www.icfpa.org.html.
9. Jain, R.K. 1993. *Indian Communities Abroad*, New Delhi: Manohar Publishers, pp.37-38.
10. Indian Embassy, Washington, D.C. 'The Indian American Community in the United States of America', http://www.indiaembassy.org/comm.html.
11. Helweg, A. and Helweg U., 1990. *The Immigrant Success Story: East Indian*, Philadelphia: University of Pennsylvania Press.
12. Min, Pyong Gap. 1995. 'An Overview of Asian American', in Pyong Gap Min ed., *Asian Americans, Contemporary Trends and Issues*, London: Sage Publications, pp.22-23.
13. Jain, R.K. 1993. *Indian Communities Abroad*, New Delhi: Manohar Publisher, pp.37-40.
14. http://www.outofindia.net/abroad/WashingtonDC/Indian_American_community.htm>SourceEmbassy of India in Washington D.C.
15. Nixon, R.M.1988. *Victory Without War*, New York, p.273.
16. *Times of India*. 2003. '200,000 NRI Millionaires in U.S.A.: Merrill', May 15.
17. Sharma, Ashok. ' India's Soft Power', http://www.ipcs.org/whatsNewArticle11.jsp?*action=showView&kValue=1946&status=article&mod=b*. Accessed on 25 January 2006.
18. Sharma, Ashok. 2007. 'Retaining Indianness in America', *Pravasi Today*, July 2007, pp. 58-59.
19. 'Indian Cusine', http:/en.wikipedia.org/wiki/Indian_cuisine.
20. http://www.thendral.com/AboutThendral.shtml.
21. http://www.mtvdesi.com.
22. http://www.adherents.com/adh_dem.html, http://www.teachingaboutreligion.org/Backdrop&Context/hinduism.htm.
23. http://www.imc-usa.org/cgi-bin/cfm/index.cfm.
24. http://www.fezana.org.

25. http://www.tpub.com/content/religion/14229/css/14229_116.htm.
26. Fisher, Maxine P. 1980. *The Indian in the New York City: A Study of Immigrants from India*, Columbia: Columbia University Press, p.13.
27. Jensen, J.M. 1988. *Passage from India: Asian Indian Immigrants in North America*, New Haven, C.T: Yale University Press, pp. 42-53.
28. Lal, Vinay. 1999. 'Establishing Roots, Engendering Awareness: A Political History of Asian Indians in the United States' in Leela Prasad eds., *Live Like banyan Tree: Images of the Indian American Experience*, Philadelphia: Balch Institute for Ethnic Studies, pp. 42-48.
29. *New York Time*, October 8, 1987 & October 12, 1987.
30. Daniel, Roger. 1988. *Asian Americans: Chinese and Japanese in the United States since 1950*, Seattle: University of Washington Press, p.51.
31. *Ibid.*
32. Pais, Arthur J.1994. 'Indians with an American Dream', *The Telegraph Magazine*, June 26, p.48.
33. http://www.ipatlanta.net/2002,khabar.html
34. *Ibid.*
35. http://www.iacfpa.org/southasia/office.html.
36. Palmer, Miles A. 2000.'Indian Americans: Numbers, Affluence are Translating into Political Power', *Congressional Quarterly*, March 18, p. 580.
37. http://www.usindiafriendship.net/congress/congress.html.
38. Mike Mcintire. 2006. 'Indian Americans Test Their Clout on Atom Pact', *New York Times*, June 5, 2006.
39. Sharma, Ashok. 2006. ' Indo-US Nuclear Deal: Intense Lobbying', Ipcs web journal, 24 June 2006, http://www.ipcs.org/US_related_articles2.jsp?action=show View&kValue=2063 &military=1016&status=article&mod=b.
40. *Ibid.*
41. *Ibid.*

4

Indian Mosaic in the Multicultural Society of Canada: The Influence of the People of Indian Origin

Lianboi Vaiphei

Introduction

The era of Globalisation has ushered the age of global village, where even the Diasporic population has emerged from the periphery to the mainstream politics. As they form an important network and linkages with the home country. In other words, the global village transcends national boundaries as global overlaps with local, and vice versa. The saga of the Indian Diaspora resonate this sentiment more apt than this. For they have become one of the most vibrant and visible community in the world, in general and particularly in Canada. The Indian Ministry of External Affairs has estimated that the total number of overseas Indian residents is more than twenty million, who are settled in more than seventy countries, including US, Canada, UK, European countries, Australia, Middle East, Southeast and Far Eastern countries in 2001. It is these overseas Indians that form the Indian Diaspora.[1]

In Canada, the Indian Diaspora forms the second highest number of immigrants. They account for more than half a million, as one in every 30 Canadians traces their roots to India. For, Canada needs to maintain an annual immigration level of around 200,000 persons to promote a sustainable growth of its population. Immigrants provide a critical importance to its labour force as it is a country of immigrants.

Moreover, the policy and practice of multiculturalism has allowed and facilitated the distinct presence Indian Diaspora in strengthening the rich mosaic of Canadian Multiculturalism. The Indian Diaspora, in turn has contributed in every walks of the Canadian Society occupying prominent positions in every field. This paper seeks to study the contribution that Indian diaspora has made in the Canadian Society in the arena of socio-cultural culture as well as economy and politics.

The Nature of Indian Diaspora in Canada

The word 'Diaspora' was originally used to suggest displacement or dispersal of a group from their homeland to alien territory under political or economic pressures; denoting the Jewish people who were subjected to conquest and religious persecution. That is how the term Diaspora has been derived, etymologically from the Greek words ***dia*** which means through and ***sperio*** which means to scatter. Thus the literal, meaning of 'Diaspora' is 'scattering' or 'dispersion'. Understandably, Diaspora has an underlying implication, of nursing an emotional link with the homeland since their parents or ancestors lived there and keeping alive the possibility of return to their homeland.

Demographically, Indian Diaspora forms the third largest in the world today after the British and Chinese Diaspora. The term Indian Diaspora is a generic term to describe the people who migrated from territories that are currently within the borders of the Republic of India. It also refers to their descendants.

The Indian Diaspora has been further characterised as Non-Resident Indians, (NRIs) – Indians who are not residents within the territory of India and also Persons of Indian Origin, (PIOs) – Indians who have acquired the citizenship of another country, but traces their sociological roots to India. Although, the Non Resident Indians and the People of Indian Origin forms the overseas Indians or the Indian Diaspora they have been distinctly characterised by the Ministry of External Affairs into different categories as follows[4]:

The Non Resident Indians (NRIs) has been distinguished by the following criteria:

(a) Indian citizens who stay abroad for employment, or for carrying on any business or vocation, or for any other purpose, in circumstances indicating an indefinite period of stay outside India;

(b) Indian citizens working abroad on assignments with foreign Governments, Government agencies or international/multinational agencies like United Nations Organisation (UNO), International Monetary Fund (IMF), World Bank (IBRD), etc;

(c) Officials of Central and State Governments and public sector undertakings deputed abroad on assignments with foreign Governments/agencies/ organisations or posted to their own offices (including Indian Diplomatic Missions) abroad.

While, the term People of Indian Origins (PIOs) has been referred to the overseas Indian citizens (not being a citizen of Pakistan or Bangladesh), if any of the following criteria is applicable:

(a) if he at any time held an Indian passport, or

(b) he, or either of his parents, or any of his grand parents was a citizen of India by virtue of the Constitution of India or Citizenship Act, 1955.[5]

The Indian Ministry of External Affairs has estimated that the total number of overseas Indian residents is more than twenty million, who are settled in more than seventy countries, including US, Canada, UK, European countries, Australia, Middle East, Southeast and Far Eastern countries, in 2001.

The Fig 1 below shows the details of the spread of Indian Diaspora in the different countries and regions of the world, where they form the major ethnic group as well as where they are in minority.

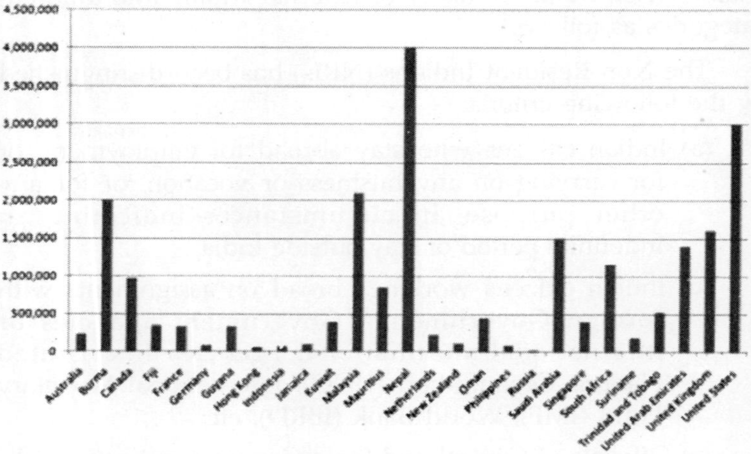

Fig 1: Regions with Significant Populations of Indian Diaspora

In some of the countries of the world, the Indian Diaspora has form a major chunk of the population of the host country, being the largest ethnic group, if not the major ethnic group and in the rest a minority. There are four countries, where they have been named as the largest ethnic groups, namely, United Arab Emirates, Mauritius, Guyana and Suriname. While in eight other countries; they have been named the major ethnic group and in fifteen other countries they are from the minor ethnic groups. Nevertheless, even in these fifteen countries, the number of populations is pretty large, as the table 1 indicates.

Table 1: The statistics of Indian Diaspora in different countries of the world

No	Largest Ethnic Group	No. of Population	Major Ethnic Group	No. of Population	Minor Ethnic Group	No. of Population
1	United Arab Emirates	1,400,000	Nepal	4,000,000	US	2,765,815
2	Mauritius	855,000	Malaysia	2,100,000	UK	1,200,000

3.	Guyana	327,000	Myanmar	2,000,000	S. Africa	1,160,000
4.	Suriname	175,000	Saudi Arabia	1,500,000	Canada	962,665
5			Kuwait	580,000	Oman	450,000
6			Trinidad n Tobago	525,000	France (2/3 in Reunion)	330,000
7			Singapore	400,000	Bahrain	310,000
8			Fiji	340,000	Australia	235,000
9					Netherlands	217,000
10					New Zealand	105,000
11					Kenya	100.,000
12					Tanzania	90,000
13					Uganda	90,000
14					Jamaica	90,000
15					Italy	71,500

The demographic profile of the Indian diasporas has been mapped by the, then President of the Global Organisation of People of Indian Origin, (GOPIO), Dr. Thomas Abraham.[6] He had estimated the population of the people of Indian origin in various countries, approximately, as follows:

Table 2 : Indian Diaspora in different regions of the World

1.	North America (Mostly US and Canada)	2.8 Million
2.	South America (Trinidad & Tobago, Surinam, Jamaica, etc.)	2.0 Million
3.	Europe (UK, Netherlands, Germany, Austria, Switzerland, etc.)	2.5 Million
4.	Africa (South Africa, Mauritius, East African countries, etc.)	2.5 Million
5.	Middle East (UAE, Saudi Arabia, Kuwait, etc)	2.5 Million
6.	Pacific Island (Fiji, Australia, New Zealand)	0.7 Million
7.	Sri Lanka and Nepal	4.5 Million

The above table shows that Canada is one of the regions, which has the highest concentration of the Indian Diaspora in the western countries of North America, mainly in US and Canada. In the North American countries, US is a larger country than Canada in terms of its population, as the former being the thirds largest and contributes around 4.54 per cent[7] of the total world's population while Canada is the 36th largest country and contributes only 0.5 per cent.

Although, the number of Indian Diaspora is higher in US, vis a vis Canada, they form the third largest social community after the Mexican and the Chinese while in Canada they are the second largest social groups; only after the Chinese immigrant groups. For the Indian Diaspora in Canada today, accounts for more than half a million, where one in every 30 Canadians traces their roots to India.

The 'Indian' Society and Culture among the Indo-Canadians

Canada is the first country in the world to officially declare multiculturalism as official state policy in 1971. The official recognition is only an official acceptance of the social reality as Canada has three founding cultures- aboriginal, British and French —later, joined by many more from around the globe. Today, multiculturalism is a touchstone of Canadian national identity and a point of pride as the fabric of the society is based on the vibrant and evolving cultural mosaic, which is premised on mutual respect for Canadians of all backgrounds and ancestry.[8]

Canada can be described as a multicultural society whose racial and ethnic diversity is expressed in different ways. In recent years, a vigorous immigration policy has attracted a growing number of applicants from non-traditional sources such as Asia, Africa, Central America, and the Caribbean. It is noteworthy that much of this diversity is concentrated in Ontario, particularly in the metropolitan region of Toronto, as well as in the metropolitan areas of Vancouver and Montréal.

Today, the multicultural societies of Canada manifest not only just the three cultures but also that of South Asian 'Indian' culture which is not only visible but has started to define its landscape as well. Interestingly, the term Indian has often been identified with the Aboriginals Canadians and still continues to be used to describe them, causing much confusion. So, all these terms that are used to describe the Indian Diaspora such as the Non Resident Indians, People of Indian Origins, Expatriate Indians of Overseas Indian have been referred to as Indo-Canadian community in Canada.[9] Therefore, even in this paper, the word Indo-Canadian is used to call the Indian Diaspora, whether they are Non Residents Indians, Expatriate or People of Indian origin.

The Indo-Canadian community has come a long way from the time they had come to Canada. For, the first Indian emigrants have been documented in 1903. The subsequent years, saw a sizeable presence of around 5,000 Punjabi forming the Indo-Canadian community in Vancouver, who formed the Khalsa Diwan Society as well as the Hindustan Association, there. The aspirations of freedom against the British Colonizers was so well reciprocated in Canada that the Paper called as 'Free Hindustan' which was published in Vancouver by Taraknath Das, following the popularity of the Ghadr Party even though it was founded in San Francisco in 1913. Moreover, with over two million Indians, who had fought the Boer War and the two World Wars as a part of the British Empire were well reciprocated and were automatically accepted as their own, when they came to Canada.

This same sentiment of allegiance was echoed even among the second immigrant who preferred coming to Canada from the Caribbean countries such as Fiji, Mauritius, Guyana, Trinidad, Surinam, Malaysia, South Africa; Sri Lanka in the nineteenth-century; where they were taken as indentured labourers.

The increasing presence of Indian Diaspora created a fear among the people in Canada which is described as the "Asian peril". Efforts were made to restrict migration through enactment of legislation, calling for a "continuous journey" from the place of origin with a stipulated amount of wealth on hand and from other ports such as Hong Kong.

It was during this period of hostility that 'Komagatu Maru incident' of 1914, occurred. The 'Komagatu Maru' is a Japanese ship, which seeks to enter the Vancouver harbour with 376 potential immigrants of Indian origin in which the majority were the Sikhs veterans of the British Army. The passengers were denied the right to disembark and were unable to enter a Canadian port and had to finally depart. This incident has drawn a lot of criticism and was interpreted as racial prejudices. However, the relaxation was made in the immigration laws, which allowed the family members of the Indian immigrants to enter Canada in 1919. Moreover, the quota system in the postwar economic expansion influenced the Canadian immigration laws and facilitated the emigrants of Indians especially among the Sikhs from Punjab, who could come and join their families in Canada.

The increasing popularity of Canada for the Indian Diasporas and with their lax laws has helped in improving the ties between the two countries, in all directions. As Canada and India develop cordial and mature relations and had heartily appreciated India's independence and welcome in the Commonwealth states.

After India gain Independence the popularity of Canada as favourite destination for the Indian Diasporas trickled down even to the unskilled workers, who were providing labour in the agricultural sector of the Canadian economy and thereby developing resources of the Canadian economy. From 7,000 south Asians of Indian origin in Canada in 1961 to around 70,000 in the next decade due to the introduction of the point system and removal of the discriminations in the immigration law.

The transition that the Indian Diaspora has made in becoming an Indo-Canadian community is not without the usual suspense and drama which is often associated when different cultures come together. The Indian emigrant as a part of the British Empire saw in Canada a kindred spirit where their aspirations of freedom was empathized and respected. The popularity of Canada among the overseas Indian and their increasing presence caused a phobia among them, in the initial years and led to attacks which were racist in nature and legislations that were aimed to control the heavy influx of the indo Canadian community. However, they were short lived as Canada liberalized its immigration laws and remove all its restrictions.

In the present 21st century, Canada has around 713, 330 people, who classified themselves as being of Indian origin, according to Statistic Canada, 2001. The figures given below indicate the nature of the Indian community that lives in Canada.[10]

Table 3 : Indian Populations in Canada

1.	Total Population of the Country	About 30 million
2.	Estimated size of the Indian community	
	(a) Indian citizens	About 150,000
	(b) Persons of Indian Origin	About 700,000
	(c) Stateless	About 1,000
	(d) Indian Community as a percentage of the population	2.8 per cent

It is not surprising that with such a huge population of the Indian Diaspora living in Canada that they form the Indo-Canadian community there. The social scene of Canada has a vibrant evidence of 'India' in the establishment of extensive and bustling commercial districts which caters to their own desires and needs such as the distinctively Indian foods, clothing, and music in its urban landscapes.

The cities of Toronto has its self-proclaimed India Bazaar on Gerrard Street, which offers a cacophonous array of colours, sounds, and Indian smells through the incense sticks to Indian clothes of sari, music from traditional- bhangra to Bollywood musicals, and food from the vegetarian to meat thalis. These street has shops which is align by the numerous jewellery shops that carry the distinctive, orangey, 22-carat gold- A scene that reflects any corner in any of the Indian city. In fact, it is in these suburbs of Toronto and southern Ontario that serves as a convergence point, where the Indian

Diaspora from both US and Canada come to shop, eat, meet friends, and watch Hindi and Tamil movies. The myriad hues and mosaic of the Indian culture exist in Canada just as it is back at home and has enriched the myraid mosiac of the multicultural society of the host country, Canada.[11]

Social and Cultural transformation of Indo-Canadian Community

The Indo-Canadian community includes not only the different categories[12] of Indian Diaspora as have been mentioned earlier but also includes the second generation of immigrants, who have come to Canada from the other Caribbean countries. In fact, the Indo-Canadian community have wide divergences of experiences based on the way they came Canada, as some of them had earlier immigrated to the former colonies of Britain and Portugal such as Kenya, Uganda and later on move to Canada; besides as indentured worker, free passenger, trader, businessmen or high skilled workers.

The transition for the social acceptance of the Canadian culture among the Indo-Canadian community is not without the culture shock as many of them are first generation rural migrants. It is natural that the sociological make up of the Indo-Canadian community has sentiments which echoes psychological roots which echoes– a mixture of insecurity, desire to assert a distinct identity, and alienation. It gets manifested in adherence to community traditions and religion, marriage and dating taboos, as well as psychological/ behavioural problems brought by alienation. However, these feeling of alienations stems from increasing emphasis on one's own separateness and religious affiliations, which has found expressions in the multicultural society of Canada more better than the *melting pot of US*.

Nevertheless, the distinct identity of the Indo-Canadian community has been well preserved among them. For the Indian Diaspora is not a homogeneous group or a monolithic lot be it in terms of their religion, language, food, and their social customs including the dress and rituals, as they also reflects the diversity of the home country, India-Unity in Diversity. Out of this population, 42 per cent are Hindu, 39 per cent are Sikh, and the remainder is Muslim, Christian, Jain, Buddhist, or no religious affiliation, in a survey conducted in 1991.

The table below shows the diversity in the religious beliefs.[13]

Table 4 : Indo-Canadian Religious profile*

No	Religion	Total Responses	Single Responses	Multiple Responses
1	Sikkhism	239,225	217,805	21,425
2	Hinduism	192,680	174,455	18,225
3	Islam	124,650	101,015	23,635
4	Christianity	117,430	65,485	51,945
5	Eastern Religions	5,875	4,785	1,090
6	Buddhism	1,435	870	560
7	Jainism	1,291	803	600
8	Judaism	655	160	500
9	Other Religions	655	540	120
10	No Religious Affiliations	30,725	16,555	14,175
	Total	713,330,581	581,665	131,665

Ethnicities among the Indo-Canadian Community

The diversity of the Indo-Canadian community is witnessed in the umbrella organisations of *the India-Canada Association* which includes people from almost all of the Indian communities. Each of the Indo-Canadian community has their own separate affiliation and organisation, as the *India-Canada Association* has other individual groups such as South Indian Cultural Association (SICA) in Ontario, Sindhi Association, Ottawa Tamil Association, Orissa Association, Malayali Association, Maratha Association, Kannada Sangh of Ottawa, and Gujarati Association Andhra Cultural Association besides the Indo Canadian Community Center, Hindu Society of Ottawa- Carlton; just to name them[4]. The reflections of the diversity of the Indo-Canadian community do not deflect the common identity and origin being 'ethnic Indians'.

The Indo-Canadian communities boast not only of the diversities that are present in India as the table given below indicates the presence of the different Indian languages in Canada. The main Indian ethnic communities are Punjabis (which account for more than half of population), Gujratis, Tamils, Keralites, Bengalis, Sindhis and others. The table below gives an indication of the different ethnicity of the Indo Canadian community.[14]

Table 5 : Indian Languages Spoken at Home in Canada

No.	Language Total:	Language spoken at home	Only speaks	Mostly speaks	Equally speaks	Regularly speaks
1	Punjabi	280,540	132.380	71,660	29,220′	47,280
2	Tamil	97,345	45,865	29,745	9,455	12,280
3	Hindi	65,890	14,175	16,075	9,0901	26,550
4.	Urdu	89,365	30,760	27,840	12,200	18,565
5	Gujarati	60,105	18,310	16,830	7,175	17,790
6	Malayalam	6,570	1,155	1,810	505	3,100
7	Bengali	29,705	12,840	9,615	2,780	4,470

Demographically, the Indian community form 2.8 per cent of the total Canadian population. The majority of the community is from Punjab, though most of the principal linguistic and ethnic groups of India are represented in the Indo-Canadian population. A survey conducted in 1991 showed that 49 percent of the Indo-Canadians surveyed were Sikh, 24 percent were Hindu and 10 percent were affiliated with other religions.

The Indo-Canadian community is not a homogeneous group or a monolithic lot be it in terms of their religion, language, food, and their social customs including the dress and rituals, for the simple reason that the Indian Diaspora have had wide divergences of experiences based on the way they came Canada, as some of the Indian Diaspora includes people of second immigrants who had earlier immigrated to the former colonies of Britain and Portugal such as Kenya, Uganda and later on move to Canada; besides as indentured worker, free passenger, trader, businessmen or high skilled workers. In fact, the migrant history of the Indian Diaspora also differs. In a way, they are microcosm of Indian diversity.

Geographical Locations of Indo-Canadian Community

Moreover, the Indo-Canadian community is widely spread across the five different provinces of Canada, out of the total ten provinces that exist there namely Ontario, Quebec, British Columbia, Alberta, Manitoba, Saskatchewan, Nova Scotia, New Brunswick, Newfoundland and Labrador and Prince Edward Island. There is a negligible presence of the Indo-Canadian community in the three territories of Nunavut, Yukon, and Northwest Territories. The Table 6 indicates the presence of the different Canadian cities, which has a large Indo-Canadian population.[15]

Table 6: Demographic profile of Indians in Canadian Provinces

No	Province	Indians
1	Ontario	573,250
2	British Columbia	232,370
3	Alberta	88,165
4	Quebec	41,600
5	Manitoba	14,860
6.	Saskatchewan	4,465
7	Nova Scotia	3,895
8.	New Brunswick	2,220
9.	New Foundland and Laabrador	1,275
10.	Prince Edward Island	255
11.	Yukon	145
12.	Northwest Territories	130
13	Nunavuit	40
14	Total	962,665

Canada follows liberal democratic traditions, with respect for human rights and dignity, with facilitating a space of expressing freedoms of religious to the cultural beliefs to its people. Moreover, with the populace of the country composing of immigrants from different parts of the world has translated the Multicultural society become a global city.

The Indo-Canadian community is highly urbanised and almost 90 per cent of them live in metropolitan areas, especially in Toronto (capital of Ontario), Vancouver (capital of British

Columbia), Montreal (the largest city in Quebec), Calgary and Edmonton. They are spread across different cities in different provinces of Canada. The table below indicates their presence across the different cities of Canada.[16]

Table 7 : Canadian Cities with large Indian Populations

No	Province	City	No. of Indian Population
1	Ontario	Toronto	484,655
2	British Columbia	Vancouver	181,895
3	Alberta	Calgary	48,270
4	Quebec	Montreal	39,305
5	Alberta	Edmonton	34,605
6	British Columbia	Abbotsford	23,440
7	Ontario	Ottawa	21,170
8	Ontario	Hamilton	14,985
9	Manitoba	Winnipeg	13,545
10	Ontario	Kithner	13,235

Today, the Indo-Canadians with its rich diversity of linguistic, regional, religious and other characteristics contributes in making the mosaic of the multicultural Canadian Society richer. Besides, the Indian ethos and spirit of *Vasudhaiva* Kutumbakam-*the entire world is one family;* has accepted Canada as their home and enshrined the values of humanity and universalism in a world of prejudices and biased which inculcates phobia of the 'otherness'

The democratic space of the multicultural society of Canada has witnessed the manifestation of the rich Indian traditions and culture and in turn contributing the mosaic of the Canadian Multiculturalism. The liberal democratic traditions of Canada have absorbed the myriad and contours of the Indian society and culture, along with the Indian immigrants. Canada provides democratization of space in providing expressions of religious and cultural freedom to its people. The Indian community has evolved into a Canadian society; which is distinctively Indian at the same time, very Canadian in its fashion of its liberal tradition.

Indian hues in the Canadian Multi 'culture' Society

India is a young nation but an old civilization, which has witnessed the amalgamation of different cultures and traditions of the world in its people. The culture of India has been shaped by its long history, unique geography, diverse demographics and the absorption of customs, traditions and ideas from some of its neighbours as well as by preserving its ancient heritages, which were formed during the Indus Valley Civilization and evolved further during the Vedic age, the south Indian Iron Age, rise and decline of Buddhism, Golden age, Muslim conquests and European colonization.

India's diversity is visible in its people, religions, climate, languages, customs, and traditions which differ from place to place within the country, but nevertheless posses a commonality. The culture of India is an amalgamation of diverse sub-cultures spread all over the country and traditions that are as old as the millennium. It is the home for well-known religious gurus and yogic preceptors. Its colourful religious festivals, age old art forms in music, dance, architecture, distinct geographic attributes and co-existence of ancient and modern cultures attract tourists from all over the world No wonder, India has adopted a policy of Integration with a catchy slogan of *Unity in Diversity*.

The Indo-Canadian community has not only retain their traditional religious belief and culture but have promoted not only among their own community but across different social groups as well as facilitate the socio-cultural exchange with the home country and globally. The different fields in which a distinct Indian cultures has contributed in making Canada a truly multicultural society has been witnessed in the following fields:

- Literature
- Dance and Music
- Entertainment in Movies, TV etc
- Religious Institutions

Literature

The saga of the Indian Diaspora from their unique experiences of negotiating the two worlds of their home country and the host country have given them the unique position of viewing both the two cultures from a birds view; has inspired many writers among the Indo-Canadian community. They have found wide readerships across different cultures and community across the globe and have even gain critical acclaim as well. It is no wonder that the works of the Indo-Canadian community writers has gained both mass popularity as well as critical acclaim.

The Indo-Canadian writers include *Ajmer Rode* - poet and playwright, *Anita Rau Badami* – novelist, *Anosh Irani* - novelist and playwright, *Jaspreet Singh*- author, *Nancy Lee*, short story writer and novelist, *M.GVassanji* – novelist, *Irshad Manji* – author, *Priscilla Uppal* - novelist and poet, *Neil Bissoondath* – author, *Robin Sharma* – author, *Shani Mootoo* – writer, *Shaun Mehta* – writer, *Harold Sonny Ladoo* - novelist and author, *Rohinton Mistry* – novelist, *Shauna Singh Baldwin* – novelist, *Shamsher Singh Sandhu* - Poet (Gazalgo)

Among the indicative list, the three writers who have achieved recognition for their work across the globe including and are well known names even in India are Rohinton Mistry, M.G Vassanji, Robin Sharma.

Rohinton Mistry have won a long list of prestigious awards like the Hart House literary prize, the Canada Governor General's Award, the W. H. Smith/ Books in Canada, first Novel Award, the Commonwealth Writer's Prize for Best Book, the Giller Prize, the Royal Society of Literature's Winfried Holtby Prize, and the 1996 Los Angeles Times Award for fiction. A Fine Balance made the short-list of nominees for the Booker Prize, on which a film was also made.[17]

Moyez Gulamhussein Vassanji or M.G. Vassanji as how he is better known as, is a Canadian novelist and editor. He has come to Canada from East Africa and has the experiences of developing countries as well as developed countries as a host country for immigrants and which have been well reflected in his literary works, such as novel *The Assassins Song* (2007). His other works has also been well received considerable critical acclaim. *The Gunny Sack* won a regional Commonwealth Writers Prize in 1990. In 1994, he won the Harbourfront Festival Prize in recognition of his "achievement in and contribution to the world of letters." That year he was also one of twelve Canadians chosen for Maclean's Magazine's Honour Roll. Vassanji won the inaugural Giller Prize in 1994 for *The Book of Secrets*. He again won the Giller Prize in 2003 for *The In-Between World of Vikram Lall*. He was the first writer to win the Giller Prize more than once. (In 2004, Alice Munro became the prize's second repeat winner.) In 2006, *When She Was Queen* was shortlisted for the City of Toronto Book Award.His latest work, *The Assassin's Song* was short-listed for the 2007 Giller Prize. In 2005, he was made a Member of the Order of Canada.[18]

Toronto-based Robin Sharma is an author of several internationally published books, besides being an expert on leadership and personality development. He had grown up in Port Hawkesbury, Nova Scotia. Among his best known books includes "The Monk Who Sold His Ferrari", *Who Will Cry When You Die, The Greatness Guide, The Greatness Guide 2, Leadership Wisdom from The Monk Who Sold His Ferrari, Daily Inspiration, Family Wisdom from The Monk Who Sold His Ferrari, Discover Your Destiny with The Monk Who Sold His Ferrari, Megaliving, The Saint, Surfer and CEO*[19]

Dance and Music

Dance is an art form that interweaves both entertainment and recreation with a distinct link to the socio-cultural traditions of a society. Dances has been categorized into two genre of Classical as well as folk dance and both of which has gained tremendous popularity in Canada.

In fact, the popularity of Indian folk dances such as Bhangra and the Classical dance like Bharat Natyam has literally made the other entire community dance to their tune. The Indian Classical Dance such as Bharat Natyam, Kathak etc is gaining wide spread popularity in Canada, not only in terms of the performances but also growing enthusiasm to learn has increased.[20]

Every area with an Indo-Canadian concentration has produced excellent Indian dance schools. Every year several concerts by Indian musicians, singers, film artists etc. are held at prominent venues in cities like Toronto, Vancouver, Ottawa and Montreal. The growing popularity of the Indian Classical Dance such as Bharat Natyam has led to their leading exponent personality like Menaka Thakar, Kitappa Pillai, and Janak Khendry becomes an icon in the city of Toronto; While Lata Pada and Sampradaya are based in Ontario, Canada. The growing interest in the Indian Classical Dance has encouraged the practice of learning and has been able to establish Dance Schools and academies where they train not only the Indo-Canadian but also people from other nationals whosoever take interest in Indian culture.

If the Classical Dance has seen a wide interest and popularity in Canada, the folk music like Bhangra is not far behind. Bhangra is a popular folk dance that is primarily associated with the Punjabi community and danced during the harvest festival of Bhaisakhi, besides weddings, New Year, and other celebrations. The popularity of Bhangra transcends across even non Punjabi community in India and has engulfed the world today. It has become hugely popular not only in Canada but also in Indian enclaves of British cities such as Manchester, Birmingham, and London (Southall) since 1980s.[21]

The Bhangra among the indo Canadian community draws on elements as disparate as the Punjabi folk genre whose name it shares, the songs of popular Hindi movies, and other diasporic dance and music's such as reggae, hip hop, and drum & bass, that often the elders in the Indo community find it difficult to recognize them, even though its related to the traditional music and dance that they so cherished. Nevertheless, has continued to gain immense popularity with a very strong fan base.[22]

The distinctive Indian Music has seen their artiste like the *Apache Indian* whose from Toronto become a global icon.

Toronto is also home *to Desi Records*, a record label devoted to music by and for the Indo-Canadian community as well as to other South Asian immigrants. In fact, an important part of these community are created by youth, for whom Bhangra and its related dance music play a central role in negotiating the complexities of their cultural and generational identities of being ethnic Indian.

Entertainment in Movies, TV etc

The Indo-Canadian community is well represented even in the creative field of art and entertainment. Many of them has transcends across Canada and are equally known in India such as Ms. Deepa Mehta, Lisa Ray, Ms. Ruby Bhatia, Mr. Mansa Ram, to name just a few of them.

In fact, Lisa ray has been conferred with "Voice Achievers Award for 2009". She is among the seven recipients to have received this award. The Voice Achievers Award is given in recognition for outstanding contributions in the fields of films, trade, medicine, literature and sports. The other award winners were: Dr Gopal Bhatnagar (cardiac surgery); M G Vassanji (arts); Meenu Sikand (social work); Raja Panjwani (sports); and Kuldip Rai Sahi (business) and Asha Luthra (business). The President of Indo-Canada Chamber of Commerce (ICCC), Ms Asha Luthra also received the award for promoting bilateral trade and investment between India and Canada.

Besides, Lisa Ray and Deepa Mehta, there are many personalities that represented in the fields of Cinema such as Manoj Sood - actor (*Little Mosque on the Prairie*), Aliza Vellani - actress (*Little Mosque on the Prairie*), Nilesh Patel - director and producer of films, Richie Mehta – director, Agam Darshi - actress and filmmaker, Samir Mallal – filmmaker, Nisha Ganatra - film director, film producer, writer and actor, Remi Kaler – actor, R Paul Dhillon - director, producer, writer and journalist, Sugith Varughese – actor, Rajiv Surendra – actor, Glenda Braganza – actress, Suleka Mathew – actress, Vik Sahay – actor, Rekha Sharma – actress, Errol Sitahal – actor, Veena Sood – actress, Melinda Shankar- actress, Raymond Ablack- actress.

In the other field of Entertainment, the Indo-Canadian community has not only represented Canada but also achieved success, like how Neelam Verma won the title of Miss Universe Canada 2002 and Sara Ghulam - Miss World Canada in 2007.

Here is an indicative list of the Indo-Canadian personalities that has made a mark *Russell Peters* - stand-up comedian, *Sugar Sammy* – comedian, *Sunny Leone* – model, *Ashwin Sood* - drummer for (and former husband of) *Sarah McLachlan, Prakash John* - R&B musician *Chin Injeti* - R&B musician, *Deesha* - R&B musician, *Devika Mathur* - singer, radio personality and *Canadian Idol* 2005 contestant, *Harbhajan Mann* – singer, *Ian D'Sa* - rock musician, Jazzy B – singer, *Cindy Daniel* – singer, Justin Singh - *Fashion File, Breakfast Television,* dabbler.ca, *Kamal Heer* – singer, RDB (Rhythm Dhol Bass) - DJ production team, *Vaughn Lal* - bassist and backing vocalist for Heavy metal band ***"Brown Brigade"*** *Karen David* - pop singer, *Koushik* - hip hop musician, *Manmohan Waris* – singer *Raji Sohal* - radio and television personality, *Nicky Mehta*– singer, *Nira Arora* -morning show radio host for CFBT-FM 94.5 in Vancouver, BC, *Nirmala Basnayake* - rock singer (controller.controller), *Raghav* R&B / desi singer, *Renee Rosnes* - jazz pianist and composer / arranger, *Shaun Majumder* - *Just for Laughs, This Hour Has 22 Minutes.*

Religious Institutions

The Indo-Canadian community has enjoyed the liberty of exercising their freedom of their religion, so much so that every community of faith has their own religious institutions. This has been well exemplified-in the city of Ontario, where there are around 50 temples which cater to the Hindus while Sikhs has their gurdwaras in the provinces of British Columbia and Ontario, such as Malton, and Ontario. There are more than a hundred Gurudwaras and temples throughout Canada, which provide a psychological haven for Indo-Canadians.

In fact, these religious institutions have become the focal points for community development. Besides the Hindus and the Sikhs, the expanding Muslim community is also equally prominent as the Ismailis have created an extensive network of social institutions, which are linked internationally to the Aga Khan and his other institutions.

Indo-Canadians celebrate their religious festivals with much fanfare. Canadian government ministers and even the Prime Minister appear at functions organised by the Indo-Canadian community. During the celebrations of the 300th anniversary of the Khalsa Panth, the majority of the Canadian Cabinet made an appearance. In the annual Baisakhi functions organised in the Canadian Parliament Complex, it is not uncommon for the Prime Minister to be present.[23]

Besides, Baisakhi, the Indian festival of lights, Diwali is also celebrated by the Canadian parliament since 1998. In Oct 17, 2009, it was celebrated by lighting the traditional lamps with Prime Minister Stephen Harper and other top leaders lighting the traditional lamps. Immigration minister Jason Kenney, finance minister Jim Flaherty, public safety minister Peter Van Loan, parliamentary secretary Deepak Obhrai, opposition leader Jack Layton and other 450 odd parliamentarians . After lighting the traditional lamp, Prime Minister Harper said the 'growing Indo-Canadian community is at the forefront of Canada's quest to build an even better country for generations to come'. 'From coast to coast our country has been and continues to be immeasurably enriched by your contributions.' [24] Mr. Obhrai, the parliamentary secretary to the foreign minister has rightly observed that Diwali can be considered as Canada's National Diwali Festival, as with almost a million-strong Indian community in Canada.[25]

These are all a natural manifestation of preserving the distinct culture and maintaining their own identity and preserving links to home country of India in the land of Canada. Once the Indian Diaspora are distanced from India, the age-old traditions, rituals, customs, festivals, religion, cultural expressions, performing arts, plastic arts, classical, folk and social dances begin to exercise a deep bond and attraction among the People of Indian Origins in Canada.

However, despite the above problems, with each passing generation, the community is becoming more integrated with the mainstream as Canada pursues more liberal and enlightened policies on immigration. The multicultural Canadian society, offers the Indo Canadian community to express their rich Indian culture and traditions, thereby giving them, an identity which they have maintain and nurtured. As, they realise its value more than their counterpart who live in their own country and has a stronger desire to pass on their values and culture to the next generation, which has help them to appreciate their roots and culture of India.

Indo-Canadian Communities in the Economy of Canada

The Indo-Canadian community has come a long way from the time they first step into the Canadian shores in 1903, when they look to the land, as a land of opportunity to the present millennium, where they has contributed tremendously in the growth of Canadian prosperity. Today, the Indo-Canadian community has occupied prominent positions in every walk of the society. The wide and diverse experiences, not to forget the diverse sociological, linguistic and religious background they have had in making Canada their home, has given them a unique position of fuelling the Canadian economy across different strata of the society. The contributions that they have made is from the bottom to the top of the economy- blue collar jobs to the invigorating the intellectual tradition such as in the academia to the decision making process of politics. In short, they have come of age. Many highly skilled workers and professionals of Indian origin have energized Canada's universities, the civil service, hospitals, and high-tech industries. They have involved themselves in all aspects of the social, political and economic life of Canada and enjoying success in all fields within the Canadian economy.

The Indo-Canadian community have settle in almost every provinces of Canada, as evidently shown in table 7. Their occupational structure ranges from the economy of agriculture to forestry in British Columbia to the major cities of Canada. Despite facing sting discriminations and barrier to job placement initially in the workplace, the People of Indian Origins as a group have an average income which is approximately equal to the Canadian average.

The economic profile reveals that the Indo-Canadian community has an average annual income, which is nearly 20 per cent higher than the national average, since they are more likely than other groups to possess a university degree. It has been estimated that over 30 per cent of them have jobs in professional and managerial positions, both within the government and the private sector, whereas 23 per cent work in manufacturing.[26]

A more detailed analysis of their educational background shows that they have a larger component of persons with mathematics, engineering and applied sciences background than any other social communities. Generally it has been observed that the students of the Indo-Canadian community perform better in technical faculties like computer science and engineering, medicine, basic sciences, etc. Only the Chinese-Canadian community competes with Indo-Canadians in the educational field. Ironically, the community also has more non-matriculates than other immigrant groups. In part, the latter is explained by the family sponsorship scheme of Canadian immigration policy. This is due to the fact that, the India is a developing country and education is one of the social sectors which are yet to meet its true potential.

However, the state of affairs in the home country does not pose any setback to meeting their potential among the Indo-Canadian community as many of them who have arrived as semi literate, goes on to become a leading figure in the academic industry. One such distinguished personalities is Asa Singh Johal, who had arrived as a semi-literate worker and has become a leading figure in the forestry industry in British Columbia, established a Chair on Forestry at the University of British Columbia, for which he received an Honorary Doctorate and later was awarded the Order of Canada. In fact, many of the Indo-Canadian community have received the Order of Canada, which is awarded to distinguished Canadians who have made an important contribution to the community.[27]

The Order of Canada was established in 1967 to mark the centenary of the formation of the Canadian Confederation. Over the last 40 years, more than 5,000 people, including many Indian-Canadians, have been given this honour. The Indo Canadian community has produced a lot of luminaries who are recipient of the Order of Canada such as Shrawan Kumar.

Shrawan Kumar is scientists who have received Canada's highest civilian award *the Order of Canada*, for his three decades of pioneering research on workplace injury and the spine at the University of Alberta. He was born in Allahabad, and an alumnus of Allahabad University where he did his masters in zoology; he had come to Canada in 1974 after his higher studies in Britain. He later on, joined the faculty at the University of Alberta in Edmonton in 1977, and has done path-breaking research, published and taught on ergonomics, occupational health and lower back pain for three decades. He was bestowed the highest Canadian award by Governor General Michaelle Jean for "his contributions to the field of rehabilitation ergonomics, in Canada and abroad, notably in his research and teachings on the causation, prevention and treatment of musculo-skeletal injuries".[28]

Besides, Mr. Kumar there has been many distinguished personalities from the Indo-Canadian community that has received wide recognition for their work globally as well as within Canada, such as Professor Asit K. Biswas, Lata Pada, Dr Arvind Koshal, M. Azhar Ali Khan to name a few of them.

Professor Asit K. Biswas, was a long-time partner with International Development Research Center on water-related research had been awarded the 2006 Stockholm Water Prize for his outstanding and multi-faceted contributions to global water resource issues, including research, education and awareness, water management, human and international relations in both developed and developing countries. The Stockholm Water Prize is presented annually to an individual, organization, or institution for outstanding water-related activities and has been founded in 1990.[29]

Lata Pada is a Bharatanatyam dancer from Mississauaga, Ontario; while Dr Arvind Koshal is a heart surgeon from Edmonton, Alberta; and M. Azhar Ali Khan, a leader in the Muslim community in Ottawa, Ontario; were included in the recent appointments made at the end of last year.[30]

With the expansion of the knowledge-based industry, the Indo-Canadian community is likely to gain in importance and strength. This would also help to expand bilateral ties between India and Canada in the hi-tech and information technology fields. However, the extra efforts are required to need to maintain their special ties and links between the communities in the two countries.

The Indian culture has a very high unique selling proposition that has launch a wide arrays of economy based on Indian culture and their experiences in the socio-cultural to the literary world. They have received appreciation across the society not only in Canada but across the globe that has led to carving out a niche, only which the Indian culture can fill. This has seen a distinct cultural identity of its own, which has not only emancipated but empowered them. This is very much evident as the otherwise would be housewife has cash in to pursue a full fledged career in not only as a performer or a teacher but also as an Administrator in running the different Academy of Dance and Music etc. The vibrant economy that has been generated among the Indo-Canadian community has given them the confidence to participate in the decision making process of the politics that has a strong implications on their community here in Canada as well as back at home in India.

Indo-Canadian Communities in the Politics of Canada

Nothing demonstrated how the destinies of the Diaspora and India were bound together, as the fact that Indo-Canadians won the right to vote soon after the same time India won its Independence from colonial rule. Indian

Independence awakened the pride of the Indo-Canadian community and gave an unprecedented welcome to the first Indian High Commissioner Shri H.S. Malik. This was well reciprocated when Nehru visited Canada in 1949.[31]

The two countries have had cordial relation based on the fact that both countries has multicultural society and share the fundamental values of an elected, democratic governments, respect for the rule of law. Therefore, they have similar institutions such as the Parliament, Courts, Civil Service and a commitment to international peace and security, through the UN systems. Like true friends, Canada has always help India in her time of needs such as the food aid program, or financing of projects and technical assistance under the Colombo Plan in 1951.[32]

It is no wonder that the feeling of white which is so prevalent among the western countries could not last long as Indian immigrants were welcomed with their industriousness nature to energize not only the Canadian economy but also provide a vibrant hue to Canadian multiculturalism. Today, the second largest source of immigrants coming from India, where around 800,000 has traced their roots to India. It is only natural that in the democratic set up of Canada, the Indo-Canadian community has a considerable influence not only as their electorates but also as the decision makers.

Indo-Canadian has made their presence felt in mainstream Canadian politics in a relatively short time, partly owing to the nature of the Canadian political system and the importance of the ethnic vote in a country of immigrants. The political prominence of Indo-Canadians is growing and plays a crucial role in determining, who gets elected to the public offices.

As a result Canadian politicians avidly cultivate Indo-Canadian ethnic groups. The Liberal Party of Canada, which has ruled Canada for most of the past century (70 out of 100 years), is known to attach great importance to the ethnic vote.

Besides, the Canadian community wants them to play a strong role in the world and keep abreast with developments in India and maintain close personal ties with politicians in India, particularly in Punjab, particularly among the Sikh community also across different countries, such as in US and UK, a trend spurred by the erstwhile separatist movement.

The Canadian Government has also given its due respect to the Indian cultures and traditions. They have accorded Heritage status and monuments to Indian temples, issuing stamp to commemorate the anniversary of the coming of Indians in Canada.

The Prime Minister Jean Chretien, along with the then Heritage Minister Sheila Copps had announced the Heritage status of the Abbotsford Sikh Temple. It is located on South Fraser Way by the then Prime Minister of Canada, Jean Chretien on July 31, 2002. The Indo-Canadians who worked at Abbotsford Lumber Company had built in 1911. The distinct wooden-frame structure of the temple was the only second structure that was built on the continent due to which the city councilors supported its designation as a heritage status. The temple was restored to its original condition, along with a museum of the Sikh history in the lower floor while the upper floor will be retained as a place of worship.[33]

On the same day the Guru Nanak Gurdwara has been designated as a historic monument by the then Canadian Prime Minister Jean Chretien and the Heritage Minister Sheila Copps and B.C. Liberal MP Herb Dhaliwal. Incidentally, the two Ministers happen to be from the Indo-Canadian community.

In order, to mark the One hundred years of Indian immigration to Canada, the Department of Canada Post released a new postal stamp of 46 cent featuring a double-edged sword, a circle and two daggers in bright gold against a blue background representing the Khada on April 19, 1999; as designed by Stacy Zabolotney. Khada is a metaphor of divine knowledge, its sharp edges cleaving truth from falsehood. Encircling the sword is the Chakra. Symbolizing God, it is a ring - a shape without beginning or end.[34]

The stamp was officially launched by the then Prime

Minister Jean Chretien of Canada; with the Post chairman Andre Ouellet and Revenue Minister Harbans Singh Dhaliwal, who's also of an Indian origin.

Dhaliwal had rightly remarked the importance of Indian mosaic in the Canadian multiculturalism in these words:*"For 100 years, Sikhs have been an integral thread in Canada's mosaic. Their dream, my dream, has been to get the recognition they deserve for the contribution they have made to build Canada. Well, it happened. Only in Canada, eh?"*[35] [36]Fully aware of the impact that his election has to the Indian community he continued to describe the freedom fighters; in the following words:

> *"They set the pattern for us to fight for freedom and democracy. We salute all freedom fighters and those who cherish social and human values."* [37]

The instances of the Heritage Minister and the Revenue Minister are not the only political leaders who represents the Indo-Canadian community. There are many political candidates, who have successfully run the elections at the local, provincial, and federal levels. At the federal level, there are politicians such as the Herb Dhaliwal, M.P., Minister of Fisheries and Oceans, and Reform Party member, the Hon. Gurmant Grewal. Deepak Obhrai British Columbia and Rahim Jaffer, who represent Alberta as Reform M.Ps. In Ontario, Gurbax Malhi has served the federal riding of Malton over the last two general elections as a Liberal Party Member.

The presence of the Indo-Canadian political leaders in the Parliament of Canada is increasing. There are nine Indo-Canadian MPs who have been recently elected to Canadian Parliament that saw the ruling Conservative Party winning, albeit short of a majority. Besides, the sitting MPs, Tim Uppal from Alberta, and Devinder Shory from Calgary Northeast won in the polls. [38] The last term of 2002, had four Member in the Legislative Assemblies in the province of British Columbia, - Sindi Hawkins, Moe Sihota, Harry Lali, and Ujjal Dosanjh. Barring Moe Sihota, Minister in the New Democratic Party (NDP) government in British Columbia, all other prominent Canadian politicians of Indian origin in public life are first generation immigrants.

The federal parliament of Canada in 2002, had 6 of its members from the Indo-Canadian community out of the total 301 member which includes a Cabinet rank Minister - *Harbance (Herb) S. Dhaliwal* who was the Minister of Natural Resources and at present is the Minister of Fisheries and Oceans; (also, the first Indo-Canadian Cabinet Minister). Besides, him there are *Gurbax Singh Malhi* from the Liberal Party, who is born and educated in India, *Rahim Jaffar* from the Canadian Alliance Party; who had come to Canada from East African, *Gurmeet Grewal* from the Canadian Alliance; born and educated in India, *Keith Martin*, also from the Canadian Alliance party; originally from Goa but born in the UK, *Deepak Oberoi* from the Canadian Alliance Party; educated in India but has East African origin.

Ujjal Dosanjh who happens to be the leader of British Columbia's New Democratic Party also became Premier of British Columbia on February 21, 2000. He is the first person from the Indo-Canadian community to hold such office in Canada. He had been sworn in as the 34th Prime Minister [i.e. Premier] by the Governor [i.e. Lieutenant Governor], Mr. G Gadown, in Victoria. While, among the Sikh community Gurbax Singh Malhi is the first person to be elected in the Canadian Parliament of Canada. He had been elected continuously since 1993, in the Canada's House of Commons/Chambre des Communes, Ottawa.

The Indo-Canadian community has a decisive role to play in the Canadian politics as they have identified themselves in the mosaic of the Canadian multicultural society. This has determined the role that they play in Canadian Politics as well as their home country in India providing the link between them.

Although the two countries have had convergence in their history based on communal issues, but there are also issues, where they have divergence, especially Post Pokhran. Canada felt betrayed as the fissile material used to construct India's first nuclear device had been obtained from the

Canadian supplied CIRUS nuclear research reactor. This had strain their relationship as Canada severed bilateral nuclear cooperation with India since 1976 and resolved to engage in nuclear cooperation only with countries that signed the Treaty on the Non-Proliferation of Nuclear Weapons (NPT) and the Comprehensive Nuclear Test Ban Treaty (CTBT), instituting full scope safeguards on their nuclear energy programme under the supervision of the International Atomic Energy Agency (IAEA).[39]

However, with India's path to Liberalization and Privatization saw the reviving of the bilateral ties of diplomacy, trade, and commerce. The 21st century has witnessed many international issues that have confronted the world today, and where both the countries can cooperate with each other, such as international terrorism like the 9/11 incident. Both the two countries has been a victim of terrorism due to the tragic event of Kanishka in 1985, which had involved them.

Ironically, the Indo-Canadian communities find themselves to faces the brunt of the antagonistic feelings that the larger community faces due to incidents such as the 9/11, even though it has occurred in US. Incidents have occurred, where Hindu temple have been burnt down in Hamilton as a reaction against 9/11. This is not the first case where misperceptions have made the Indo-Canadian community the victim, in particular and the people of Canada at large.

The liberal traditions of Canada have made them vulnerable to any kind of terrorist activities which involve any of the community. The Kanishka incident in 1985 had occurred as a response for misusing places of worship in Canada. However, following the defeat of the cross-border sponsored terrorism in Punjab; these militant trends have abated significantly.

The political leaders of the Indo-Canadian community have played a positive role in renewing the ties between the two countries, as they have manage to influence the Canadian Federal government to identify issues which would be of common interest with the Indian government even when the international community have gone ahead in trying to isolate India by restricting its ties with India. They have even revoked international interest in India by engaging in dialogue of multilateral issues in the international community, which India is in a position today and rightful belongs. However, there are still many areas if concern in which they need to play a proactive role such as the issue of Terrorism.

Indo-Canadian Community and Indo-Canadian Relations:

The Indo-Canadian community has definitely given an Indian flavour through its myriad colours for the eye, vibrating with the melody of traditional Indian music and keeping them in sync with the tapping of the feet from the classical Indian dance to the folksy beat of Bhangra. The Indian influence does not only resonates in the shores of Canada but has echoed through the pulse of the Indian politics, where they have come to acknowledge that the Indo-Canadian community have not only sought to shape but has influence the bilateral relations between the two countries of India and Canada.

In order to know, how the Indo-Canadian community has influenced the Indian Politics, it is important to trace the relations from the historical diplomatic relations, it has shared. The different issues in which they have converge and diverged. Even in the issue of divergence, Indo-Canadian community has been able to play a constructive role of building a friendly and cordial relation for the simple reason that they were also part of the Canadian legislatures and were the policy makers.

The main issue of convergence comes also from the historical fact of commonality of being under the subjugation of the British Empire. Later, when the two country-India and Canada became independent nations; they continued the cordial relation based on the fact that both countries has multicultural society and share the fundamental values of an elected, democratic governments, respect for the rule of law. That is why; they have similar institutions such as the Parliament, Courts, Civil Service and a commitment to international peace and security, through the UN systems.

Besides, the fact that there is a very vibrant Indo-Canadian community which forms a sizable chunk of the Canadian mosaic in their multicultural society.

Issues of Convergence

The convergence of interest and commitment between the Indian and Canadian government had been witnessed over a wide range of issues, from the Korean War armistice, the International Control Commission to the Suez crisis, be it in the United Nations or the Commonwealth. Moreover, the bilateral relations between India and Canada was all the more enhanced during the early period from 1940s to 1960s due to the personal ties that developed between the first Indian Prime Minister Jawaharlal Nehru with Canadian Prime Minister, Louis St. Laurent and Lester B. Pearson who had served over those years:

A friendly personal relation between the two head of state translated for the states as well. It was not a surprise when Mr. Nehru emphasized on "meeting of minds" in his speech which he made to the Canadian Parliament on 24 October 1949. Quoting his speech, he had said that -

> *I am revealing no secret when I say that our point of view and that of Canada are identical or very near to each other on almost every issue. In particular, I should like to refer to the spirit of understanding shown by our government and your representative at the meeting of Dominion Prime Ministers, held in London last April, in the determination of our future relationship with the commonwealth.*[40]

Canada started sending aids whenever India was in need such as the food aid program, or financing of projects and technical assistance from Canada under the Colombo Plan in 1951, when India was at its nascent stage of seeking self sufficiency of independence to tide over the food security problem that India had faced. In fact, over the past five decades Canada has given the largest single bilateral aid programme to India which amounted to over three billion Canadian dollars.

Although, the interests shared by the two countries have

converge on many fruitful issues, it has also diverge through distinct periods of time which has been sharply demarcated by precipitous declines caused by significant disagreements between the Canadian and Indian governments over substantive issues.

Issues of Divergence

The main issue of divergence of interest began after India pursued its "peaceful" nuclear explosion of May 1974 in Pokhran. For Canada felt betrayed as the fissile material used to construct India's first nuclear device had been obtained from the Canadian supplied CIRUS nuclear research reactor. This had strain their relationship as Canada severed bilateral nuclear cooperation with India since 1976 and resolved to engage in nuclear cooperation only with countries that signed the Treaty on the Non-Proliferation of Nuclear Weapons (NPT) and the Comprehensive Nuclear Test Ban Treaty (CTBT), instituting full scope safeguards on their nuclear energy programme under the supervision of the International Atomic Energy Agency (IAEA).[41]

The detonation of five nuclear devices in two sets of tests on 11 and 13 May 1998 had surprised Canada along with the international community. Canada had temporarily withdrawn the High Commissioners office from New Delhi and ban military exports, suspending non-humanitarian development assistance and had restricted official contact. The same was done with Pakistan as well as the latter had reiterated with an alleged six nuclear detonations on 28 and 30 May, 1998. According to the Canadian Foreign Affairs Minister Lloyd Axworthy, it was a clear and fundamental threat to international security regime including that of Canada's.

Canada remains a member of the multi-country South Asia Task Force (SATF) established by the G8 Foreign Ministers in June 1998 to address nuclear proliferation and in mid-May 1999, the then Secretary of State (Asia- Pacific), Raymond Chan paid one-day working visits to Pakistan and India to reinforce Canada's views on nuclear proliferation.

Despite these disagreements over India's nuclear policy, bilateral relations grew in some areas of mutual interest during 1999 and 2000. In June 1999, the Canadian Supreme Court hosted the Chief Justice and a delegation of the Indian Supreme Court for the first meeting of the Indo-Canada Legal Forum with the principal theme of Human Rights and Court Efficiency. The second meeting was held in India in early February 2001. Moreover, the Canada-India Working Group on Counter-Terrorism was established in 1997 and the meetings are conducted with the participation of several departments and agencies of both the governments.

It is during these phase that both the two countries have had their episodic lows but the political bonding that the two country share did not cease due to the social bonds that existed between the two countries. The social bond was fermented by the Indo-Canadian community who have helped to mitigate the disagreements and promote an overall positive relationship, as they has help to renew their economic interest in India and revive the economic ties, especially after the economic transformation of the 1990s.

The beginning of the last decade of the 20th century witnessed India taking a path of Liberalization and Privatization opening up to the waves of globalization. The economic transformation of India has renewed economic interest and revived economic ties. This has been illustrated when the Prime Minister Jean Chretien along with his Team Canada mission visited India in January 1996. The team Canada comprise of two Cabinet Ministers, Premiers from seven Provinces along with 300 business persons.[42]

The visit of the Canadian Prime Minister was well received and led to renewing of visits by the dignitaries and furthering diplomatic ties. After 8 months of visit of the Canadian Prime Minister, in September 1996 the then India's external Affairs Minister Inder K. Gujral paid an official visit to Canada. The move taken up by India had been reciprocated in equal measures if not more, when the Foreign Affairs Minister of Canada, Lloyd Axworthy who visited India in the following year in January 1997 and inaugurated the Office of the Canadian High Commission in a new city besides the one existing in Delhi in Chandigarh, Punjab.[43]

The Canadian government opened another High Commission in Chandigarh; specifically cater to the Indo-Canadian community as many of them traces their homes in Punjab. This would also help facilitate their visits from the home country with that of the host country. Besides, the inaugurations of the Canadian High Commission in Chandigarh, the Canadian government have also sought to expand Canadian representation in India by opening up a Trade Office in Bangalore and appointing Honorary Consuls in Chennai and Kolkata. [44]

The next year also witnessed a cultural exchange when the Former Governor General Romeo Leblanc visited India in March 1998 along with a cultural delegation. The cultural visits soon progress to ministerial visit and participation in issues of commonality.

The first official visit was made by the Indian Minister of Environment and Forests, T.R. Baalu. He made the first official bilateral visit to Canada after being invited by the Canadian counterpart and participated in the GLOBE 2000 environmental exposition in Vancouver where he met his Canadian counterpart David Anderson and the then Secretary of State (Asia-Pacific), Raymond Chan. Even in the official visit of the Indian Minister there has been a subtle but definite role that the Indo-Canadian community has made in influencing the relation between the two countries; especially when Minister T.R Baalu traveled to Ottawa to meet the Minister of Fisheries and Oceans, Harbance Dhaliwal or is popularly known as Herb Dhaliwal participated in a technical program.

The visits of the Canadian Prime Minister followed by the dignitaries and later engaging in the discussion on issues of commonality such as environment has definitely brought in an alteration from the diverging issue that the two country took a stand has finally converge.

In fact, the converging of issue has been best stated by the DFAIT'S (Department of Foreign Affairs and International Trade) assistant Deputy Minister Joseph Caron, when he address on Asia-Canada relations on 19th October 2000. He eluded the change of Canadian approach to India in his speech, which has been quoted as follows:

> *"Without compromising our steadfast opposition to India's nuclear weapon program, Canada stands ready to engage in co-operative exchanges in other areas, to our mutual benefit. We are also considering a much more proactive strategy to pursue dialogue with Indian officials and civil society on non-proliferation and the human security agenda. There must be consistent messages to Canadian business, including the increasingly influential Indo-Canadian community that the Indian market offers huge prospects for them, which the government ids fully prepared to support."*[45]

The change of Canadian approach to India was becoming evident as the proactive strategy of pursuing dialogue and engage in co-operative exchanges to the mutual benefit of the two countries has been seriously taken up. In the very next year in March 2001, the Minister of Foreign Affairs John Manley announced the plan that the Government of Canada seeks to pursue a broadest possible political and economic relationship with India.

Stating that the Canadian government would henceforth encourage bilateral visits in the ministerial level and resume full developmental cooperation program in India and provide support to any cultural and athletic exchanges. In his announcement, the Foreign Affairs Minister Manley, had pledged to build a strong historical ties between the two countries and seek to work together in the international organization from the Commonwealth, the United Nations to the World Trade Organisation on multilateral issues of mutual concern, such as peace keeping, trade and development.

The announcement brought in active and vibrant bilateral relations after almost a three year long period of setting to take off. It is interesting to note that the Canadian government has sought to revive the relation with India without compromising on the main issue of reservation that they have had and yet seeking to continue building relation on mutual issues of interest. Manley had maintained restrictions on the export of military goods and on nuclear cooperation with India and expressed concern about the nuclear proliferation in South Asia.

The seriousness of the Canadian Government in engaging their relations was also seen when the Deputy Prime Minister John Manley visited India across the various cities of Amritsar, Chennai, Mumbai and New Delhi. In fact, he had sought to visit India when he served as Minister of Foreign Affairs that is why India was the first country he visited after becoming the Deputy Prime Minister. [46]

Manley visited the cities extensively as well as had meeting with all the head of the state and important leaders in the country such as the then President Late K.R. Narayan, Prime Minister Atal Bihari Vajpayee, Minister of External Affairs Jaswant Singh, Home Affairs Minister L.K. Advani and Leader of the Official Opposition Sonia Gandhi among others.[47]

He had also visited Universities like the Canadian Studies Division in the School of International Studies of the School of International Studies, Jawaharlal Nehru University where the author had been a student. He had delineated the area of common concern that the two countries shares on the various subjects of political, economy, energy and environmental issues. [48]

He had delineated on the different issues of concern such as political, economic, environment and energy issues. On the political issue, he stressed the need of cooperation in countering Terrorism, consultations on international security issues including the problems of small arms, landmines and human smuggling. Besides, he stressed on the benefits of cooperation between the major cities and expressed his desire to deepen institutional exchanges between the Parliamentarians, Supreme Courts, Election Commissions and the other professional communities.

In the economics issues, he stressed the need for growing synergies where the two countries has a comparative advantage – Fibre Optics and telecommunications for Canada and Business operations, Outsourcing and software applications for India. In the issue of environment and energy sector, the resources and the technology that India needs to enhance its energy generation, transmission and distribution while Canada has the specialization in the environmental technology and with both the countries already working closely on the issues of environmental sustainability, has a promise of developing potential collaborations. Besides, Infrastructural development and financial services and investment are other sectors that hold great promises for the bilateral trade.[49]

The visit of the Deputy Prime Minister, John Manley was closely followed by the visit of two Canadian Federal Ministers, the then Minister for International Trade; Pierre Pettigrew and the Minister of Intergovernmental Affairs, Stephane Dion. The Minister Pierre Pettigrew had visited India to seek trading relations with India as he was accompanied by Canadian business delegation of around 150 individuals. They had come to engage with their business counterparts in the metropolitan cities of Mumbai and Delhi, while the smaller Canadian business delegates visited cities of Bangalore and Hyderabad. The then, Minister of Intergovernmental Affairs, Stephane Dion had visited Delhi and Bangalore and was engage in a programme of events which focus on discussions about the conceptual issue of federal system and practical approach in the national governance.[50]

It has been clear that the Indo-Canadian community has managed to influence the Canadian Federal government in identifying issues which are of common interest with the Indian government even when the international community had isolated India, by restricting their ties with India. They had contributed in revoking international interest by engaging the federal government of Canada and thereby engaging India in various dialogues on different multilateral issues in the international community, which India is in a position today and rightful belongs.

Conclusions

Canada being an immigrant country needs to maintain an annual immigration level above 200,000 persons to promote a sustainable growth of its population. The population is of critical importance to the economy as they are contributes to the much required labour force. It has been predicted that by 2026, the Canadian population would be around 36 million, where immigration will play a major role. In that scenario, one in among four Canadians will be an immigrant. With India already maintaining a steady position of number two in sending immigrants to Canada, the people of Indian origin in Canada has an increasing and influential role to play in the Canadian society.

The liberal and multicultural tradition of Canada has made the Indo-Canadian community progressed in achieving success in different field across the society. As the then Deputy Prime Minister of Canada, Manley had remarked that *'the community is playing an increasingly important and influential role in the Canadian society'*. For they have reach a position, where they could not only influence the public policy of the Canadian government but also of the international community at large.

The Indo-Canadian community has comes of age. They have influenced and brought a strong Indian flavor , not only in the society but also in the issues that has emerge be it in domestic politics as well as the foreign policy of Canada.

However, a lot depends on how the immigrant population of the 'Indian Diaspora' continues to grow. As this will not only determine the Canadian Policy in various issues of interest both domestic as well as in its foreign affairs. It will also have a strong impact on the issues of commonality, whether they diverge or converge, as has been witnessed.

India and Canada have always had commonality of interest be it, on political, historical and cultural relations and this is where the Indo-Canadian community will continue to play important mechanisms of building bridges. Moreover, with the Canadian foreign policy becoming more democratic, it has opened up new windows of opportunities which express Indian mosaic in not only the Canadian multiculturalism but also offer the democratic space for viewing Indian's perspectives and be an exemplary for the world.

Endnotes

1. 'Indian Diaspora', http://www.indiandiaspora.nic.in.
2. *Ibid.*
3. *Ibid.*
4. Non-Resident Indian Investment, http:// *www.thebharat.com.*
5. *Ibid.*
6. *www.gopio.net/NRI_PIO_Talk_Mumbai.html.*
7. From the US Population Clock about the US Census Bureau in its official website, http://www.census.gov/main/www/popclock.html. Retrieved 2008-04-29.
8. *Making the Mosaic: Multiculturalism in Canada,* http://archives.cbc.ca/celebrations/topics 3517.
9. The different terms categories used to describe the Indian Diaspora.
10. Chapter 14, *Report of the High Level Committee on the Indian Diaspora, http://www.indiandiaspora.nic.in/diasporapdf/chapter14.pdf.*
11. *'India', http://*www.bindi.com.
12. *Ibid.*
13. *Statistic Canada,* http://www12.statcan.ca/census-recensement/index-eng.cfm.
14. 2001 Census *of Detailed Languages spoken at Home* , http://www12.statcan.ca/english/census01/products/standard/themes/RetrieveProductTable.cfm?Temporal.
15. *Statistics Canada,* op. cit.
16. *Ibid.*
17. http://www.contemporarywriters.com/authors/?p=auth73.
18. http://www.ryerson.ca/library/events/asian_heritage/vassanji.html.

19. http:// www. robinsharma.com/robinsharma_about_sli_about.htm.
20. 'India', http://www.bindi.com.
21. Warwicks, Jacquiline. 2000. 'Make Way for Indian Bhangra Music and South Asian Presence in Toronto', *Popular Music and Society*.
22. *Ibid.*
23. 'Baisakhi Celebrations', http://www.sikhnet.com/community.
24. *'Canadian Parliament Celebrates Diwali'*, http://www.sulekha.com.
25. *Ibid.*
26. Chapter 14, Report of the High Level Committee on the Indian Diaspora , *http://www.indiandiaspora.nic.in/diasporapdf/chapter14.pdf.*
27. *Ibid.*
28. *Shrawan Kumar gets Canada's Highest Civilian Award,* 04 Jan, 2010; http://www.digitallearning.in/news/news-details.
29. *Asit K. Biswas Wins Stockholm Water Prize,* 18 April, 2007; http://www.idrc.ca.
30. 'South Asians Awarded the Order of Canada', Vol 3, no. 7, Feb 2009. *Indo Canada Outlook.*
31. *Documents on Canadian's External Relations,* www.dfait-maeci.gc.ca/department/history-histoire/.../details-en.asp?
32. Carrick, James. 2002. 'Braided Paths India –Canada's Relations: 1947-2002', Lecture delivered on 9th May in the Indo-Canadian Conference at the Centre for American And West European Studies, Jawaharlal Nehru University, New Delhi.
33. *Pioneers of Asian Immigration,* www.lib.ucdavis.edu.
34. *Ibid.*
35. *Ibid.*
36. *Ibid.*
37. www.lib.ucdavis.edu/punjab/chrono.
38. *Nine Indo-Canadian MPs Elected to Canadian Parliament.,* http://www.encyclopedia.com.
39. Manley, John. 2002. 'India and Canada: Partners for the 21st Century', Lecture delivered on Jan 21, 2002, Jawaharlal Nehru University, New Delhi.

40. Jawaharlal Nehru's speech in his visit to the Canadian Parliament, http://www.international.gc.ca/department/history-histoire/dcer/details-fr.asp?intRefid=613.
41. *op. cit.*
42. *Ibid.*
43. *Canadian PM's Visit : Consulate Opened in Chandigarh*, in India New Online, www.Newsindiamart.com.
44. *Ibid.*
45. *op. cit.*
46. 'Canada's Deputy PM Visits Golden Temple', *The Tribune*, January 21, 2002, Chandigarh.
47. Robinoff, G. Arthur 'Canada's Re engagement with India', *Asian Survey*, vol. 42, no. 6, Nov. - Dec., 2002, pp. 838-855.
48. *op. cit.*
49. *Ibid.*
50. *Ibid.*

5

Contribution of Indian Diaspora in Francophone

Ajay Dubey and Jyoti Tyagi

Introduction

The Indian Diaspora today constitutes an important and unique force in the world economy. People of Indian Origin (PIOs) have been extremely successful in their host countries. Today, PIOs live in almost every country of the world and they have made their mark in almost all professions and occupations. Indian Diaspora world over is no longer seen as humble migrant but as community holding high post in politics, universities and industries and other professions. It is amongst the best educated and successful communities in the world. In every part of the world the overseas Indian community is recognised and respected for its hard work, discipline, non-interference and for successfully integrating with the local community. Indian Diaspora has made significant contributions to the economy of the country of residence and has added in considerable measure to knowledge and innovation.

The present article is divided into four parts. The first part will very briefly discuss the world- wide spread of Indian diaspora in general and Francophone in particular followed by a brief discussion on history of migration in the second part. The contribution of Indian Diaspora in Francophone is discussed comprehensively in the third part. This section is divided once again into three, that is, Political Contribution, Economic Contribution and Socio-cultural Contribution. The last part will deal with the response of the Indian Government.

World wide Spread of Indian Diaspora

India has the second largest Diaspora in the world. The overseas Indian community estimated at over 20 million is spread across every major region in the world, particularly in the West, Middle East, Africa, West Indies, South and South East Asia, Australasia and Oceana.[1] Table 1 shows that there has been a phenomenal increase in the total volume of the population of Indian Diaspora since independence. In 1920s the estimate was 2.4 million; it increased to 7 million in 1960s. From 1980s to 2000 the number of Indian diaspora has doubled from 10 million to almost 20 million. This increase has been due to demand of labourers in West Asia and migration of professionals to west especially in Information Technology sector.[2]

Table 1 : Overseas Indians' Population Estimates

Year	Total Estimates
1920s	2.4 million
1930s	3.51 million
1940s	4 million
1950s	4.34 million
1960s	7 million
1970s	7.9 million
1980s	10.64 million
2000	20 million

Source: Sahadevan, P. 1995. *India and Overseas Indians: The Case of Sri Lanka,* Delhi: Kalinga. p.15 & www.indiandiaspora.nic.in

At present PIOs are in majority in Mauritius (almost 70 per cent) and Guyana (51 per cent); the single largest ethnic group in Fiji (Less than 50 per cent) and Suriname (37 per cent). In Trinidad and Tobago, Indians are the second largest group (40 per cent). In several other countries the Indians' position is third or fourth in the population ranking–Malaysia (9 per cent), Singapore (6.4 per cent), Srilanka (5.5 per cent).[3] In these countries, Indian communities have been politically very strong.

Francophone as a region consists of French speaking countries. It includes France, French West Indies: Guadeloupe and Martinique and almost twenty five countries of Africa which includes Indian Ocean territories (refer to Table 2). Overall the Francophone Indian Diaspora constitutes over 5 per cent of the total Indian Diaspora.[4]

Table 2 : Estimated Size of Overseas Indians in Francophone

Countries	PIOs	Indian Citizens	Stateless	Total
Algeria	5	40		45
Benin	450			450
Burundi	300			300
Cape Verde	4			4
Cameroon	250			250
Comoros	50			50
Cote d' Ivoire	30	270		300
Djibouti	280			280
France	55000	10000		65000
Guadeloupe	40000			40000
Madagascar	25000	3000	1000	29000
Mauritius	704640	11116		715756
Reunion Island	220000	55		220055
Morocco	25	350		375
Seychelles	2000	3000		5000
Tunisia		70		70

Source: *Government of India*. 2001. *Report of High level Committee on Indian Diaspora*, www.indiandiaspora.nic.in

Historical Background

In the study of Indian Diaspora, writers generally distinguish between two phases of migration, that is, "Colonial Phase" and "Post Colonial Phase". It should be emphasized, however, that the emigration of Indians has a much longer history than what the reference point of colonialism seems to suggest. It is well known that Indian saints and monks undertook long journeys to spread knowledge, peace and love. Fifty years after Buddha's death (483 B.C.) his disciples went to the neighbouring countries (Central and Eastern Asia) to spread Buddhism and settled there. Maritime history of pre-colonial India records evidence of continuous contact between the kingdoms of the Coromandel coast and the islands of South-East Asia. The contact of the Palas of Bengal with the Sailendra kings of Indonesia and the expeditions of the South Indian Cholas which vanquished the great Indonesia Empire of Sri Vijaya are repeatedly referred to by scholars like Huge Tinker. Apart from Monks and *Bhikshus* India's mercantile connections led to permanent settlement in East Africa. These early migrants to East Africa belonged mainly to small trading communities like the *Ismailis, Bhoras* and *Banyas* of the Gujarat region. Similarly Indian traders went to Ceylon, Burma, Malaya, Thailand, and Indonesia and settled there. They were mainly *Nattukkottai Chettyars* of *Chettinad* in the Tamil region of South India.[5]

However, the most crucial phase of Indian migration started in the colonial era. The industrial revolution in Europe brought revolution in transportation and communication as well. This facilitated the large scale emigration of Indians to far off lands. As European mercantile class grew new areas for raw materials and new markets were discovered in Asia, Africa and Latin America. By nineteenth century, slavery was abolished. This created an enormous demand for a cheap and regulated labour force.

This made India a reservoir of cheap, docile, and dependable labour, especially to work on the plantations. Tinker provides one of the most comprehensive surveys of the emigration of Indian labour overseas during the colonial era. Broadly three distinct patterns of Indian emigration are identifiable in this period: (1) "indentured" labour emigration, (2) kangani and maistry labour emigration, and (3) "passage" or "free" emigration. The indentured labour emigration was a contract signed by the individual labourer to work on plantations. It was officially sponsored by the colonial government. It began in 1834 and ended in 1920. The overwhelming majority of the labour emigrants under this system were recruited from North India. These labour emigrants were taken to the British colonies of British Guiana, Fiji, Trinidad and Jamaica; the French colonies of Guadalupe and Martinique; and the Dutch colony of Surinam. The kangani (derived from Tamil kankani, meaning foreman or overseer) system prevailed in the recruitment of labour for emigration to Ceylon and Malaya. A variant of this system, called the maistry (derived from Tamil maistry, meaning supervisor) system was practised in the recruitment of labour for emigration to Burma. Under these systems the kangani or maistry (himself an Indian immigrant) recruited families of Tamil labourers from villages in the erstwhile Madras Presidency. Under these systems the labourers were legally free, as they were not bound by any contract or fixed period of service. These systems, which began in the first and third quarter of the nineteenth century, were abolished in 1938. Emigration from India did not cease after the abolition of indenture and other systems of organized export of labour. There was a steady trickle of emigration of members of trading communities from Gujarat and Punjab to South Africa and East Africa (Kenya, Tanzania and Uganda), and those from South India to South East Asia. Most labourers immigrated to East Africa to work on the railroad construction. These emigrants were not officially sponsored: they themselves paid their "passage" and they were "free" in the sense that they were not bound by any contract.[6]

France recruited indentured labourers from Pondicherry and Karaikal to Reunion and Seychelles. Recruitment to the French colonies like Reunion continued through French ports in India without the knowledge of British Indian authorities. It was only in 1860 that France was officially permitted by the British authorities to recruit labour for Reunion at the rate of 6,000 annually. Indenture was for five years and return passage was provided at the end of indenture. The Governor- General was empowered to suspend emigration to any French colony if any abuse was detected in the system.

Nearly 68000 indentured Indian labourers were brought to the French Caribbean islands of Guadalupe and Martinique between mid 1850s and late 1880s. Descendants of those indentured workers now constitute a significant part of island's population.

Recruitment to British Colonies, however, was different from recruitment to French Colonies. The British authorities allowed freedom in the sphere of language, culture, and religion to the emigrants. Proper records of departure from India and arrival in colonies were still maintained in the archives. Unlike Britain, France has always followed the policy of assimilation in their colonies. French ruled their colonies as extension of their empire. Under this policy the subject population was to be fully acculturated in the mainstream French culture in terms of language and culture. Thus, in the French colonies under the assimilation policy the language, culture and religion of emigrants were often changed. There was no checking of abuses of emigration rule as well as the conditions of emigrants in the French colonies. In the Francophone region all records of emigration and even numbers of arrival were deliberately destroyed.

Apart from Indentured labourers Indians especially Gujarati went as "free traders". Madagascar is one country where they are quite successful. Similarly they went to Reunion and Seychelles.

A new and significant phase of emigration began after India became independent in 1947. The large-scale and steady emigration of doctors, engineers, scientists and teachers to the industrially advanced countries of the West is essentially a post-independence phenomenon, and particularly so of the late 1960s and the 1970s. It somewhat declined with the adoption of stringent immigration regulation by the recipient countries. This pattern of emigration, often described as "brain drain," is essentially voluntary and mostly individual in nature. With the second and subsequent generations having emerged, and the emigrant population enjoying economic prosperity and socio-cultural rights, this stream of emigration has resulted in vibrant Indian communities abroad. To be contrasted with the above is the emigration of skilled and unskilled labourers to West Asia in the wake of the "oil boom" there. This emigration is voluntary in nature, but its trends and conditions are determined by labour market vagaries. It is a predominantly male migration, characterized by uninterrupted ties with the families and communities back in India.[7] Recently Professionals are going to France, especially in Information Technology sector.

Indian Diaspora in Francophone

The present article deals with the contribution of Indian Diaspora in Francophone particularly in France, Mauritius, Reunion, Seychelles, Madagascar, Guadalupe and Martinique where one can find PIOs in substantial number. The contribution will be discussed under three heads Political, Economic and Socio-cultural.

Political Contribution

A Francophone country where PIOs have been most active politically is Mauritius. When British took over the colony Indians were the dominant ethnic group. It is till today the most significant group that dominates the political life in Mauritius. It is the only country in the world where PIOs are in a majority (68 per cent of population). The first of these Indians arrived in 1834 as indentured labourers to work in the sugarcane fields. They came mostly from Bihar (both Hindus and Muslims) and to a lesser extent from Gujarat and Bombay. French brought Tamils and Telegus as skilled workers. Often referred to as "coolies", PIOs in Mauritius today are controlling the political landscape of Mauritius.[8]

By the mid -19th century some important members of Indian community such as Sinnatambou Chettiar and Moonisamy Mudaliar were appointed to District Committees. By 1850, Pitchen, Pragassa, Rayapa and Sandapa families were on the electoral lists. Gyanadicrayen arlanda was nominated to the Council of Government in 1886. Dr. Haseen Sakir, a Muslim from the lascar community was successfully elected as a municipal councillor in Port Louis in 1900.[9]

By 20th century, many Indian intellectuals started making their voices heard. Ramkelawon Boodhun, the son of an immigrant railway worker, and a barrister educated in Britain, stood in the general elections of 1921. He failed in winning the seat but was nominated by the governor to represent Indo-Mauritians along with Dr. Haseen Sakir. Indians actively played political role. They campaigned against the retrocessionist movement, which sought to achieve a renewed attachment to France. Rajcoomar Gujadhar and Lollah were elected in 1926 general election under the banner of l'Union Mauricienne.[10]

During economic depression of 1930s, Indians were the first one in Mauritius to unite working classes. Dr. Maurice Curi founded a labour party in 1936. Trade unions were also formed. Another important name in this regard that mobilised Indian community to raise the number of voters was Basdeo Bissoondoyal. Due to his efforts, the number of electors rose from 10000 to more than 70000.[11]

One cannot forget the name of Seewosagur Ramgoolam, medical doctor by profession, was the son of a sirdar from Bihar. Ramgoolam, with respect called 'chacha' (uncle) and revered as the father of the nation, held the position of Prime Minister for a number of years. He introduced free education at all levels and various social aid provisions. His son, Navin Ramgoolam also served as prime minister himself and as leader of the opposition. The two main political formations – the MSM of Sir Aneerood Jaugnauth and LP of Navin Ramgoolam – have been alternately forming governments in Mauritius since the exit of Sir Seewosagur Ramgoolam. Sir Aneerood Jaugnath is current President of Mauritius.[12]

Thus, Indian community in Mauritius is politically very active. Indians comprise the largest group of voters and therefore, the community is able to dominate politically.

Similarly, in Reunion Island one finds a very active Indian Community. Reunion Island is an overseas French Department. It is not an independent country but like other French overseas possessions, it is headed by French 'Prefect'. It has elected representatives in central and regional councils. It is not considered as a colony. All of its inhabitants are citizens of France. However, a French visa would not enable a foreigner to visit Reunion, one needs special permission from France to do so.

Reunion has substantial population of 220,000 PIO in the island. PIO form over 30 per cent of the island's population. Among the Indian community, Tamils constitute the largest group. Their main occupation is agriculture.[13] In 1920, Indians were granted French nationality. This meant equal opportunities for Indians in all fields, i.e., business, education, participation in administration, etc. With these rights PIOs became active on political front. Jean Paul Viapoulle became the mayor of Saint Andre and the first Vice president of General Council of Reunion. Second and third Vice presidents of the same general council were also Indians – Saminandan Axel Kichenin and Nadia Ramasammy. Another example of this kind was Denise Nilameyon who became Deputy Mayor of Tampon. Thus, Indians have utilised well the available opportunities at political level.[14]

In French West Indies too -Guadeloupe and Martinique – PIOs have made their mark politically. Guadeloupe an island in the Atlantic Ocean and a French Department had traditionally been a bone of contention between the French and the British. The British occupied it from 1759 to 1763. In 1763, it was restored to France in exchange for all French rights to Canada. It was finally designated as territory of France through The Treaty of Paris in 1815. It was represented in the French parliament for the first time in 1871.[15] It became a French Department on 19 March 1946. Martnique is an island in the eastern Caribbean

Sea. Like Guadeloupe, Martinique is also an overseas department of France. The Indian community in Guadeloupe is estimated to be around 55000 in a population of about 400000. Thus, Indian community constitutes a substantial number of voters and no one can ignore them. Some of the Indians have also occupied the significant positions. Henri Bangaou held the post of Senator from Guadeloupe in the French Senate. Ernest Moutoussamy has been the Depute of Guadeloupe in the National Assembly of France.[16]

PIOs in Francophone, therefore, have contributed immensely at political level. However, the contribution of PIOs is not only limited to political arena but also to the economic. PIOs in Francophone are actively involved in the development of their host nations.

Economic Contribution

World over the Indian Diaspora is a vibrant and industrious diaspora. This is also true in Francophone countries. Irrespective of their numbers, PIOs in Francophone have been very successful economically. Whether it is in France, Mauritius, Madagascar, Seychelles, Reunion, PIOs have made their presence felt. Let us comprehensively discuss the economic contribution of PIOs in Francophone.

Most of the Indians in France migrated from former French colonies in India; Pondicherry, Karaikal, Yanam, Mahe and Chandranagore. Later, they arrived in France from other Francophone areas including Mauritius, Seychelles and Madagascar. The Indian community in France is estimated at 65000 or 0.11 per cent of the total population of 59 million.[17] Indian community has made their place in France. During the First World War, over 130000 Indian soldiers served in France. In the post Second World War period, Indians provided the labour that helped rebuild France. At present, about 6000 members are estimated to have taken up jobs in army and police forces. About 12000 members are in the French government service. Approximately, 9000 Indians are working in a managerial capacity in French private company.[18] A large majority of Indian community are mainly engaged in private small businesses. Some are running restaurants. Indian cuisine is quite famous. Most of the People of Indian origins residing in France belong to the middle class. The businessmen also market handicrafts, home furnishings, fabric and garments, gems and jewellery, rice, spices, ethnic groceries, fruits and vegetables etc. from India. Gope Hathiramani, a sindhi businessman, is the richest Indian in France.

The success of People of Indian Origin is most notable in the Information Technology sector. Realising the importance of Indian workforce, France is working hard at increasing the number of Indian student studying there. Besides, certain reforms such as making work permits easier for Indian students who finish courses in France are also being introduced. Annually there are about 250000 foreigners coming to study in France. Out of this, only 1700 are from India. Jerome Bonnafont, the Ambassador of France in India said that with India playing an important role amidst growing globalisation, France is keen on many more young people from India going to France to study and being exposed to the French culture and way of life. Besides, French multinational companies are also keen on hiring larger numbers of highly skilled Indian workers for their global operations. France is making big efforts towards a three-fold increase in the number of Indian students going to study in France annually. He adds that the French government is making some immigration policy reforms that will allow foreign students to remain in France for some months after they finish their studies to look for jobs. Recently, work permit rules have been eased to allow Indian students, who finish a course in France, to stay back for 6 months to look for a job on their existing student's visas.[19]

Thus, Indian Diaspora in France has become prominent with a significant presence in various businesses and high-skill professions, such as information technology and medicine.

In Mauritius, during the French rule (1721-1810), Indians (as slaves, servants, workers) played an important role in the development of Mauritius. With the help of Indian labourers, French developed Mauritius as a key sugar exporter.

Free artisans, slaves and soldiers were brought from India by the colonial rulers. Some were awarded land grants and became employers of slaves and respected members of the coloured elite. Indians took every opportunity that came in their way. They became quite successful as contractors, traders and sometimes as colonial administrators too. They were also employed in the service of French East India Company. Skilled workers from India also played a key role in development of infrastructure – the harbour, homes, storehouses, administrative buildings, defence works, roads to transport goods and canals. Thus, masons, carpenters, dockers and sailors were recruited from India. They were known as 'Malabar workers'.

Many Indians, under the British rose on the economic and social ladder. One such Indian was Veliavel Annasamy, who was part-owner of a sugar estate in 1822. Rama Tiroumoudy was another name in this regard. He became a part-owner of the estate Bon –Espoir. Indians also rose up to important positions in the British administration.[20]

Gradually Indians started rising economically. In 1845 the Sinnatambous controlled the Mauricia estate, and by 1852 Tiroumoudy took over Bon espoir plantation. Arlanda family owned the estate of Lemencia. The economic advancement of these Indians was noticed by Gujarati traders. Merchants from Gujarat, especially Surat started opening shops. Memane Bazaar developed around Reine and Royale streets and a Surtee bazaar began on Rue de la Corderie.[21]

Indians also got their hands in money lending and real estate. Merchants from Gujarat also started investing in sugar cane cultivation. The rise in the economic status brought prestige and social status for Indians and wealthy individuals played important role in raising the status of the community as a whole.

In any discussion on economic contribution of Indian Diaspora in Francophone, one cannot afford to neglect Madagascar. Indians in Madagascar came as traders, most of them coming from Gujarat Bombay belt of India and from a caste that is famous in India for its commercial and trading skills – the Banias. Though Indians made their presence on the island even before the British and French Colonial power did, they established themselves firmly by 1900. *Sakalava* King of Boina region in Madagascar founded Mahajanga in 1745, a town on the north-west coast of Madagascar, for the merchants. Indians first settled there.

Trade and shop-keeping are the principal occupations of the Indians. The majority of the Indians, both Hindu and Muslims, took to trade, commerce and shop-keeping, which continued to be the pursuits of their descendents.

The People of Indian Origin (PIOs), being mostly traders, are heavily concentrated in towns and small trading settlement. A high degree of urbanization forms an important characteristic of the Indian population. Unlike the European settlers and natives, the Indians have been precluded since the early days of their settlement, from acquiring extensive land rights. Deprived of any opening in the agricultural sector, they turned more to the urban and commercial enterprises. Such commercial leanings, favoured and sustained by the circumstances that did not allow the Indians to own and acquire cultivable land on an extensive scale. However, nothing could prevent them from maintaining commercial transactions with the natives living in rural areas. There was, again, considerable discrimination against Indians in public employment throughout the colonial period. French mistrusted them, as Indians came from a British colony. When Madagascar got independence in 1960, subsequent governments were apprehensive about Indian emigrants.

The economic importance of PIOs in Madagascar far outweighs their number. According to the L.M. Singhvi's Report on Indian Diaspora, Indians in Madagascar, constituting around 2 per cent of the population, controls around 50-60 per cent of the economy. When French left Madagascar, the vacuum was filled by the Karana (Indians are known as 'Karana' in Madagascar) business houses in the economic field. They are present everywhere. They got hold of Madagascar's foreign trade. Karanas have made their mark in almost every economic activity – commercial transport sector, textile companies, retail sector (between 50-60 per cent of the retail business and almost 90 per cent of the gold shops in Madagascar are controlled by Karanas).[22]

Thus, the small Indian community of Madagascar is conspicuous by its economic importance. Unlike other countries in the South West Indian Ocean, where most Indians arrived as slaves or indentured labourers, Indians in Madagascar arrived as free traders. It continued to grow and prosper at such a rate that today it controls more than 50 per cent of the country's economy.

In Seychelles too, Indians played an important role in the creation of Seychellois economy from the outset. The conversion of Seychelles into plantation society in the late 18th and early 19th centuries led to the large –scale introduction of agricultural workers, chiefly from India. Seychelles is a tiny island nation of 81000 people in the middle of Indian Ocean. The Indian diaspora constitute over six per cent of the country's population.

Indians came to Seychelles along with the first French settlers in 1770. Seychelles and Pondicherry in India were both French colonies at the time and many of the sailors on French ships were Indian. Thus, contact with Seychelles was inevitable. The first Indian settler was Ramalingam, who, in 1789, was sent as an advisor to the governor of Seychelles. He was endowed with large areas of land and under the French many Indians became landowners. The first Indian settlers were mainly from Western and Southern India who settled inter-married and laid the foundation for the growth of the Indian influence here.[23]

During that time the Seychelles owed its importance to its strategic location between India and East Africa and it is this location that inevitably drew Indians in the last quarter of the 19th century.

Together Seychellois Indians and expatriate Indians, who came mainly from Tamil Nadu, Kerala, Gujarat, Karnataka and

Andhra Pradesh, number about 5000 in a population of 80000. Their area of control is retail trade and construction. About a half a dozen of these companies, employing a large number of people, have garnered most of the major building projects in the country. Indians also dominate education and health sectors and hold key positions in major private enterprises.

Similarly in Reunion, PIOs have played an important role in the development of the economy of Reunion. Most of the Indian settlers came as indentures labourers. The first contingent of Indians landed in Reunion around 1670. Gradually cash crop cultivation developed in Reunion and thus need for slaves grew. In 1709, around one-fourth of the slave population was of Indian origin. During the 19th century, new waves of Indian migration took place, coinciding with the development of the sugar industry on the island. In the aftermath of abolition of slavery the French government signed an agreement with the British government (1860) to import Indian indentured workers to work on plantation. Indian labourers played a crucial role in the continued economic growth of the island. Most of the indentured labourers were from the region which is now known as Tamil Nadu.[24]

Free immigrants arrived from Pondicherry, chiefly masons and carpenters. As the economy of the island started growing, Gujarati merchants started taking notice of it. They established themselves in wholesale and retail trade from mid-19th century onwards, including some families who moved to the island from Mauritius. Gujaratis dominates some of the key sectors of the economy. Some immigrants have had a significant impact on the economy of reunion. One such Gujarati was Moussa locate, who arrived on Reunion around 1870 from Surat suburb with his eight sons. He set up a successful business in Saint-Paul. Today his descendants head a group of companies with important interests in the fields of medicine, consumer goods and appliances.[25]

Similarly, Ismail Mamodjee Omarjee, arrived in Reunion in 1875 and set up a shop Rue des Bons Enfants at Saint-Pierre, where the huge family business is still headquartered.

He is remembered for his charitable work, including distributing food and drinks to families during Spanish flu epidemic of 1919.[26]

Another well-established Muslim business family is the Ravites. The founder's son expanded the family business until the store became well known for its huge range of household goods.

In Guadeloupe and Martinique, Indians played an important role turning the physical landscape of the two islands. When cash crops developed on the islands need for labourers grew. The French government adopted the policy to bring Indian indentured workers to work on sugar plantation in Guadeloupe and Martinique. Indian immigration to Martinique continued until 1883 and to Guadeloupe until 1889.

Whereas in non-French Caribbean region Indian migrants were primarily from North India, in the French Caribbean, the picture was different. Sixty per cent of the Indian population in Guadeloupe and up to hundred per cent in Martinique were from South India. They came from wide range of districts in Madras Presidency, and from the French colonies of Yanam, Karaikal and Pondicherry. French brought labourers on contract basis. However, many chose to stay back. They bought land and settled on the islands.

Thus, the economic contribution of Indian Diaspora in Francophone is commendable. Similarly PIOs have contributed in social and cultural arena.

Socio-Cultural Contribution

Indian Diaspora, by integrating themselves with the society and culture of the host nations on the one hand and by retaining their identity on the other, have contributed in the development of the society and culture of the host countries. This transition has been so beautifully done that they have become a proud community in many Francophone countries.

In Guadeloupe and Martinique, the Indian community is completely integrated culturally with the rest of the population.

However, at the same time there are several associations to promote Indian culture in Guadeloupe. These associations, run by mostly People of Indian Origin are fairly active in organising cultural activities in all principal towns, namely, *Pointe- a-Pitre, Le Moule, Port Luis, Capesterre-Belle-Eau and Sain-Claude.* One such prominent group is *Association Culturelle Guadeloupeeenne des Armis de L'Inde,* which has over three hundred members and two hundred associates. Indian community is so prominent on the island that recently 150nd birthday of the arrival of Hindus Tamil in Guadaloupe was celebrated with much pomp and show. In memory and homage to the contribution of those from India who founded the multicultural Guadeloupe of yesterday and today, the Regional Council, erected the First Day Monument, on the occasion of the 150th anniversary of the arrival of first Indians in Guadeloupe. The monument weighs more than six hundred kilograms is made by Indrajeet Sahadev. He is an Indian born sculptor residing in France. The monument is a combination of symbolic representations of the long *Kalapani* Journey, a boat with Lord *Ganesha's* figure at the prow, masts with lord Shiva's trident and *damru* engraved in gold obliquely sectioned at the top to form *Om*. The art piece stands on a circular lotus *mandala* base, the whole monument resting on a marble *yantra*. On the four sides of the rectangular base block are figures of a conch, a golden sun with the date 1854 in the middle, and sugar cane shoots - the bitter reason that brought the Indians to the island. Dr. Henry Bangou said on the occasion that the contribution of the Indians to the evolution of Guadeloupe and its population is incalculable. Today Indians in Guadeloupe are to be found in all sectors of society, from agriculture to politics. Their painful integration, in spite of all the hardships and persecutions, is considered today a success. This is due to their non-violent attitudes and determination in the work place, since the time of the sugarcane fields.[27]

In Seychelles too, for well over 200 years the Indian settlers became well integrated with the local population resulting in inter-marriages and some conversions also. They became well versed in the local Creole language also. In the course of this development their traditional values including language, religion and culture took a back seat in the land of their settlement.

In the 1980's, however, there was renewed interest of Indians in establishing religious and cultural centre. It was only in 1984 that *Seychelles Hindu Kovil Sangam* was established. The main purpose of this organization was to build a temple. *Navasakti Vinayaga Temple* was consecrated in May 1992. It is the only Hindu temple in Seychelles. Among the most prominent families are Adam Moosa, Chaka, Oliahji, Valabhji, Afif, Suleman and Jivan Shah. Many receive a proud mention in the "Who's Who" of the Seychelles in a publication of the former Seychelles president James Mancham.[28]

Likewise in Mauritius, Indian community is very active. Dookhee Gunga, who made millions in construction business, donated large sums of money for the construction of Hindu temples and cremation grounds throughout the country. He also founded the Gita Mandal, in association with other wealthy Indians, which was set up to administer a number of hindi schools in Mauritius. He also financed the first Hindi publications to be printed. A government school was also named in his honour.[29]

Similarly, Muslim community also established many organizations and places of worship. A Kutchi Memon society was set up in 1850 and ran the Jummah mosque, built in 1852. In 1863, two mosques were built at Rose Hill and Rose Belle. In 1892, the Sonee Surtee Mussalman Society was founded. Bohra Muslims too constructed their own mosque and established a cemetery.

Vikash Dhorasoo, an indo-mauritian football player, made his international debut in 2006 FIFA World Cup, becoming the first PIO to be in the World cup.

Indian Diaspora has made Indian cuisine quite famous in all the Francophone countries. Indian curry and *Chikkan Tikka* have become delicacies in many households of many non-Indians. In France Indian restaurants are very popular.

The discussion on contribution of Indian diaspora in Francophone, henceforth, has brought into focus two key facts. First, there is a large expatriate population of skilled people from emerging economies in the Francophone and second, PIOs are significant resource for the development of the countries of origin. Having said this, let us also see the response of Indian Government.

India's Diaspora Policy in Francophone

Arguably, the response has not been very favourable to Francophone countries. From the Nehruvian era of total neglect of Indian diaspora till today when Indian government is now making a "conscious effort to woo her diaspora", one does not see any constructive effort from the Indian policy makers to involve PIOs in Francophone.

Indian policy makers, while formulating policies towards PIOs, have taken a myopic view from two angles. First, they see diaspora only through the looking glass of remittances and financial flows and second, this has led them to look toward west and basically Anglophone countries. Not all expatriates need to be investors and their development impact should not be measured only in terms of financial contributions to the home country.

There are around five per cent of Indian diaspora globally in the Francophone region. But there is a lack of information about them for a long period of time due to the loss of their culture and language (because of assimilation policy). As a result, The Indian policy makers are ignorant about their problems and expectations. All the policy measures of government of India are targeted towards Anglophone diaspora. It is completely neglecting the Francophone diaspora. Though L.M. Singhvi's committee report voices the demands and expectations of Indian Diaspora, less importance is paid to PIOs in Francophone.

It is important for the Government of India to engage with the Diaspora in a sustainable and mutually rewarding manner at all levels:- economic, social and cultural. To create conditions, partnerships and institutions that will best enable India to connect with its Diaspora in francophone countries. In this globalised world, India cannot afford to neglect her diaspora living in francophone and the time has come for a strong and sustained engagement between India and PIOs in francophone.

Conclusion

The present article has, thus, traced the increasing important role of Indian diaspora in Francophone. There is a substantial number of Indian diaspora in Francophone region. There are around sixty-five thousand of them in France, around fifty thousand in French West Indies territory of Guadeloupe and Martinique and around a million in Francophone Africa. Indians have contributed significantly to the economy, society, politics and culture of these countries. Indian labourers have been main force in transforming physical landscape of many Francophone countries like Mauritius, Reunion, Seychelles, Guadeloupe and Martinique. The Indian diaspora constitute an important and unique force in these countries with a significant presence in various business and high-skill profession. PIOs are extremely successful in knowledge based sectors particularly in Information Technology. They have also done extremely well in owning and running small business like in Madagascar. Indian community has also been active on political front.

Endnotes

1. Mathews, K. 2001. 'Indian Diaspora in Africa', *World Focus*, vol.22, no.3, p.5.
2. Sahadevan, P. 1995. *India and Overseas Indians: The Case of Srilanka*, Delhi: Kalinga Pub., p.16.
3. *Ibid.*
4. Dubey Ajay. 2005. 'Identity Issues of Indian Diasporas in the Francophone: A Study from the Third World Regions in Africa and Carribean', Paper presented in the International conference on *Indian Diaspora: Trends, Issues and Challenges* organised by the Centre for the Study of Indian Diaspora,

University of Hyderabad, 24th to 26th February, p.1.

5. For details see, Motwani et. al. eds. 1993. *Global Indian Diaspora: Yesterday, Today and Tomorrow*, New York: GOPIO, p.1-33.

   Abraham, George. 1993. 'Indians in South-East Asia and Singapore Experience', in Motwani. et.al., *Op.Cit.*

   Desai, Niranjan. 1993. 'The Asian Influence in East Africa' in Motwani.et.al., *Op.Cit.*

6. For details on migration during colonial period see, Kondapi, C. 1951. *Indian Overseas: 1838-1949*, New Delhi: Oxford University Press, pp.8-29.

   Indian Indentured System, www.wikipedia.org.

   Lal, Brij V.et. al. 2006. *The Encyclopedia of Indian Diaspora*, Singapore: Editions Didier Millet, pp.44-65.

7. Pant. G. 2001. 'Gulf NRIs: From Expatriates to Entrepreneurs'. *World Focus*, vol.22, no.3. March, p.9.

8. Government of India. 2001. *Report of High Level Committee on Indian Diaspora*, www.indiandiaspora.nic.in.

9. Marina Carter. 2006. 'Mauritius' in Lal, Brij V.et. al. *Op.Cit.*, p.269.

10. *Ibid.*

11. *Ibid.*, p.270

12. *Ibid.*

13. Government of India. 2001. *Report of High Level Committee on Indian Diaspora*, www.indiandiaspora.nic.in.

14. *Ibid.*

15. Thaniyayagam, Xavier S. 1968. *Tamil Migrations to Guadeloupe and Martinique, 1853 to 1883*, Paper presented at Second International Conference of Tamil Studies, Madras,

    www.tamilnation.org/diaspora/guadeloupe.htm,

    www.freebase.com/view/en/indians_in_guadeloupe.

16. Government of India. 2001. *Report of High Level Committee on Indian Diaspora*, www.indiandiaspora.nic.in.

17. *Ibid.*

18. *Ibid.*

19. 'Young Indians turning to France', http://economictimes.indiatimes.com/features/the-global-indian-takeover/Young-Indians-turning-to-France/articleshow/2939601.cms.

20. Marina Carter. 2006. 'Mauritius' in Lal, Brij V.et. al. *Op.Cit.*

21. *Ibid.*

22. Government of India. 2001. *Report of High Level Committee on Indian Diaspora*, www.indiandiaspora.nic.in.

    Also see Thompson Virgina and Richard Adloff. 1965. *The Malagasy Republic.* Stanford, California : Stanford University Press.

23. Lal, Brij V.et. al. 2006. *Op.Cit.* p.272.

    Also see, Bissoondoyal. U. And Servansing, S.B.C. 1989. *Slavery in South West Indian Ocean*, Moka, Mauritius: Mahatma Gandhi Institute, p.65.

24. Government of India. 2001. *Report of High Level Committee on Indian Diaspora*. www.indiandiaspora.nic.in.

    Lal, Brij V.et. al. 2006. *Op.Cit.* p. 273.

25. *Ibid.*

26. *Ibid*

27. Thaniyayagam, Xavier S. 1968. *Op.Cit.*
    www.freebase.com/view/en/indians_in_guadeloupe

28. Government of India. 2001. *Report of High Level Committee on Indian Diaspora*. www.indiandiaspora.nic.in.

29. Lal, Brij V.et. al. 2006. *Op.Cit.* p. 273.

6

Indian Contribution to the West Indies/Caribbean

Kumar Mahabir

Introduction - Becoming West INDIANS

The abolition of slavery in the early 1830s in the British, French and Dutch colonies of the West Indies/Caribbean led to a severe shortage of labour in the sugarcane plantations. The ex-slaves had exercised their right of freedom of choice to discontinue working on the sugarcane even for a wage. The subsequent shortage of labour served as a catalyst for the introduction of a system of imported contract labour. The British first introduced labourers from India to the Caribbean through a semi-slave system of contract labour, lasting five to ten years, known as Indentureship. In 1838, Britain sent the first Indian labourers from the port of Calcutta to British Guiana (now Guyana) based on the success of the system in Mauritius.

Initially, the Caribbean initiative met resistance, since accusations were levelled at the harsh treatment of the newly-arrived workers. Nevertheless, with lobbying by John Gladstone and other British planters, the system continued and expanded. It was later extended to Trinidad and Jamaica [1845] and then to other Caribbean islands like St. Lucia [1856], St. Vincent [1856], Grenada [1857] and St. Kitts [1861]. The system was also adopted by the French and Dutch who took Indians to Martinique [1853], Guadeloupe [1854], French Guiana [1855], St. Croix [1862] and Suriname [1873]. By the time Indentureship system ended in 1917, about 400,000 Indians came to the Caribbean colonies, most of them chose to settle in the islands in the New World.

Most of the indentured immigrants to the Caribbean came from North India, primarily Uttar Pradesh and Bihar, with lesser numbers from South India. The majority of immigrants to the French territories originated from South India and spoke Telugu and Tamil. Northern Indian immigrants spoke the Hindi dialects of Bhojpuri, Urdu and Bengali. The vast majority of these immigrants were Hindus, with about 10 per cent Muslims. Many factors in India encouraged migrants to leave and seek their fortunes elsewhere. Severe famines in India were one such factor. Describing the living conditions of peasant farmers, Dutt writes:

> *The appalling poverty and joylessness of his life under such conditions cannot be easily pictured ... It is literally a fact and not a figure of speech that agricultural labourers and their families in India generally suffer from insufficient food from year's beginning to year's end. They are brought up from childhood on less nourishment than is required even in the tropics, and grow up to be a nation weak in physique, stunted in growth, easy victims to disease, plague and famine.*[1]

The land revenue system, which benefited the land-owning classes and the colonial rulers of India, compounded the problem for peasants in India. Bajpai writes:

> *The state was seen to connive with the exploitative elements of the agrarian society of Uttar Pradesh which was engaged in siphoning off the products of the peasants' toil ... the agrarian crisis deepened in these decades with indebtedness becoming widespread as well as deep, as the debt was passed on to succeeding generations.*[2]

The exploitative nature of the relationship between peasants and landowning classes is aptly reflected in numerous, seemingly arbitrary taxes. Examples include *dhururai* or dust cess, for dust raised as cattle passed the landlord's estate; and payment of presents, called *nazar,* in festivals such as Dusshera, Holi and Eid; *neota* or invitation cess, when villagers were asked to join in celebrations. There were also taxes for the variety of cane produced. *Nazarna* was payment due for permission to build or modify existing houses. The term *nazarana* was also used to describe an extra rent premium, which was taken as a gift payment. So severe was the system of taxation that the practice of *kanya vikray* [sale of daughters, typically very young girls, to be married to much older men] developed to enable peasants to withstand conditions of extreme deprivation. These factors reflect the economic and social circumstances of India in the years of indenture. They served as push factors to encourage migrants to depart their homeland in search of a better future.

In the early days of indenture, when the passage from India to the Caribbean took at least three to four months, conditions on the ships were deplorable. Many Indians did not make it to their destinations, but died on the ships as a result of disease and lack of medical care. Apart from physical discomfort, Indians also faced psychological and emotional distress on board of the ships which traversed the Middle Passage. Many Indians regarded departing from India with horror and referred to the passage from India to the West Indies as the dreaded *kalapani* or dark waters. Caste endogamy broke down on the ships as well as on the plantations on the New World. Due to the harsh conditions that Indians faced, they became united in their struggle for survival. Despite these cruel living conditions, Indians eventually produced a middle class of small farmers and shop owners.

By the time indentureship ended in 1917, many Indians did not exercise their option to return to India. They chose, instead, to remain as permanent settlers in the Caribbean where they got, bought or rented land to do agriculture and rear cows. By the end of World War 1, those who chose to settle in the colonies easily constituted about half the population of Guyana, Suriname, and Trinidad (and Tobago). They also formed the largest minority in Jamaica, Grenada, St. Vincent, St. Lucia and St. Kitts. Today, they constitute over 1.5 million in the region, settling in the territories of the Caribbean from Cuba and Jamaica in the North West to Guyana and Suriname in the South East. They form a visible ethnic group that has changed the face and form of culture, religion, music, food, architecture, politics and the economy in the Caribbean.

The social circumstances of the early years were exceedingly difficult. Not only were Indians, thousands of miles from the land of their birth, they also faced an apprehensive and sometimes hostile host community of non-Indians and non-Hindus. Despite the loss of many valuable traditions through the death of their elders and the inability to resist the dominant Afro-European culture, several aspects of Indian cultural heritage have survived. The growing presence of Indians saw the rise of racial, cultural and religious trends that have contributed to the creation of a uniquely cosmopolitan Caribbean society at the beginning of the twenty-first century. Notwithstanding their impoverished means and limited opportunities, the Indian presence has demonstrated steady social advancement in every field of endeavour, including agriculture, literature, music, art, sports, business and the media.

Agriculture – Sugar, Cocoa, Flora and Fauna

Most historians believe that it was the arrival of the indentured labourers from India that saved the failing sugar industry from ruin in the Caribbean. With the abolition of slavery and competition of beet sugar from Europe, planters placed all their hopes on Indian labourers. Their cheap, abundant and reliable labour in the fields was complemented with the introduction of various varieties of sugarcanes from India. Indians also contributed considerably to the expansion of rice cultivation in Guyana, Suriname, Trinidad and Jamaica. In Jamaica, Africans honed the skills of rice cultivation by learning from the success of Indians. Indians' production in this agricultural sector may have influenced the adoption of rice as a staple food for all peoples in the Caribbean. Indians also introduced marijuana ("ganja") as a medicinal and sacred herb, particularly to Rastafarians in Jamaica.

Cocoa became the most valuable export crop in Trinidad, and even surpassed sugarcane during, and just after indentureship. Indians were at the forefront of this agricultural enterprise as indentured labourers, but more so, as free Indians in the role as contractors and small proprietors during indentureship. Indian indentured labourers also contributed to coconut cultivation on the coasts of Cocal and Ortoire along the Manzanilla-Mayaro Road, and Coromandel and Icacos on the south-west peninsula of Cedros in Trinidad. Scores of Indians were also recruited as indentured labourer on rubber estates in Trinidad (and perhaps Guyana).

Indian immigrant labourers were brought with animals on the same ship to the Caribbean. It is recorded that large lop-eared goats, for instance, were the survivors of the ship "Lapwing", which was wrecked near Barbados on its way to Guyana. As agricultural workers, during indentureship (1838-1917), Indians worked alongside cattle in the fields, and they also kept private animals as property and pets. Small mongooses were also imported from India to Jamaica, at first, and then to other Caribbean islands to control rat infestation on the sugarcane plantations.

Indians have also contributed a fair share to the region's flora. Hindus in particular, cultivate consecrated trees in sacred groves to protect the species from destruction and extinction. Plants like the tulsi/basil, neem and papal/peepar/banyan are cultivated near the *jhandi* (yard shrine) as *in situ* germplasm preservation/collection centres to sustain individual and communal needs. Indian contribution to plants was numerous and diverse. They introduced or cultivated several types of *bhaji* [spinach], and some exotic plants like amrak/bilimbi/cucumber tree, lowkee/bottle gourd, chalta/elephant apple and jinghee/angled loofa. To this day, Hindus grow flowers, fruits and vegetables which they offer during worship, use for domestic consumption, and sell extra supplies on the wayside or in the market.

Food - *Roti,* "Doubles," and Other dishes

There are dozens of dishes that Indians have introduced or invented in the Caribbean. Among all the type of breads, *daal* [pulses and legumes], *sabji* [vegetables], chutney and *aanchar* [pickles], snacks and *meethai* [sweets and desserts], *roti* seems to be the most popular, and has spread beyond ethnic and geographical boundaries. There are many types of *roti* - all uniquely Caribbean, and different in appearance and taste from the traditional *puris* of India. In this carte du jour, *daal puri* is at the top of the menu because of its extreme popularity. Filled with finely-ground *daal* [split peas], *daal puri* is lighter and fluffier than its ancestor, and does not contain potato or any other filling. The next favourite is *paratha roti,* referred to as "buss-up-shut" in Trinidad because of its resemblance to a bursted-up shirt. It is made on a *tawa* [baking stone] with the usual flour, baking powder, margarine, and vegetable oil or *ghee* [clarified butter]. It is basted with a *puchara* [stick with cloth strips at the end] and pounded with a *dabla* [pallet] or end of a *belnaa* [rolling pin]. Both *daal puri* and *paratha* roti are usually eaten with curried vegetables or meat.

Indians have created completely new dishes to add to the colourful Caribbean culinary potpourri. Sometimes their ingredients, method of preparation, cooking technique or presentation style are different from that of their originals. One example is the delightful "doubles" which is uniquely Trinidadian and a gift to the world. Traditionally Indian in ancestry, 'doubles' is singularly the most nutritious, cheapest and tastiest snack. Made mainly from flour, yeast, *haldi* [tumeric] and *geera* [cumin], it is essentially a *channa* [chick pea] sandwich made with *vada* [patty]. It is sold hot mainly from street vendours who serve it with a dash of chutney, *kuchilla* [shredded pickles] or pepper. In North America where it is also sold in West Indian shops, "doubles" is referred to as "channa burger."

Another distinctive food offering is *choka,* which is any roasted, mashed and seasoned vegetable. Yet another Indian contribution to the culinary arts is "chownkay," which is the preparation of adding hot oil to uncooked food, or vice versa. But garlic, onions and hot peppers are first heated in the oil until golden brown. This particular preparation method is used when making curries, and some believe that if the curry is not 'chownkayed' properly, it will not "eat good." Indians have also contributed curry to the Caribbean with popular preparations being curried goat in Jamaica, and curried chicken and duck in Trinidad and Guyana. Indians were the first to curry fruits in the Caribbean like green bananas and pommecythére. But it is with green mangoes that Indians have been able to demonstrate their creative skills in cooking. Nowhere else in the world has any group been able to curry the fruit to create a delicious delight.

Indians in Trinidad have discovered and popularized the use of shado beni or bandaniya (a type of cilantro) to flavour almost any dish. The pungently scented herb has become the standard ingredient in almost any *talkari* [vegetable] and chutney. Indians have been able to give a distinct flavour to their foods through the use of spices like cardamom, cinnamom, clove, cumin, karapule, lovage, fenugreek, massala and nutmeg. Interestingly, the Hindi names have been retained for most of the food items and preparations (e.g. laung/luong, geera, methi, haldi, aloo, baigan, kurma, partan, etc). Cooking items and utensils have been retained in their original forms after four generations, complete with their original names (e.g. *daal gootni, bilna, chulha, sil, lorha, kalchul, belnaa, chowkee,* etc.)

Language - Varieties of Hindi (Bhojpuri)

Indians introduced Arabic and Hindi in the Caribbean 169 years ago. Arabic and Hindi are an important medium today in the rediscovery of an essential part of the region's religious and cultural heritage. Like Trinidad Spanish and Trinidad French Creole, Trinidad Hindi (Bhojpuri) has moved from a language of the majority, to a language spoken only by elderly people at least 80 years old who live in isolated rural communities[3]. The survival of Hindi in Trinidad may be retained only in its lexical form, and it would persist only in so far as it is used in Trinidad Creole English[4]. However, it is without doubt that Hindi is the second language of Trinidad, Guyana and Jamaica. It is entrenched in Caribbean

English vocabulary; it is present in the language of all nationals regardless of race or ethnicity when they use words like *roti, sari, dulahin and nani.* It is a living language and it is used more frequently than French or Spanish - the two foreign languages taught in most secondary schools[5].

All Caribbean peoples are exposed daily to Hindi through conversations with elders at home, through sermons and songs by pundits and their choir, and through music on cassettes and CD players, loudspeakers ("mikes"), cinema, videos, television, and radio. There are also Hindi/Indian cultural concerts and competitions, plays, and poetry performances taking place. In Trinidad, there are six television channels that broadcast Indian cultural programmes weekly, and seven radio stations that air Hindi music twenty-four hours a day, seven days a week. Hindi is so important to Trinidad, that the Hindi Foundation hosted the First Hindi Conference in the Western Hemisphere in 1996 in the island. Trinidad was again successful at hosting the Fifth World Hindi Conference in 2002.

Literature – Naipaul, Selvon, *et al.*

Indian novelists, poets and playwrights have inscribed their unique style and ethnic presence in the imaginative literature of the Caribbean. Perhaps the person who has made Indians in the Caribbean visible to the world is the novelist, V.S. Naipaul. He has won almost every major literary award in English in the world including the prestigious Booker Prize. In 1990, Naipaul was knighted by Queen Elizabeth II, and in 2001, he won the distinguished Nobel Prize for Literature. He has written more than twenty books in the last forty-five years, but perhaps his most popular novel is *A House for Mister Biswas,* which is based on the author's early life in Hindu Trinidad. Sir Vidia is the son, older brother, uncle, and cousin of published authors Seepersad Naipaul, Shiva Naipaul, Neil Bissoondath and Vahni Capildeo, respectively.

Samuel Selvon is the second most recognized imaginative Indian writer from the Caribbean after Naipaul. He was different from Naipaul in the sense that he was more 'creolized.' His landmark achievement was the publication of *A Brighter Sun* in 1952 which considered, for the first time in Caribbean fiction, the notion of Indians and Africans working together to build a new nation. Selvon also invented a narrative medium based on Creole, rather than Standard English. Selvon was also the first writer to seriously consider West Indian immigrants as a subject of fiction in his ground breaking novel, *The Lonely Londoners* (1956)[6].

Distinguished Indian women writers include Rosanne Kanhai, Ramabai Espinet, Shani Mootoo, Ryhaan Shah and Lakshmi Persaud. Persaud has published four novels: *Butterfly in the Wind, Sastra, For the Love of my Name,* and *Raise the Lanterns High.* The Centre for Translation and Comparative Cultural Studies at Warwick University in the UK has established a Research Fellowship in her name. These and other writers like David Dabydeen and Rabindranath Maharaj capture the experience of being an Indian, and ethnic minority in the Caribbean. The moral values, religious rituals and customs their narratives describe are distinctly Indian, and have little in common with anything African. Yet, their works are undeniably Caribbean in its social context of cultural sensitivity, civil insecurity and political powerlessness.

Song, Music, Dance, Drama and Film

Indians in the Caribbean consider music to be an integral part of their culture which they have sustained and improvised since their first arrival in the New World in 1838. They had brought with them in the immigrant ships musical instruments that were previously unknown in the West Indies. These included the *tassa, tabla, dholak, majeera, bansoori, sitar* and harmonium. Indians introduced songs like *bhajans, ghazals* and *qawaalis*. With the introduction of the Hindi cinematic movies like *Bala Joban* [Sweet Youth] in 1934, Indians began to include renditions of film songs in their repertoire. It is also widely believed that Indian rhythms contributed to the creation of soca - a dance music version of calypso.

Some of their music evolved from folk songs ("tan singing") and wedding songs into a new musical genre called chutney. The fast-paced, saucy and suggestive songs were first sung in the privacy of women during Hindu wedding ceremonies primarily to tease the bride. The songs have now made their way to dancehalls and concerts and are now taken over by male bards. Some popular chutney artists include Drupatee Ramgoonai, Terry Gajraj, Rikki Jai, Sarika Mahabir and Adesh Samaroo. Chutney fetes are held almost every weekend at several venues in Trinidad. This distinct musical form of Hindi mixed with English lyrics, is a silver string that binds Indians together in their new diasporas around the world to weave a memory of their homeland in the Caribbean. Indians have successfully used chutney to negotiate space and identity in Carnival in Trinidad, to the extent that "the national festival" has been re-defined to include Chutney Monarch, Chutney Brass, Chutney Soca, Chutney Calypso, Chutney Glow, and Chutney Mardi Gras.

Indians have introduced both folk and classical dances to the Caribbean. These have been taught by teachers from India and local experts who have studied in their ancestral land. They have adopted Odissi, Bharat Natyam, Kathak and Kuchipudi styles of dancing to the country of their birth. In addition to the folk and Bollywood dances, Indians have created the chutney dance that is associated with the song of the same name. Chutney dances are performed solo, in pairs, or large groups, and the choreography integrates dance-form fusions from classical, folk, as well as movements inspired by Afro-Caribbean styles. Like the song from which it is derived, chutney dancing has evoked both revulsion and admiration because of the skimpy navel-baring costumes, and the moves that are often overtly sexual.

Indians have popularized the playing of the tassa drum in the Caribbean. Tassa has become a symbol of racial and ethnic unity in Trinidad and Tobago. The drum is played by a wide cross-section of people which is clearly dramatized during Hosay/Muharam in St. James year after year. Tassa was brought to, and re-invented in Trinidad through the influence of Shi'ite/Shia Muslims to commemorate Hosay. The tassa choir consists of at least a set of four pieces: (1) the cutter: the lead instrument which, because of its crisp sharp tone, varies the rhythmic pattern ("hand") at counterpoint; (2) the fooley: it resembles the first but is lower in tone. (3) the *dhol*: the huge bass drum which gives a full booming effect; and (4) the *jhanj*: a pair of large brass cymbals. Tassa choirs also perform every weekend at fetes, competitions, weddings, variety concerts and even in Carnival bands and fetes. Tassa has become the unofficial national instrument of welcome for heads of state and visiting foreign delegates.

"Ram Leela" is perhaps the oldest living form of free outdoor folk theatre in the Caribbean. It definitely holds the unrivalled record of being the only play to have been performed at dozens of venues for over 100 consecutive years in the region. "Ram Leela" is performed in serialized acts over several nights. Produced by community groups throughout the country, villagers all serve without the expectation of payment. The attractions include the performances of actors in their glitzy costumes, their opening parades through the streets, their rhythmic stylized dancing, the colourful stage décor, the spectacular giant effigies, and the thunderous tassa drumming. Villagers play the roles of animals, clowns, humans, saints, gods and demons through masks, costumes, props, gestures and body movements. They do not speak but mime to the songs and dialogues of a *pundit* [priest] who narrates through a loudspeaker in Hindi and English. "Ram Leela" is performed in a large flat space on a playing field fenced off by bamboo trunks. The final scene of the play climaxes with the torching of the 30-foot effigy of the giant demon, Ravan. He turns into a towering inferno in the dark night until he totters and comes crashing down to the ground with thunderous applause from the audience.

Indian actors and actresses have excelled on stage and in film in the Caribbean, Canada, England and Hollywood. The actor who has earned the honour of starring in the most Hollywood films is Errol Sitahal. He portrayed a business executive in the comedy *Tommy Boy* (1995) starring Chris Farley. Sitahal was also the mysterious Indian servant with a pet monkey in the movie *A Little Princess* (1995). The engaging family drama is ranked as one of the finest children's films in the 1990s. He appeared as a stern father who is an Indian medical doctor in another Hollywood blockbuster, *Harold & Kumar Go To White Castle* (2004). Also making her extraordinary appearance as an actress on stage and in cinema is Grace Maharaj. She starred in scores of stage performances, numerous television commercials, four television serials, and four full length movies.

Architecture, Sculpture, Fashion, Arts and Crafts

Indians have introduced new styles of sculpture, art and architecture in the Caribbean, particularly visible in the temples in Trinidad. One such temple is the richly-decorated mandir in Edinburgh in Chaguanas with its many miniature sculptures adorning its walls and panels. There is also the magnificent mural of natural art in the sanctums of the Trevini Mandir in Williamsville, which has not been duplicated anywhere else in Trinidad or the Caribbean. At the Hare Krishna temple in Longdenville, there is an altar of breathtaking beauty with unique motifs of deities and saints, in addition to peacocks, feathers and flowers. At the Dattareya Yoga Centre and Temple in Carapichaima stands a gigantic Hanuman *murti* [statue] which towers over 85 feet (25 metres) tall. In the same area is the monumental Temple-in-the-Sea known world-wide for its exceptional history, design and location. With a bicycle as his only means of transport, one man built this temple 500 feet (150 metres) off the seashore. This is a proud monument in Trinidad that would one day be declared a World Heritage Site by UNESCO.

Indians have enriched the Caribbean in the field of fashion with the wearing of dhotis, kurtas, Nehru jackets, saris, shalwars, nose-pins, necklaces, bangles, anklets, eyeliners, me*hendi* markings and forehead *tikkas/bindis*. During ethnic occasions like Hindu weddings and "Ramayana Yagnas," every person in Indian wear is transformed into a model of elegance and grace. Most women dress themselves in beautiful saris – some with two-tones, some with multi-colours, and others plain, but all complemented with matching jewellery. Some *saris* are bordered in splendid sequins while others drape in thick, rich folds. Indian garments have become famous for their majestic tapestry. Fabrics are decorated with sparkling sequins in an array of colours to suit figure, taste and tone. Jewellery pieces like the *nak-phul* [nose rings], *bayra* [bangles] and anklets serve as finishing touches to complete the attire of Indian women. The choice of garment reflects elegance, sets the mood, and speaks directly to the degree of modesty, grace and sanctity ascribed by Indian society to the adornment of the human body.

Indians have also introduced the fine art of mehendi as a form of temporary tattoo. *Mehendi* has become the latest craze in Indian fashion among teenagers in the Caribbean. The artistic touch of *mehendi* adds a sensual appeal to women who finish "dressing-up" by decorating their hands and palms with artistic lines of paint. Indians have introduced many designs like floral patterns from the Middle East, geometrical shapes from North Africa, and the block outlines from South Asia. However, the popular choice in the Caribbean is the intricate lacy inter-woven lines that are the hallmark of the Indian and Pakistani styles. A growing number of women artists, who operate from their homes and beauty salons, do intricate creations at an affordable price.

Of the entire Western Hemisphere, it is perhaps only in Trinidad that one can find the craft of bamboo bending that Indians have introduced. During the festival of *Divali*, illuminated split bamboo tubes are transformed into magnificent works of art that are displayed in yards, parks and streets. Indians also use bamboo tubes to make ball-less cannons that explode with a flare and an ear-splitting boom! This recreational pastime appears to be unique to the country, and mainly children "buss bamboo" in their yard or on street side-walks to herald the Festival of Lights.

Indians introduced the traditional art of pottery-making in the Caribbean. The traditional craft has been kept alive by a cluster of Indian families in Trinidad. The potters pursue the craft with a full-time passion. They produce highly-skilled utility and aesthetic vessels of clay such as jars, pots, goblets, saucers and *deyas* [clay lamps]. These skilled potters have no formal training, but they create vessels of exquisite beauty. It is a marvel to watch them work with their bare fingers, seemingly playing with the clay, their busy minds spinning artistic designs, and their wheels singing with joy.

Indians have created or re-created artistic symbols to mark their ethnic identity in the Caribbean. One example of such a symbol is the *jhandi* [Hindu flag], which can be seen fluttering on public roadsides leading to ceremonies and celebrations. *Jhandis* are usually seen near temples and beaches. Their display at the homes of Hindus is unique to the Caribbean – and is not an import from India. The *jhandi* has become an affirmation of presence, visibility and cultural struggle and triumph in a hegemonic Christian society. With its bamboo poles firmly planted in the earth, the *jhandi* signifies the rootedness of a people, and their claim for space in a land that has to be shared by all other groups in the multi-ethnic society.

Festivals – Indian Arrival Day, Divali, Eid-ul-Fitr, etc.

Indians commemorate the arrival of their immigrant ancestors to the Caribbean annually. In Trinidad, Indian Arrival Day has been declared a public holiday on May 30th every year since 1994. The heritage day takes the form of prayers, speeches, songs, music, dances and plays in communal as well as public spaces. The spirit of the day is invoked at various beaches with the re-enactment of the landing of the first boat-load of "pioneers" who gave birth to the Indian community in the region.

But it is Divali (in October or November) which is undoubtedly the largest Indian-based festival in the Caribbean, particularly Trinidad. Divali is also the second largest national festival after Carnival in the island. The Hindu Festival of Lights is celebrated mainly in honour of Mother Lakshmi, Goddess of Wealth and Prosperity. Divali is marked by the lighting of thousands of *deyas* [clay lamps] on decorative designs of split bamboo tubes, unique only to Trinidad. The lights twinkle in the shadows of free public performances by actors, models, drummers, dancers, musicians and singers.

During the days and nights preceding Divali, non-Hindus and non-Indians actively join in the celebration by lighting *deyas,* wearing *saris* and *kurtas,* and partaking in preparing and eating traditional Indian foods and sweets. The festival climaxes with a display of resplendent fireworks on Divali night, which has been pronounced by the state since 1966 as a public holiday. The major event takes place for one week at the Divali Nagar [Divali Village] in central Trinidad where thousands of visitors converge to create a bustling Indian bazaar.

The second largest Hindu festival is Phagwa or Holi celebrated (in mid March) after Carnival. The festival is marked by lighting of bonfires, playful squirting of tinted water (*abeer*) and smearing of coloured powder (*gulal*) on the bodies and clothes of participants. The sea of revellers becomes washed in hues of colours that make it impossible to distinguish their individual racial identity. Bands of *chowtal* singers parade with drums and other percussion instruments stages built on temple grounds and sports fields. A recent entry into *Phagwa* has been the lively *pichakaree* song competition largely in English that dwells on themes of religion, society and contemporary Trinidad politics. *Phagwa,* with its pervasive red colour symbolizing fertility, also signals the beginning of the harvest season.

Other major Hindu festivals include Shivratri (in February) held a few days away from Carnival. It takes the form of an all-night vigil in over 200 public temples across Trinidad. From midnight, offerings are made to Lord Shiva, the Remover of Obstacles, whose form is an oval stone, symbolizing the abstraction of God. Kartik is a water festival (in October or November) in which Hindus converge to rivers and seas to perform *puja* [worship], bathe and make offerings of flowers and fruits. Ganga Dashara (in May) take the form of a pilgrimage to a river in Blanchisseue. There, the sacred Ganges is invoked through rites and rituals to reconnect with the world's oldest river festival.

The largest festival for the 6 per cent of Trinidad's Muslims is Eid-ul-Fitr, which has been declared as a national holiday. The morning begins with devotees dressed in ethnic wear congregating at mosques and large open sites. The thanksgiving service mainly celebrates the end of a month of prayer and fasting from dawn to dusk, which began with the sighting of the new moon. The Morning Prayer is followed with lavish feasts of Indian dishes with family members and friends, and the distribution of food (especially *halwa* and *sawine*) to neighbours and the needy.

Muharram/Hosay – A Street Procession and Spectacle

Indians have introduced Muharram (called Hosay) to the Caribbean which has a very long tradition as a folk street procession. Indeed, it is as old as indentureship itself. Its history in Trinidad dates back to the 1850s in the Philippine estate where the first *taziya* [ornate imitation tombs] was made[7]. In the 1920s, it was not unusual to see about eighty-three *taziyas* being paraded in any one place[8]. These sometimes-forty-foot tall structures were placed on carts and wagons and were drawn by two, four or six mules (*The New Era* 1871). Muslim designers preferred floral motifs but drew even these in an abstract style. They applied their mastery of the exact sciences - mathematics, astronomy, optics, *etc.* to the architecture of the *taziya*. The rival *taziyas* competed for admiration in the splendour of their designs so much so that it prompted a colonial journalist in *The Trinidad Sentinel* of 1857 to admit to "the remarkable taste of the coolie in these matters." In Guyana, the Sunni Muslims lobbied to have legislation passed to ban the procession there about forty years ago. In Jamaica, however, cultural continuity has led Hosay to become one of the great national events, with Clarendon having the best organised and most elaborate procession[9]. In all three islands, Hosay was/is characterized by the parade of *taziya*, and the performance of *marsiyah* songs; tassa drumming; *gatka* stick-fights; and rod, broom and moon dances.

Carnival – The Greatest Street Show in the World

According to newspaper reports of the 1850s (e.g. *Trinidad Sentinel* 1857:3), Muharram/Hosay was the first (religious) festival to bring together Indian Hindus and Muslims, and Africans, in one colourful procession. Indeed, laws were passed in 1884 to restrict Hosay to Muslim participation alone for fear of potential solidarity and revolt against a hegemonic planter class. It is highly probable then, that Hosay evoked in the ethnic memory of Africans, art-forms in their traditions that would have almost disappeared. Hosay, perhaps, also provided a resource and an inspiration from which artists drew new ideas to weave into their cultural material for Carnival. In the heart of Carnival is to be found the vernacular tradition of drama and visual pageantry which has one of its roots in the Indian cultural tradition. There is the comparable masquerade "tent" for example - a temporary structure built in the yard to house the *taziya* during its "dressing," and under which visitors accommodate themselves nightly to watch the act of creation[10].

Another such recognizable feature is the undoubted influence of the tassa drum in the making of the steelband. The similarities in their metal cylinders, two striking sticks, heating to provide tonal qualities, posture of the musicians, and thongs around their necks have been studied by scholars versed in the phenomenon of cultural cross-fertilization. UNESCO's historian-researcher, W. Austin Simmonds and later, anthropologist, J.D. Elder were the first to make known their discovery[11]. Another Indian contribution to Trinidad Carnival is the *somaree* [horse] dance. Choreographer Molly Ahe[12] argues that the mounted papier-mâché steeds with rich brocade skirts over bamboo frames, complete with reigns, accompanied by singing and drumming, is "a distinct contribution from Indian mythology." There is too, the Indian stickman [*gatka*] of the Hosay procession in his costumed breast-plate of satin, mirrors, bells and ribbons, who extended his fighting mêlée to the "gayelle" [stage] of Carnival drama. Indian musical elements in the calypsos of Ras Short I, Sparrow, Barron, Dave "Booker" Martin, Wanderer and others would have to be the study of an entire paper. The incorporation of primitive technical devices into carnival wire-bending skills derived from the making of huge effigies in *Ram Leela,* floats on which *taziyas* are wheeled, the bold use of colours in Phagwa, etc – have to be examined objectively to test the hypothesis of Indian origin/inspiration. In Jamaica, anthropologist Judy Bettelheim (1980) has found that the character of Babu in the Jonkonnu (John Canoe) festival was inspired by Indian immigrant labourers to Westmoreland.

Sports – Wrestling, Stick-fighting, Horse-racing and Cricket

As indentured immigrants, Indians brought traditional games like *kabaddi, gulli danda, luha/lohar, eka buka, guli danda,* wrestling and stick-fighting to the Caribbean. They were played on the long voyages on the ships and the lonely estates on the sugar plantations as a form of recreation. Most of these games have almost disappeared. There have been attempts by at least three cultural groups in Trinidad to revive some age-old Indian games like *maakhan chor* [building a human pyramid].

Wrestling is one of the game that is recorded in history as having been played in the depot in Calcutta when the immigrant labourers were awaiting departure on the ship bound for the Caribbean during Indentureship[13]. Indian wrestling was a popular sport in the Caribbean up to the 1960s. Large crowds gathered to witness the highlight of the day, which was preceded by performances by musicians, dancers, magicians, puppeteers (*kataputli*) and acrobats. There were Indian sweetmeats and delicacies on sale. The wrestling matches were as popular as the open-air theatres of "Ram-leela" and "Kanse-leela." Indian wrestling (*kusti*) was different from other styles is that it was characterised by more "high-falls" and "pinnings" and less "choke-holds." Indians still form a substantial segment of the spectators who watch the sport – now all-foreign fights - on television. There is no local Indian organisation, like the Wrestling Federation of India, to encourage, promote and develop this traditional Indian sport in the Caribbean.

Indians brought a unique style of stick-fighting – called gatka to the Caribbean. It was played particularly during the Shi'ite Muslim funeral re-enactment of Hosay/Muharram. Combatants fought with a shield (*fenner*) and a stick (*lathi*) in postures varying from standing to bending on one knee to rolling on the ground. The two duelers would move towards each other, touch hands ceremoniously, dance in circles to the rolling rhythm of the tassa drums, "gran-charge," and then charge. The gatka style of stick-fighting later became creolised during Carnival. Indian stickmen eventually joined their African counterparts in the gayelle [arena] as allies and as opponents to the rhythm of bongo drums and the frenzied chants of kalinda songs. Both Indian and African styles of stick-fighting have become a dying art form and are now played mainly in a few villages in the Caribbean.

It was noted that as early as indentureship, Indians in Trinidad, Guyana and Jamaica were particularly attracted to horse racing as spectators, jockeys, trainers and owners. In Jamaica, Indians participate in extraordinary numbers in breeding, grooming and riding of horses. The best known stud farm is owned by Henry Jaghai in Bushy Park in St Catherine. In Trinidad, Emile Ramsammy, Ricky Jadoo, Wendell Bharath and Rajpaul Rajkumar are champion jockeys; and Roland Khan, Balkrishen Maraj, Maniram "Boboy" Maharaj, Bertwin Samlalsingh, Jagdis Suratsingh, David Mahabir, Shaffique Khan and Ricky Jadoo are known racehorse owners. Some owners give Indian names to their horses like "Adawar" and "Indian Decision."

It is in the field of cricket that Indians have scored their mark in sports locally, regionally and internationally. They brought their unique style of spin-bowling to the game. Sonny Ramadin of Trinidad was the first Indian to be selected to play in the West Indies team in 1950. It was a stroke that turned into an upward sweep for all aspirants of the game. It was Ramadin who introduced *doosra* [reverse spin] to the world, later popularized by Murali Muralitharan of Sri Lanka. Ramadin contributed to the West Indies scoring its first victory in an international series (against England). Ramadin was followed by Rohan Kanhai from Guyana. In 1972 to 1973, Kanhai was appointed the first Indian captain of the West Indies team, to be followed by Alvin Kallicharan in 1978. Kanhai also played in the first Cricket World-Cup final against Australia in 1975. Following the footsteps of Ramadhin, Kanhai and Kallicharan came a new generation of cricketers like Raphick Jumadeen, Inshan Ali, Ranjie Nanan, Shivnarine Chanderpaul, Ramnaresh Sarwan and Darren Ganga. Chanderpaul, a former West Indies captain in 2005, is one of the top ten best batsmen in the world. His batting style is like that of Larry Gomes (Trinidad) and Sourav Ganguly (India). Sarwan's contribution to the game is his singular batting skill (like Kanhai), coupled with his amazing leadership skills as a captain. In 2007, Ganga received the Humming Bird Medal from the government of Trinidad and Tobago for his contribution to sport.

Business, Trade and the Professions

Indian labourers who worked for paltry wages on the sugarcane estates in the Caribbean soon became a thrifty, energetic and industrious people. They were able to rise from their deplorable condition to be equal to, and sometimes better than, the freed slaves whom they had replaced on the plantations. Most Indians grew to become small farmers in their own right, others became market vendors and cattle owners, and some went into the retail trade and real estate. Some of them retained and practised skills that they had inherited from their legacy of the caste system in jewellery, pottery and money-lending. Others went into new areas of entrepreneurship like transportation that began with carts, and then progressed into cab-taxis, lorries/trucks and buses. In the 1950s, a fair number of Indians went into the wholesale business, and by the 1970, there were a significant group in medicine and law – professions that brought considerable wealth and high social status.

Today, the vast majority of Indians work in non-agricultural jobs as labourers, taxi-drivers, salespersons, clerks, teachers, and police officers. Yet, many engineers, accountants and general contractors in the Caribbean are Indians. A few families control the local manufacture of aerated soda drinks in Trinidad. To this day, Indians dominate the retail trade with their dry-good shops, supermarkets and hardware stores. They still dominate the jewellery, auto-parts and foreign-used car industry. Except for the Hindu Credit Union in Trinidad, they have not yet been major players in the financial sector (banks and insurance companies) of the economy. The success of Indians in business and the professions have provided a platform for them to participate with power and influence in other areas of the society.

The News Media – Radio, Television, Newspaper

In Trinidad, the airing of Indian music on radio was introduced by Moen Mohammed in the 1960s, and in Guyana, it was pioneered by Rajkumari Singh on Radio Demerara. Since 1993, seven Hindi/Indian music radio stations have been established in Trinidad. Before the advent of these stations, "about half of the entire population served a token one or two hours of daily programming - insufficient to reflect the deep religious and cultural strengths" of more than 50 per cent of the population[14]. Besides news and interviews, these frequencies feature Indian music - local and Hindi – Hindu and Islamic religious songs, and broadcast live *yagnas* [congregational worship] and other Indian cultural programmes. "Radio Jaagriti" is the last of seven Indian ethnic stations to come on air in January 2007; it is the first Hindu radio station in the Caribbean, and the Western Hemisphere.

Indians have produced thousands of half- and one-hour weekly local performance programmes on television in the Caribbean. The most popular, "Mastana Bahar," was first aired in 1970 in Trinidad. The show-contest was first produced by Moen Mohammed and his Jamaican-born wife, Hansraji Maragh, to highlight the talent of local singers, dancers and musicians. Indians feel that there is a dire need for a local Indian television channel to complement "Zee TV" on the foreign cable network.

Indians in Trinidad have produced ethnic newspapers like *The Indian Koh-i-Noor Gazette* (1898), *The East Indian Herald* (1919), *The East Indian Patriot* (1925), *and the East Indian Weekly* (1928). These newspapers were produced to give voice to Indians who felt that they were politically marginalised in society, and whose representative views and culture were consigned to the margins of the mainstream press. The *Weekly* diligently reported the activities of Mahatma Gandhi which influenced Indo-Trinidadians to press for greater representation in the politics of the British colony. The *Weekly* launched the writing career of the short-story writer Seepersad Naipaul, father of the Nobel laureate V.S. Naipaul, and the journalist Patrick Chokolingo, pioneer of tabloid newspapers in the island. Indian newspaper journalism was revived with the publication *Sandesh* (1985-1990). With the advent of the Internet, the print news media have given way to easily-produced and accessible electronic newspapers, journals and newsgroups like *jahajeedesi2005@yahoogroups.com, Bhatcha-man@yahoogroups.com* and *indiancaribbean@yahoogroups.com*.

Conclusion

To do justice to the topic of Indian contribution to the Caribbean would at least take the length of an entire book. The book would have to be divided thematically into chapters (agriculture, cuisine, literature, language, etc.), or country by country in the Caribbean (English-speaking, French-speaking, Dutch-speaking, etc.). The thematic format would be more challenging since one can take a variety of approaches with appropriate headings and sub-headings. One approach can be the arrangement of information into social, political and religious organisations (e.g. British Guiana East Indian Association, Democratic Labour Party, Maha Sabha). Another approach can take the form of theoretical concepts (e.g. caste, panchayat, extended families). And yet another approach can be the documentation of profiles of prominent Indians in the region (e.g. V.S. Naipaul, Balram Singh Rai, Rajkumari Singh, Basdeo Panday). Each format would have its advantages and disadvantages.

The format I have chosen in this essay is the thematic approach based on easily recognisable categories like arts, sports, festivals, business, etc. This format integrates Indians from thirteen or more countries in the Caribbean into a single community which becomes the unit of analysis. This format engenders the challenge of inclusion/exclusion and emphasis/de-emphasis – what should be left out, or merely mentioned; and how much should be written about an issue, event or person. It was a responsibility that I have made using my lens of objectivity to direct my hand in judgement. It was agonizing for me, for example, to resist the temptation of sketching a profile of Anand Ramlogan, a young, bright attorney who is fighting for the equal rights of Indians and other discriminated groups. Equally painful was the act of excluding the achievement of Dr. Savitri Ramcharan's contribution to the world in the development of the Walnut Creek birth control pill (Ranahan 1981). I felt some distress in not writing about extinct folk-dramas like *Indar Sabha, Harischandra, Rahasmandal* and *Sarwaneer*; and the Indian contribution to folk medicine (e.g. massage, mantras, jharay) and folklore (e.g folktales, myths, spirits). But I felt no angst in leaving out a section on politics because so much has been written on the topic already (see Ramharrack, Siewah, *et al.).* Whatever format or approach I had chosen would not have been without shortcomings and it fair share of criticism. I have made a commitment that my contribution to the literature on Indians in the region must be refreshing, innovative and new, like my grandparents' re-creation of India in the Caribbean.

Endnotes

1. Dutt, R. C. 1969. *The Economic History of India in the Victorian Age,* vol. II, New York: August M. Kelley Publishers.
2. Bajpai, Gita 2001. 'Colonialism and emigration: The movement of people from north India to Trinidad during 1870s and 1900', Unpublished paper, Department of History, The University of the West Indies, St. Augustine, Trinidad.
3. Chandoo, Ann Marie . 1989. 'East Indian' Influence in the Language of Trinidad with Special Emphasis on Lexicon', UWI, St. Augustine: Caribbean Studies Project.
4. *Ibid.*
5. Mahase, Radica. 1996 'The Potential of Hindi as a Language of Study in the Curriculum in Trinidad', UWI, St. Augustine: Caribbean Studies Project.
6. Birbalsingh, Frank. 2000. *Jahaji: An Anthology of Indo-Caribbean Fiction,* Toronto: TSAR Publications.

7. Grant, K.J. 1923. *My Missionary Memories,* Halifax, Nova Scotia.

8. *Ibid,* p. 69.

9. Mansingh, Laxmi and Ajai Mansingh. 1999. *Home Away From Home: 150 Years of Indian Presence in Jamaica 1845-1995,* Kingston, Jamaica: Ian Randle Publishers.

10. Gibbons, Rawle A. 1979. *A Traditional Enactments of Trinidad: Towards a Third Theatre,* M.Phil. Thesis, St. Augustine: University of the West Indies.

11. Mahabir, Kumar. 1984. 'The Influence of the Tassa in the Making of the Steelband: The East Indian Contribution to the Trinidad Carnival', Trinidad: Phagwa East Indian Cultural Promotions Brochure, pp. 12-22.

12. Ahe, Molly. 1978. *The Dance in Trinidad and Tobago,* Port of Spain: Golden Heritage, Heritages Culture Ltd., p. 72.

13. Mahabir, Kumar. 1985. *The Still Cry: Personal Accounts of East Indians in Trinidad and Tobago during Indentureship (1845-1917),* New York: Calaloux Publications, p. 152.

14. *Newsday.*1998. Ahamad , Riyaz. 'Chairman's Message', 12 July, p. 2.

7

Indian Diaspora in Caribbean: Their Economic Role and Contribution

R.L. Chawla

Introduction

According to available information, more than one million Persons of Indian Origin (PIOs) are spread over the Caribbean region. Most importantly, Trinidad and Tobago (T&T) has 500,600 PIOs, which constitute 40 per cent of its total population; Guyana with 395,350 PIOs has 51 per cent of its total population; Suriname with 150,500 PIOs accounts for 35 per cent of its total population and Jamaica with 61,500 constitutes 2.5 per cent of its population. French West Indies with 42,000 and Barbados with only 2,200 are some of the other parts of Caribbean region inhabited by the PIOs. By 1987, among the Indians in T&T, the Hindus formed 65 per cent of the population, the Muslims 15 per cent and the Christians 20 per cent. In Guyana, 70 per cent of the Indians followed Hinduism; 18.3 per cent Islam and 10.6 per cent Christianity in the same year. The Surinames Indians comprise of 76 per cent Hindus, 20 per cent Muslims and 4 per cent Christians.

It may be important to recall that by 1890, about 85 per cent of Indians were Hindus, 15 per cent were Muslims and Christians accounted for 0.1 per cent of the total Indian population in Guyana. Thus, over the next 100 years, Hindus were converted into Christianity and the plausible reason adduced by the scholars is that Hinduism was polytheistic, diffused and a household religion. Although the Christian converts were caricatured as 'rice Christians' and 'belly Christians', conversion provided them with greater possibilities of social mobility and economic benefits and also could advance the educational opportunities for their children in missionary schools abroad.

Tracing back the origin of these immigrants, they were forcefully recruited when sugar plantation had emerged as the major economic activity in the Caribbean region during the European colonial rule. Before sugar plantation was introduced in the Caribbean, it may be recalled that this crop had grown and flourished in the Northeast of Brazil (1550-1700). However, the Dutch found it economical and less expensive to develop sugar industry in the Caribbean region. Somewhat later on, the British and the French developed the sugar estates in the Caribbean region. While the process of recruiting Indian indentured labour is traced back to the 1830s, but it gathered momentum by the 1860s. It was because of the fact that abolition of slavery seriously led to the shortage of labour on the sugar plantation and the demand for the Indian immigrants was what is usually described as 'Factor Augmentation Process' in the plantation economies. Thus, Indian labour emigrated to Guyana (1838), T&T (1845), Grenada, St. Lucia & Vincent (1856), St. Kitts (1861), Suriname (1872) and Jamaica (1873).

This paper is a preliminary survey of the Indian diaspora's economic role and contribution in the post-colonial select Caribbean nations. While historical, social and political dimensions of Indian diasporic community, in general, have been well-documented and elaborately researched by Indian and foreign scholars, their role and contribution in the process of economic development of their respective countries have received little attention.

After analysing some broad macro-economic and social indicators of these select nations, our effort is to highlight the role of Indian diaspora in their respective nation-building exercises. For example, Indian entrepreneurship in economic development processes of these countries, particularly during 1990s, has come to be recognised. Also, while White minority continues to be engaged in services sector (mainly banking & financial sectors), the Indian community, by and large, has already made inroads in trade and tourism, small businesses, hotel and entertainment activities in the region. These post-colonial societies themselves underwent sea-change in their economic structures, development strategies and even economic performance during the past four decades or so. Natural questions that needs to be asked are how 'ethnicity factor' affected the performance of different groups so as to alleviate their poverty, reduce inequality and increase employment opportunities and what has been the relative performance of education/health indicators of various ethnic groups of these nations?

Post-Colonial Caribbean Economies

Majority of the Caribbean nations got their independence from colonial regimes – mainly the British, French and Dutch during 1960s. Early scholarly writings of the Caribbean School of Development such as those of Oxaol, Blomstrom and Hettne analyse the nature of these tiny and small islands economies in 'dependency framework'. Notwithstanding the differences in level of development, size of the market, resource endowment and locational base, these Caribbean economies exhibit certain general structural features, having impacted upon their course and pattern of development over a period of time. By and large, these countries have suffered from dependency in perpetuity, curse of monoculture and Dutch disease syndrome, distorted industrial structure, even de-agriculturisation and disproportionate size of services sector in their post-colonial period.

While summarising a quick survey of the development processes and contours of development strategy of these countries, one can say that they have had aid-driven development strategy in 1960s and 1970s and thereafter these countries moved from aid to trade during 1980s and 1990s, the period being characterised as the 'Decades of Policy Reform', Structural Adjustment Programmes (SAPs) formed the basis of their development strategy during this period. External support and initiatives, such as Caribbean Basin Initiative (CBI) launched in 1982, are pointers in this direction[1].

Major Macro Economic Indicators

During 1983-92, Guyana (-0.1 per cent) and T&T (-3.1 per cent) showed the extreme case of negative growth rates, these were however, followed by somewhat high positive average annual growth rates in the rest of 1990s. Further, while Guyana and Jamaica recorded annual inflation rate of more than 10 per cent but below 50 per cent during 1983-92, T&T has shown this rate varying between 5 and 10 per cent (except 13.2 per cent in 1993) during the above period. Suriname remained an exception; its average inflation rate was 18 per cent per annum in 1983-92, but witnessed staggering 143.3 per cent in 1993; 368.5 per cent in 1994 and 233 5 per cent in 1995. Nonetheless, its average came down to 18.4 per cent during 1997-2000 (IMF, World Economic Outlook, May 2001, p.182). Trends in savings-investment ratios in this region show that while these averaged more than 20 per cent in 1975-90, the same were recorded less than 20 per cent in 1995-98. Exceptions were, however, Guyana, T&T, St. Kitts and Nevis which maintained an average of more than 20 per cent during 1995-98. Similarly, investment ratios hovered in the range of 35-40 per cent in Guyana, Jamaica and Grenada during 1990s, whereas T&T was the laggard to maintain an average of 20 per cent per annum during the same period. In T&T, FDI inflows as percentage of gross capital formation which averaged 16 per cent during 1987-92, recorded an unprecedented spurt to reach 109 per cent in 1997 from a low of 35 per cent in 1995-96 and 55 per cent in 1993-94.

In absolute terms, net FDI in the Caribbean maintained a rising trend; $163 million in1988; $459.1 million in 1990; $923 million in 1994 and $1395 million in 1998. T&T has been the topmost recipient, followed by Jamaica, Guyana, Barbados and Organisation of East Caribbean Countries (OECS). USA, EU, Canada, China and Taiwan have been the major investing countries in the region. One distinct trend in FDI inflows in the region is that there have been wide variations in the levels of FDI across countries. For instance, during 1988-98, T&T recorded average annual FDI inflow of $354.9 million; the same was less than half in Jamaica ($142.7million); Guyana ($78.8million) had slightly more than half that of Jamaica and Barbados one-seventh of the level of Guyana. Among the major markets of CARICOM, US and EU absorbed an average of 65 per cent of its exports in 1980-85 but their share went down to an average of 55 per cent in 1995-97 and a low 52 per cent in 1998. The intra-CARICOM exports constitute one-fifth of their total exports in 1998. Again, US and EU were the major suppliers to these markets and their combined share rose to more than 60 per cent in 1997-98 from a low of 43.6 per cent in 1980; 56.7 per cent in 1990 and nearly 58 per cent in 1995. Intra-CARICOM imports averaged 9.5 per cent of their total imports during 1980-98.

Social Indicators in Caribbean Region

Information culled from various issues of Human Development Report show the present socio-economic status of the Caribbean region as follows:

First, life expectancy in the Caribbean increased from an average of 57 years in 1960 to 68 years in 1992. While country differences are quite marked, Guyana's life expectancy is the second lowest in the region i.e., 65.2 years in 1992 compared to 56.1 years in 1960. Haiti has the lowest, averaging around 56 years in 1992.

Second, infant mortality rate fell from 100 per thousand to 38 per thousand between 1960 and 1992 in the Caribbean. However, the same declined to 48 per thousand in 1992 from a high of 100 in 1960 in Guyana.

Third, total enrolment at all levels increased for the Latin American and Caribbean nations during the decade of 1980. In Guyana, for example, this ratio rose slightly from 61 per cent in 1980 to 65 per cent in 1990. In Haiti, this ratio was 30 per cent in 1990.

Fourth, GDP per capita varies considerably across the region. During 1980s, average annual per capita growth rate fell sharply in the region and showed negative trends from a high of –4.3 per cent in T&T to -3.9 per cent in Guyana and –3.2 per cent in Suriname. Barbados and Jamaica were the exceptions to register positive per capita GDP growth rate of 1.2 per cent and 1 per cent respectively in 1980s.

Economic Role and Contribution of Indian Diaspora

Historically, after the abolition of slavery, mostly in the first half of 19th century in the European colonies in Caribbean, there occurred severe shortage of labour in sugar and coffee plantation in that region. Not only there was demand for more labour to work on plantations, but development of the colonial economies also created several commercial and low level industrial opportunities at those points where the colonial powers inter-acted with the indigenous rural economy. The economic opportunities abounded in retail trade and manufacturing of simple consumer goods demanded by peasants and rural workers. These goods were, however, not supplied by foreign business enterprises. Local population lacked the entrepreneurship to tap these limited lucrative opportunities. Thus, it was the Indian and the Chinese enterprises which offered these services in the nook and corner of the Caribbean region.

Thus, according to a study by R K Jain, the economic activities of the migrants were largely a function of their original migration purpose and motive and have only gradually changed in nature among the descendent communities in recent decades[2]. At the time of each migration and in each geographical context, the Indians occupied an ethnically based economic niche. For example, indentured Indian migrants to the West Indies became rural labour and independent farmers especially in the sugar industry and rice plantations in Guyana over the years.

Till the colonial regimes in the Caribbean, there was very little or no involvement of Indians in the political life of their respective countries. However, after the independence it was realised by Indians that it was not only important for them to play their due role in their adopted country, but also to safeguard their rights as equal citizens. Like Fiji in the most recent years, Guyana and T&T had also witnessed periods of turmoil and civil strife along the ethnic divide and it made imperative for the Indian community to stand on its own. The message has been that like Fiji, other countries might not find Indian community soft and easy targets.

Again politically, having been ruled for more than a century and with a respectable majority in some of these countries, it was but natural that second or third generation Indian leadership must emerge to lead these countries. In this context, Cheddi Jagan, President of Guyana and now Bharat Jagdev, and Hasan Ali and Vasudev Pandey, Head of State in T&T occupied the highest positions in their respective countries. Another well-known PIO, Shridath Ramphal remained Commonwealth Secretary General for a number of years. The Noble Laureate V.S.Naipaul, and Jit Samaroo the well-known exponent of pan music have brought laurels not only to the Caribbean nations but also to their country of origin. The Indian community's role can not be better described in this region except what the noted Barbadian novelist George Lamming has put in his words:

"These Indian hands-whether in British Guiana or Trinidad have fed all of us", Lamming has recognised, "there can be no creative discovery of this civilisation without the central and informing influence of the Indian presence. There can be no history of Trinidad and Guyana that is also not a history of humanisation of those landscapes by Indian labour."[3]

Indian diaspora's participation in transition process and drawing up the political and economic vision of the liberated countries can hardly be gainsaid. There is also no less temptation to draw comparison with the past and to stress historical continuities in the presence of globalisation forces. For a long time, the Caribbean has been a major contributor to the formulation of global markets for goods, services and factors of production and financial assets.

For the Indian diaspora, it has been a long and arduous journey from servitude to resistance to freedom, and professionally from indentured labourers to entrepreneurs in their adopted countries. While doing so, they have adjusted and woven themselves in the socio-economic fabric of their respective countries despite the fact that the indentured system and its abuses have had left a legacy of distrust and dislike between the Afro-Guyanese and Indo-Guyanese. The latter's role in the agriculture development and agrarian reforms remained critical in the post-colonial societies. In this respect, even Cheddi Jagan's programme for the economic development of Guyana placed primary emphasis on the peasants and the betterment of their lot. Ever since the end of their indenture, many of the enterprising rural Indian workers through hard work and savings managed to buy some land and started growing sugarcane. Over the years, they themselves became small planters and now own a large chunk of sugar plantations and rice fields. While comparing the Caribbean with the African continent, it is apparent that there was relatively less threat of racial and economic discrimination and nationalisation in the former colonies.

Indian Diaspora's Role in the Business Activities

From trading in rural areas to managing modern corporate sector in urban competitive environment, the role of the Indian business community can hardly be underestimated in the Caribbean in general. Many Indians are heading banks, airlines, consultancy firms, IT companies besides being the core professionals like doctors, engineers and architects and well-versed with accountancy, pharmacy and business management practices. Their economic strength and professional achievements have begun to exert their voice and influence in politics , culture, business and the social life of the host country. As thrifty and savers, they have been the important source of capital financing in the manufacturing and construction activities. The Indian trader, besides performing its usual role of supplier of goods, has also been engaged in supply of high and middle level manpower resources for industrial projects. In short, their contribution and achievements have been of a high order. While starting initially at the lower rungs of the economic ladder in their adopted countries, they rapidly climbed up the hill top. In the phase of liberalisation and privatisation of the Caribbean economies during 1990s, the Indian entrepreneurs have carved a new role for them and show all the needed attributes to manage modern corporate sector to grow regionally and globally in tune with the needs and aspirations of local economies. To achieve and gain respectability in alien land, launching of educational facilities was one of the main contributory factors of success of second and third generation PIOs.

Educational Facilities, Achievements and Returns

The indentured labourers from India saved from their pitiable earnings to establish the very first schools where their children could study along with the children of the indigenous population. The basic idea was that this might enable them to look for a better life than what they have had experienced. After attaining independence, some of the indigenous leaders have been the products of these institutions and occupied exalted positions in public life.

A number of recent studies show the attainment of the educational level on the basis of ethnicity as well as gender. For example, a study by Reed and Addington shows that for Indians, both working and non-working, the average educational attainment levels for men and women are 9.75 and 9.27 years respectively while those among other ethnic groups, the corresponding levels are 10.86 and 10.84 years. For Africans, these have been 10.07 and 10.17 years for men and women respectively.

With respect to differences in returns by educational level, only Indians are observed to receive significantly better returns on post-primary education. Further, largest differences in the returns to education are seen across the three ethnic groups.

It is not only the educational attainments but also in terms of sector employment, labour market characteristics, relative poverty and inequalities, Indians have performed better compared to other ethnic groups. One factor contributing to this success is the rising proportion of Indian middle class in its total share of the population in the recent years.

Sectoral Employment

A glance at employment statistics in Guyana shows that agriculture accounts for a third of total employment; 58.6 per cent of the poorest are employed in agriculture; and most of the poor are self-employed in agriculture. Public service absorbs 15 per cent of the total employed persons and one-third of these employees fall below the poverty line. Commerce with 14.7 per cent and manufacturing with 12.2 per cent employment have considerably lower proportion of poorest (7.5 per cent). Similarly, services, transport, mining, construction and finance constitute lower proportion of the total employment and significantly lowest ratio of the poorest.

If we look at the type of employment in Guyana, it is clear that nearly 42 per cent are employed in the informal sector including self-employed; 51 per cent are employed on regular wage/ salary and 11 per cent as casual labour. The size of the informal sector in the Caribbean ranges from a low of 8 per cent in Antigua to 36 per cent in Jamaica and in Guyana the same is 23 per cent of the labour force.

In the absence of data on ethnicity and employment, it is hard to measure the employment share of each ethnic group at sectoral level. However the thumb rule would suggest that the Indian diaspora constitute nearly 45 per cent of the total population, the same weight should be used in deriving the proportionate share at sector level with some adjustment.

Characteristics of Labour Markets

In the post-colonial societies, labour market gains were registered by the non-White population (Reed and Addington). During 1960s, however, research conducted at the University of West Indies revealed persistence dominance of top jobs in T&T by the White, despite their declining presence in the labour force. A study by J. Harewood attributed this bias to colour-based outcomes, to historical discrimination, opportunities from family affiliation and access to capital. The University of West Indies Centre for Ethnic Studies has found that small businesses in T&T still engage in discriminatory hiring practices, preferring co-ethnics for positions at senior management levels.

Ethnicity and Poverty in Guyana

According to a World Bank study, 87.5 per cent of the Amerindian populations are below the poverty line, followed by 43 per cent of the Afro-Guyanese and 33.7 per cent of the Indo-Guyanese. Comparing the other Caribbean countries such as T & T, the World Bank data show that the headcount index of poverty for Afro-Trinidadian is 24.8 per cent, Indo-Trinidadian 17.3 per cent and households headed by persons of mixed race 27.4 per cent. As a share of total population who are poor, households headed by Afro-Trinidadians account for 46.7 per cent, Indo-Trinidadians 35.7 per cent and mixed race 17.7 per cent. The pattern of ethnic poverty in T&T is similar to that prevailing in Guyana.

Summary and Conclusion

While summing the main findings of this study, we can say that the role and contribution of the Indian diaspora in the Caribbean has not been insignificant. However, at the beginning of the new millennium, the whole of Caribbean and not particularly the Indian diaspora encounters challenges thrown by the forces of globalisation.

In the traditional sector such as agriculture, there is a perceptible decline in the productivity, marked by unequal distribution of land, shortage of credit for small farms and the problem of agro-industries producing for exports but lacking links with the domestic agriculture sector. However, the onslaught of globalisation has shifted the focus on tourism, natural resource based exports and transition from import substitution industrialisation to export processing activities.

Even though the challenge can be met to shift the economic pendulum, there is no surety for the international forces to accommodate these exports when the rules, regulations and procedures both at multilateral and regional levels are being redefined. The disproportionate burden of adjustment would fall on the Indian diaspora because of their involvement in industrial and other businesses at great length in the region.

Endnotes

1. This section heavily draws on a previous paper titled "Caribbean Economics : Dependency, Regionalisation and Globalisation" presented by the author at a seminar on "Indians in the Caribbean and the Recent Developments in the Region" at the University of Goa on 22nd February 2002.
2. Jain, R.K. 1993. *Indian Communities Abroad : Themes and Literature*, New Delhi: Manohar Publications and Distributors.
3. *New World Quarterly*, vol. 2 no.1,1996 p.69.

8

Contributions of People of Indian Origin to East Africa

Rajneesh Kumar Gupta

Introduction

The Coast of East Africa was known to the Indians since ages. '*The Periplus of the Erythrean Sea*', a Greek guide for sailors compiled about A.D. 100, bears witness to the existence of a close-knit network of Indian ocean trade and the role of the Indian seaman and merchant along the East Coast of Africa.[1] Throughout the history, migration to East Africa for trade purposes was an un-disrupted phenomenon for people living in North West Coastal region of India. Prof. Mangat, writes about such trade linkages, "Indian merchants supplied cloth, beads and simple manufacturers in exchange for ivory, gold, gum copal, incense, and after the fourteenth century, slaves."[2] The writing of the Venetian traveler, Marco Polo, also produces proof of the trade relations between the Malabar Coast of West India and Zanzibar in East Africa in the time of his visit.[3] Since, movement of *dhows* (Gujarati term for sailing ships) were dependent on monsoon winds so they had to stay in East African coast for several month. This led to temporary settlement of Indians in East Africa. At this point, it is noteworthy that presence of Indians was not limited to coastal region; they also ventured inner-land. Cynthia Salvadori gives detail account of this settlement, she writes-

When Vasco da Gama sailed into Mombas in 1948 he noted

the presence of 'four vessels belong to Christians from India', and it was a Badala Muslim pilot from Cutch whom da Gama encountered in Malindi who showed the pioneer Portuguese navigator the way to India. A Dutch traveller noted 'Mesticos' (i.e. Goans) along with 'Portingales' in Mombasa in the 1580's. A Badala captain is recorded to have settled there in 1705; another Cutchi Muslim pilot was noted as being in the employ of the Sultan of Mombasa in the early 19th century. In the records of the brief British Protectorate that captain Owen declared over Mombasa there are numerous references to the 'sizeable community of Indians (e.g. Muslims and Banyans)' then in the town.[4]

However, migration and settlement of Indians in the region is certainly linked with the expansion of British colonialism in both regions. In 1841, British established consulate in Zanzibar, in 1872 they introduced a regular steamer service between Bombay and Zanzibar and a British Indian Post Office at Zanzibar. In 1873, Bombay High Court acquired appellate jurisdiction over British Indian subjects in Zanzibar. In the same year the control of Political relations with Zanzibar and of Consular appointment it w as transferred from the Bombay government to the government of India. All above development facilitated trade linkages and so free migration and settlement. By the 1887, population of Indian settlers in East Africa reached 6345 and Business communities of India like Khojas, Bohras, Sindhis, Memans, Parsis etc. emerged richest and the most influential businessmen in the region.[5]

Later, Indians migrated to East Africa as 'indentured labours' for the construction of 'Uganda Railway'. And thereafter, to grab opportunities materialized in government services, crafts, commerce and wholesale and retail trade. In 1939, the Asian population in East Africa exceeded 100,000. Their number had increased, both by a free flow of immigrants attracted to East Africa by prospects of economic betterment, and by natural growth estimated at two to three percent per annum. By 1948 Kenya had a population about 97,000 Indians, Uganda 35,000, and Tanzania 62,000 the greatest proportionate increase since 1921 having occurred in Uganda.[6] This trend was continued till the independence of these countries. Rattansi and Abdulla estimate that by 1963 the Asian population in East Africa was placed at 372,000 with the distribution between the three countries as follows: Kenya 180,000, Tanzania 110,000, and Uganda 82,000 - the rate of increase between 1948 and 1963 was on average 4.2 per cent per annum.[7] But, after the independence of these countries large number of PIO's has migrated further to American and European countries. Therefore, population of PIO's in East Africa declined sharply and according to recent estimates their strength in whole East Africa is about 170,000, country wise their population is-85,000 in Kenya, 85,000 in Tanzania and 7,000 in Uganda.[8]

Contributions to the Country of Adoption

Peoples of Indian Origin in East Africa, constitute a tiny minority and their total population do not exceeds even 0.5 per cent of the total population in either of the countries of East Africa.[9] They have migrated in different capacities and in different bursts and do not form a homogenous group. Inspite of this diversity one thing is common among all PIO's and that is their contributions to the land of their new destiny. They have contributed positively to every stratum of East African economy, polity and society. They participated in national movement and made significant contribution in the nation building process. The success stories of entrepreneurs are legendary and they are playing a key role in industrialization process of these countries. From hi-tech manufacturing industries to traditional restaurants, from renowned hospitals to famous educational institutions, from popular games to leading think-tanks -everywhere contributions of PIO's is visible, which is an obvious result of skill, dedication and hard work. For the purpose of this study contributions of PIO's have been broadly outlined under four subheadings : economic, political, cultural and philanthropic activities.

Economic Contribution

Long association of Indians led to tremendous

contribution in East Africa, which is most visible in economic terms. It is well accepted fact that East Africa was a difficult region in terms of human settlement as Gideon S. Wee and Derek A. Wilson points out "...There were large tracts of arid, waterless desert and semi-desert. There were areas dominated by the *Tse-Tse* fly and the Malaria carrying mosquito. There were the forested mountains and highland regions. There were the steep escarpments of the eastern and western rift valleys...."[10] Only Indians had the courage to venture in internal land of East Africa and successfully operated their business and trade for centuries. But, unlike British power, they concentrated on commercial activities and never tried to colonize the region. Later, in the colonial phase many Indian went to East Africa as a victim and not as free commuter. Nevertheless, author observed during his field visit to Kenya that PIOs are well appreciated by local people due to their positive contribution to the economy of East African countries.[11] Broadly, their economic contribution can be underlined in following sub-headings:

Construction of Railway Link

First and foremost contribution of PIO's, during this period, was construction of Railway link between Lake Victoria to Indian Ocean at Mombasa, commonly known as 'Ugandan Railway'. This was not an easy job, complexities and involved dangers in the work were well described by Lieut. Col. J.H. Patterson, then an engineer engaged on the construction of the Uganda Railway, in his book "The Man-Eaters of Tsavo and other East African Adventures."[12] According to Uganda Railway committee, 319,883 indentured servants were imported to work on the railway. Of these 163,12 were repatriated after the expiration of their contracts or through dismissal, 6,454 were invalided to India and 2,493 died.[13] Due to hard work, skills and dedication of indenture labours, 572 mile long railway link was completed within short span of time. It will be interesting to quote Sir Charles Eliot who has acknowledged important contribution of Indian indentured labours in these words-

"The railway was built almost entirely by coolies brought over from India; and though the cost of transport and of providing the food to which men were accustomed was considerable, I do not think the necessary labour could have been provided in any other way. After nearly nine years the natives have become so familiarized with the railway, and the idea of working for Europeans, that they are able to perform the class of work required for maintenance; but it may be doubted if even now they could be used for purpose of construction and it certainly was out for the question when the railway commenced. The jungle which surrounded the first part of the line is particularly uninhabited and to have brought labour down from Uganda would probably have been a more lengthy and difficult task than to bring it from India, to say nothing of difference in efficiency".[14]

Evolution of Market Economy

Equally important is contribution of PIO's in the evolution of market system in East Africa. Indians were pioneer in the establishment of *'dukas'* (derived from the Gujarati word *'Dukan'* means a shop), local trading centers and bazaars in different localities. The introduction of a variety of imported items to the local population and later on the rupee as currency provided incentives for greater production as well as a transition from barter to money based economy.[15] They established their *'duka's'* in every corner of East Africa and there was a time when term *'dukawallah'* became synonymous for PIO's. Despite of, several difficulties *"dukawallah"* carried the mechanism of monetary economy in the interior to create new methods in the process; he introduced a set of new values of mark for money, to produce for the market, to cultivate economic crops and to manufacture other goods not merely for exports but also for the expanding domestic market.[16]

However, post independence period has seen phenomenal change in this image. Successive governments of these countries imposed several restrictions on the involvement of the *alien* in local retail trading especially in remote areas. So majority of PIO's moved to other options for their livelihood. Some of them entered in wholesale business or manufacturing sectors and made tremendous success. A major junk of PIO's joined private sector for employment as availability of government jobs for them was very difficult. Number of PIO's, who were professionally qualified opted to work independently as architect, doctor, engineer etc. They all are contributing positively to the economy and society of East African countries as per their capacity.

Unavoidable Segment of Economy

'Five Pillar Theory', advanced by Pheroze Nowrojee for Kenyan economy, could be the best way to explain importance of PIO's in the East African economies in present context. According to Nowrojee- "...capital in Kenya consisted of five main pillars: firstly, international capital, controlling finance, agriculture and agro business; two, domestic capital which was Asian African, and invested principally in light industry and business properties; and three, domestic capital which was black Kenyan and private, and invested principally in financial institutions, light industry, business and residential properties; four, domestic capital which was black Kenyan through the collective and cooperative sector including KFA, KCC, the tea growers, coffee growers and the cooperative unions; and five, domestic capital which was black Kenyan and public, being governmental and parastatal holdings in every sector of the economy".[17] Nowrojee prefers to use term 'Asian African' for the PIO's while 'black Kenyan' to the indigenous segment of society as he considers native to all of those who are born and grownup in the land. Nowrojee's proposition is based on circumstances prevailing in Kenya during 1980s. However, it is equally applicable for other two countries of East Africa and is significant for the present time as well. Fallout of the Ugandan economy after Idi Amin's expulsion of Asians in 1972 and continuous appeal of Amin's successor Musevini to expelled Asians to return shows that PIO's have become an unavoidable segment for the economy of East African countries.

Successful Entrepreneur

Now, People of Indian Origin in East Africa are often branded as economically most successful community. On an average, they are economically well off than their counterpart indigenous or European ethnic groups. Firms like Chandaria, Madhvani, Manji and Mehta group etc. hold significant share in East African economy. Their entrepreneurship skills are well acknowledged by scholars. For instance, David Himbara, in his book "Kenyan Capitalists, the State and Development", writes about success of PIO's in Kenya, "Some of the determining factors that distinguished the Indians from businessmen in other Kenyan communities were their commercial skills, as evidenced by an ability to survive in remote areas on modest resources and by sheer determination and hard work; their vision of the potential mass market and the patience to transform it into an actual market; their general efficiency and competitive edge; and the role of family units and collective organizations in providing mechanism to engender discipline and cohesion."[18] Gijsbert Oonk refers to one of his friend's explanation to relatively better economic performance on Indian community, he writes, "You see, when an African earns 20 dollars, he likes to live as he has earned 25 dollars. An Indian, however, will spend only 5 dollars and save 15 for further investment..."[19]

Technological Advancement and Enhancement of Employment Opportunities

Legendry success in business and trade is also a big economic contribution to the country of adaptation. People of Indian Origin are largest share holders in the revenues of these countries as they pay taxes in various forms. They are bringing technological advancement in the country and most importantly they are one of the biggest employers of local population. As employers Indians are often more employee friendly and humanistic in nature than their counterparts. 'Asian Foundation' registered as a limited company in the Kenya, have become a major catalyst for technological advancement and enhancement of employment opportunities for indigenous people in Kenya. Asian Foundation built famous 'City Park Market' at Nairobi in 1991, within three years of its existence. This market was built to provide a permanent place for street hawkers selling vegetables and fruits in temporary kiosks and stall in Nairobi. Over the years a number of other commercial activities have also developed on site. At present over 600 Hawkers are getting livelihood opportunities in 'City Park Market'. Presently Asian Foundation is engaged in the 'Linking Jua Kali (MSE) to the Formal Sector' project in Kenya in the collaboration of the United Nations Development Programme (UNDP), Ministry of Labour and Human Resources Development, Kenya Motor Industry Association (KMI), Kenya Association of Manufacturers (KAM), Ministry of Trade and Industry, Kenya Industrial Research Development Institute (KIRDI) and Federation of Kenya Employers (FKE). Total cost involved in the project is US$ 100000, which is one of the biggest projects in Kenya for the skills development of the human resources.[20]

Political Contribution

Most of the PIOs in East Africa, willingly or unwillingly, migrated from India for reasons that were economic in nature. There were hardly any political motives involved in migration process. But, they made significant political contributions especially since the beginning of 20th century. Initially, they were united for the demand for better work condition, then they begun protest against racial policies of colonial government. As movement against colonialism got momentum in India, they became integral part of the movement in East Africa. In later phase, they participated in independence movements of East African countries together with African leaders and played important role in the nation building process.

Trade Union Movement: In late nineteenth and early twentieth century, a junk of Indians migrated to work for railways and other industrial sectors. Those were owned by colonial powers and Indians were recruited merely as employees. Working condition was harsh, there were no job security for them and sometime they were treated as machine and not a human being. So, first political assertion of PIO's manifested in the form of demands for proper working conditions in the industrial sector. Such political assertion has been labeled as 'trade union movement'. Since, 1900 onwards, several trade unions came to existence in East Africa and adopted effective tool of strike. In 1914, a weeklong strike was launched in Mombassa by Indian railway and public works department workers in combination with Africans.[21] In the 1930's the trade union movement in East Africa took a new turn under the leadership of Makhan Singh and his organization- Labour Trade Union of Kenya (LTUK).[22] Two successive newspapers were soon launched-'*The Kenya Worker*' and 'The *East African Kirti*'-edited respectively by Makhan Singh and Mota Singh. In March 1937, the LTUK was renamed the Labour Trade Union of East Africa (LTUEA).[23] Through trade unions, leaders like Makhan Singh, Pio Gama Pinto, Chanan Singh etc. attempted to unite African and Indian workers at East African level and forced employers to improve working conditions and assure as well as job security. Involvements and sacrifices of PIO's for workers right's is duly appreciated by scholars and even Kenyan historian Bethwell A. Ogot accepts that 'trade unionism' in Kenya from 1935 to 1950 owes its success, the vision, dedication and selflessness of one person i.e. Makhan Singh.[24]

Formation of Political Associations: Apart from trade union movement, contribution of PIO's is also noticeable through other political activities which start from the formation of 'Indian Association' in various parts of East Africa. In 1900, 'Mombasa Indian Association' was organised on the initiative of L.M. Salve. He was joined in this enterprise by three of the wealthiest businessmen in East Africa- Allidina Visram and the brothers Alibhoy and Tayabali Mulla Jeevanjee.[25] Later A. M. Jeevanjee became president of the Mombasa Indian Association. On 1 April 1906, he called a mass meeting of the Indians at Mombasa.[26] Such associations were also established in Kisumu, Eldoret, Nairobi, Dar-es-Salam, Zanzibar, Arusha, Jinja, and Kampala etc. In 1909, A. M. Jeevanjee became the first Indian to be nominated as member of the legislative council of Kenya.[27] Indian political activity became more organised after the establishment of the East African Indian National Congress (EAINC) in 1914. During 1920s and 1930s political assertion of these associations were focused on the colonial policies of land reservation, the communal system of representation and segregation, and the provision of separate services for different races. Though, initially sometimes PIO's asserted their Indian identity and wanted to be linked them to India. But, when African leaders formed local organizations like Kikuyu Central Association (KCA), they extended full support and assistants to them and worked together for the cause of East African interests. During this period, the colonial printing works owned by Girdharilal Vidyarthi, became the official news centre of the Indian community and his papers, *The Colonial Times* and *Habari Za Dunia* were champions for the cause of PIO's as well as indigenous people.[28]

National Movement: By 1940s, nationalism became a vital force in East Africa and after World War II, mass movement against colonial power got strength more then ever. PIO's in East Africa collaborated with local people for their demands and aspirations. PIO's owned newspapers gave publicity and encouragement to the national movements. M.A. Desai, the editor of 'East African Chronicle', helped to print articles and pamphlets in Swahili for Harry Thuku, sometimes referred to as the father of African nationalism in Kenya. PIO's assistance was also given for printing the newspaper 'Muiguithano' edited by Jomo Kenyatta. There were also a handful of radical PIO nationalists of a political sophistication, beyond that of any African politicians at that time, who significantly influenced developing African nationalism in the early days.[29] Tom Mboya acknowledged involvement of PIO's in the national movement of East Africa in these words-"The overwhelming majority of the Indian community in Kenya supported the African stand…as friends and allies in the struggle for freedom and democracy".[30]

Since, national movement shaped modern nationalism in the East Africa and had for reaching consequence, it would be relevant to discuss role of PIO's in the national movement in little detail. Just after World War II, in mid December 1945, Indians and Africans were confronted by the British government's new scheme for the closer union among the three East African territories; namely Kenya Plan for establishing a settler dominated British East African Dominion. PIO's acted promptly and extended their wholehearted support to indigenous people. The Colonial Times wrote editorials against this plan. The British government acted authoritatively and arrested members of the Colonial Times staff i.e. G.L. Vidyarthi, W.L. Sohan and Haroon Ahmed.[31] Emphasizing on Unity between PIO's and African people Jomo Kenyatta asserted that the Indians and the Africans have politically many things in common and a common platform can be built where the members of the two communities can work together on completely equal footing.[32] Soon after Kenya witnessed a revolutionary movement called *'Mau Mau'* under the leadership of Jomo Kenatta and demanded 'land for freedom', Colonial government declared a state of emergency and arrested Kenyatta and ninety-eight others and KAU was banned. Jomo Kenyatta was charged for conspiracy against government. During the trial of Jomo Kenyatta a group of lawyer came forward to defend Kenyatta. PIO's like F.R. S. De Souza and A. R. Kapila were associated with this group.[33]

In Tanzania, PIO's helped to institute the Tanganyika African National Union (TANU) in 1954 and afterwards to further its progress. Surendra and Randhir Thaker, devoted their printing works to issuing the TANU weekly *Mwafrica* and in 1959 established their own newspaper Ngurama (Thunder) as a voice of African independence. The Indian's involvement in the nationalist movement of Uganda began in 1952 when the Uganda National Congress (UNC) was formed.[34] In 1958, a group of young Indian Intellectuals, including Gurdial Singh, Rajat Neogy and Natoo Karia- known as *'Young Turks'* with Dr. Muljibha Motibhai Patel as their guru formed the Uganda Action Group (UAG). Their principle aim was to explain to the African and Indian inspirations, and to collectivize, channelize and mobilize both communities for independence. Associating with the more

Africans, they contributed to Milton Obete's rise and to the breakaway from the UNC in 1959. This led to the founding of Uganda People's Congress (UPC) led by Milton Obete. Later most of the Indians in the UAG, above all Gurdial Singh and Ahafiq Arian worked closely with Obete and the UAG supported the UPC's demand for independence under a common roll and universal adult franchise.[35]

Role in Post Independence Politics - Though, in post independence period numerical disadvantages and unwillingness of political elite to accommodate in political space of East African countries discouraged PIO's to contribute in political domain and very few PIO's got chance to serve in political post or getting elected in representative bodies. But whenever they were able to do so they have contributed very positively. F R S De Souza became first deputy speaker in Kenyan parliament and Krishna Gautama and Amin Walji served as member of Kenyan Parliament. In Uganda, Jay Tanna is presently serving as Member of Parliament and in Kenya Kamlesh Pattni is all set for contesting election in forthcoming election. Professor Yash Pal Ghai, a PIO, headed 15-Member, "Parliamentary Constitutional Review Commission" instituted by then President of Kenya HE Daniel Arap Moi to review the Kenyan constitution.

At the time of independence, a large number of PIO's were working as bureaucrats in all three countries. Especially, Goan community had been known as administrative community within PIO's, and according to Sir Charles Eliot, 'the District Officers were usually "assisted by a Goan or more rarely by a European clerk. In the coast towns there is also a customs official generally a Goan".[36] But after independence they became victims of *Africanization of bureaucracy* and now participation of PIO's in the permanent set up of the government i.e. bureaucracy is almost invisible. In Judiciary also, PIOs have made significant contributions in the past and there were number of judges, lawyers and other staffs from the PIO community. Though, today none of the serving judge in the Supreme Court in either of the Kenya, Tanzania or Uganda belongs to PIO, but some of the best lawyers of whole East Africa come from PIO community. And, number of prominent PIO's like Pheroze Nowrojee, Neera Kapila, Zarina Patel, Usha Shah etc. are engaged in the promotion of democratic ethos of political system in these countries, without being part of formal governmental structure.

Cultural Contribution

PIO's in East Africa have not only preserved their cultural ethos but also have influenced local communities in cultural terms. From religious practices to, food habits, from Indian craft to cloths, dance to music nothing is unknown to the people of East Africa. And Indian communities too have adopted several norms and practices of East African culture, which is clearly visible in their everyday life. As a result of this interaction a 'mosaic culture' is evolving in East Africa and in-depth understanding between PIO's and other communities is developing. Ms. Zarina Patel points out

> *"...We are not a monolithic community with a cohesive leadership. We are a conglomeration of many diverse communities, languages, religions and customs. Occupationally though predominantly business-oriented, we also are professionals, artisans and service workers. Conditions of insecurity have tended to band us together but gradually as social and political conditions allow for greater interaction, we are increasingly able to identify with other...As people with a common citizenship we share common interests and concerns, including work related interaction".*[37]

Religious Beliefs - People of Indian Origin in East Africa belong to either of Hindu, Muslim, Sikh, Jain, Christian or Parsi faith. Hindus are in majority among PIO's in East Africa. Hindus are further divided into several sects and sub-sects-Arya Samajee, Sanatan Dharmi, Vaishnav, Shakt, Swami Narayan Panth etc. All of them have their presence in different parts of East Africa. Sikh community is the second largest group among PIO's in East Africa. Sikhs have their presence in all three countries but majority of them are settled in Kenya. Sikh community, have established *Gurdwara* in various places of East Africa such as Nairobi, Kisumu, Eldoret, Mombasa, Kericho, Makindu, Meru, Nakuru, Thika, Arusha, Zanzibar, Kampala etc. Most of the PIO's Muslims in East Africa belong to one of three sects of the- Ithna'shri, the Bohra and the Ismaili Khojas. The Ismaili Khojas are predominant there. Among Christian PIO's, Roman Catholic is predominant group; most of them migrated from Goa. Jainism is another important religion of PIO's in East Africa. Majority of Jain does belong to The Svetambara (white clad). Shree Sthanakvasi Jain Mandal, Jain Sangh, Svetamber Derawasi Jain Sangh, Visa Oshwal Community etc. are major Jain's associations in East Africa. Among PIO's in East Africa, Parsi's are also in significant number.

These religious beliefs have made deep impact on the socio-cultural life of the peoples of East Africa. Today, the skyline of every major town in East Africa is decorated with the graceful curves of a Hindu Temple, a Muslim Mosque or a Sikh Gurudwara. In Nairobi alone there are more than ten temples, six Gurdwara's and an equal numbers of Mosques.[38] These places are activity centres of PIO's and many indigenous people also not only attend the functions here but also actively participate. Mr. Shastri Mwangi Arya, a priest in Arya Samaj, Nairobi who belongs to indigenous community and has worked comprehensively on Vedic text, is a great admire of contributions of PIO's especially through institutions like Arya Samaj.[39]

Food Habits and Medicinal Practices - PIO's contribution in food habits is also noteworthy. There are restaurants in every major towns of East Africa, offering Indian foods. Delicious North Indian, South Indian, Gujarati and Punjabi foods etc. are easily available and people of all walks of life enjoy them. Due to influence of PIO's several indigenous people have adopted vegetarian food habits. JKS Makokha, accepts that Indian food items like *'Chapatti'* have become integral part of food in the life of indigenous people.[40] PIO's have introduced numerous crops, vegetables and fruits in East Africa, now they grew well here and sold in the green vegetable markets. Indian utensils and condiments and most other items of daily needs are available in a plentiful supply. Even traditional Indian mouth freshner *"Paan"* (betel) has made place in East African food habits and *Pan* Shops can be seen in various parts. Indian medicinal practice *'Yoga'* and *'Ayurveda'* is very popular here and during recent visit (in the month of August-September 2007) of Indian *'Yoga icon'* Swami Ramdev series of *'Yoga camps'* were organized in Kampala, Mombasa, Nairobi and Dar es Salaam and attended by large number of PIO's as well as indigenous people.

Music and Films - Indian music and films are very popular in the region. There are two *'drive-in cinema hall'* in Nairobi, Mr. Suresh Kapila, an architect by profession, informed during interaction that every weekend they show Hindi movies.[41] Other cinema hall too shows *Bollywood* movies because this is very profitable business for them. In recent past many *Bollywood* actors/actress have visited these countries, Salman Khan's shows of July 2007 in Nairobi was a major hit. A disc of one Swahili song *'Malaika Nakupenda Malaika'*. (Oh, fairy like my beloved, I love you very much) sung by Lata Mangeshkar in Swahili has become tremendously popular. Some African musicians have made a pleasant musical blending of Indian film tunes and native African music. A few enterprising PIO ladies have started classes in Indian classical dances like *'Bharatnatyam'*, *'Kuchipudi'* and others where apart from PIO's a few African ladies also have shown keen interest in learning this Indian art form.[42]

Philanthropic Activities

Literally, 'philanthropy' means 'love of mankind', which involves service of humanity as per capacity of individual or group. Philanthropy has been an integral part of Indian way of life. People of Indian Origin in East Africa have been actively engaged in philanthropic activities through establishing educational institutions, hospitals, giving donations to the poor and needy people and providing relief in natural or manmade calamities. It would be noteworthy to quote Robert G. Gregory's remark on philanthropic activities of PIO's-

> *"Unlike in Western societies, where philanthropy, at least in the industrial age, has been associated with a relatively few, affluent members of society, philanthropy among the Asians tended to be general through the society. It was not confined to any one religious community, nor to people in any distinct level of capital accumulation. On the whole, it was practiced by both rich and poor. It was as though everyone had assumed an obligation to give, and to give according to his means. Thus Asian philanthropy is explained not so much by factors that determined the unique motivation of individuals, as by those that affected the society as a whole."*[43]

Education- The first and for most among the PIO's philanthropic endeavors, is their contribution to the promotion of education in East Africa. Initially PIO's established their own community schools to educate their children in accordance with their own cultural ethos, as colonial educational setup was inadequate and unsuitable for them. Later, they started admitting children of indigenous community as well. Now, Schools like Arya Boy's School, Arya Girl's School, Shree Sanatan Dharm School, Ismaili School, Goan School, Khalsa School, Allidina Visram High School, Aga Khan Academy etc. are primarily established and funded by PIO's and they are providing cheap and quality education to the children of PIO's as well as to children of indigenous people. During the establishment of University of Nairobi, PIO's were major contributor in terms of funds as well as intellectual resources. In-fact proposal to establish a university for providing higher education to citizens of East Africa was first mooted by PIO's. Leading industrialist Nanji Kalidas Mehta wholeheartedly supported this idea and expressed his view that "We should go in for a scheme of East African University to commemorate the name of Mahatma Gandhi...There could be no discrimination. Indians, Africans, Arabs, Europeans and in fact any person who calls himself or herself an East African citizen should have full freedom to avail of this facility".[44] Apart from this, PIO's have established libraries such as Desai Memorial Library, Asian-African Heritage Trust Library, Oshwal Library, East African Ramgarhia Board Library etc.

in various parts of East Africa with the substantial collection of books and other resources.

Medical Facilities - It is a well established fact that healthy citizens leads to prosperous nation. Health is duly regarded as an important criterion of the development. The Human Development Index (HDI), released by United Nations Development Programme on early basis considers health in three most important segment of human development. Adequate medical facilities are for most necessity to maintain good health of the people. Adequate medical facilities consist of establishment of well equipped hospitals, availability of skilled doctors and other medical staffs, and costs of medical care in the reach of ordinary citizens. PIO's contribution is noticeable in every aspect of adequate medical facilities. To provide proper and affordable medical facilities they are running various hospitals, dispensaries and clinics such as M.P. Shah Hospital, Aga Khan Hospital, Parkland Nursing Home, Pandya Memorial clinic, Guru Nanak Hospital etc. In these hospitals qualified medical staffs take care of health of the people and majority of the beneficiary are indigenous people. Ethnic organizations of PIO's like Hindu Council of Kenya, Ramgarhia Youth Club, Associations of Ismaili Khojas and believers of Agha Khan also organize Free Health Camps on different occasion.

Relief Works - In case of any calamity PIO's undertake voluntary services and often reach to victims to provide them relief. Here two of such examples can be cited, first is linked with manmade calamity and second is related to a natural calamity. In August 1998, PIO's organized "All Africa Hindu Conference" in Nairobi, as opening session was underway on 7th August, news came that there is a major bomb blast in the city centre of Nairobi at American Embassy. Organizers got together and suspended further programmes of All Africa Hindu Conference and diverted all attention to the national tragedy. Immediately all food that was prepared for the participants of the conference were taken to the bombsite to help the rescuers. A 24-hour food centre was set up immediately and people were immediately requested to donate blood as the extent of this blast became apparent. In 2006, when Kenya was facing severe famine situation Hindu Council of Kenya launched "Food for Education Programme" and reached over 200,000 children within a period of eight weeks and with the collaboration of Eagle Foundation, Switzerland distributed 400 tones of highly nutritious food.[45]

Conclusion

In the centuries old existence, People of Indian Origin have made numerous contributions to the East African economy society and state. In past they introduced the monetary economy, built railway line, played significant role in nation building process and participated in national movement. Now, they are playing vital role in the socio-economic transformation of these countries. Hard work, skills and passion have made them successful in entrepreneurship, services and other activities and they are sharing their economic prosperity with the needy people of the society by various philanthropic activities apart from generating significant revenue to the state. Substantial numbers of PIO's are descendent of those who migrated fourth, fifth or some time sixth generation ago. They are born and nurtured in these countries and deems East Africa as their land of destiny. But, at the same time PIO's have not neglected socio-cultural values of motherland and are very cautious to retain their identity, which manifests in their day to day life.

Endnotes

1. Bhushan, Kul. 1993. 'Indians in Kenya' in J.K.Motwani, M. Gosine and J. Barot-Motwani, eds. *Global Indian Diaspora: Yesterday, Today and Tomorrow*. New Delhi, p. 127.
2. Mangat, J.S. 1969. *A History of the Asians in East Africa c. 1886 to 1945*, London, p.1.
3. The book of Ser Marco Polo tr. Henry Yule (London: 1903), pp.411-12. Cited in, S.A.I. Tirmizi. 1998. *Indian Sources of African History*, New Delhi, p.9.
4. Salvadori, Cynthia. 1989. *Through Open Doors-A View of Asian Culture in Kenya*, Nairobi, pp. 7-8.
5. Gregory, Robert G. 1992. *The Rise and Fall of Philanthropy in East*

Africa, New Jersey, p. 18.

6. Mangat, J.S. *Op.Cit.*, p.140.
7. Rattansi, P. and M. Abdulla 1965. 'An Educational Survey' in Dharam P. Ghai, eds. *Portrait of a minority Asians in East Africa*, Nairobi: Oxford University Press. pp. 127-28.
8. Government of India. 2001. *Report of the High Level Committee on the Indian Diaspora*, Ministry of External Affairs, New Delhi, p. 94.
9. *Ibid.*
10. Wee, Gideon S. and Derek A. Wilson. 1974. *East Africa through a thousand years*, London, p. 5.
11. Author got these impressions during his visit of Kenya in June-July 2007.
12. Patterson J.H. 1919. *The Man-Eaters of Tsavo and other East African Adventures*, London.
13. Cd. 2164, *Final Report of the Uganda Railway*, p. 13.
14. Eliot, Charles.1966. *East Africa Protectorate*, London, p. 215.
15. Desai, Niranjana.1993. 'Asian influence in East Africa' in J.K. Motwani, Mahin Gosine and J.B. Motwani. eds. *Op.Cit.*, p. 127.
16. Ramchandani, R.R. 1976. *Uganda Asians: The End of an Enterprise*, Bombay, p.90.
17. Nowrojee, Pheroze. 2001. *Asian African Business-The National Perspective*, Speech given at IFRA, Nairobi on 2 May.
18. Himbara, David . 1994. *Kenyan Capitalists, the State and Development*, Nairobi, p. 35.
19. Gijsbert, Oonk. 'Towards a Historical Explanation of the Economic Success of a Middlemen Minority', *Awaaz*, Issue III, 2006, p.8.
20. *Asian Foundation Newsletter*, Issue 1, May 2007, pp. 2-3.
21. Gregory, Robert G.1993. *Quest for Equality; Asian Politics in East Africa 1900-1967*, New Delhi, pp. 125-126.
22. Gupta, Vijay. 1981. *Kenya: Politics of Independence*, New Delhi, p.65.
23. Gregory, Robert G. *Op.Cit.*, p. 130.
24. Rattansi, P. M. 2004. 'Rebel with a Cause'. *Awaaz*, Issue I, p. 18.

25. Government of India.2001. *Report of the High Level Committee on the Indian Diaspora,* Ministry of External Affairs.New Delhi, pp.96.
26. J.S. Mangat. *Op.Cit.,* p.103.
27. Kala, A.S. 1980. 'The Role of Asians in Kenya's Nationalist Movement', in R. R. Ramchandani. eds. *India and Africa*. New Delhi, p. 208.
28. April, Seidenberg D. 1983. *Uhru and the Kenya Politics,* New Delhi, p.89.
29. Desai, Niranjana. *Op.Cit.,* p. 123.
30. Mboya. 1963. *Freedom and After,* Boston, p. 178, Cited in Gregory, Robert G. *Op.Cit.,* p.71.
31. Gregory, Robert G. *Op.Cit.,* p. 83.
32. *Ibid.* pp. 80-81.
33. Interview: FRS De Souza, 10 July 2007.
34. Gregory, Robert G. *Op.Cit.,* pp. 106-112.
35. *Ibid.* pp. 112-113.
36. Bhushan, Kul. *Op.Cit.,* p. 129.
37. Patel, Zarina. 2004. 'I am a Kenyan South Asian', *Awaaz,* Issue III, p.42.
38. Bhushan, Kul. *Op.Cit.,* p. 128.
39. Interview: Shastri Mwangi Arya, 13 July 2007.
40. Interview: JKS Makokha, 11 July 2007.
41. Interview: Suresh Kapila, 8 July 2007.
42. Pathak, A. R. 2000. *Indo-Kenyan Cultural Ethos,* Nagpur, pp. 65-66.
43. Gregory, Robert G. *Op.Cit.,* p. 206.
44. *Ibid,* p. 127.
45. *Virat Hindu Samagam Souvenir,* 14 January 2007, pp. 61-64.

9

Contributions of Indian Diaspora in Development of South Africa

Vidhan Pathak

Introduction

'Diasporas' are ethnic groups of different geographic origins residing and acting in host countries but maintaining strong sentimental and material links with their countries of origin. Most often they are ethnically distinct and differ from the population of the host countries in race, religion, culture and language.[1] In the host countries, Diasporas mostly remain minority groups and preserve their ethnic, religious identity and solidarity. This solidarity serves as the basis for maintaining and promoting constant contacts among the Diasporic groups and has economic, social and cultural significance for the host countries as well as homelands.[2] This is also the basis for the organized actions of the Diasporas. One of the purposes of these actions is to create and increase the readiness and ability of the Diaspora to preserve an interest in economic, political and cultural exchanges with their homelands. The networks created by the ethnic Diasporas are becoming more important in the international arena and have peculiar and interesting characteristics due to their being part of a complex triadic relation with their host countries and homelands.[3] In the contemporary international relations,

'Diasporas' are now recognized as an international force. This is because scientific and technological advancement has reduced the distance and broken the communication barriers. The ongoing race for globalization has created an environment to look beyond rigid national boundaries for economic and other development aspirations of the people.

Diaspora has significant presence in the political scene of some of the countries even though in terms of number, it might be small percentage of the total population. In countries like Mauritius, Indians who are in majority occupy significant positions in political arena, while in other countries, the minority status of diaspora usually means that they are left out of the top political post. The presence of diasporic leader in a state has a direct bearing to the status of international relations of that country, whether through the more favorable foreign policy or through the pro-diasporic perception it helps to create. Diasporas have managed to overcome hostilities and discrimination in the host country to become the influential community, and essentially dictate the policy of that country, making it more favorable to diasporic community worldwide. The concern and interest for diasporic community by the home country can also affect the international relations between the host-home countries to a certain degree. The relations of host and home countries of diasporic communities are also influenced by the treatment of diaspora in the host country. Diasporas can be active actors, influencing the foreign policies of their adopted homelands. Diasporas, especially those in liberal-democratic societies, often organize as interest groups and operate as ethnic lobbies in order to influence the foreign policy of their adopted homelands vis-à-vis their homelands. More generally, diasporas are increasingly able to promote transnational ties, to act as bridges or as mediators between their home and host societies, and to transmit the values of pluralism and democracy as well as the "entrepreneurial spirit and skills."

Although diasporic communities have direct implication to international policies, in particular, the most visible and powerful link is economic in nature. The Diasporas economic strength is of more significance. The dominant economic roles of Diasporas in different countries, therefore, make them a force to be reckoning with. Thus, Diaspora in a sense has become a variable in the game of international relations purely due to their contribution to the GDP of the respective country. Outside the economic aspect, the social network and transnational interdependence of the Diasporas binds them together all over the world. The members of diaspora see their counterpart as some sort of culturally similar people and feel some degree of kinship towards them. The diaspora though distant from their homeland, they still maintain their transnational link, regardless of their loyalty. The common cultures also enable each and every member of diaspora to relate more closely to one another, particularly in time of crisis. Thus, the significant presence of diaspora in different countries provides better integration between these countries. The diasporic links also become an interlinking nerve network, which propagate concern of one country to the rest of countries. In international relations, therefore, the diaspora consideration is another important variable.

Indian Diaspora is a generic term referring to the people who migrated from territories that are within the borders of the Republic of India. Indian migration to the different parts of the world is not a new phenomenon. Indian migration started more than five thousand years ago, when saints and seers moved in different directions, although not in large numbers. It continued with the migration of Indian traders who travelled throughout the world for trade and business. During the colonial period after the abolition of slavery by the British parliament, Indians migrated to various parts of the British colonies to form an alternative labour force to fulfill the needs of the European settlers. A large number of Indians migrated as indentured labourer to countries like Mauritius, South Africa, Fiji, Trinidad and Guyana to work on sugar plantations. Indian migration continued after independence, with the migration of professionals like doctors, engineers, chartered accountants and businessmen to the west. This is also known as the brain drain wave because most of the migrants have been professionals.[4] The Indian Diaspora is currently estimated to number twenty million, composed of NRIs (Non-Resident Indians) and PIOs (People of Indian Origin). Most Indian settlers are in Africa, the Caribbean and Oceania. Among all these regions, Africa is an important area due to the large numbers of Indians there. As per parameters laid down by the Government of India, an overwhelming proportion of Indians in Africa fall within the category of PIOs as most of their families had gone to the African territories before independence of the Indian state. The existing literatures on the Indian Diaspora in different parts of the world inform us about certain aspects of the PIOs. India, in terms of culture, languages, dialects, regions, social morels and religions, is as diverse a country as no other. And this is abundantly clear in that emigration to other countries was as varied as India's regions and people. The historical contexts, causes and consequences of immigration have also been varied; even social characteristics such as class, caste, place of origin and level of education have been very different. PIOs have wide divergence based on language, religion and geographical regions from which they emigrated. They are not a monolithic lot. PIOs have adopted and integrated themselves into the social and economic fabric of the countries to which they have migrated. They worked with great perseverance, dedication and commitment in contributing to the cultural enrichment and economic development of their adopted homelands. Many of them endowed with strong entrepreneurship capability have been successful in establishing flourishing business concerns. Many of the Indian migrants have become one of the richest persons in their country of adoption. This paper is an attempt to assess the overall contribution of Indian settlers (PIOs) in the development of South Africa i.e. their contribution in the economic, social and political spheres of that country. There are several factors that determine the contribution of diaspora to the country of their adoption. It includes the profile of the diaspora i.e their education, skills, status and duration of stay, political and socio-economic context of their settlement and coping up strategy. In certain countries, diasporas are vibrant communities and play significant role in wide spectrum of political, economic and socio-cultural areas where as in certain other countries they have limited space to play, where the strict law or adverse conditions does not allow them to play any role in the political and cultural sphere. However, in spite of being minority in numerical terms, Indian Diaspora has made significant contribution in every strata of human life of the Rainbow Nation South Africa. To understand the contribution of Indian diaspora in South Africa, it is important to have an idea of the migration pattern and composition of Indian diaspora in South Africa.

Indian Migration and Settlement in South Africa

South African Indians have a long history of settlement in South Africa. Cyril Hromnik, a Czech historian claims in his book, *Indo-Africa: towards a new understanding of the history of Sub-Saharan Africa*, (Johannesburg: Juta & Company Ltd.) published in 1981, that Indians had settled in Southern Africa more than two thousand years ago to exploit gold and other minerals. According to him, the term "Bantu" comes from the Sanskrit word "Bandhu" (relative), which the Indians used for their African helpers or servants.[5] Researches on slavery in South Africa by scholars from South Africa, Britain and United States have shown that Indians were taken to the Cape from the 1650s to be sold as slaves and that their descendants may well outnumber the Indians in South Africa. Many of the prominent Afrikaner families have Indian ancestors. The coloured community of almost four million has perhaps more ancestor from India than from any other country or region. People from Bengal, Coromandel and Malabar are related to the Afrikaner and coloured people of South Africa and perhaps even to the Africans.[6] Greek navigation manuals refer to Indian access to Africa in pre-Christian era.

In colonial period, Indians in South Africa came from two different sets of migrations, the first consisting of indentured labourers and the second made up of 'passenger

Indians' (so-called because they paid for their own passage on the boat), who were mainly higher caste Gujarati traders and merchants.[3] A large scale migration of Indians to South Africa took place under the indentured system, which was introduced to replace slave labour for agricultural work. After the setup of large sugarcane farms by European settlers for the commercial production of sugar, a steady supply of labour was required. It was decided, through enabling ordinances and rules in both South Africa and British India, to obtain supplies of cheap Indian immigrant labour under an 'indenture or labour contract system'. The first shipment of Indian indentured labour reached Durban on 17 November 1860.[7] Most of the indentured workers who went to South Africa were from South India but a substantial percentage of them were also from Bihar and U.P. Though they were semi skilled workers suitable for agricultural works, they were treated very badly by the local colonial powers and kept at the lowest strata in socio-economic structures of their new home. The working conditions of the indentured laborers were harsh. The plantation owners demanded long hours of work in the oppressive humid climate of Natal. Harsh punishment was meted out on labourers who could not keep up with the heavy workload. Their problems were compounded by the fact that they were living in a foreign land with a foreign culture and they also had to contend with many foreign languages. Not everyone could cope with the severe demands. But those who did became land-owning free Indians, considered to be wealthy by the standards of their homeland. At the end of the initial contract (3 to 5 yrs) the indentured laborers were offered land in lieu of the cost of their repatriation i.e., a free passage back to India or agricultural land equivalent to the value of a passage back to India. It led to a spectacular growth in Indian settlements all over the country. Given the choice of re-indenture, a free passage home to India or freedom and a small plot of land, the 'free' Indians, after the end of their contract, usually chose their freedom and the land. Owning land was an unlikely event in their homeland of India and it is understandable that the majority preferred to remain in South Africa. However, in spite of the provision for a grant of land in lieu of a return passage home, only a few Indians were granted plots. Thus, free Indians became free labourers on the sugar and coffee plantations, domestic servants, gardeners, fisherman, storekeeper and traders. They tried to move into all economic spheres and shifted towards industrial sector and as a result their proportion in agriculture fell to less than a quarter about 17 per cent in 1951.

After the expiry of their indentures, many Indians moved to the cities, becoming established as a thoroughly urban population. However, because of the apartheid system the majority tended to remain poor, with few opportunities for improvement. The forced removals programme caused great disruption and social hardship for Indian people. The extended family system was largely destroyed, with negative consequences for many, resulting in various social problems. However, the indentured workers worked very hard. They had a culture of saving. They gave utmost priority to education of their children even when they were just struggling to survive under a hostile exploitative colonial rule in a new country. The mother country India was also under colonial rule so no help came from it. Pushed against the wall to survive, inheriting the culture and tradition of India, which believed in work is worship (karma) and having the inner faith and confidence of belonging to an eternal civilisation with resilience and ability to overcome the most adverse situation, they decided to put the best of them for their new home. For them the ship to go back India was burnt. The immigrant labourers helped to generate in South Africa a sugar and agricultural boom. The immigrant labourers were the pillars of white economy and prosperity. They struggled, grew and came up in the socio-economic ladder of the country.

Indentured immigrants were followed by Indian traders, merchants or petty businessman presumably to supply them with spices and other goods. They were called 'Passenger' Indians. They were also called 'Arabs' as a majority of them belonged to the Gujarati Muslim trading communities.[8] But their number was very small and their presence did not change the social status or treatment of Indian indentured workers.

However, unlike indentured workers who lost their contact with India, these merchants kept very close ties with their families in India.

Despite measures adopted to restrict Indian immigration and to curb population growth through steps such as the imposition of licence fees on Indian traders and taxes on children who reached the age of majority, Indian population soon outdid the European population. By 1885, only 2,000 Indians were in the hub of Durban city. They increased to 10,335 in 1889 and to 30,135 in 1892. It worked against them after they (46,000) exceeded the English (45,000).[9] According to the first census of 1904, there were 100,918 Indians in Natal as against 97,109 Europeans. In Natal, there were three categories of Indians, indentured, free and passenger whereas in the Transvaal only two categories of Indians (free and passenger) were present. The "free Indians" were not only more numerous compared to the indentured labourers, they were also providing competition to Europeans farmers and traders. Therefore, the Europeans were strongly opposed to the presence of the Indian tradesman and free Indians. At the turn of the 19th century, a small number of accountants, teachers, lawyers and priests joined other Indians. After the ban on Indian immigration in 1913, only a small number migrated to South Africa as educated Indians who were exempted from the ban on Indian immigration. All the later immigrants formed an economic class that is middle class.[10] By the end of the 19th century ethnic Indians constituted a sizeable community in Natal, in Transvaal and in Cape colony of South Africa.[11] In fact KZN's (KwaZulu-Natal) largest city, Durban, has the largest Indian population in Sub-Saharan Africa.

Discriminated against by apartheid legislation like the Group Areas Act, Indians were forcibly moved into Indian townships and had their movements restricted. The infamous Group Areas Act 1950 reinforced the racial segregation for business and residence. This Act forced the Indian families displaced from one location to another resulted the resettlement of the evacuated traders. However, despite the widespread restrictions, the Indian traders prospered and many also set up businesses in the Transvaal. They were not allowed to reside in the Orange Free State and needed special permission to enter that province. They were also, as a matter of state policy, given an inferior education compared to white South Africans.

Thus, from a humble beginning as indentured labourers, the South African Indians have progressed to a point where in spite of their minority status, they have contributed and played a significant role in the political, economic and social transformation of South Africa.

Contribution and Role of Mahatma Gandhi in South Africa

One of the Gujarati businessmen hired barrister Mohan Das Karam Chand Gandhi for legal help in South Africa. Gandhiji went to South Africa as a lawyer for his client Abdulla Sheth in May 1893 and was subjected to existing practices of racial discrimination by colonial master and White settlers. Europeans called Indians 'Coolies' and Gandhi himself was called a 'Coolie' barrister.[12] Gandhi had firsthand experience of the tyranny and inequality in South Africa. Already at that time, over 150, 000 Indian immigrants were settled in various places in South Africa.[13] Their near slavery condition and discriminatory treatment in the racially structured society of South Africa drew Mahatma Gandhi into active politics. He opposed this racist practices and discriminatory system. While opposing the colonial rule and powerful White settler administration, he developed tools and tactics of mass mobilization and non-violent struggles. It was the indignity of racial discrimination suffered on the soil of South Africa by the father of the Indian Nation, Mahatma Gandhi, which provided the impetus for his philosophical and spiritual transformation.[14] Mahatma Gandhi evolved and made the maiden use of many of his tactics of non-cooperation, civil disobedience, satyagraha and peaceful protests in South Africa, long before he used them in the Indian freedom struggle from 1920.[15] Gandhi's satyagraha was directed against anti-Indian laws like the Asiatic Registration Act and Immigration Restriction Act. On Gandhi's call, Indians in South Africa publicly pledged themselves as early as 11 September 1906 to resist the draft Asiatic Ordinance, which he called "the Black Act". Thus, was born Gandhi's technique of non-violent resistance or non-violence as corporate action. The most intense phase of the satyagraha began in 1913, when over 5,000 Indian coalminers and railway workers struck work and joined the Great March – a peaceful protest march from Natal to the Transvaal under the leadership of Gandhi, H.S.L. Polak and Herman Kallenboch. On 21 January 1914, the historic Gandhi-Smuts agreement was signed.[16] It was the first ever systematic, determined fight against racism in the modern world. Gandhi's struggle in South Africa was one of the most remarkable manifestations in the history of the spirit of passive resistance. When colonialism was in its heyday and there was nothing like world opinion, it required rare courage of conviction, fearlessness, determination and dedication to initiate and carry on a peaceful resistance movement against racial-arrogance and tyranny in a far off country. Thus, Gandhi mobilized the Indian community against the colonial rulers and started the process of liberation struggle, which was later taken over by the native African Community. Gandhi also founded the "Natal Indian Congress" on 22 May 1894 and a newspaper "Indian Opinion".

Gandhi was not only able to foster a kind of unity among Indians workers and traders, but also had some impact on Black unity and movement. In fact, he not only contributed substantially for the causes of the indentured labour class, but also laid the ground by generating awareness among all groups, which in the subsequent period took the form of a united progressive struggle against apartheid. Nelson Mandela declared at a rally in Durban on 25 February 1990: "A strand in the struggle against oppression began with the formation of the first black political organization in Africa- the Natal Indian Congress founded in 1894 by Gandhi..." He also mentioned "the long tradition of cooperation between Africans and Indians against racial discrimination and other forms of injustice and oppression".[17] Mandela, during his visit to India in October 1990, recalled that it was Gandhi who pioneered the struggle against racial discrimination in South Africa. "Mahatma Gandhi showed us the way". The historic and peaceful transition from the brutal system of apartheid to multi-racial democracy in South Africa in the mid-1990s signifies the continuing influence and relevance of Gandhi to South Africa and as to the rest of the world.[18]

Political Contributions of Indian Diaspora in South Africa

Indian Diaspora has been politically influential in South Africa. Today, the South African Indian origin community numbers around 1.2 million and constitutes about 2.5 per cent of South Africa's total population. The community with such low percentage has shown remarkable achievements in the political field of the country. They contributed a lot to the struggle for freedom and human rights in South Africa. A small minority earned much recognition by its sacrifice, competence and contribution. The Indian passive resistance of 1946-48 was a landmark in the history of the South African liberation struggle. It initiated the mobilization of world public opinion in support of freedom in South Africa. It helped to prepare the way for an entirely new stage in the struggle against racism. The South African Indian Congress worked in close alliance with the African National Congress (ANC) which came into being in 1912 and was initially inspired by the Gandhian ideology of non-violence. The alliance between the Transvaal Indian Congress, the Natal Indian Congress and the ANC was made in the famous "Three Doctor Pact" signed by Dr. A.B. Xuma, Dr. Yusuf Dadoo and Dr. G.M. Naicker.[19] The South African Indian Congress had strong bases in the Natal and Transvaal. Dr. Yusuf Mohamed Dadoo, Dr. G.M. Naicker, Parsee Rustamjee, Thambi Naidoo, Ahmed Mohammed Cachalia, Yusuf Akhalwaya, Prakash Napier, Surendra (Lenny) Naidoo, Krishna and many more are symbolic of thousands of people of Indian origin who gave their lives or spent long years in prison, restrictions and exile in the struggle for the liberation of South Africa from

Apartheid and racism. Many members of the Indian community such as Ebrahim Ismail Ebrahim, Mac Maharaj, Yousuf Pahad etc were deeply involved in the armed struggle launched by the ANC against the apartheid government.[20] South African Indians made valuable contribution in organizing international support for the liberation struggle in South Africa.

PIOs in South Africa after initiating the resistances, civil disobedience and peaceful agitation against the racist regime joined hand with the majority black community in South Africa who were the worst victim of racial discrimination. The majority of PIOs joined ANC formation to oppose apartheid and many of them emerged as top leaders of this party over the years. Indians in South Africa, has valuable contribution in organising international support for the liberation struggle in South Africa. A multi-racial people's delegation from South Africa led by Dr. A.B. Xuma and including H.A. Naidoo, Serbajee Rustomjee and H. Basner arrived in New York to assist the Indian delegation to the United Nations. The issue of apartheid was raised by India and twelve other countries in 1952 in the United Nations and succeeded in the appointment of a U.N. Commission to study the racial situation in South Africa.[21]

South African Indians followed Gandhian as well as revolutionary activities in their freedom struggle. The contribution and role of the PIOs in the release of political prisoners and unbanning of political organizations was significant. The "one million signature campaign" led by Jay Naidoo, played a crucial role in spreading awareness among the people of South Africa about the collapse of the apartheid economy as a whole. This step in turn was followed by mass campaigns for the release of political prisoners. Militant activities of the Indians as it found its expression in trade unions and its methods of successful strikes, sabotage of government property etc brought the normal life and government offices standstill. This atmosphere forced the white government to compromise for negotiation for peaceful transformation of South Africa.[22]

Different political forums such as Natal Indian Congress (NIC), Transvaal Indian Congress (TIC) and Colonial Born Indian Association (CBIA) were formed by the Indians to express their strength in the freedom struggle. In the apartheid period Indians were found in different political formations and contributed for the struggle against apartheid. Forums like trade unions, student unions and teacher unions were also used by the Indians to fight against the apartheid regime. There was also revolutionary participation of South African Indians in the struggle. They either used weapons or stood behind the revolutionaries and their guerrilla activities. Prominent activists like Ahmad Kathrada, Indres Naidoo, Reggie Vandeyer and Sirish Nanabhai, Vijay Ramlakan, Jude Francis, Mac Maharaj and Derek Naidoo were involved in the revolutionary activities. Indian women in South Africa also participated in the struggle and followed the peaceful mechanism. Women participation during 1950s particularly in Defiance campaign of 1952 was significant. Freedom fighters like Ms. Zainab Asva, Veeramah Pather, Khatija Mayat, K. Goonam, Z. Gool, Fatima Meer were either arrested or jailed and tortured or beaten up while protesting and fighting against apartheid policies.

South African Indians played an important role in the anti-apartheid struggle and a few rose to positions of power after the 1994 elections in South Africa. The Indian community in South Africa has made its way through its tremendous input and contribution to the political life of the country.

Contribution and Role of Indian Diaspora in Post-Apartheid Politics of South Africa

In spite of the difficulties of the transitional period in the process of social transformation, economic arrangements and political structures, Indians are part and parcel of South Africa. Being Indian in ethnic identity does not contradict their citizenship and loyalty to the host country. Overall, given their small numbers they had a significant contribution to the struggle for non-racial democracy and till today continue to make vital contribution in the development of South Africa.

South African Indians in the transitional phase of apartheid (1990-94) participated in the negotiation process, which led to dismantling of apartheid and holding of first democratic non-racial elections in 1994. A South African Indian, Ahmad Kathrada, was member of the Negotiation Committee along with Nelson Mandela, Oliver Tambo and Walter Sisulu. Many prominent PIOs participated in the CODESA (Convention for a Democratic South Africa). They were Ahmad Kathrada, Mac Maharaj, Omar Abdullah, Frene Ginwala, Jay Naidoo, Mohammed Vallimoosa and Judge Ismail Mohammed. Judge Ismail Mohammed even co-chaired the initial meetings of the CODESA. The role of Ms. Frene Ginwala is not only significant for her contribution during apartheid period but also in the transitional phase of democracy. She was spokesperson of the ANC in the UK and was also an active member of CODESA. Pravin Gordhan was one of the public faces in the MPNF (Multi-party Negotiation Forum). Individual Indians played a wide range of activities within transitional Executive Council and also outside the Council. Jay Naidoo was a secretary of the COSATU, Valli Moosa, secretary of the ANC's Negotiations Committee, Gora Ibrahim, Foreign affairs secretary of the PAC and Strini Moodley was a key spokesperson of the AZAPO. South African Indians also participated in the drawing up of the new constitution of South Africa. The chief justice of South Africa, Ismail Mohammed, also comes from the Indian community.

In the post apartheid era, South African Indian's participation and contribution in the political process has been heterogeneous in nature. They are found in different political parties such as ANC, NP (Nationalist Party), NNP, DP (Democratic Party), IFP (Inkatha Freedom Party), MF (Minority Front) and DA (Democratic Alliance). They were elected from different political parties for the National as well as Provincial Assemblies and were also found in the National and Provincial governments from different political platforms such as ANC, NP, DA, IFP and MF. The South African Indian community was well represented with 42 elected members in the National Assembly and 9 members in the National Council of Provinces and many of them get important portfolios in the government of National Unity. Most prominent among them were Ms. Frene Ginwala who was the speaker of the National Assembly. She also held other offices like head of the Research Department, head of the ANC's Commission for the Emancipation of Women and convener of the Women's National Coalition. Mohd. Omar Abdullah was the minister of justice and was also engaged in drafting of new constitution and preparation of party documents for the ANC. Mr. Jay Naidoo, minister of post and communication, was a major force in drafting and implementing of the RDP (Reconstruction and Development Programme) and was also acclaimed as a major negotiating partner in the NEF (National Economic Forum). Being in charge of these plans signifies the important role played by an Indian. The RDP was supposed to be pivotal to the aspiration to create a "better life for all" which was the ANC's 1994 electoral slogan. Naido's job was RDP enforcer.[23]

There were seven cabinet ministers and three deputy ministers of Indian origin in Mandela government and at least eight ministers in the provincial governments including Kwazulu Natal in 1994. In Mbeki government, there were five cabinet ministers and two deputy ministers of Indian origin including two important positions, Essop G Pahad (Minister in the Presidency) and Ebrahim K. Ebrahim (Advisor to Deputy President) and eight ministers in provincial governments with 31 elected members of Parliament in 1999-2004. There were other coveted positions held by South African Indians including Mewa Ramgobin, Member of Parliament and chairman of phoenix settlement Trust, Fatima Meer, Director of Institute of Black Research, Logie Naidoo, Deputy Mayor of Durban, Vasu Gounden, Executive Director of ACCORD and Prof. William Malegapura Makgoba, VC of University of Kwazulu Natal. President, Thabo Mbeki after third national election in August 2004, nominated a leader of the Indian origin, Ebrahim Rassool, as Premier of the Western Cape Province.[4]

Though PIO's have contributed significantly in the

political domain of South Africa, very few PIO's got the chance to serve any political post or get elected in representative bodies. However, whenever they were able to do so they have contributed very positively towards the development of the country. Indian community in South Africa has glorious political record during the anti-apartheid struggle and is equally supportive in the ongoing efforts to rebuild the nation. For the vast majority of Indians South Africa is their natural home. Indians have earned true citizenship of South Africa through their tremendous input into the political life of the country and above all through their moral contribution to the lives in South Africa.

Economic Contributions of Indian Diaspora in South Africa

From the sugar fields, the South African Indians have reached a level to compete with the big industrial houses in the country. Almost all of them, whether indentured worker, free passenger, semi-skilled or skilled worker or business community, have done economically and professionally quite well in South Africa. The early nineteenth century South African economy was pre-capitalist economy, which was largely centered on slave labour based production of wine, wool, hides, ostrich feathers and consumer crops. There was shortage of labour without which land resources could not be developed. Thus, the Natal colonists welcomed the first boat load of indentured Indian immigrants with great joy on 16th November 1860. Among this group of Indian immigrants were blacksmiths, weavers, traders, mechanics, gardeners, barbers, carpenters, accountants etc.[24] Indian labourers contributed considerably to the growth and prosperity of the sugar industry in the Natal. The export value of sugar from the Natal increased from Rand 2009 in 1857 to Rand 100000 in 1864.[25] During this period Natal's revenue increased fourfold and the per capita revenue for the white population rose from Rand 4 to Rand 40. Moreover, the presence of Indians benefited the exchequer by keeping down the price of African labour.[26] The diligence, industry and skill of the Indian immigrants rapidly transformed the economy of Natal. The immigrant's labourers helped to generate a sugar and agricultural boom in South Africa. They worked hard and helped in establishment of the sugarcane farming industry in South Africa, which constitutes the largest segment of agricultural sector and a major foreign exchange earner. The immigrant labourers were the pillars of the white economy and prosperity. Thus, economically, a number of remarkable transformations were affected over two or three generations. Through sheer perseverance, labour and thrift, and most significantly by a calculated withdrawal into their culture, in which they found forces of sustenance, Indians successfully laboured to give their children and grandchildren better economic futures, and they in time came to capture the trade and commerce of their new homeland South Africa.

The economic profile of the Indian Diaspora in South Africa is heartening. While around 40,000 could be termed rich, the rest are all earning members of the society. There is not much poverty among the Indian community. The average household income of Indians is three times that of the Africans and more than twice of coloured and half that of the whites. Indians in South Africa constitute a major segment of an economically advanced class since the 1960s. The proportion of Indians living in urban areas increased from 69.5 per cent in 1936 to 83.2 per cent in 1960 and 91 per cent in 1980. Their dependence on agricultural occupation (in terms of the per centage of Indian workers involved) sharply declined from 38 per cent in 1936 to 12 per cent in 1960 and less than 4 per cent in 1980. At the same time, industrial jobs became increasingly more important. About 41 per cent of the Indian workforce was engaged in manufacturing in 1970 as against only 19 per cent in 1936. Although the proportion of Indians engaged in commercial activities did not change appreciably during 1936-60 period, it did change significantly between 1960 and 1970 from 18 per cent to 24 per cent.[27] Indians in South Africa constitute the second most prosperous community after the whites and they have significantly contributed to the South African economy. The Indian community earns a per capita income of at least 40 per cent that of the whites whereas the African community earns only 18 per cent of that amount.[28] The changed status of Indians is a tribute to their strong community service and self-help policies that enabled them to make grant strides in education and employment. Indians are engaged in various sectors of economy namely farming, trade, manufacturing (small and medium level), transport, government services and other professions like medicine, law, accounts and teaching etc. In commerce, they are largely retail proprietors and assistants. Around 12 per cent are traders involved in food, clothing and general dealership while the 10 per cent of the professionals are teachers. Today, Indians are among South Africa's highly successful businessmen, professionals, civil servants, academics, corporate managers and even politicians. There is no poverty in their ranks.[29] According to the Common Country Assessment of the UNDP, Indians who are under poverty are 5 per cent. About 40 per cent Indians are engaged in industrial activities, which include textile, leather, woods, gold, and construction. Further 15 per cent in service sector, 30 per cent in agriculture and market, gardening and associated activities. And the remaining 15 per cent are involved in small business or daily wage workers. In the service sector, Indians are largely seen in IT, medical and legal practices.[30] Chartered Accountants play an important role in the economy. In the post apartheid South Africa, there are well over a thousand Indians in this profession in comparison to approximately two hundred each from blacks and coloureds community. Similarly over 70 per cent of lawyers and attorneys come from Indian community. Indians also occupy leading positions in various organizations representing legal practioners. Indians are now also dominating the computer service industry.

In past decades, job reservation for whites and the thirst for education produced a substantial pool of Indian academics and professionals in South Africa. They possess high and good educational skills, entrepreneurial capability, capital power and also work ethics. Many Indian businessmen are also taking on black partners. All these are ideally suited to boost economic growth and poverty reduction in South Africa. Furthermore, the Indians are well suited to fill the vacuum created by the many skilled whites who left or are leaving the country because of prevailing political and economic uncertainty in South Africa.

Thus, Indians are contributing and playing a major role in the post apartheid South African economy. The Indian community has made its way through its tremendous input and contribution to the economic life of the country. Their presence makes South Africa a vibrant economy in the African continent. As they obtained higher education and professional training, they became a major source of skilled workers in the South African economy.

Social and Cultural Contributions of Indian Diaspora in South Africa

The Indian community in South Africa has undergone a significant transformation in socio-cultural field. South African Indians have developed their own identity, tied to South Africa, and disentangled from India by differences of perception, moral conduct, expectations and notions of self. The present generations of Indians in South Africa were born there and are very much integrated into the mainstream of the South African society. South African Indians have adopted several norms and practices of South African culture, which is clearly visible in their everyday life. In fact, there has been increasing transformation of cultural identity of South African Indians to one that seems to be an amalgam of Eastern, Western and African along with Indian identity. On the other hand, Indians have also influenced the local communities in cultural terms. From religious practices to food habits, from Indian craft to cloths, dance to music nothing is unknown to the people of South Africa. People of Indian Origin in South Africa are mostly either Hindu or Muslim. While a few still speak Indian languages like Telugu, Tamil and Gujarati, which have constitutional protection, most younger Indians speak English exclusively and use Afrikaans or Zulu as a second language. The 1996 Constitution of Republic of South Africa states that 'The Pan

South African Language Board must promote and ensure respect for languages, including German, Greek, Gujarati, Hindi, Portuguese, Tamil, Telugu, Urdu and others commonly used by communities in South Africa and Arabic, Hebrew, Sanskrit and others used for religious purposes'. The religious beliefs of South Africans Indians also have impact on the socio-cultural life of the peoples of South Africa. PIO's contribution in food habits of South Africans is also noteworthy. There are many restaurants in South Africa who offer Indian foods. As a result of this interaction between different communities in South Africa, a 'mosaic culture' is evolving which is clearly visible in the everyday life of South Africans.

Indian films and music are also popular in South Africa. Bollywood films with english subtitles and television programmes are immensely popular among South Africans. These are broadcast both by the South African Broadcasting Corporation's SABC 1 television channel for a few hours each week, and by the DStv satellite television service, which carries Zee TV, B4U, NDTV and an Indian-language Sony channel, as well as South Indian channels, introduced in 2004. DVD and video versions of Bollywood films are widely available and large movie theatre chains like Ster-Kinekor increasingly show Bollywood films. The South African Broadcasting Corporation (SABC) also has an Indian-oriented radio service called Lotus FM.[31] The post-1994 South Africa shows the government participation by introducing a one FM Radio Channel broadcasting Hindi songs, news, commentary and discussion. A number of South African Indian filmmakers, musicians and visual artists have been active and have contributed in their respective field. South African Indians like Junaid Ahmed, Usha Seerjaram and Omar Badsha are some of the many who have produced work, which could be said to engage with the countries pluralism. By combining Indian music and instruments with western forms of expression, for instance, bhangra (folk song and male dance from Punjab, India) is an ideal example of a hybrid culture.

South African Indians have increased their profile and brightened their prospect with respect to greater involvement in the development of black communities in South Africa. Philanthropy has been an integral part of Indian way of life. People of Indian Origin in South Africa have been actively engaged in philanthropic activities through establishing educational institutions, hospitals, giving donations to the poor and needy people and providing relief in natural calamities. The first and foremost among the PIO's philanthropic activities, is their contribution to the promotion of education in South Africa. PIO's initially established their own community schools to educate their children in accordance with their own cultural ethos, as colonial educational setup was woefully inadequate. Later, they started admitting children's of indigenous black community as well. The Indians teachers are also teaching African students voluntarily. PIO's contribution is also noticeable in providing adequate medical facilities. To provide proper and affordable medical facilities they are running various hospitals and clinics. In these hospitals qualified medical staffs take care of health of the people and majority of the beneficiary are indigenous black people. In this regard certain religious organizations such as the Rama Krishna Vedanta Society and the Divine Life Society have spearheaded the movement of building schools and clinics in Black areas. They have also made arrangements with Indian practitioners to provide medical services free of charge in the severely poor areas in Black townships.

South African Indians have contributed and played useful roles in the process of transition in diverse field of their expertise.[32] Junaid Ahmed as secretary of the congress of South African writers, Frene Ginwala as chairperson of the National Coalition of Women, Samba Ramasamy as chairperson of the National Olympic and Sports Congress, Aswini Trikamjee as head of the Soccer, Ebrahim Patel as head of Rugby and Krish Mackerduj as head of Cricket Federation contributed significantly in their respective field.

Conclusion

In the post-apartheid South Africa, definite and significant changes have occurred not only in the power structure but also in all walks of life for the Indians and black people as well. There has been a tremendous scope for South African Indians to rise up with the structural changes in the South African society, polity and economy and contribute for the development of the country. On account of their illustrious political, cultural and economic achievements over the years, they can play a constructive role in the development and transformation of South Africa.

The vital concern in South Africa today is on how to incorporate the different racial groups in South African society. Association is necessary for reconstruction and reconciliation of a new South Africa where Blacks, Whites and Asians could amalgamate in the community. The PIOs who are in the middle section of socio-economic and political structure have to identify themselves not only with the ideology of emancipation of the black community but become an integral part of their struggle and endeavours to move forward. The government of South Africa is striving for nation building through the concept of a "rainbow nation". Thus, South African Indians should also move with the rest of South Africa for a meaningful integration of the rainbow nation.

Endnotes

1. Weiner, Myron. 1986. 'Labour Migration as Incipient Diaspora', in Gabriel Sheffer, eds., *Modern Diaspora in International Politics*, London :Croom Helm, p.47.
2. Sheffer, Gabriel. 1986. 'A New Field of Study: Modern Diaspora in International Politics' in Gabriel Sheffer, eds. *Modern Diaspora in International Politics*, London: Croom Helm, p.1.
3. Dubey, Ajay K. 2000. 'India and Experience of Indian Diaspora in Africa', *Africa Quarterly*, vol.40, no. 2, p. 88.
4. Aggarwal, Baleshwar. 2001.'Indian Diaspora', *World Focus*, vol. 22, no. 3, March, pp. 3-4.
5. Reddy, E.S. 1997.'India and South Africa', *Mainstream*, Jan 11, p. 20.
6. *Ibid.*

7. Jain, Prakash C. 1999. *Indians in South Africa,* Delhi:Kalinga Publications, p.3.
8. *Ibid,* p.8.
9. Dharampal, 1992. 'South African Indians, India and New South Africa,' *Economic and Political Weekly,* Oct.24-31, p.2357.
10. Gupta, Vijay. 1993. 'Indians in South Africa', *Strategic Analysis,* January.
11. Ramchandani, R.R. 1998. 'Some Aspects of India's Africa Policy', *Indian Africanist,* January-March, 1998.
12. Dubey, Ajay. 1998. 'India-Africa relations and Indian settlers in Africa', *Indian Africanist,* April-June.
13. *Ibid,* p.17.
14. Mukherjee, Pranab Kumar. 1997 'India-Africa and South-South Cooperation' in N.N. Vohra and K. Mathews. eds. *Africa, India and South-Africa Cooperation,* New Delhi: Har-Anand Publications, p.41.
15. *Ibid.*
16. Gangal, S.C. 1992. 'Gandhi and South Africa', *International Studies,* vol. 29 , no. 2, p.195.
17. *Africa: South of Sahara,* 2002. London: Europa Pub.
18. Mathews, K. 'A multi-faceted Relationship: A Synoptic View', *Africa Quarterly* , vol. 37 no. 1&2.
19. Beri, Ruchita. 1998. 'Indo-South African Relations in the Post Apartheid Era', *Strategic Analysis,* May, p.283.
20. M.K. Lokesh. 1999. 'A Profile of Indian Community in Kwazulu-Natal', *Africa Quarterly,* vol. 39, p.64.
21. Dubey, Ajay.1998. 'India-Africa Relations and Indian Settlers in Africa', *Indian Africanist,* April-June.
22. Srivastava, A. 1990. 'Ethnic Indians and Struggle Against Facism', *Bulletin of Academy of Third World Studies,* vol.2, Oct. p. 149.
23. *Statesman's Who's who.* 1996. London: Macmillan.
24. Naicker, N.P. 1971. 'Indians in South Africa', in Anirudha Gupta. eds. *Indians Abroad: Asia and Africa,* New Delhi: Orient

Longman, pp. 261-62.

25. Narin, Iqbal. 1985. *The Politics of Racialism: A Study of Indian Minority in South Africa, Down to the Gandhi-Smuts agreement*, Agra: Shiva Lal Agarwal Pub, p.66.
26. *Ibid*, p. 65
27. Carriam, Yunus. 1994. 'Indian South Africans in the Transition to a Post Apartheid South Africa', *Africa Quarterly*, vol. 32, no. 1-4, p.52.
28. Minnaar, A de V. 1991. *Conflict and Violence in Natal/Kwazulu: Historical Perspective*, Pretoria, S.A.: HSRC Publishers, pp. 40-41.
29. Padayachee, Vishnu. 1999. 'Struggle, Collaboration and Democracy, the Indian Community in South Africa, 1860-1999', *Economic and Political Weekly*, Feb. 13, p.394.
30. Common *Country Assessment: South Africa*, New York: UNDP, 1999.
31. See, http://en.wikipedia.org/wiki/Asians_in_South_Africa, Accessed on 15 September 2005.
32. Andrew Reynolds. eds. 1999. *Election 99: South Africa from Mandela to Mbeki*, Oxford: James Curry, p. 137.

10

The Indian Diaspora in Mozambique and Madagascar: Analysis of Socio-Economic and Political Contribution

Sasmita Mohanty

Introduction

The study of Diaspora is of much importance at current conjuncture than it was in the earlier decades. Gradually, the study of Diaspora phenomenon has come to attract more attention.The origin and meaning of Diaspora is much contested like many other concepts of social sciences. This is due to the fact of its multi dimensions. The word Diaspora is the combination of two words derived from the Greek verb *Speiro* (to sow) and the preposition *Dia* (over). The notion of Diaspora is often used in an untheorized and undertheorized way. To some, Diaspora meant migration and colonization and for others, especially, Jews, Africans etc., it signified a collective trauma, banishment. This is due to one's dream of home but lived in exile. This is now a form of identity formation.[1] In this article, the term 'Indian Diaspora' is used in a way, which is synonymous with the PIOs.

Diaspora is defined as the scattering of people with a common origin, background, and beliefs. Though the word was referred to in the context of the dispersion of the Jews after the Babylonian exile, in recent times, it refers to the involuntary migration of people as slaves, indentured or contract labour. This is the new area, which needs further exploration especially in post-colonial states of Asia and Africa. The earlier areas of research interest in these countries were on the impact of colonial rule on the economies of these countries. The migration of Indians to the far-flung parts of the world was due to a variety of reasons. In fact, migration of people across the globe is an inseparable part of human history.

The origin of modern Indian Diaspora lays mainly in the subjugation of India by the British and its incorporation into the British Empire. Many other colonial powers also played significant role in exporting Indian labourers to far off countries of Africa. Many Gujarati traders left for East-Africa in large numbers in the early parts of the twentieth-century. In the post Second World War period, the dispersal of Indian labourers and professionals has been a nearly world-wide phenomenon. The study of Indian Diaspora is very recent like the study of Diaspora itself.[2]

Looking at the impact of Indian Diaspora, they have contributed immensely to the countries of its adoption in different sphere not only in Africa but across the globe. It may be in the area of science and technology or labour force which engaged in various developmental work or IT sector or trade and business. And the Indians are also contributing immensely to the global culture through Hindi films and through the celebration of festivals. This can also be implied in the case of Mozambique and Madagascar.

In many cases, it happened that the Indian Diaspora supported democratic regime and fought against the authoritarian regimes. Diasporic population sometimes play pertinent role in bringing stability in their adopted countries when any sort of violence occurred. They transmit the value of pluralism and democracy to their adopted countries or I would rather say to their home countries. They have the skills and entrepreneurial spirit, which their home countries lack.

For this reason, the Indians occupy highly paid jobs in western countries.

Unlike the West European countries, India - its people and its Government - have always recognised that the interests of the African people of this country are paramount, that the PIO cannot claim any right in conflict with those of the African people, and that their destiny is with the African people. That was the firm advice of our leaders like Mahatma Gandhi, Rabindranath Tagore, Sarojini Naidu and Pandit Jawaharlal Nehru, and the firm and consistent policy of the Indian Government ever since independence.[3]

Within this backdrop, my attention in this article is mainly directed towards the socio-economic and political contribution of the Indian Diaspora towards these two adopted Countries, Mozambique and Madagascar, which will help in understanding the involvement of Indians in their adopted countries as a whole. There can be no true progress in these two countries of Africa, unless and until the contribution of its entire population is recognized. There is a lot of literature on the contribution of the Indian Diaspora towards India and other developed countries of the world like USA, UK and Australia but not much research has been done on the contribution of the Indian Diaspora towards the countries of its adoption in Africa. This paper, therefore, promises to address this unexplored area of research.

Madagascar is the fourth largest Island in the world, situated in the east coast of Africa. Before independence, it was a French colony. Now also it is considered as the France Overseas territory and France has a greater influence on Madagascar. Despite great deforestation, it is still a very beautiful Island, full of greenery, beautiful beaches and unexplored mineral wealth. It is also blessed with a small population, little over 16 million. Of this number, PIOs comprise some 25, 000[4]. They came as traders around the year 1900. Majority of them run merchant shops. Some Indians, especially traders, came from other African countries like Zanzibar and Kenya[5]. On the other hand, Mozambique is a country of Southern Africa. It was a Portuguese colony. Around 20,000 Indians are there in Mozambique. The Indians migrated from Goa, Daman and Diu and from some parts of Gujarat (Portuguese call it as Northern Province) to Mozambique and from Mozambique to Lisbon (Portugal). Some of them settled down in Mozambique and some in Portugal. All this happened during the Portuguese colonial period in the 19th Century as these provinces of India and the country of Mozambique were under Portuguese rule and shared same colonial experiences. This does not mean that there was no migration of Indians to this country before colonial period. Only during the colonial period, their migration intensified and the Indians especially Goans found it quite advantageous to migrate to Mozambique located in the East African coast across the Indian Ocean.[6] Indians first migrated to this country long back, when trade and commerce started across the Indian Ocean region. There is a long history of the migration of the Indian merchants to this region as well as the Goa-Mozambique relation. If one were to trace its history, one would see with the Portuguese controlling the Indian Ocean, Goans started to be active in the commerce of wood, tea, coffee, spices, and cinnamon in the Goa-Mozambique-Lisbon triangle. Since the 16th century, they, with the Gujarati traders, played an extremely important role in consolidating Portugal's control over the hinterland. Until 1752, Mozambique was under the direct administration of Goa[7]. So, it was the Goans who first came to Mozambique. The Goans are in majority among the Indian population in Mozambique and have made remarkable progress in the socio-economic and political sphere, and have higher social status in the Mozambican society.

Contribution of the Indian Diaspora in Mozambique and Madagascar

Chief Lutuli, in his Nobel lecture, quoted - "a distinctive contribution to human progress and human relationships with a peculiar new African flavour enriched by the diversity of cultures she enjoys".[8] Indians of the Mozambique and

Madagascar contributed to this African flavour immensely and have left their foot prints on the sands of time.

The Indians made a notable contribution to the development of these countries and can make an equally significant contribution to the future development as part of the whole Mozambique and Madagascar nations. They have the cultural heritage of many regions of India and have developed skills, largely by community's own effort, which others can imbibe from them to have a better future.

Economic Contribution

In the economic field, the Indian Diaspora in both the countries has relatively contributed more than the other indigenous populace. In Madagascar, although the PIOs constitute only 2.5 per cent of the total of 15 million populations, they control a significant proportion of economy. It is estimated that they run more than 50 per cent of the country's economy. Indians are to be found in all areas of economic activities but their involvement in professions such as medicine, law and teaching is not significant because of their low interest and advancement in education[9]. Economic dominance creates resentment against the Indians. In this way they are contributing largely to the Madagascar society especially in the economic sphere. Their economic wealth also means that this community should have some social responsibility. The Indian Diaspora community is aware that it must play a greater role in the development of Madagascar and involve itself in works of charity, and so on.

On the other hand, the Indian Diaspora keeps contributing to the Mozambique society long before the colonial period, especially in the economic sphere. Indians migrated to these country decades ago, when trade and commerce started across the Indian Ocean region. There is a long history of the migration of the Indian merchants to this region and Goa-Mozambique trade relation. With the Portuguese controlling the Indian Ocean (from 1498, when Portuguese under Vasco Da Gama discovered the sea route to

India), Goans started to be active in the commerce of wood, tea, coffee, spices, and cinnamon in the Goa-Mozambique-Lisbon triangle. Since the 16th century, they with the Gujarati traders played an extremely important role in consolidating Portugal's control over the hinterland. Until 1752, Mozambique was under the direct administration of Goa.[10]

The Goans played a pioneering role in Mozambique and did help to buttress the colonial structure in that country in a major way. Goans are very rich compared to the indigenous Mozambican people and undertook such tasks, which the White men could not perform in East Africa in general and in Mozambique in particular. Goan pioneers played a role in different countries of the globe, and their involvement in Africa is well known. But less is heard of Portuguese speaking Africa[11].

The vast river Zambezi and its tributaries irrigate Mozambique's central region. It is a very fertile region with luxuriant vegetation but with abundant mosquito larvae too. Local inhabitants lived in small huts made of sticks, and dry grass called 'palhotas'. In this region of high fever and poisonous snakes, the Goan immigrants lived, toiled, and colonized the same, working shoulder to shoulder with the Portuguese. Other Portuguese researchers argue that none could surpass the Goan immigrants of Mozambique in shrewdness in their commercial excursions, business transactions and in their labour output in the exploration of gold mines. Louis Fernando da Carvalho Dias says the Goan emigrants were "so courageous" that they continuously moved across the forests, opened new roads, faced great perils and kept up the commercial and economic connections between Goa and Mozambique. Many Goan emigrants worked in the Zumbo gold mines and carried on the ivory trade between Goa, Mozambique and Portugal. Such were the close links between the Goans and Mozambicans that even *'achars'* (i.e. pickles of various kinds), *caju feni* and dry salted fish were regularly transported by ships from Goa to Mozambique to be consumed by the natives[12].

Portuguese language is the main obstacle for the Indian traders in this region. Still the Indian traders are more successful compared to the indigenous traders and the

Portugal traders. According to a recent estimate made by FICCI, there are about 900 persons of Indian nationality and over 16,000 persons of Indian origin, holding Mozambican and Portuguese passports. A majority of the persons of Indian origin are engaged in the wholesale and retail trade and originally hail from Gujarat, Goa, Daman and Diu as mentioned above. Along with other Asian communities, they control about 40 per cent of the trade in Mozambique[13].

Social Contribution

Both Madagascar and Mozambique are the heterogeneous societies comprising of various religious and social groups like India.

The 25,000 Indians of Madagascar can roughly be divided into the following social and religious groups: Hindus 3,000; Bohras 7,000; Khoja 6,000; Ismaeli 3,000 and Sunnis 1,000. Out of these, most Hindus are Indian nationals as are some of the Bohras and very few of the Khoja community. The rest are either the French nationals and in some cases, Malagache nationals. There are as many as 1,000 who are stateless.[14]

As far back as 1900, predominantly Gujarati Indians from the Saurashtra region had arrived in small sailing boats at the port of Hahajanga, located in the Northwestern part of this Island. In the initial phase, Muslims migrated to this island predominantly, consisting of Khojas, Ismailis and Daoudi Bohras as mentioned above. A small number of Hindus also followed them and settled down in other parts of Madagascar.

As mentioned above, during colonial period migration was intensified. Even after independence Indians in Madagascar are descended. They are mostly from traders who arrived to the newly independent nation looking for better opportunities. The majority of them came from the west coast of India known as Karanes (Muslim) and Banian (Hindu). Although the Indians in Madagascar greatly influenced by the policy of *assimilation* of the France like other indigenous people and generally speak fluently French but still they did not forget their Mother tongue and majority speaks Hindi or

Gujarati, and though some of the other Indian languages are spoken. Nowadays the younger generations speak at least three languages French, English, Gujarati and Malagasy. A large number of Indians are highly educated in Madagascar, particularly the younger generation, who try to contribute their knowledge to the development of the Madagascar[15].

Most of these Indians in Madagascar fulfil their cultural needs through religious institutions such as temples, mosques etc. In some of these places attempts are made to teach Gujarati, Urdu etc. They are eager to form an Indian cultural centre in the capital, Antananarivo so that the younger generation does not lose its cultural links with India (Pala 2003:99). Indians belong to the middle strata of the Madagascar society. On the other hand, Mozambique Indians enjoy high status in the society, especially the Goans. The Indian Hindus use to read *Ramayan* and *Mahabharat,* our famous mythological scripts and practice their rituals on regular basis[16].

The Goan emigrants have not only left their footprints on the sands of time but also their imprints on the habits, customs and traditions of their descendents and on the natives who lived under their influence. They were men and women of extraordinary physical resistance and had exceptional strong temperament, lived in the regions of Zambezi river. In those days to live in the regions of Zambezi River was a very risky venture. Lobato argues that if the Portuguese possessed Alta Zambezia, they owed it in great part to the emigration policy, to which the Goans "contributed immensely"[17]. Goans are completely integrated into the prevailing cultural and ethnic environment of Mozambique.

The 19th century presented a golden era in Mozambique as Mozambique's outward perspective has widen, seeking to attract foreign investments and technological know-how to key industrial sectors and to promote the beautiful coastline as a global tourist destination. The new wave of Indian migrants included administrative officers, lawyers, doctors, engineers and also fishermen, craftsmen and traders landed in this country. Jose Vincente da Gama, from Saligao, is said to be the author of the first printed book in Mozambique, published in 1859. And he was an Indian migrated from Goa[18].

Hindi movies are very popular in both Madagascar and Mozambique in particular and in Africa in general. Bollywood considered as Hollywood in the African countries. They are very much fascinated towards Indian culture. Sometimes the Indian Diaspora community in Africa invites Indian artists to perform in their soil. Indians use to celebrate festivals like *Holi* and *Deewali* and invite their neighbours.

There are various associations formed by the Indian community in Mozambique and Madagascar to have greater cooperation and coordination among them. Among those some are Hindu associations and some are Muslim associations.

Political Contribution

In both Madagascar and Mozambique, democratic government has been set up. Madagascar has the experience of transition from the authoritarian regime to a democratic regime in 1990s and a new Constitution was formed.

Recently, in the year 2003, in the Madagascar legislative elections, two Persons of Indian Origin have been elected as deputies to the 160-member National Assembly, coincidentally in the same proportion as the population[19].

The Indians were the real heroes in Mozambique. They use to over shadow the Portuguese officials in administration and other professions. Some of them were local chiefs and some were efficient and renowned administrators.

Indians from Goa (Goans) played pivotal role in Mozambique political life as well. One among them was Pedro Caetano Pereira. This man was a trader who established himself in the regions of Zambezi succeeded by his foresight in acquiring such a prestige and influence among the local people. He controlled and dominated over the rich territory of Macanga, became its chieftain and was given the title of Camatowa (destroyer) by the natives, which was a kind of Mozambican counterpart of Shiva in the mundane sense of the term. The first coloniser of Zumbo (a region of the left bank of the river Zambezi situated 330 kilometers from Tete and belonging to the old empire of King Monomotapa) was a Goan, surnamed Pereira[20].

The Goans have greater participation in Mozambican politics as compared to the Gujaratis. The Gujaratis are more into business. Economically, Indians are quite well off compared to the indigenous people. Some of them are eminent industrialists, politicians, bureaucrats and press persons.

Conclusion

It is beyond doubt that the Indians in these two countries, Mozambique and Madagascar, immensely contribute, especially in the economic field, towards the development of the country. The PIOs of Mozambique in contrast to the PIOs of Madagascar are remarkably successful not only in economic field but also in the social and political sphere. Compared to the PIOs of Madagascar, the PIOs of Mozambique are much more educated and actively participate in the public and political sphere barring a few. Indeed, the entire world will watch with the greatest of interest, the emergence of these two countries of Africa with their own distinctive culture to which people from many lands have made a contribution, in particular the Indian Diaspora community, in a very significant manner.

Endnotes

1. Cohen, Robin. 2001. *Global Diasporas: An Introduction*, Oxon: Routledge.
2. Mohanty, Sasmita. 2007. 'Indian Diaspora in Mozambique and Madagascar: A Comparative Analysis'. Unpublished M. Phil Dissertation submitted to Jawaharlal Nehru University, New Delhi, p. 7.
3. Speech opening the exhibit on the 'Art, Culture and Social Reality' at the Wits Spring Festival, University of Witwatersrand, 1991, http://www.anc.org.za/un/reddy/culture.html. Accessed on 15 September 2008.

4. Pala, Adavjee Anilkumar. 2003. 'Indian Community in Madagascar', *Africa Quarterly*, vol. 43, no. 1, p. 99.
5. Dubey, Ajay. 2003. 'Indian Diaspora in the Francophone Africa', *Africa Quarterly*, vol 43, no.1, pp.88-89.
6. Karnik, Sharmila S. 1998. 'Goans in Mozambique', *Africa Quarterly*, vol. 38, no. 3, p. 95.
7. Isaacman, Allen and Isaacman, Barbara. 1983. *Mozambique: From Colonialism to Revolution, 1900-1982*, United States: West View Press, p. 15.
8. Speech opening the exhibit on the 'Art, Culture and Social Reality' at the Wits Spring Festival,University of Witwatersrand, 1991, http://www.anc.org.za/un/reddy/culture.html. Accessed on 15 September 2008, p. 2.
9. Dubey, Ajay. 2003. 'Indian Diaspora in the Francophone Africa', *Africa Quarterly*, vol. 43, no. 1, pp. 88.
10. Isaacman, Allen and Isaacman, Barbara. *Op.Cit.*, p.15.
11. Frederick Noronha. 1999. 'News Feature Goa: Goans in Mozambique', http://www.goacom.org/news/news99/sep/msg00013.html. Accessed on 23 June 2007.
12. *Ibid.*
13. Mohanty, Sasmita. 2007. *Op.Cit.*
14. Pala, Adavjee Anilkumar. 2003. 'Indian Community in Madagascar', *Africa Quarterly*, vol. 43, no. 1, p. 100.
15. Mohanty, Sasmita. 2007. *Op.Cit.*
16. Lal, Brij V., Peter Reeves, Rajesh Rai. eds. 2007. *The Encyclopedia of the Indian Diaspora*, Paris: Editions Diddier Millet and National University of Singapore.
17. Frederick Noronha.*Op.Cit.*
18. Xavier, Constantino Hermanns. 2006. 'A Little Goa in Southern Africa', Unpublished Seminar Paper presented at CIPOD, School of International Studies, Jawaharlal Nehru University, New Delhi.
19. Pala, Adavjee Anilkumar. 2003. 'Indian Community in Madagascar', *Africa Quarterly*, vol. 43, no. 1, p. 99.
20. Karnik, Sharmila S. 1998. *Op.Cit.*, p.98.

11

Mauritius : Contribution of People of Indian Origin (PIOs) to National Development until 1992

Chit Dukhira

Introduction

PIOs have struggled for self socio-economic uplift and to contribute to the national development of Mauritius.[1] Mauritius, an 1865-square kilometer island of volcanic origin discovered around 1500, lies in the South-West of the Indian Ocean on the African continent shelf. PIOs represent about 75% of its plural population of 1.2 millions. It includes inhabitants of European, mainly French, African, Malagasy and Chinese stock.

Mauritius was retained for some time by the Portuguese as a port of call. The Dutch came later, but also left after two vain attempts at settling. Holding the island from 1721 to 1810, the French named it Isle de France. During this period, Indians came as slaves, contract artisans or free immigrants. Having conquered Isle de France in 1810, the British renamed it Mauritius, as the Dutch had done initially. After introducing their administrative pattern of public services and justice, they abolished slavery in 1835. Indians were then shipped in indenture to work in the fields of the powerful Franco-Mauritian sugar magnates. French culture and private laws have persisted. Besides, the Franco-Mauritians are still dominant economically.

The present PIOs' ancestors, massively indentured, also comprised free immigrants who earned their livelihood through self-employed occupations. Of Hindu, Muslim or Christian faith, they hailed from various regions of India. Most of them came from the Bhojpuri-belt of western Bihar and eastern Uttar Pradesh (UP). Even before the PIOs' campaign for their own, and national, advancement, a few visitors, mostly from India,[2] or the Non-Resident Indians (NRIs), had paved the way for the struggle. Glaring injustice had been meted out in the past to the Indo-Mauritians by not only the White oligarchs and other inhabitants as the Coloureds[3] generally, but also by those of non-European ancestry, including most of the Indo-Christians. Although still bearing Indian family names, the Indo-Christians have for the most part integrated the General Population.[4]

A struggle had to be engaged in order not only to raise the socio-economic status of the Indo-Mauritians but also to overcome the constitutional and legal obstacles hindering them from having the least say in, let alone managing, the national affairs. The part played by two topmost PIOs in this endeavour is stressed here - one leading the country to Independence in 1968 and the other making it a Republic in 1992. The paper underlines the contribution made in various fields by PIOs, in general, and a few prominent ones in particular.

Most Prominent PIOs

In the NRIs' footsteps, a few endogenous Indo-Mauritian leaders emerged. They were the descendants of indentured labourers, like Dookhee Gungah, the first social worker of national importance, Cashinath Kistoe, the first PIO national leader, R.K. Boodhun, the first PIO barrister, Sir Seewoosagur Ramgoolam (SSR), the Father of the Nation, as well as the Bissoondoyal brothers - Basdeo, the unparalleled PIO missionary, and Sookdeo who allied with SSR as from 1965 to win Independence in 1968. These protagonists included free Indian immigrants, as Sir Abdul Razack Mohamed (SARM) who, born and bred in Calcutta, contributed towards the achievement of Independence since even 1959 when he had forged a political alliance with SSR. These PIO stalwarts, among others, have excelled in promoting the country's socio-economic, cultural and political progress.

Gratefully called, in Mauritius, the Father of the Nation, as Mahatma Gandhi in India, whilst, like Jawaharlal Nehru, affectionately named Chacha, SSR, an indentured labourer's son, is the architect of modern Mauritius. As the two foremost Indian barrister-leaders, he studied in the UK. He qualified as a medical doctor in London, where he also stayed for a much longer period than Nehru and Gandhi. Of Eastern, not to say Indian, background and imbued with Western, specially British, culture, coupled with his socio-political experience, SSR was the ideal person, of all the country's democrats, dead or alive, irrespective of ethnic origin, to champion constitutional reform in plural Mauritius. His public career is outlined below, followed by that of Sir Anerood Jugnauth (SAJ), the President of the Republic since 2003, who succeeded SSR as Prime Minister in 1982.

Being in dire financial straits, SSR spent 14 years in London where he also devoted much time to socio-political, journalistic and literary activities. He was actively associated with the Indian National Congress and its leaders in London, especially Vithalbhai Patel. Having proofread the work, "The Indian Struggle," of Subhas Chandra Bose, he was privileged to be handed over an autographed copy in 1935 before leaving London. A nominated legislator and an elected municipal councilor as from 1940, he was Mayor of Port-Louis in 1958. An elected legislator sitting on the Executive Council since 1948, he was associated since then with the voting of progressive legislation and government projects. In 1948, he formally joined the Mauritius Labour Party (MLP), founded in 1936 and was made leader of the Party in 1951. It was the majority party in the legislature until 1982. He was successively Liaison Officer (for education), Minister of Finance, Chief Minister, Premier and Leader of the House as well as Prime Minister. An eminent democrat, parliamentarian, humanist, journalist, professional, intellectual and statesman, SSR overcame various sorts of obstacles and even suffered humiliations on account of his Indian parentage. He has bequeathed to the people dignity, identity and a Welfare State. SSR led Mauritius to Independence after the decisive victory of 1967 at the polls when his MLP was allied with two other parties, both led by PIOs, SARM's Comité d'Action Musulman[5] (CAM) and Sookdeo Bissoondoyal's Independent Forward Bloc (IFB). It was whilst finally serving as Governor-General since 1983 that he passed away in 1985. His only son and the elder of his two children, Dr Navinchandra Ramgoolam, a medical doctor and barrister, who took over the MLP leadership in 1990, is the current Prime Minister after having held this post in 1995-2000. He had served as Leader of the Opposition during two mandates, in 1991-1995 and 2000-2005.

A barrister, first elected to the national legislature in 1963 under the IFB, Sir Anerood Jugnauth SAJ was in 1976-1982 the Leader of the Opposition as the then chairman of the Mouvement Militant Mauricien (MMM). He first became Prime Minister in 1982. In that year, his then leftist party, the MMM, along with the now defunct Parti Socialiste Mauricien (PSM), an MLP splinter group led by Harish Boodhoo, won the elections. The MMM-PSM Alliance unseated SSR and routed his MLP. Within four months after forming his own party, the Mouvement Socialiste Mauricien (MSM), SAJ now allied with the MLP, led by SSR himself, and the Parti Mauricien Social Démocrate (PMSD), headed by Sir Gaëtan Duval (SGD). After his first nine-month term as Prime Minister, he was re-elected as such - in not only 1983 but also 1987, when his MSM was again allied with the MLP and the PMSD. He triumphed again in 1991 and 2000, now together with the MMM. After SAJ's five mandates as Prime Minister, between 1982 and 2003, the MMM leader-founder, Paul Bérenger, of French extraction, who had started his public life as a trade unionist, succeeded him for two years (2003-2005). During

SAJ's prime ministership in the mid-1980s, as planned by his Minister of Finance, Vishnu Lutchmeenaraidoo, also an MMM MP earlier,[6] the MSM-MLP-PMSD regime, taking advantage of the public infrastructure put in place by SSR, removed Mauritius from an economic abyss, in which it had been plunged before 1982, when recession was raging worldwide, into a buoyant economy.

Start of Awakening

Representation in the Legislature 1886-1936

The country's first general elections were held from 11 to 20 January 1886 according to the new Constitution of 1885. It remained in force till 1948. Only British male subjects aged 21 years and above with the ability to read and/or write English could vote. Franchise was also based on narrow property qualification.

Of the country's 365,000 inhabitants, the electorate totalled less than 12,000. Only 253 PIOs (129 Hindus and 124 Muslims) could then vote. Of the elected legislators, all were Whites, except one Coloured. A flourishing trader and planter of Pondicherrian origin, Louis Gnanadicrayen Arlanda, was appointed the first Indo-Mauritian legislator. His daughter's husband, Dr Marius François Xavier Nallétamby, was nominated legislator in 1891. Kistnasamy Narainsamy, a marine broker, was made such a nominee in 1901.

For the appointment of the Swettenham Commission (1909), Dr Eugène Laurent, a Coloured progressist, who was the leader of the Action Libérale, a political group of some moderate Whites and the elite Creoles,[7] was instrumental. The NRI Manilal Doctor actively supported him in his campaign to set it up. Although no mention was made in its terms of reference about the Indo-Mauritians, Manilal Doctor could plead for their grievances before the Commission. Whilst granting a loan of £115, 000 to the sugar magnates, the British Government specified the allocation of £15,000 to the small Indo-Mauritian planters. The Commission exposed the glaring absence of Indo-Mauritians in the country's socio-political and economic life.

Abdulla Dustageer, popularly called Abdulla Khalipa, a real estate owner, in vain, fought the general elections in Savanne in 1896, 1901 and 1906. The Indo-Mauritian community was indifferent to politics at the time. In the ensuing elections of 1911, a number of other Indo-Mauritians tried their luck, but also without success, though belonging to the progressive political group that was then the Action Libérale. Amongst them were Harry Seewoodharry Bhuguth, a sworn land surveyor (in Plaines Wilhems), Boodhun Lallah, attorney-at-law (in Pamplemousses), Sirkissoon Dassyne, proprietor (in Moka), and Goolam Mamode Issac, trader and planter (in Rivière du Rempart). In 1911, Dr Hassen Sakir, a member of the Action Libérale, was appointed to the Council of Government. He was the first non-Christian Indo-Mauritian legislator. No Indo-Mauritian even appeared on the list of the official candidates in the 1916 elections.

For the 1921 elections, R.K Boodhun, barrister, and Rugbur Ramloll, attorney-at-law, stood as candidates in Grand-Port and Pamplemousses respectively. Both lost by a slender margin. Boodhun served as a nominee in 1922-1925. He was also the first Indo-Mauritian Hindu legislator. Serving since 1911, Dr Sakir was re-nominated in 1921 and replaced by Goolam Mohamed Dawjee (GMD) Atchia in 1926.

In January 1926, Dunputh Lallah, attorney-at-law, was returned to Grand-Port. He was the first elected Indo-Mauritian legislator, defeating Gaston Gébert and Marie Fernand Louis Morel. In the same elections, of 1926, Rajcoomar Gujadhur, sugar estate and mill owner, defeated Pierre Montocchio in Flacq. However, barrister Dhiraj Seetulsingh was defeated in Grand-Port, just as Ibrahim Beebeejaun, a landowner, in Rivière du Rempart and Ramrattan Hawaldar, a sworn land surveyor, in Pamplemousses.

Already meagre numerically, the Indo-Mauritian electorate further dwindled in the late 1920s because of the prevalent economic depression. A good number of these voters, previously eligible, had their names struck off the electors' list, as they no longer satisfied the wealth criterion. Not even one Indo-Mauritian contested the 1936 general elections.

First National Indo-Mauritian Platform 1935

In 1935-1936, a national voluntary committee, illustrative of Indo-Mauritians' diversity, afterwards known as the Indian Cultural Association (ICA), celebrated the centenary of the first arrival of the Indian indentured labourers. R.K Boodhun and Rampersad Neerunjun (later Chief Justice and Sir) were chairman and secretary respectively. Kissoonsingh Hazareesingh (later Dr), a self-made man, was the joint secretary.

Representing the Madras-based Indian Colonial Society, T. K. Swaminathan, delegated by Rabindranath Tagore who then patronised it and with whom Hazareesingh had exchanging correspondence, was the Chief Guest. In his inaugural address, on 29 January 1935, he qualified the memorial as "translating into a concrete shape the abstract idea of Love and Gratitude towards those pioneers of our countrymen who have laid the foundation on their blood and bones for the increased wealth and prosperity of this colony which has earned for itself the enviable name of the 'Pearl of the Indian Ocean.'" This memorial should be considered, he pointed out, "as underlying the awakening of the national consciousness of the Indians of Mauritius."[8]

Chairman Boodhun gave an account of the Indo-Mauritian history, with legal references about the gross injustice to which the indentured labourers were subjected. He stressed that Indo-Mauritians "are not mere materials as they have been treated in the past that is to say, as human cargoes or cattle, but are moulders and fashioners; yes, moulders of the destinies of the colony." He quoted the Swettenham Report 1909, which had concluded that "the importation of Indian labour has saved Mauritius from impending financial ruin and is responsible for whatever measure of prosperity she has enjoyed, notwithstanding repeated visitations of cyclones, droughts and epidemics...." He added, as remarked therein, that "the prosperity of the island depends on the Indian people who form the majority of the population.'" Boodhun asked for "the abrogation of all laws, statutes, ordinances or proclamations in force in Mauritius imposing on persons of Indian or African origin, although free, civil and military restrictions which were inoperative in the case of those of European descent." He deplored: "It is pitiful to think of the political condition of Indians in Mauritius." Although "in the matter of political governance of the colony, there is no preferential legislation between the Indians and non-Indians, and the former consequently enjoy equal political rights under a common franchise system," he urged that "the policy of the government today should be to update this system by lowering the standard of electoral qualifications so as to provide a more adequate safeguard for Indian representaion, which is an indispensable factor in the consideration of general public opinion."[9]

Speaking on "A Century of Indian Life in Mauritius" on 12 January 1936, Hazareesingh dwelt on the Indo-Mauritians' untold miseries from the beginning in 1834 until the end in 1922 (*sic*). He praised their perseverance, philosophy of life and interest in education, which had helped the community register some socio-economic progress. After appreciatively referring to the fusion of the Eastern and the Western cultures in the country, Hazareesingh cautioned: "We must not live in water-tight compartments that can blur our vision, but must rather blend with Mauritian life, in order to secure that harmony so necessary for the welfare of the heterogeneous community."[10]

On this occasion, Aunuth Beejadhur[11] published his book, *Les Indiens à Maurice* (Indians in Mauritius), believed to be the first work by a PIO on Indians overseas. The NRI Pandit Lakshmi Narayan Chaturvedi, a scholar in Hindi and Sanskrit, of Ballia, who stayed for about 23 years in Mauritius, too, came out with his collection of narrative poetry, *Shatabdi*

Saroj (The Centenary Lotus), describing the Indo-Mauritian struggles.

The article, in the ICR first issue, 'Sons of Immigrants,' of SSR "was going to become his political manifesto," Hazareesingh later remarked.[12] He served as the ICA secretary and edited the ICR till the end, with SSR as chairman. A public officer, who was the first PIO to head a government department, Hazareesingh also closely, collaborated with him to make Mauritius a Welfare State.

Print and Audio-Visual Media

Mauritius has a long tradition of written press, starting as early as on 13 January 1773. It has been French-dominated and even conservative until recently.

The *Islamisme* of the Indo-Mauritians, A. Ibrahim Atchia and Noormamode Nooraya, came out in 1906-1914. The first socio-political Indo-Mauritian paper, launched by Manilal Doctor, *The Hindustani*, appeared in 1909-1914. Initially a tabloid in English and Gujarati, this weekly later became an English and Hindi daily. It championed the cause of Indian immigrants and their descendants. Atchia and Nooraya put their printing press at Manilal Doctor's disposal. The Arya Samaj's fortnightly in English and Hindi, *Arya Patrika* (1911-1913), first edited by Khemlall Lallah, was printed at the press of *The Hindustani*. In 1912, the *Oriental Gazette*, founded by Ramloll Tiwari, appeared in Hindi and English, and so did Hossen Khan Naudeer's *The Indo-Mauritian*, a political weekly.

Subsequently, other papers, in English and/or French and Hindi, or in Hindi exclusively, contributed towards the emancipation and uplift of the masses. *The Mauritius Indian Times* appeared in 1920-1924. It was a political daily in English, French and Hindi, with the motto "Union is Strength," founded by R. K. Boodhun and Kailessursingh. H. Dwarka edited the English-French section, whilst Pandit Ramawad Sharma was the editor of the Hindi section. The Gujadhurs' *Mauritius Mitra* (Friends of Mauritius), in English, French and Hindi, was edited successively by Pandit Ramawad Sharma and Pandit Chintamanee Mookteram Chatterjee. It came out during the period 1924-1932.

Cashinath Kistoe founded the *Mauritius Arya Patrika* in 1924 and the *Arya Vir* in 1929. Another weekly, the *Jagriti* (Awakening), appeared during the period 1939-1945. From 1945 to 1950, the two papers came out under the title of *Arya Vir-Jagriti.* Since 1950, the publication has been appearing fortnightly as *Aryodaye* (The Rise of the Aryans). The *Sanatan Dharmak,* a bi-lingual weekly of the orthodox Hindus, also appeared as the *Arya Patrika* and the *Arya Vir,* in English, French and Hindi. Noormamode Nooraya's new paper, *Réveil Islamique,* came out from 1929 to1934.

The daily *Advance* (1940-1984), in English and French, initiated by Jaynarain Roy, but later actually launched and first edited by SSR and Aunuth Beejadhur respectively, fought for political progress, particularly targeting those of Indian stock. It later became the mouthpiece of the MLP. The Hindi bi-weekly *Janata,* or *The People* (1947-1982), first edited by Jaynarain Roy, too campaigned for emancipation. So did the Bissoondoyals' *Zamana* (1948-1977), or *The Times,* a fortnightly in English, French, Hindi and Tamil, which promoted Hinduism. *Zamana* was preceded by *Sangram* (The Struggle) and *Sainik* (The Soldier), both published equally by the Bissoondoyals.

Beekrumsingh Ramlallah's *Mauritius Times,* founded in 1954, remains a militant weekly. A former civil servant, who later became an MLP MP (between 1959 and 1982) and Minister (1967-1982), Kher Jagatsingh (later Sir) co-edited it for some time. In the early days, Somdath Bhuckory often wrote the editorials before he served as Municipal Chief Executive Officer of Port-Louis (1960-1980). Ramlallah's Hindi fortnightly, *Nav Jeevan* (New Life), edited by Soorya Prasad Mungur Bhagat, appeared from 1962 to 1965. The organ of the Comité d'Action Musulman (CAM), edited by Swalay Mohabeer, *The Star,* came out in 1963-1973.

The Congress (1964-1970), the organ of the now defunct All-Mauritius Hindu Congress, led by Premchand Dabee, a former MLP MP, coming out daily in separate editions in

Hindi, English and French, was also in favour of constitutional evolution. *Advance, Mauritius Times, The Star* and *Zamana* were at the helm of the fight for Independence.

The television system, promised since 1959, was launched on 8 February 1965 by Premier SSR. Colour television was partially introduced in 1975, and in the following year "studio-based programmes together with video programmes"[13] were started. From 1953 to 1966, Pandit Oomashankar Geerjanand served as the first Indian Programme Organiser. Parmamand Ramlackhan replaced him until his retirement in 1987.

Moving Out of Destitution

Economic Progress 1820s-1910s

First a few Indian free immigrants flourished even in the early 1820s. Annassamy, a prosperous trader, bought in 1822 "two plantations encompassing 765 arpents, together with 285 slaves, a steam-driven sugar mill and its appurtenances, 55 heads of cattle, 12 mules, seven carts and other items" for \$178,850, of which he effected a down payment of \$20,000.[14] The number of such Indian merchants, of South India, Parsee and Gujarati, rose from seven in 1851 to 33 in 1861. It soared to one-third of the country's mercantile class by 1881.

The Parsees Bickajee and Pestongee Manackjee were successively prosperous importers of Indian foodstuffs. Bickajee was also involved in shipping as well as immovable property and money lending transactions. Unlike Bickajee, Manackjee invested also in sugar plantations. These two Parsees were instrumental in attracting Gujarati merchants to Mauritius from Kutch and Surat. They both advanced money to them. Thus, Bickajee made an advance to Ismaljee Mamoojee in 1846 and Manackjee to the same Mamoojee and Daoujee Moossajee in 1850.

Ismaljee Mamoojee and Daoujee Moossajee were among the first Surtees to turn to agriculture after being engaged in trade. These Gujarati retailers, and later merchants, having arrived from far-off Indian villages with scanty funds, borrowed from the local market to carry out their trading activities. One of the first Surtee merchants, Ajum Goolam Hossein, was the only one to have disembarked with his capital. The Meiman and the Surtee *bazaars* operated from the 1860s. A tiny number of Hindu Gujaratis came mostly as *sonars* (jewellers) or traders in textile and grocery. Keesundas Mayaram was the first jeweller to come from Kathiavar. The Muslim merchants employed *Mehtajees* (chief clerks), who were Hindu Gujaratis supervising their commercial transactions, especially book-keeping. A few Hindu petty traders too disembarked from Sind, which now forms part entirely of Pakistan. A strong contingent also hailed from the then Madras Presidency.

The Gujarati Muslim merchants were engaged in fierce competition with the European and other local importers and exporters to meet the demands of the ever-increasing number of the families of the Indian indentured labourers. They imported grains and textiles from India where they exported sugar. The Surtees first settled in the countryside where they worked as retailers before moving, as merchants, to the urban areas.

Thanks to the system of *morcellement* (parcelling of land), a number of indentured labourers became small planters. A few Indian immigrants were already landowners even at the start of the 1840s, "but the nature and extent of their activity has remained hidden from view."[15] By 1881, when he died, Seewoodharry Bhaguth, Indian immigrant No. 152217, who had arrived on 10 June 1855, was already a noticeable landowner and businessman in Plaines Wilhems. He "not only helped to inaugurate the large-scale subdivision of sugar estates and other properties known as the *grand morcellement*, but also heralded the active role Indian immigrants were to play in this process of social and economic transformation."[16] Other Indians also got involved in business, besides land cultivation and transactions. Taking advantage of the *grand* (large*) morcellement* of or around 1875, they purchased land to such an extent that "by 1900, if not before, Indians may have accounted for as much as one-third of the value of all property changing hands."[17]

By 1910, the smallholders owned 27,928 arpents under cane, representing one-fifth of the land used for sugar production. Together with the estate owners, they farmed "54,000 arpents in cane compared to 35,480 arpents just six years earlier. These developments, coupled with the expansion of *métayage,* meant that by 1920 the responsibility for cultivating almost 45% of all the land devoted to cane rested in Indian hands."[18] A large majority of the small planters relied upon temporary work on the sugar estate to supplement their income derived from selling their own cane for their livelihood.

As they were short of funds, the planters were exploited by moneylenders, middlemen and other usurers. They were charged exorbitant rates of interest, often exceeding 12% monthly, irrespective of the period of loan. No institution existed to grant soft loans so as to enable them to earn their livelihood and incur expenditure on the various agricultural activities during the six-month inter-crop season. Many poor planters, being unable to repay their debt as a result of the system of *vente à reméréé,* a conditional sale contracted when the loan was obtained from moneylenders, had their land expropriated.

Co-operatives 1913-1952

As recommended by the Swettenham Commission 1909, the Co-operative Credit Societies Ordinance was passed in 1913. The Long Mountain Co-operative Credit Society was created on 25 May 1913. Pandit Baloram Mookteram was the founder secretary of this oldest among the country's existing co-operative societies.

In 1938, Abdool Latiff Osman and Seeparsad Seerbookun were nominated legislators on account of their involvement in co-operatives. They were the credit society's secretaries for Morcellement St André and St Julien d'Hotman respectively. Osman was chosen to represent the labourers engaged in the sugar industry, and Seerbookun for the small planters.

The department of co-operatives was set up on its own in 1947. G.E.Bodkin, a retired director of the department of agriculture, was the first full-time registrar of co-operatives. His assistant Mohabeer Burrenchobay, who later became deputy registrar, "displayed relentless efforts for the progress of the movement and the uplift of its members."[19]

The first co-operative stores were successively opened at Eau Coulée, Morcellement Saint André and Curepipe in 1947. But the one at Eau Coulée soon closed down. The consumer society running the Morcellement Saint André Co-operative Store is the oldest in the sector. Started by Kaleechurrun Ramdewar in 1946, Ramparsad Ramdewar and Jagdeosing Chundunsing were its respective founder chairman and secretary.

Early in 1948, 15 co-operators, all PIOs, including Jagdeosing Chundunsing, Manilall Ramdin, Hurrynarain Madhun, Maheeputh Jusrut, Hossenjee Edoo, A. H. Yadally, M. Patel and Jagdeo Roodermun, decided to form a co-operative bank. On 8 October 1948, the Mauritius Co-operative Central Bank Ltd (MCCB) was founded with Chundunsing (of Morcellement Saint André) and Manilall Ramdin (Pont Coleville) as chairman and vice-chairman respectively. Leon Julien, senior co-operative officer, was its first manager for a brief period. Appasamy Govindasamy Pillay, an inspector in the department of co-operatives at that time, succeeded him.

As approached in 1949 by Assistant Registrar Burrenchobay, the Barclays Bank in London authorised its branch in Mauritius to provide facilities to the MCCB, enabling it to increase its funds and, thus, focus on the development of savings for ten years. By virtue of the Brokers Act 1945, all the sugar producers had to market their produce through a broker. Since the MCCB was an institution, the broker had to be its general manager. The brokerage earned was distributed proportionally among the co-operative societies by way of "B" shares according to the tonnage of sugar handled by every one of them. Ultimately these were turned into "A" shares. In the meantime, the small planters agreed to great sacrifices, as they did not claim any dividend to enable their bank to flourish. By 1985, a capital of about Rs250 million had been built up. In 1971, the MCCB became a proper banking institution. However, its activities were confined to co-operative societies. By 1976, the MCCB began operating as a commercial bank. Mootoosamy Sidambaram was its General Manager from 1957 until his retirement in 1986. Sidambaram made a model of the bank for not only Africa but also the Southern Hemisphere. This co-operative bank, however, was liquidated in 1996 owing to mismanagement.

On 16 August 1950, the Mauritius Co-operative Agricultural Federation (MCAF) was registered. Mohun Parsad Kisnah, who later, after retiring as a government primary school head teacher, became an MLP elected MP and the spokesman of the country's co-operators, initially chaired it. Jagdeosing Chundunsing held the post of the MCAF secretary from the start to his retirement in 1970.

Access to Education

Primary

There had been a dire lack of government provision for primary education. Thus, many PIOs, individually or in groups, started setting up primary schools all over the island.

In 1895, Ibrahim Sulleiman Atchia, assisted by Noormamode Noorooya, opened in Rose-Hill the Mohamedan Aided School, a primary institution providing general education. Noorooya was its first head teacher. The Surtee Soonnee Mussulman Society set up in 1912, near the Central Market of Port-Louis, a primary school, called the Soonnee Surtee Aided School, for both boys and girls. Closed in 1962, the school was later shifted to the Taher Bagh, in Port-Louis itself. In the 1920s, the Kutchee Meiman Society provided free elementary primary schooling on the premises of the Port-Louis Jummah Mosque, offering Islamic studies, besides general education.

Thanks to a donation of both land and building by Chicooree Adnath, a primary school was opened at 8th Mile, Triolet, in 1911. Pandit Ramlall Tiwari helped him in running the school. Hindi, Indian culture, English and French were taught. Other such institutions included the Young Men's Hindu Aided School in Port-Louis, the Aryan Vedic School of Vacoas, now named after Pandit Cashinath Kistoe, its founder, the Saraswati Hindu Aided (now Gopeechand Chuttur Government) School at Ecroignard and the Laventure (now Ramsaroop Ramgutty) Aryan Vedic Aided School. Chuttur and Ramgutty helped set up the school at Ecroignard and Laventure respectively.

Under the influence of Basdeo Bissoondoyal around 1940, the Shree Shambhoonath Shivalaye, at Camp Fouquereaux, that had long been providing free tuition in Hindi, started free private general primary schooling for all classes. Khooblallsingh Ruhee, Soogrim Tiwari Baramdoyal and Parsad Bheenick were the prominent benefactors. Later, the authorities became responsible for the institution, now called Shree Shambhoonath Government School. From 1943 to 1953, a primary institution was run, under the auspices of the Arya Sabha, at Goodlands, the Victoria School, which later became the Goodlands Government School, and now is named after Doorgachurn Hurry, the initiator of the project. Seemurthan Haradhun had donated the land. Free classes were held. Hindi was taught outside the normal class hours.

On 6 November 1951, Sookdeo Bissoondoyal pressed in the legislature for the construction of cheap school buildings for potential primary pupils in villages. At the end of 1955, Veerasamy Ringadoo moved for Government to re-examine the question of intake of pupils in primary schools so as to increase the number of admissions in January1956. His project, however, did not materialise. Accordingly, Ramlallah and his *Mauritius Times* launched a nationwide campaign to press the government to build such schools in as many places in the country as possible, thus, educating all children of primary school-going age. A shift system was introduced; the class preceding the first standard was abolished to accommodate the maximum number of children. Most of the required primary schools were built by 1960.

Renganaden Seeneevassen became the first Minister of Education in 1957. Without delay, he enacted the Education Ordinance 1957, whereby the Minister "shall have control of the educational system of Mauritius and shall be responsible for the general progress and development of such system."

Secondary and Further Education

Founded in 1924, the Bhujoharry College located in Port-Louis was the country's first non-denominational private secondary school. In 1932, the New Eton College opened its doors in Rose Hill. Goinsamy Venkatasamy was the founder-rector. Shantilall Dhanjee worked there as, in turn, administrative secretary, teacher and assistant or deputy rector before setting up in 1954 his own institution, the Dhanjee College, which operated until 1974. Many such secondary institutions were later opened in both urban and rural areas.

In 1929, Rohenee Rughoo, later Ms Jaynarain Roy, was refused admission to the Loreto College, although she had won the Junior Scholarship. Such schools were reserved for Christian girls. Winner of a bursary in 1943, Mokshda Kistoe too was denied admission to the Loreto College. Her father, Cashinath Kistoe, had to intervene personally with Director Ward to enable her to be accepted.

In 1945, the Vedic Vidyalaya was founded in Curepipe, with the help of the Arya Sabha Mauritius. A private venture until 1947, it was a girls' primary school where only Hindi was taught. Ramsawock Ramdoyal and his son Bissoondoyal were the promoters. As from 1948, it provided both primary and secondary general education. When an exclusive secondary section was created in 1951, it was named Hindu Girls' College. In 1962, the Dayanand Aryan Vedic College was founded in Port-Louis by the Arya Sabha.

The Islamic Cultural College, starting in Curepipe in 1949, was moved to Port-Louis in 1953, as helped by the Kureeman-Toorab Benevolent Society. The Islamic Cultural Association, founded by Dr Hassenjee Joomye in 1945, had set it up. Besides general education, Islamic studies are ensured there.

Created in 1951, the Queen Elizabeth College, as named in the following year, was the country's first state secondary institution for girls. The Surtee Soonee Mussulman Society started its Muslim Girls' College in 1964 at its headquarters, at the corner of Corderie and Rémy Ollier Streets, Port-Louis. Later, the Muslim Girls' College moved to a new building, on the Society's other plot of land at the corner of Dauphine and Dr Eugène Laurent Streets, also in Port-Louis. Its construction had been funded by the Kathrada family. The college provides both general education and Islamic studies.

A few private secondary school managers or principals, as well as some teachers, mostly of Indian origin, coached students outside normal working hours for a nominal fee, if not free of charge. They even paid the external examination fees of poor students. Since the 1960s, the Ministry of Social Security pays the external fees, on grounds of poverty, of deserving students. Some individuals also gave private tuition more or less free of charge. Among them were Sookdeo Bissoondoyal, Alex Bhujoharry and Shantilall Dhanjee.

In 1968, after Independence, SSR's government caused the University of Mauritius to be set up. Between 1971 and 1973, it instituted the Mahatma Gandhi Institute, the Mauritius College of the Air and the Mauritius Institute of Education. The Indian languages are taught full-time in primary and secondary schools. Besides, in 1976, SSR made secondary education free for all students, irrespective of government-run or private schools, including the confessional ones.

Oriental Studies

Dookhee Gungah (1867-1944) was the pioneer of the free teaching in Mauritius of Sanskrit, Hindi and Hindu culture. He ran no less than 12 schools between the first and third decades of the 20th Century. Besides providing the premises, where both Hindi and Sanskrit were taught, Gungah personally met all the expenses, including the salaries of teachers and inspectors. After the examinations, he issued certificates and even prizes to deserving pupils. In 1927, he donated a plot of land with building at Dr Eugène Laurent Street, Port-Louis, to the Gita Pracharak Maha Mandal. With branches in Forest Side, Curepipe Road, Saint Paul and Beau Bassin, the Mandal propagated countrywide the teachings of the Gita and culture in general.

Around 1910, the Shree Shambhoonath Shivalaye of Camp Fouquereaux set up a school, under the chairmanship of Moorlidhar Pandey Geerjanand and with a generous donation from Madun Raut, for the teaching of Hindi. The other promoters were Deoduth Ram, Indurjeetsingh Seerattun, Ramparsadsingh Seenundun and Mahabul Leela.

Cashinath Kistoe was the first professional Indo-Mauritian preacher and Hindi teacher. The Arya Paropkarini Sabha founded in 1918 the Aryan Vedic Vidyalaya in Vacoas. The Kistoe family occupied an outhouse in the precincts of the school. Ms Radica Duljeet-Kistoe, Cashinath's wife, gave free private tuition in Hindi to pupils attending this school, now known as Pandit Cashinath Kistoe Aryan Vedic Aided School.

Prof Basdeo Bissoondoyal, who considered Kistoe as his guru, later became a great champion of Hindi in Mauritius, personally devoting himself to its teaching. Under the auspices of the Arya Sabha Mauritius, Pandit Srinivas Jugduth opened the Mesnil Girls' School, in 1936, where he voluntarily trained Hindi teachers, male and female.

The Long Mountain-based Hindi Pracharini Sabha (HPS), initially known as Teeluck Vidyalaye, was the most equipped institution propagating Hindi across the country by the early 1950s. Then Jaynarain Roy and Soorya Prasad Mungur Bhagat were its president and secretary respectively. With over 450 branches by 1961 all over the country, the HPS has been organising examinations, under the aegis of the Hindi Sahitya Samelan of Allahabad, India, as from 1946.

It was recommended in the Ward Report 1941 to stop the part-time teaching of Oriental languages (Hindi, Urdu and

Tamil) in the primary schools, imparted in the wake of the Kunwar Maharaj Singh[20] Report 1924. For Ward, such teaching should be ensured by the relevant communities. However, after the intervention of SSR in the legislature, such teaching continued and improved, and it was even better organised as from 1948.

Christian pupils were daily offered religious instruction. Those of other denominations were denied such facilities. In some private secondary establishments, such as the New Eton College, evening classes were organised to impart Hinduism, Islam and Christianity to the students, depending upon their faith. Since 1944, teachers with the necessary knowledge were allowed to impart instruction on Indian culture. 94 Oriental language teachers were recruited in 1950, when the relevant branch at the Teachers' Training College, Beau Bassin, was established. Soon afterwards, Prof Ram Prakash, a linguist from India, introduced a systematic plan for the teaching of Indian culture and languages at governmental institutions. He also coached teachers of Oriental languages at the then Teacher Training College, now integrated into the Mauritius Institute of Education.

The Presidency College of Curepipe, a private institution set up by Yogi Rummun in the early 1950s, was the first to cater for classes in Hinduism in 1965. Only in 1977 was Hinduism accepted as a subject for external examinations by the Cambridge University.

In 1956, Abdool Wahab Foondun set up the Jamia Urdu Examinations of which he became the superintendent. Recognised by the Aligarh Muslim University, India, the certificates delivered are officially accepted in Mauritius.

The All-Mauritius Tamil Examinations Syndicate runs classes up to the *Tamil Mani,* a course higher than the advanced level of GCE in Tamil. The "Union Tamoule de Maurice" encourages the teaching of Tamil in its 50 branches in the country. Such institutions as Annadurai Tamil Palli, Sockalingum Meenatchee Ammen Palli and Kistnen Mestree Tamil Palli organise free Tamil courses.

In the 1960s, under the Mauritius Marathi Mandali Federation's auspices, the Vacoas-based Marathi Dharmic Sabha and the Cascavelle-based Marathi Prem Wardhak Mandal provided free tuition in Marathi across the country. Currently, the Marathi Sahitya Parishad and the Maratha Mandir, among other organisations, offer the same facilities.

The Andhra Maha Sabha, established in 1946, runs evening classes in Telugu in its 62 branches. The Jyoti Maha Sabha also contributes to the advancement of Telugu culture.

Towards Independence and Republic Status

Before 1945

In 1935, for the first time in Mauritius, the inhabitants of Indian origin, especially the elite, were aroused by feelings of patriotism. They were made to be interested in both their culture and national politics thanks to the ICA and its organ, the ICR.

The proletariat became conscious of worker and political rights, as led by Dr Maurice Curé, who fathered the MLP in 1936 together with his lieutenant Pandit Sahadeo Rama. After Curé, the MLP was chaired successively by Emmanuel Anquetil and Guy Rozemont. A labourer who worked as an agent of the MLP in the beginning, Hurryparsad Ramnarain soon became the country's most renowned trade unionist. Assisted by Mohun Parsad Jugdumbi, he headed both the then largest union, the Plantation Workers' Union, and the then most powerful national workers' federated body, the Mauritius Labour Congress.

Back from India where he had pursued higher studies, Badeo Bissoondoyal embarked upon his *Jan Andolan* (mass movement) which, culminating in the gigantic Maha Yaj of 5 February 1942, shook the masses, making them conscious of their rights at the grass roots. SSR's speeches in the Council and press articles, besides addresses at private and public gatherings, made an impact on the population at large. Jaynarain Roy's writings too contributed to alert the elite and the authorities about the need for changing the political set-up. Besides, the liberalising effects of World War II and the British Labour Party's coming into power in London favoured patriotic sentiments.

To elect the legislature, before 1945, out of a total population of 419,000, all 11,437 voters were males. Those of the General Population amounted to 7392. The number of the electors among the PIOs, though totaling about 70% of the population, was insignificant - Hindus (2317) and Muslims (1621).[21] The Chinese voters numbered 107.

Constitutional Consultative Committees of 1945 and 1946-1947

In 1945, Governor Sir Donald Mackenzie-Kennedy laid before the Council in Mauritius his first draft revised Constitution. SSR championed the proletariat's cause, supported by Renganaden Seeneevassen, who had been an appointed legislator since a year. The other progressive Indo-Mauritian members comprised Abdool Latiff Osman, G. M. D. Atchia. SARM and Anquetil, too, made reformist proposals. As reported in *l'Oeuvre* of 20 March 1945, SSR found nothing worthwhile in the Governor's proposals for the advancement of workers. He condemned the reserved seats, found exaggerated the number of nominees and official members and differed from the views about the Governor and the Executive Council's powers. Not only was he against educational qualification for voting but also advocated adult male suffrage. For SARM, who also demanded male adult suffrage, it would be the sole requirement to satisfy the Indo-Mauritians. Otherwise, he argued, any man aged 21 years and above being able to fill the electoral inscription form in his own handwriting in any language should be entitled to vote.

The PIOs Ramnarain, Jugdambi, Sookdeo Balgobin, Harilal Vaghjee (later Sir), Aunuth Beejadhur, Ramawad Sewgobind, GMD Atchia, Renganaden Seeneevassen, SARM and SSR, together with Emmanuel Anquetil, Dr Willy Dupré, Dr Edgard Millien, Guy Forget and Raymond Rault, were generally, among others, opposed to both the Governor's proposals and those contained in the memorandum submitted by the conservatives.

In his press articles, later published in booklet form,[22] Roy criticised the Governor's proposals and put forward his suggestions. He dealt with such subjects as race and politics, the executive, the legislature, distribution of seats and the franchise. Concerning adult suffrage, he evoked the Moody Report (1943), according to which "the Government has no effective means of keeping contact with the people" and "the illiterate masses were less to be blamed than the highly educated employers." Roy was convinced that the primary purpose of the Constitution was "the problem of establishing a better system of Government," so that "we send to the Council the right type of persons - persons who can ensure the right approach to the reforms that are now being proclaimed from housetops."

Governor Mackenzie-Kennedy set up a Second Consultative Committee after the receipt of the draft Constitution from the Secretary of State for the Colonies. The proposals now pertained to plural voting, female suffrage, franchise for ex-service men and pensioners, additional powers to the Governor, increase in the number of officials on the Executive Council and the appointment of a Speaker to chair the Council. The Standard VI Certificate was maintained as a voting criterion, whereas the qualification concerning the annual payment of rent decreased from Rs. 300 to Rs. 240.

SSR told the Committee on 15 January 1947, "We are not against female suffrage, if it is extended to all women in the country without distinction of creed or class."[23] After a week, he pointed out to it, "We should not lose sight of the fact that the Council is semi-representative and that if the Constitution is to be changed, it should make an advance towards the composition of a Legislative Council that is fully representative."[24] SSR advocated a representative government, together with an increase in the number of elected legislators and a decrease in that of nominees. Seeneevassen pleaded for universal suffrage, thus allowing all, including women generally, to vote. On 29 January 1947, SSR told the Committee, "The right to vote should be given to the man or woman who is able to fill in the electoral form in any language current on the Island, the Letters Patent to provide that in ten years' time this matter be reviewed to see whether adult suffrage cannot be contemplated, because we firmly believe that that is the final solution to our problem....It is true that lack of political knowledge and experience will handicap the voters in the beginning, but this will not cause a revolution, as they will vote for the same kind of people as were in power before. Their standard of values will take time to change, and they will only learn to use the vote by using it. They will make mistakes, as even educated democracies do at times; but they will learn something from their mistakes and gradually build up some stock of political wisdom." SSR also commented that "in every country where a change of Constitution has taken place, people have always taken a conservative stand and have usually returned people of the old gang. The history of this country will also show that, despite the fact that certain classes of people, even certain communities, having a majority in certain districts, they have not made use of it to return members on communal lines in an election."[25]

During the debate on the subject in the Council on 29 January 1947, SSR urged that "we must do away with property qualification altogether, and deal with man as a man, as an essential and good citizen who is able to play his part in the life of the island just as everybody else."[26] He continued, "When discussing education, medical services, employment, transport and all other ingredients of civilised life, politicians must take account of the voters. What we want in this country is that men and women should be given this right and privilege."[27] On 5 February 1947, he said that he was against the enfranchisement of women only holding the Standard VI Certificate. The conservatives opposed universal suffrage because of the illiteracy of the overwhelming majority of the inhabitants at that time. Yet, they were in favour of the enfranchisement of women, but only those with the Standard VI Certificate. This qualification was then held by almost all the Franco-Mauritian, and very few, privileged Coloured women. Hardly any woman of African, Malagasy or Asian origin possessed it.

In his despatch No. 14 of 21 April 1947 to the Secretary of State for the Colonies, Governor Mackenzie-Kennedy expressed the view that "the bulk of the people were unprepared for democratic institutions and did not understand them." He commented that in Mauritius "society was divided horizontally into economic and social classes and vertically by racial and religious differences."

At the last session of the Committee, held on 14 February 1947, SSR personally gave to the Governor a memorandum summarising the salient points raised by his progressive friends and himself during the previous meetings. A letter dated 5 March 1947 signed by Seeneevassen, Osman, Vaghjee, Sewgobind, Beejadhur, Balgobin and SSR,[28] was despatched to the Governor on such issues as the Executive and the Legislative Councils, Franchise and Plural Voting. Under Plural Voting, they remarked, "We believe that no proposals can hope to propound a solution to the constitutional problem of Mauritius which are not based on adult suffrage, although we are prepared to accept, in a spirit of compromise, that the right to vote be restricted to such of the male and female population who are able to fill their application form in anyone of the languages, European or non-European, in use in the Colony, the Letters Patent to provide in a preamble to our Constitution for the introduction of both male and adult suffrage at the end of ten years from the date of the coming into operation of the new constitutional scheme."

A new Constitution came into force on 19 December 1947. In 1982, Prime Minister SSR, thus, reminisced about the Constitutional Consultative Committees 1945-1947, "Finally, I managed to have the property qualification removed entirely and successfully proposed a compromise over the Standard VI qualification," through "a simple literacy test."[29]

Literate Vote 1948

Popular elections, although not yet based on universal adult suffrage, were held for the first time on 9 and 10 August 1948. Because of World War II (1939-1945) and the delay taken in deciding upon a revised Constitution, general elections could not take place after the normal five-year term of the legislature in either 1941 or 1946.

Franchise was extended to all , male and female, aged 21 years and above, who could pass a simple literacy test in any language spoken in the country - "English, French, Gujarati, Hindustani, Tamil, Telugu, Urdu, Chinese and the Creole commonly in use in the Colony." [30]During the literacy campaign involving Basdeo Bissoondoyal, Renganaden Seeneevassen, Beekrumsingh Ramlallah and others, the illiterates were taught to sign in the Indian languages in use in the country. Out of a population of 419,000, a mere 72,000 was allowed to vote. In 1936, the number was as low as 11,000, composed mainly of Franco-Mauritians and members of the Coloured bourgeoisie.

Some 15,000 female electors were registered in 1948. As reproduced in *Le Cernéen-Le Mauricien-Advance* of 16 September 1947 from a despatch from the Governor, those "literate in English and French characters" totalled 61,289, of whom the General Population (Whites, Coloureds and Chinese) numbered 40,904, whilst Indo-Mauritans, although of much greater numerical strength, were a mere 20,385.

A group of progressive contenders - SSR, Vaghjee, Beejadhur, Ramsoomer Balgobin and Roy - presented a 20-point manifesto. They pleaded for self-government, democratic local government, equal opportunities for all, a balanced economy through diversified agriculture, encouragement for trade unionism and replacement of the poll tax by income tax. The MLP manifesto included compulsory education, a tax on revenue, social insurance and minimum wages.

The press played a decisive role among the intellectuals. *Advance* supported "the Indian intellectuals," whereas *Le Mauricien*, "still headed by Rivet, backed the Creole elite and some Franco-Mauritians" and *Le Cernéen* "backed the Franco-Mauritian elite."[31]

After the elections, a group of the newly elected legislators comprising not only SSR, Vaghjee, Beejadhur, Ramsoomer Balgobin and Roy but also Raymond Rault, Guy Forget, Dr Edgard Millien, Sookdeo Balgobin, Juggurnauth Bedaysee and Seeneevassen formally joined the MLP. Its chairman, Guy Rozemont, who had succeeded Anquetil upon his death in 1946, ranked first in Port-Louis. He was the MLP only elected candidate. In 1948, for the first time, the legislature was composed of a significant number of progressists, including Bhagwan Gujadhur and Sookdeo Bissoondoyal.

Championing Further Constitutional Reform 1950-1952

In *Advance* of 14 February 1950, under the pen-name of Thumb Mark II, SSR warned the conservatives: "Your time is done. It is best that you leave it to the rising proletariat to clean the Augean stable you will surely leave behind you - your remnant of corruption, your social injustices, your inequalities, your nepotism and your grab-and-take practices. We want to build up a society, which will not be your oyster. We want to renew humanity and, in this natural process, your skeleton is required for the museum of the future, so that posterity can realise what monsters you had been and how stupid we had been to allow you to usurp our heritage for so long."

On 18 July 1950, SSR told the Legislative Council that "the time has come to implement fully universal suffrage in the colony, and the time has come fully to give responsible government to this country, to the people of this country; the time has come fully to implement what the Right Honourable Secretary of State has said from time to time that the intention of the Home Government is to provide self-government to the colonies whenever that is found possible."[32]

On 12 December 1952, SSR tabled his motion on universal suffrage and responsible government, requesting that "a delegation of seven members of the Council be appointed as soon as possible" to meet the Secretary of State "for discussion of the various points in issue." He pointed out that "in this century, every man and every woman should have the right to vote, and we believe that this time has come now when this right should be accorded to them, so that every one may be standing equally on this land." Regarding responsible government, SSR remarked, "this country has had a systematic and consistent parliamentary education for over a century, and no one can gainsay that." He referred to those who were enfranchised, despite their illiteracy, because of their wealth, offices or property. For him, the illiterate, just as the former servicemen, who had been lately given the right to vote "even if they did not know how to write or read," should be granted franchise in view of their experience and ability to rear a family, among other criteria. He deplored that "no opportunity has been given to them" so as "to get the right to vote." For him, "the right to choose is the essence of democracy. That right cannot be withdrawn from the people simply because there is a minority in this country who think that they are entitled to a privileged position politically."

The debate was first adjourned. After being prorogued on 19 December 1952 until 3 February 1953, the Council was eventually dissolved on 30 June 1953. The MLP battle-cry at the legislative elections of 1953 was universal suffrage. It won 13 of the 19 seats.

Universal Adult Suffrage 1959

Emphasis was laid in the MLP manifesto for the 1959 general elections, held on the basis of universal suffrage, on Mauritianism, socialism with an egalitarian society, dominion status with full autonomy, franchise to those aged 18 years, the appointment of a Speaker, the nomination of a member to represent Rodrigues and the town councils to be fully elective. In its pre-election agenda, Sookdeo Bissoondoyal's IFB dwelt on adequate wages, judiciary reform, trade unionism, responsible government and an Executive Council exclusively composed of elected members.

Allied with SARM's CAM, the MLP won 31 of the 40 new single-member constituencies. For the first time, the elected legislators had a majority on both the Legislative and the Executive Councils. Seven members of the 12-strong Executive Council belonged to the MLP-CAM Alliance. As there were 37 progressive legislators, the MLP-CAM Alliance urged for immediate internal self-government and complete Independence in 1964. The six elected members of the IFB were also favourable.

On 22 October 1959, SSR told *Reuters* that people in Mauritius wanted Independence within the Commonwealth and his party was keen on getting it as soon as possible.[33]

Political Campaign 1963-1967

After the 1961 Constitutional Conference in London, the grant of internal self-government was agreed to in two stages - in 1961 and 1964 following the general elections scheduled for 1963.

When he returned home from London on 8 September 1961, Chief Minister designate SSR was given "the heartiest reception of (his) life" at the airport.[34] From 26 September 1961, he began to "bear the title of Chief Minister, in addition to his appointment as Minister of Finance," as specified in the Government Gazette of the same date.

For the 1963 general elections, the MLP made the grant of full autonomy, to be followed by Independence, its clarion call. On the other hand, the Parti Mauricien (PM), precursor of the PMSD, fought for not only the integration of Mauritius within Great Britain but also separate electoral lists and proportional representation. With the CAM as its ally, the MLP secured 25 seats out of the 40 - 19 (MLP), 4 (CAM) and 2 independents (pro-MLP). Eight and seven candidates of the PM and the IFB were returned respectively.

On 9 March 1964, Chief Minister SSR flew back from London, where an agreement had been reached after the constitutional talks for the formation of an all-party government. He was acclaimed at the airport by an enthusiastic crowd of over 50,000; it was reported in the press. On 11 March 1964, a new Constitution was published in a special edition of the *Government Gazette*. The legislature and the Executive Council were re-named Legislative Assembly and Council of Ministers respectively. Though still Governor-chaired, the topmost official executive body now consisted of the Leader of the House and 13 Ministers. Finance Minister and Chief Minister SSR, who had also become Leader of the House, was made Premier, being empowered to chair the Council of Ministers in the Governor's absence and recommend its summoning. Moreover, the Premier was to be consulted by the Governor in the appointment and revocation of Ministers, as well as the summoning, prorogation and dissolution of the Legislative Assembly. The all-party government (MLP-CAM-IFB-PM), formed on 13 March 1964, was short-lived.

In its memorandum to the Secretary of State for the Colonies for the September 1965 Constitutional Conference in London, the MLP pressed for the early grant of Independence. It also insisted on franchise for all those of 18 years and above, ministerial collective responsibility, a Leader of Opposition, independent service commissions, vote by two-thirds of all legislators to amend the Constitution and a chapter therein on fundamental rights. Harilal Vaghjee (later Sir) drafted the memorandum. At this Conference, chaired by British Secretary of State for the Colonies, Sir Anthony Greenwood, the MLP, the CAM and the IFB urged for full Independence. Both the best loser system for the safeguard of minorities and the creation of an Ombudsman, as demanded respectively by the CAM and the IFB, were supported by the MLP.

The best loser system was accepted by all the parties present, including the MLP, at the 1965 London Conference so as to ensure, as asked by the CAM, a reasonable representation at the legislature of each segment of the plural Mauritian society. This was "to avoid any frustration leading to instability,"[35] later pointed out Sir Satcam Boolell who had also participated in the Conference. According to him, the MLP had supported this electoral device introduced in 1967 "not to favour any split between Muslims and Hindus, but because it had found in it the ideal answer to the under-representation of minorities." The IFB demanded a High Powered Tribunal to check abuses of power and corruption in general. But it opposed the introduction of separate electoral lists.

However, the PMSD wanted continued association with the UK, a status like that of Reunion Island,[36] to safeguard minority rights and continue the shipment of sugar from Mauritius to Great Britain if the latter joined the European Common Market. Dreading Hindu hegemony, the PMSD believed an association with Great Britain would facilitate emigration to UK and Europe as a whole. The CAM, meanwhile, favoured a separate electoral roll for Muslims. The British cast aside not only the demand for association of the PMSD but also a Referendum, which it subsequently asked. They rather pronounced on a general election, which would be decisive for Independence. Later, Sir Satcam commented, "It was the first time in the annals of colonial liquidation that such a mishmash was announced instead of the straightforward grant of Independence."[37]

The Banwell Report was completed at the end of January 1966. Twenty constituencies each returning three members on the main land and a two-member constituency for Rodrigues, the electors having to vote on the basis of the block system, or voting for three candidates in Mauritius and two in Rodrigues, and the creation of an Electoral Commission were among the recommendations. Besides, the percentage of votes polled by each party was to determine the number of seats in the Legislative Assembly, known as the corrective system. As opposed by the MLP, which was backed by the CAM and the IFB, this system was soon substituted by the electoral mechanism of eight best losers.

As from 1966, the Premier, upon whose advice the Governor appointed the 12 Ministers, led the Council of Ministers.

Achieving Independence in 1968

At the head of the Independence Party (IP), grouping the MLP, the CAM and the IFB, SSR triumphed in the decisive elections of 7 August 1967 when around 90 per cent of the electorate voted. The IP obtained 53 per cent of the votes polled. About 44 per cent of the electorate were against Independence, preferring an Association with Great Britain, as championed by the PMSD and its new populist lawyer-leader, Gaëtan Duval (later Sir). He was actively supported by his mentor and predecessor, the respected towering long time barrister-parliamentarian and gifted public orator, Jules Koenig.

Tabled by SSR on 22 August 1967, the motion for Independence was seconded by the MLP deputy leader, Guy Forget (later Sir). At a later stage of the proceedings, all the PMSD members, except Yvon St Guillaume and Tangavel Narrainen, walked out of Parliament on the twin grounds that there were petitions filed in the Supreme Court against some elected members of the IP and the time for Independence was not opportune. St Guillaume and Narrainen even voted the motion for Independence.

The inaugural independence ceremony was held on 12 March 1968, when the first Prime Minister, SSR, hoisted the Mauritian national flag. The national anthem "Motherland" was then also officially released. Krishna Menon, India's Defence Minister in the late 1950s and early 1960s, and Cheddi Jagan, then Leader of Opposition in Guyana, were among the official guests at the Independence celebrations in Mauritius.

Accession to Republican Status in 1992

As early as 6 February 1971, mention was made in the daily *l'Express* of the possibility of Mauritius becoming a Republic.

Opening the Legislative Assembly on 6 September 1983, the Governor-General, Sir Dayendranath Burrenchobay, announced the Government's intention, as demanded by the PIO during the previous electoral campaign, to make Mauritius a Republic within the Commonwealth. At the sitting of 16 December 1983, whilst steering the Bill, Prime Minister SAJ described it as "another landmark in the political emancipation of Mauritius." He appealed to the House to cast aside political partisanship and vote unanimously for the Bill to make Mauritius a Republic on the Indian model, as it "is the cherished wish of the entire nation that SSR should be the First President of the Republic. This is a fitting tribute to the person who has been commonly known as Father of the Nation, to a man who, throughout his life, struggled for freedom, democracy, dignity, peace, love, brotherhood and tolerance; and, if what Mauritius is today, it is thanks to this man which history cannot ignore in this country."[38] However, the Assembly rejected the Bill. The constitutional requirement of three quarter majority was not met.

In 1992, following the victory won by the MSM-MMM coalition in the previous year's general elections, Mauritius finally became a Republic. The presidential regime follows the Indian pattern. In Mauritius, the National Assembly, as the Mauritian unicameral legislature is now called, elects the President, upon a proposal of the Prime Minister and with the support of "a majority of all members of the Assembly."[39] The Westminster-form of parliamentary democracy, with the Prime Minister as Head of Government, has been retained. Rule of law still prevails and multi-party politics is the normal practice. Mauritius remains a member of the British Commonwealth of Nations.

Cassam Uteem, formerly MMM deputy leader, Minister and Lord Mayor of Port-Louis, who had been an MLP-CAM municipal councillor in Port-Louis, became the first elected President of the Republic. Appointed on a motion tabled in the Assembly, he took over from Sir Veerasamy Ringadoo, an elected MLP MP (1951-1982), Minister (1959-1982) and the last Governor-General who had briefly continued as the First President.

Endnotes

1. The Republic of Mauritius comprises the outlying islets of Rodigues where live some 38,000 inhabitants, mostly of Malagasy and African origins, Saint Brandon and Agaléga. It continues claiming its sovereignty rights over Chagos and

Tromelin, the former occupied by the British and the latter by the French.

2. Of European descent, Adolphe de Plevitz crusaded to alleviate the indentured labourers' miseries. Delegated by Mahatma Gandhi, Manilal Doctor battled for Indo-Mauritians on the socio-economic, legal and political fronts. Dr Chiranjiv Bhardwaj and Pandit Atmaram Wishwanath, both of whom came at his request, continued his missionary work. The latter died in Mauritius in 1947.
3. The Coloureds are actually of mixed ancestry, White, Indian and African.
4. According to the 1st Schedule of the Constitution of Mauritius, Hindus, Muslims, Sino-Mauritians and General Population (GP) comprise the Mauritian citizenry. "Every person who does not appear, from his (sic) way of life, to belong to one or other of these three communities (Hindu, Muslim and Sino-Mauritian) shall be regarded as belonging to the GP, which shall itself be regarded as the fourth community," it is also laid down.
5. Muslim Committee of Action.
6. After having been an MLP unfortunate candidate in 2000, Lutchmeenaraidoo, the MSM-MLP-PMSD Finance Minister from 1983 to 1991, has now again joined the MMM as its Shadow Finance Minister.
7. The elite Creoles are intellectuals and professionals, or others of upper middle class, of mixed (African or Indian) ancestry, being neither White nor Chinese, as the Coloureds, but of darker complexion.
8. *Indian Centenary Book*. 1976. second edition, Mauritius: Mahatma Gandhi Institute, pp. 40-41.
9. Extracts, reproduced from *Indian Centenary Book*, Op.Cit., pp. 55-73.
10. *Ibid*. p.15.
11. Beejadhur was later the first editor of the daily *Advance* before becoming a parliamentarian, a Minister and then the first Governor of the Bank of Mauritius.

12. Hazareesingh, K. 1991. 'Preface' in *Kisoonsingh Hazareesingh at 80*, Port Louis.
13. *Indradhanush*, September 2000, p.245.
14. Allen, Richard. 1999. *Slaves, Freedmen and Indentured Labourers in Colonial Mauritius*, Cambridge: Cambridge University Press, p. 152.
15. *Ibid.* p.138.
16. *Ibid.* p. 136.
17. *Ibid.* p.144.
18. *Ibid.* p.168.
19. Extract from Minister Laventure's speech at the 50th anniversary celebrations of the Mauritius Co-operative Movement (1913-1963) - reproduced in the Souvenir Book edited by P. Maureemootoo, then Secretary of the Mauritius Co-operative Union.
20. Maharaj Singh spent six months in Mauritius, on mission, as sent by the British Indian Government, to better the Indo-Mauritians' lot.
21. The Indo-Christians made up the General Population, as even as they do now.
22. *The Constitutional Proposals (An Analysis of the Revision Plan)*, 1945.
23. Hazareesingh, K. 1979. *Selected Speeches of SSR*, Macmillan, p.44.
24. *Ibid.* p.42
25. Selvon, Sydney. 1986. *Ramgoolam*. Mauritius: Editions de l'Océan Indiens. pp. 39-34.
26. Hazareesingh, K. 1979. p. 46.
27. *Ibid.* p.47.
28. Published in *Le Cernéen-Le Mauricien-Advance* of 27 March 1947.
29. Mulloo, A. 1982. *Our Struggle, 20th Century Mauritius, SSR* - Vision Books. Delhi, p.70.
30. Second Schedule, Constitution 1947.
31. Smith, Adèle S.1982. *Modern Mauritius*, Indiana University Press. p.10.

32. *Advance* of 14 February 1950.
33. Koenig, Jean Antoine . 1992. *Jules Koenig – Une Vie pour la Justice*, Mauritius: Editons de l'Océan Indien, p.48.
34. Mulloo, A. *Op.Cit.*
35. Sir Satcam Boolell, *Mauritius Times* of 23 December 2005.
36. A French overseas small island department, found in the Indian Ocean, separated from Mauritius by half an hour's flight.
37. Sir Satcam Boolell, *Mauritius Times* of 16 August 2002.
38. Debates in Council – 16 December 1983. p.21113.
39. Constitution of Mauritius. p.28 (2) (a).

12

Contributing to the Success of Entrepreneurship: Indian Diaspora in United Arab Emirates

Prakash C. Jain

Introduction

India's historic trade links with the Arab World, including the United Arab Emirates, are well known. Settlement of Indian traders mostly engaged in pearl trade began in the early 19th century, concentrated initially around the ports of Dubai, Fujairah, Sharjah and Dalma Island. Until the early 1960s, there were only a few hundred Indian families settled in the UAE. However, as the UAE started receiving oil revenues and undertook massive development programmes, a large number of Indian labourers, professionals and businessmen started taking up jobs and business in the UAE. The inflow of Indians increased steadily until 1995-96. In 1996 before the amnesty, the number of Indians in UAE was estimated at 1.2 million. Since 1996, due to diminished employment opportunities, considerable number of labourers returned to India. But the migration flow has again picked up since the year 2000, mainly because of the start of various developmental projects involving construction activities and the growth of tourism and service sector. The present strength of Indian community in UAE is estimated at around 1.3 million. It is estimated that about 30 per cent of the total population and over 50 per cent of the work force in UAE are Indians.

Economic Profile

The Indian population in UAE consists of labourers, skilled/ semi-skilled workers, professionals and businessmen. It is estimated that 25 per cent of the Indian working population in the UAE are in the category of unskilled labourers, 50 per cent are semi-skilled/skilled workers (i.e. fitters, plumbers, carpenters masons, salesmen and women, nurses, etc.) and the remaining 25 per cent are professionals (i.e. doctors, engineers, chartered accountants, IT professionals, executives, office managers and businessmen). Family members/ dependents constitute about 25 per cent of the Indian population.

Since the late 1980s there has been a gradual shift in the socio-economic profile of the Indian migrants to the Gulf. The preponderance of unskilled and semi-skilled workers in the construction industry and other sectors has been slowly reversed. A survey done in the UAE indicated that there has been an upward flow of migrants in white collar jobs. Indians have a stranglehold on textile, gold, electronics and construction industries. A sizeable number of them also operate hotels and restaurants. According to figures provided by the Indian Ministry of External Affairs, skilled and un-skilled workers accounted for about 70 per cent of Indian migrants, white collar workers for about 20 per cent and professionals had a 10 per cent share in 1998.

Contribution of Indians in UAE's Development Process

The role of Indian Community is limited largely to economic activities. Indian community commands respect from the older generation of UAE citizens for the role played by it in the development of the infrastructure and economic growth as well as for running educational institutions, hospitals and providing other services.

There are a number of well established Indian business establishments in the country. The majority of the Indian population in the country is salaried class. The economic condition of the employees is considered good, except in the case of unskilled labourers, who work under hard climatic conditions.

Indians have been playing a major role in the economic development of the UAE over the last 35 years. Professionals and technically qualified Indians are engaged in huge numbers in the knowledge-based sectors such as information technology, Dubai Healthcare City, Dubai Internet City, Dubai Media City, Free Trade Zones, etc. There are a number of well-established Indian business entities in the country which are respected for their professionalism and reliability.

The Indian community, in so far as the business is concerned, is engaged mainly in trading. There is now growing diversification into manufacturing, especially in the numerous Free Zones in UAE, in particular the Jebel Ali Free Zone (JAFZ), which has attracted a number of companies from India. Registered community associations provide a platform for interaction between visiting Indian dignitaries and influential locals. The Indian Business/Professional Group, Abu Dhabi, Indian Business and Professional Council, Dubai, Indian Business and Professional Council, Sharjah and Indian Sports Clubs are active in organizing such interaction and facilitating visits of Indian leaders/delegations.

The NRIs in the UAE are one of the richest communities in the Gulf region. Estimatedly, they own up about $20 billion. Most of this wealth is sourced through work and work-related accomplishments, particularly as technology entrepreneurs, physicians and health care providers, small business owners, and corporate executives. They account for some 65 per cent of the high net worth category of individuals. According to the 2005 World Wealth Report of Merrill Lynch, there were 47,000 millionaires in the UAE in 2003 and 52,000 millionaires in 2004. Of these the NRIs numbered about 8,000 in 2003, according to one estimate. The same source suggests that the largest majority of Gulf Indians made their first million from their core business or performance bonus if they were employed. In the recent past, Resurgent Bonds and Millennium Bonds issued by the State Bank of India have made new millions for some people. The UAE has the higher density of millionaires than the US and is the wealthiest country in the region.

What accounts for this extraordinary success of the Indian entrepreneurs in the UAE? The following three factors can be associated with the success of Indian entrepreneurs in the Gulf countries in recent decades. In the context of the UAE these are: (i) the existence of old-time Indian traders, (ii) a network of Indian associations and (iii) world class infrastructure and investment climate, particularly the free trade zones. These are briefly discussed below.

Indian Trading Communities

India had a very close maritime trade relations with the Persian Gulf countries since the days of the Indus Valley civilization. The medieval sources, however, provide more concrete evidence of the presence of Indian traders in this region. These sources reveal that "Hindu merchants were present in the port of Shiraj on the Persian shore of the Gulf at least in the ninth century and that they also frequented the coast of Oman, Socotra and Aden"[1]. Similarly, Gujarati merchants, both Hindu and Muslim, played a dominant role in maritime trade and finance across the Indian Ocean[2]. Since at least the middle of the eighteenth century Sindhi merchants also played an important role in the trade with the Gulf countries[3]. The British administration in the Gulf from the early 19th century onwards further helped settle a number of Indian business communities in the Gulf countries.[4] In this section we can consider profiles of some of the major Indian trading communities which are relevant in the context of the UAE.

Sindhi Traders

Since at least the 18th century some Sindhi Hindu trading castes have been active in overseas trade, especially in the Gulf and the Red Sea region. Among these the Lohanas, Bhatias and Khatris are particularly important. The three castes happen to be *Banias* and are close to each other. In the pre-partition Sindh, the Lohanas were dominant in terms of population as well as social status. Among the Lohanas, the trading segments are generally known as *Bhaibands* (group of brothers) that are contrasted with *Amils* who were mostly in government service and enjoyed relatively a higher status in the community. Two *Bhaiband* trading groups, whose business acumen has been legendry, are Shikarpuri shroffs and Sindwork merchants of Hyderabad. These two groups along with Thattai Bhatias constitute a Sindhi Hindu Diaspora that extended their activities far and wide, especially following the annexation of Sindh into the Bombay Presidency in 1847[5]. The networks and the trading activities of the three Sindhi business sub-communities are briefly discussed below.

Shikarpuri Traders

The Shikarpuri international trading network developed during the period of the rise of the Durrani Afghan Empire and consolidated itself in the Central Asian Khanates between 1800 and 1870. The Shikarpuri merchants also played an important role in Russian Central Asia between 1880 and 1970, in Chinese Sinkiang between 1890 and 1933 and in southeastern Persia during the inter-war period. The Russian revolution of 1917, the 1933 rising in Sinkiang and the partition of India in 1947 had a great unsettling impact on the Shikarpuri network. So much so that the Shikarpuri network, which was basically confined to Central Asia, virtually disappeared from the scene. "It appears that most Shikarpuri banias relocated themselves after 1947 in India, using the dense network of the so-called 'Multani' banking firms to get work".[6] Some of them had also relocated themselves in the Gulf countries.

Hyderabadi Sindworkies

In contrast to Shikarpuri network the rise of the Sindworkie network dates back to the post-annexation years in colonial Sindh, and its global expansion to 1870s. Unlike Shikarpuri traders, the Sindhworkies specialised into silk trade and the curio trade. According to Marcovits[7], "Their specialization was not the result of particular predisposition, but occurred, one might say, serendipitously, because they found themselves in Egypt at the right moment, that of the birth of modern tourism, and were able to provide tourist with craft products which satisfied their taste of exoticism. They often followed the major maritime routes, established shops in the ports where international travelers called in, and in the process, extended their trade almost to the entire world."

Today major Sindworkie communities (both professional and trading) are located in the USA, Canada, Spain, Algeria, Hong Kong, Singapore, Indonesia, Philippines and the Gulf countries. Like Shikarpuris, the Sindworkies too were relocated in India after the partition.

Thattai Bhatias

Thattai Bhatias are perhaps the oldest trading community in relations to the Gulf countries in general and the UAE in particular. During the medieval period Arab traders often visited Thatta, the native place of Thattai Bhatias, for trading pearls with textiles and spices. Thattai Bhatias believe that it was these Arab traders who invited some of the Bhatias to settle and trade in the Gulf Emirates.

Thattai Sindhi Bhatia community derives its name from the city called Thatta, now in Pakistan. Bhatias trace their genealogy from the *Chandravansi/Yaduvanshi Kshatria.* Their social history of the past millennium, in terms of the change of religion and occupation, the rise and decline of the city Thatta, the migration and remigration of Bhatias on account of Muslim invasions, partition of India and their subsequent migration to the United Arab Emirates and other Gulf countries is extremely interesting.

Originally a Rajput caste from Jaisalmer, Thattai Bhatias changed their occupation from warriors to traders after settling down in Thatta in the 13th or 14th century. In the 16th century they got converted to *Pusti Margi Vaishnavism*. Mostly vegetarian now, their principal deity is Krishna and Nathdwara in Rajasthan is their major pilgrimage centre.

Well settled in the United Arab Emirates and some other Gulf countries, the Thattai Bhatias have come to monopolise the wholesale and retail trade in textile in the Gulf countries.

They are also into general trade, trade of electronic goods and foodstuff, etc. The latest community census, (*Thattai Bhatia Vasti Patrak)* done in 2002, suggests the presence of over two thousands of them in the UAE. Theirs is truly a success story in the face of their migration and remigration from Jaisalmer to Punjab, Sindh, Bombay and then to the Gulf countries.

Of the 689 Thattai Bhatia families in the UAE listed in the *Vasti Patrak* about ninety per cent live in Dubai and about as many are headed by male members. The total population of the community in the UAE is about 2,100. They are divided into 42 endogamous *Nukhs* (surnames/subcastes). About 30 per cent of them are into business, about 40 per cent into service and other professions and rest of them are widows and retirees. Their preferred business appear to be textile trading – wholesale and retail. In the Gulf region, Bahrain and Oman also host small Thattai Bhatia communities. In India, Mumbai is their headquarters since at least the partition.

Sonis

Apart from the Sindhis, the Sonis of Gujarat constitute an important segment of the merchant community in the UAE. The Sonis, or goldsmiths are a dominant caste in Gujarat, and they originate and are concentrated in the districts of Kutch and Saurashtra (old Kathiarwar) respectively[8]. They belong to two separate *varnas* and *jatis,* one called baniya or vaniya. Sonis recognize their descent and status within the *Vaisya varna* (trading castes and classes) and the other called *parajiya.* Sonis are recognized as *Kshtriyas* (fighter castes and classes). Outside India they are concentrated in Dubai and Bahrain. They migrated to these destinations sometime in the late 19th century, most probably around 1890. Since then they have been an affluent segment of the business community in the Gulf countries.

Parsis

Compared to the Bhattia and Bohra communities, Parsis constituted a very small yet significant trading community in the Gulf, especially in Yemen and Bahrain. Soon after the British occupation of Aden in 1839, a few Parsi businessmen from Bombay established themselves there supplying various provisions and services to the British establishment. Thus, in 1842 there were 38 Parsis in Aden[9]. Their number increased to 61 in 1856 and 121 in 1872.[10] According to Gavin,[11] "in 1846 they began to move into the gum, hides and coffee trade, and they seemed to be the only members of the commercial community with large enough capital at that date to buy the cargoes of American ships".

Besides traders, Parsis in Yemen also consisted of an educated segment who worked for the British administration. Needless to mention, some of the Parsi traders rose of political as well as economic prominence. The current Parsi population in Yemen is not known. What is certain about them is the fact that all of them are today naturalized citizens of Yemen.

In Bahrain, the Parsi population in the early 1980s was estimated at only 50 persons who were organized through the Bahrain Zoroastrain Anjuman[12]. Most of the members of the Parsi community in Bahrain were educated, highly skilled people drawn from urban India.[13] In the case of Bahrain, however, we do not have any definitive information about the size and the activities of the community. The same can be said about the Parsis in other Gulf countries.

Bohras

In India the Mustalian Ismaili Shiites are known as Bohras. The term is derived from the Gujarati word *vohoru* (meaning trade), signifying the major occupation of the first converts. The Bohras were further divided into two sub-sects of *Sulaymanis* and *Daudis*. The split occurred "over the succession to the twenty sixth Supreme Dai, who died in 1591. The Mustalians remaining in Yemen favoured Sulaymon Ibn Hasan as his successor while most of those in India favoured Daud Burhan al-Din"[14]. In spite of their further sub-division over succession to the twenty-ninth and fortieth Dais into Alias or Nagoshis and Hiptias, the Daudis are by far the largest group. "Most Bohras in India, and nearly all those in Bahrain and the rest of the Gulf, are Daudis". [15]

The Khojahs

The Khojahs are a sub-sect among Muslims whose religious headquarters are at the present time in India, but of whom a number reside in the Persian Gulf. The Khojahs have been authoritatively defined as follows: "a sect of people whose ancestors were Hindus in origin, which was converted to and has throughout abided in the faith of the Shi'ah Imami Isma'ilis, and which has always been and still is bound by ties of spiritual allegiance to the hereditary Imams of the Isma'ilis".[16]

The present Khojah sect has descended from Hindus of Sindh and of Kutch, who, in the 15th century of the Christian era, were converted from Hinduism to the Isma'ili form of the Shia faith. The Isma'ili Dai or missionary by whom the ancestors of the Khojahs were converted was one Pir Sadr-ud-Din, who is said to have been sent from Khurasan to India by Shah Islam Shah, an ancestor of the present Agha Khan and sixteenth from him in the ascending line.

From its original seat in Sindh and Kutch the Khojah faith spread or was carried by emigrants, to Gujarat, Bombay, East Africa and the shores of the Persian Gulf, but this process cannot be assigned to any particular period. The Khojahs differ to some extent from the Isma'ilis of Persia and other countries in ritual, and possibly in dogma; but those among them who adhere to their original tenets still regard the Agha Khan as the unrevealed Imam and as the head of their faith.[17]

The word "Khojah", in the present application, is understood to mean "honourable or worshipful convert". The Shia Imami Ismaili Muslims, generally known as the Ismailis, live in over 25 countries including India, Pakistan, Iran, Afghanistan, Syria, Kenya, Uganda, Tanzania, Canada, the United States, the United Kingdom, and in parts of China and Tajikistan. His Highness Prince Karim Aga Khan is the 49th Imam (spiritual leader) of the Ismaili Muslims, and is a direct descendant of the Prophet Muhammad.

In common with other Shia Muslims, the Ismailis affirm that after the death of the Prophet Mohammad, his cousin and son-in-law Ali became the first Imam of the Muslim Community. Ismailis believe that this spiritual leadership, known as the Imamat, continues through the hereditary line of Ali and his wife Fatima, the prophet's daughter.

Table 1: Distribution of Khojahs in the Gulf countries, late 19th Century

Territorial division	Port	Number of souls
Oman Sultanate	Quryat	5
Oman Sultanate	Matrah	1050
Oman Sultanate	Barkah	A few
Oman Sultanate	Maana'ah	A few
Oman Sultanate	Suwaiq	30
Oman Sultanate	Khaburah	125
Oman Sultanate	Sohar	16
Trucial 'Oman	Ras-al-Khaimah	33
Trucial 'Oman	Sharjah	158
Trucial 'Oman	Dubai	23
Persian Coast	Lingoh	56
Trucial 'Oman	Bandar 'Abbas	67
Trucial 'Oman	Minab	17
Persian Makran	Chahbur	140
'Oman Sultanate	Gwadar	250
Total		**1,969**

Source: Lorimer (1970: 2379-84).

Allegiance to the Imam and adherence to the Ismaili Tariqah (persuasion) of Islam has given the Ismailis bonds of unity and a common identity. They are known for their principles of self-reliance and entrepreneurship, as well as for their participation in contribution to the societies in which they live.

Throughout the course of history, the Ismailis have made significant contribution to Islamic civilization in those parts of the world where they have settled, such as the Arabian Peninsula, the Middle East, Persia, North Africa and on the Asian subcontinent and Central Asia. During the Fatimid Caliphate (l0th to 12th Century AD), this contribution included the building of the cities of Cairo and Mahdiya (Tunisia), and the founding of various learning centers including the University of Al-Azhar, which, at over a thousand years old, is reputed to be one of the oldest universities in the world.

This period was also distinguished by the development of maritime trade between the lands comprising the Fatimid Empire (Egypt, Syria, Corsica, Malta and Southern Italy) and by the quality of its scholarship, which drew upon people of all creeds including Christianity and Judaism. The influence of early Muslims was far-reaching and their observations, experiments and traditions broke new ground and had a significant influence on modern science. The legacy of their intellectual development left a lasting mark on the history of disciplines such as medicine, optics, astronomy, geography, philosophy, music and architecture.

During the late 19th century there were about 2,000 Khojahs in the Gulf countries, particularly in Oman and the Trucial States (UAE) (See Table 1). Accordingy to Lorimer, "At Gwadar the Khojahs are said to be still for the most part of altogether Agha Khanis, that is, Imamiyah; but at Matrah, which is their principal place, it is reported that nearly all have seeded and have become ordinary Ithnah-Ashari Shi'ahs, not Sunnis as at Bombay. The seceders at Matrah have preserved some of their ancient social and other usages, and the term Khojah continues to be applied to them, there are elsewhere, on account of their antecedents. In Oman, as a whole, about 90 per cent of the Khojahs are now Ithanah-Asha-riyah. The Agha Khan maintains regular communication, through agents in the Gulf, with the Khojahs who have remained faithful to him." In the context of the Khojahs it can be said that wherever they are settled, they are generally accompanied by their wives and children. World-wide Khojahs are involved in a number of developmental and philanthropic activities. These are conducted under the aegis of Agha Khan Foundation which is incorporated in Geneva, Switzerland, and is a non-denominational international development support agency with programmes in South and Central Asia and Africa. It supports programmes in the fields of health, education, rural development, poverty alleviation, and infrastructural developments, etc.

Malabaris

The latest groups of entrepreneurs to have arrived in the Gulf are the south Indians, popularly known as "Malabaris" (literally meaning Indians from Malabar Coast). In the Gulf context, these include Syrian Christians, Mopla Muslims and even Hindu Chettiars. Most of them migrated to the Gulf countries during and after the 1970s in the wake of oil price boom. Gulf Malabari entrepreneurs have gone into wide variety of fields including supermarketing, health care, IT, electronics, education, hospitality etc. a large number of them have also been successful as medium and lower level entrepreneurs throughout the Gulf region.

Early Traders and the Social Capital Formation

Scanty accounts available of the early Indian traders in the Gulf countries conclusively establish the fact that there had evolved a strong personal and community bonds between them and their hosts, including the ruling families. The ruling families not only invited many Indian traders to settle down in the Gulf Countries, they provided every conceivable help to them with respect to their business and personal life. "Friendship" would be a more appropriate word to describe this relationship. Business was conducted on trust – so much so that in the earlier days there was no need for the deal to be put down on papers.[18]

The Gulf rulers particularly in the Trucial Emirates were always available for hearing any grievances of the Indian traders. In fact, in Dubai the successive rulers knew many

Indian traders by their names. At the same time as the British subjects the Indian traders enjoyed certain privileges and security in the Gulf countries. Even otherwise there was minimal crime in those countries, a situation that still continues.

Mutual respect in regard to socio-cultural and religious activities was another salient feature of the then Gulf societies. Thus, Indians would often greet the Sheiks during Eid, and in turn the Sheiks would visit the homes of Indians at Diwali and New Year. During 1950s and 1960s such festivities were also observed on the occasion of Indian Independence and the Republic Day. In most Gulf countries plots of land were given for the Indian communities for building temples, Gurudwaras and Churches, schools and cremation grounds. It was on the strength of such goodwill and friendship on the part of the host society that the Indian community could preserve their character and culture in the Gulf countries.

In the case of Indian traders the use of "ethnic resources" is another factor that accounts for their entrepreneurial success. With the competitive advantage of "ethnic resources", a typically large Indian company thus employs a sizeable Indian workforce at various levels of its operations. Indians also have a large number of socio-cultural and business and professional organizations in the Gulf which facilitate their entrepreneurial activities through networking. In short, the social capital, thus, generated has gone a long way in making the Indian community successful and prosperous.

Network of Indian Associations

This section profiles the major socio-cultural and business associations of expatriate Indians which are there in the UAE, the oldest one being more than half-a-century old. These associations have been very helpful to the newly arrived Indian immigrants and entrepreneurs. Their presence and continuity has consolidated the nascent Indian Diaspora in the Gulf countries.

Indian Association, Dubai

Indian Association of Dubai is one of the oldest organisations that was established way back in 1940s. It was on 10th January, 1958 the Indian community members met at the residence of an Indian trader Mr. Dhamanmal Isardas. The purpose was to select an interim committee and to have a workable constitution for the Indian National Association.

It was to the wishes of Mr. N. Bhavandas, Indian Consul in Muscat, Mr. K.K. Bhatia, the then Hon. Secretary of the Indian National Association. The association was the only official Indian organisation instituted to co-ordinate matters relating to Indians with the British Political Agency and Indian Mission in Muscat. The association was then situated in old Bastaki Villa opposite the Dubai Museum. The pilot committee was headed by Mr. G.P. Padiyath. The association liased with the British Political Agency in Obtaining NOC's for Indian visitors, and acted as a mediator to solve trade disputes involving Indians and raised funds for local bodies. The association screened weekly films shows for recreation besides some other cultural activities. The association celebrated the Republic Day that was attended by the members of the Royal Family as well as UAE nationals. Entertainment and cultural programmes formed permanent feature.

Indian merchants community had organised a primary school Bharat High School, under the guidance of Mrs. Hemkalaben. The school later on expanded and reorganised as the Indian High School, Dubai. The Indian Association office is shifted to Old Pakistani Counsel Area. It has expanded its functions phenomenally and holds cultural programmes lavishly year round. It also helps Indian expatriates in getting passport related formalities done at nominal charge.

The Indian Association has well represented executive material help in India in cases of earthquakes, drought, floods, etc. They have provided many services to Indians evacuated from Kuwait and Iraq during the Gulf war and have done a lot in getting safe passage to thousands of Indian, who were living in United Arab Emirates without legal documents and Visas.

Indian Association Dubai organises welcome functions for Indian leaders, financial and business experts, taxation and investment consultants and cultural personalities of varied talents. Indian Association also organises Indian Fairs and participates in Dubai Shopping Festival with Indian cultural shows.

Indian Association, Sharjah

Indian Association, Sharjah is one of the largest associations of expatiate Indians anywhere in the world. The Indian Association Sharjah has been a regular venue for meetings, seminars, conferences and now with the construction of the prestigious Community Hall with added facilities matching to the modern techniques, it will be able to cater all the needs of Indians including super style stage for entertainments. Indian community in Sharjah was deeply grateful to H. H. Dr. Shaikh Sultan Bin Mohamed Al Qassimi, Supreme Council Member and the Ruler of Sharjah, for donating the plots of land on which Sharjah Indian School and Indian Association Sharjah Community Hall now stand.

Since its formation in 1979, the main concern of the Indian Association Sharjah has been the welfare of Indian community. The Indian Association Sharjah did creditable work in revitalizing the community involvement in educational, social, cultural, recreational and other fields. In all these areas the community has been giving special stress for strengthening Indo-UAE relationship that has been deep rooted over centuries.

Present Activities: Sharjah Indian School and Gulf Rose Nursery, which are owned and managed by Indian Association Sharjah, have emerged as the most prestigious educational institutions in Sharjah. Indian Association Sharjah renders supports and financial help to the needy people both inside and outside UAE through its distress relief programmes.

Cultural Activities: Until the formation of Indian Association Sharjah, there was no common platform for the

Indian community to get together and develop their talents. Since its inception Indian Association Sharjah could establish its undisputed leadership in the cultural front through organising Inter-School Cultural Meets and the Inter-Organisational Cultural Competitions. The most important among them was cultural competitions conducted for the Indira Gandhi Memorial Rolling Trophy, instituted by Indian Association Sharjah.

Social and Humanitarian Services: Indian Association Sharjah spares no effort in extending help to the needy. Indian Association Sharjah has been able to take up numerous issues concerning the expatriate Indians, with the Government of India, State Governments and other concerned authorities and on many issues positive responses were received. The association also liaise with Indian Embassy, Indian Consulate, and local Government authorities and render its help to stranded Indians. Timely help has always been rendered to the sick and needy. The service rendered by Indian Association Sharjah during Amnesty, in repatriating the stranded Indians has been widely appreciated by the Embassy, Consulate, the local Government Authorities and all concerned.

Educational Activities: There are two educational institutions running under the ownership and management of Indian Association Sharjah - Sharjah Indian School and Gulf Rose Nursery. They were established with the prime intention of meeting the traditional needs of Indian children residing in Sharjah and neighbouring emirates. These institutions were built on a plot of land most graciously donated by His Highness Dr. Shaikh Sultan Bin Mohamed Al Qassimi, Supreme Council Member and the Ruler of Sharjah. Sharjah Indian School is currently having a strength of about 4,000 students, is the largest in Sharjah Emirate and is conducting classes from K.G. to Class XII.

Office Complex: A long cherished dream of Indian Association Sharjah and Indian community to have an office of its own is being fulfilled. Office Complex with a conventional RCC structure comprising of ground floor and first floor incorporating modern architectural features having 840 sq.m. built up area has already been occupied.

Community Hall: A multi purpose Community Hall with all the modern facilities to cater the needs of Indians is under construction. It is built over a plot of land measuring 100 x 100 - roof cladded with insulated aluminum sandwich panels. Total built up area is 672.71 sq.m and a height of 13 mt. The following facilities are available in the Community Hall.

Mini Auditorium/Business Center: A business center to accommodate more than 250 people where large business conferences, promotions, presentations and Audio/Visual facilities, comfortable seats, stage, echo free sound systems, projectors etc. will be provided. These facilities will enhance the promotions of products to a large number of customers and dealers.

Indoor Sports Hall: Indoor sports Hall is designed to provide Volley ball / Badminton / Shuttle-cock/ Basket ball courts and provided with casters synthetic flooring from Germany. Spacious Gymnasium with qualified instructor will provide training to both Association members and non-members who wish to enhance their Physical strength. Most modern equipment will be provided for training.

Multi-Tiered Spectators Gallery: It provides seating for about 1,500 individuals.

Stage: A total area of 60 sq.m covers fourth side of sports court, synthetic flooring, green rooms on both sides, stores, lavatories. Shade of arc lighting and sound are special attractions of the hall. Sound proofed wall with acoustic wall lines and mutating acoustic suspended ceilings with a facility to accommodate 1,500 people.

Library/Reading Room and Television Room: A large number of books in different Indian languages and in English variety of subjects are available. Most of the periodicals and newspapers will also be provided.

T.V. Room: A separate room will be provided to those who are interested in watching T. V. programmes and news update.

Advertisement Display Boards All Around Community Hall: Display boards of size 2 ft x 6 inches will be available on three sides of Community Hall, with proper lighting. Establishments can make use of these centrally bit boards for promoting their products and establishments.

An estimated cost of 5.2 million dirhams will be needed to complete both the above ambitious Projects. Indian Association Sharjah has faith in the Indian community in UAE and is confident that the members of the community will contribute to make this venture a great success.

Indian Social Center, Abu Dhabi

During the late 1960s Abu Dhabi was witnessing an all-round development. The population of Abu Dhabi was increasing by influx of people coming in from various parts of the world for jobs in new development projects, Government Departments and Private Organizations. The need for an institute or a club with social and recreational background was then felt very strongly. A small group of Indian community met in a residential flat and the discussions resulted into an idea of forming a club or organization, where middle class people could gather with their families for an evening relaxation and entertainment. Such early initial meetings and gatherings ultimately gave birth to a Club which was christened as UNITY CLUB in 1967.

Until the end of 1969, the Club functioned in a rented place in the new Market of Shaikh Hamdan Road and then it shifted to another rented place near Police Head Quarters. Subsequently, a plot of land was given by the Government of His Highness Shaikh Zaid bin Sultan, where today stands this new structure built by the Indian community. The name of the Club has had to be changed, on their moving to the new premise on instructions from the Labour and Social Affair Ministry of Govt. of Abu Dhabi, to Indian Social Center.

Indian Business and Professional Council (IBPC), Dubai

Indian Business and Professional Council (IBPC) Dubai is the only recognized representative organization of Indian businessmen and professionals in Dubai. It was formed in 2003 following the unification of three Indian business organisations: (i) Indian Business Council (ii) Overseas Indians Economic Forum, and (iii) Business and Professional Club. The Council is licensed by the Dubai Chamber of Commerce. This new unified body was formed mainly to represent the Indian business and professional community in Dubai with all the activities of the earlier organizations. This formation of a single entity was in the larger interest of the Indian business community in Dubai. Indian Business and Professional Council work with the mission:

1. To promote economic co-operation between UAE and India.
2. To promote strong business relationship between UAE and India and to strengthen co-operation and develop business relationship between the UAE national businessmen and professionals and Indian businessmen and professional community.
3. To provide the opportunity for Indian businessmen and professionals to meet on a regular basis and to act as a unified forum for the exchange of information related to current or expected business or professional opportunities in India and UAE.
4. To provide link with organizations in India and UAE dedicated to the development of international trade and investment both in India and UAE.

Similar organizations exist elsewhere in the UAE and other Gulf countries. Thus, in the Sharjah emirate the association is known as the Indian Business and professional Council Sharjah and had a membership of 95 companies as of December 2004. The membership of the Abu Dhabi- based Indian Business and Professional Group about the same time was 155. Besides these general associations specialized associations representing a single trade also exist in the UAE. Thus, Texmas is the name of the textile merchants group. As of January 2005, there were 326 members, overwhelming majority of them being Indians, particularly the Sindhis. For the past couple of years efforts are being made to relocate the textile merchants from Bur Dubai to a newly built Dubai Textile City. According to informed sources there are at least 600 wholesale and retail textile merchants in Dubai of which at least 450 are Indians. Dubai Gold City is another similar project which is being carried out in the Emirate. Media, electronics and some other sectors of the economy have been receiving similar treatment from the Government.

Indian Sports Club, Dubai

Saturday 15th August 1964 is an important day in the history of the Indian Sports Club, Dubai on which day the Club titled initially as INDIA CLUB was formally inaugurated. This happened in premises comprising of 4 rooms near the Customs House on the Dubai Creek side. There were 35 to 40 Founding Members of the Club.

Dubai during the late 1960s did not have the image which it casts on the world scene today. The entire business and residential area was spread over 3-4 km on Dubai and Deira side of the Creek with Abra points in the centre. The total population was a little over 25,000 with 20 per cent coming from India, engaged mostly in trading and business activities.

Those were days when one had to live in conditions close to nature. The miracle of electricity reached Dubai in 1969. Till then brass lamps and hurricane lanterns lighted the evenings and nights and the day ended quite early. With family members away in India owing to the lack of education facilities for children the need to meet people socially was very acutely felt. In 1957, on the occasion of the Centenary of India's freedom struggle of 1857 six like-minded people gathered together and pledged to have recreation facilities for the community. They even decided that the new institution would be called INDIA CLUB.

The Club stated functioning initially with facilities for badminton, table tennis, carrom darts and a bar. Social functions like Housie were frequently held. Ladies joined the functions on occasions.

The membership was steadily increasing and so were the social and sports activities. By 1973, the membership had reached more than a hundred and the limited space was inadequate to meet the growing needs of the Club. The organisers approached H. H. (the late) Sheikh Rashid bin Saeed Al Maktoum, the then Ruler of Dubai who generously donated a plot of land and blessed them to go ahead with the building.

The building work at the new premises started in right earnest during 1973. The first building (the old Club House now demolished) which housed the main bar and restaurant was completed well on time for the Annual Day on 15th August, 1974. It was indeed a memorable evening. The Club was on its own land. The name of the Club was therefore suitably changed to INDIAN SPORTS CLUB.

In December 1975, the first two badminton courts were built with interest free loans from the members and business community. Along with badminton the club could organise many more social and cultural activities. The first tennis court was built in the same year. In October, 1980 the swimming pool was ready. Two more tennis courts were added at the same time along with sauna/steam and a gymnasium. As facilities increased so did the membership.

The role played by the Indian Sports Club and many local and expatriate sponsors helped to raise the standard and popularity of various games and promoted healthy relations between the UAE nationals and the members of the Indian community. Several other sports activities were organised on a regular basis for the members with the cooperation of local and expatriate sponsors. Two more badminton courts and two squash courts were built in a new complex and inaugurated in December 1984 by the then Indian Ambassador to the UAE Mr. Ishrat Aziz.

The Indian Sports Club Dubai looks to the future with confidence and has further improved the facilities by building a new Club House which was inaugurated on 11th October 1992 with modern amenities and many more comforts for the members. The Indian Sports Club, Dubai is rated one of the best of its kind for the expatriate Indians around the world.

Free Trade Zones

Apart from the existence of the old Indian trading communities and their networks of associations that made it convenient for the newer Indian entrepreneurs to grow and prosper in the Gulf countries, the UAE provides a very conducive atmosphere for entrepreneurial growth. This includes not only the first rate infrastructural facilities but also extremely low tax regimes. The free trade zones, particularly in the UAE offer various incentives to investors, including the right to 100 per cent foreign ownership; the absence of taxes, import or export duties; and the right to fill repatriation of profits and capital, as well as an ample supply of cheap labour. Not surprisingly, a large number of Indian companies have been taking full advantage of these incentives.

United Arab Emirates is a strategic location for international trade. Since its inception as a federal state, the government has opened up the economy for foreign investors and global traders. In furtherance of this each emirate has established at least one free zone to promote international trading. Free zones in UAE offer the following incentives to investors:

- 100 percent foreign ownership:
- No corporate taxation for 15 years, renewable for an additional 15 years;
- Freedom to repatriate capital and income;
- No personal income tax; Full exemption form import duties;
- No currency restrictions;
- No bureaucratic red tape;
- No recruitment problems;
- Modern efficient communications;
- State-of-the art infrastructure;
- Abundant energy; and

- Attractive working environment.

In general, most of the free zones issue different types of licences, namely trading licence, industrial licence, and service licence. Currently there are 10 Free Trade Zones instituted in the UAE, which are as follows: Jebel Ali, Dubai Airport Zone, Dubai Technology, E-Commerce and Media Free Zone (Dubai Internet City), Sharjah Airport International Free Zone, Hamriya Free Zone, Ajman Free Zone, Fujairah Free Zone, Ahmed bin Rashid Free Zone, Ras Al-Khaimah Free Zone, Saadiyat Market (Saadiyat Free Zone).

In addition to the three free zones already established in Dubai, the Government of Dubai has launched the following exclusive Trading zones: Dubai Customs Automobile Zone (Ducamz) - established in a 50,000-square metre business complex in Al Aweer, with 240 car re-exporting companies to boost the country's automobile trade.

Carpet Free Zone (CFZ) is proposed to be built in Deira Dubai and will target the handmade carpet sector. Dubai Textile City — with an aim to establish Dubai as the region's largest and the most convenient textile trading centre is more or less ready.

The Saadiyat Free Zone is located on Saadiyat Island off the coast of Abu Dhabi. Saadiyat Market is an international market place designed for a junction for global capital financial and commodity flows. It is intended to become a leading financial centre bridging the time zone gap of 3-5 hours a day between London and Singapore/ Hong Kong, enabling for the first time, a financial cycle of 24 hours a day, 7 days a week including Saturdays and Sundays.

It is designed in such a way to enlarge the market for international companies and traders by creating new opportunities for the trading and distribution of commodities and products into and from key markets of the GCC and other West Asian countries, North and East Africa, Indian sub-continent, South East Asia and the CIS countries. Saadiyat market will include an international stock exchange, a futures and options exchange, a commodities trading exchange, and a clearing house. Beside the common incentives offered by existing free zones in UAE, the Saadiyat Free Zone offers other outstanding incentives to investors. Participants in the following activities are also included: investment and financing; insurance; commodities; transportation; companies seeking listing; and service providers.

Table 2: Free Trade Zones in Dubai

	Jebel Ali Free Zone	Dubai Airport Free Zone	Dubai Inter-Net City
Location	Dubai	Dubai	Dubai
Established	1985	1999	2000
Kms from Dubai International Airport	40	1	5
Size of Zone	100 million sq. mtrs.	4 million sq. mtrs.	4 million sq. mtrs.
Lease Period	15 yrs (renewable)	15 yrs (renewable)	50 yrs
Ownership	100 per cent	100 per cent	100 per cent
Company Formation Period	20-30 days	10-20 days	3-4 days
Companies Registered	1504	87	120
Types of companies which can be formed	Branch of a Foreign Company, Branch of a UAE Company, Free Zone Establishment (FZE), Free Zone Company (FZCO)	Branch of a Foreign Company, Branch of a UAE Company, Free Zone Establishment (FZE)	Branch of a Foreign Company, Branch of a UAE Company (including other free zone UAE Licences, LIC (single shareholding), LIC (multiple shareholding)
Activities allowed	Number of activities are restricted. No General Trading Licence is issued. However, a company can obtain additional trade licence with difference activities.	Limited to high-value low-volume products, high-tech/IT Companies, high industry/assembly operations and activities related to aviation industry are preferred.	Information Technology, Electronic Commerce, Telecommunications and Media services are preferred.
Facilities offered	Warehouse/Factory Units, Office Units, Plot of Land.	Waterhouse, with or without Office, Office Units, Plots of Lands.	Office Units, Plots of Land
Types of Licences Issued	Trading, Service, Industrial, National Industrial	Trading, Service, Industrial	Not Specified

Table 3: Free Trade Zones in Sharjah and Ajman

	Sharjah Airport International Free Zone	Hamriya Free Zone	Ajman Free Zone
Location	Sharjah	Sharjah	Sharjah
Established	2000	1995	1998
Kms from Dubai International Airport	25	35	20
Size of Zone	1 million sq. mtrs.	10 million sq. mtrs	1 million sq. mtrs.
Lease Period	25 yrs (renewable)	15 yrs (renewable)	20 yrs (renewable)
Ownership	100 per cent	100 per cent	100 per cent
Company Formation Period	3-4 days	3-4 days	3-4 days
Companies Registered	432	105	454
Types of companies which can be formed	Branch of a Foreign Company, Branch of a UAE Company, Free Zone Establishment (FZE), Free Zone Company (FZCO)	Branch of a Foreign Company, Branch of a UAE Company, Free Zone Establishment (FZE), Free Zone Company (FZCO)	Branch of a Foreign Company, Branch of a UAE Company, Free Zone Establishment (FZE), Free Zone Company (FZCO)
Activities allowed	Not Specified	Not Specified	Not Specified
Facilities offered	Warehouse/Factory Units, Office Units, Plot of Land	Waterhouse, with or without Office, Office Units, Plots of Lands	Office Units, Plots of Land
Types of Licences Issued	Commercial, General, Trading, Service, Industrial	Commercial, Service, Industrial, National Industrial	Trading, General Trading, Service, Industrial, National Industrial

Dubai Shopping Festival

About a month long Dubai Shopping Festival started in 1997 has emerged as a major business event in the Gulf region. In the past couple of years the Festival has attracted about 3.5 million visitors annually. The UAE-based big Indian entrepreneurs such as the Jashanmals, EMKE Group, Joy Allukas Group, Jumbo Electronics, etc. have been among the foremost promoters of the event that in turn further generates not only big business and investments but also tourism and goodwill among the people.

Table 4: Free Trade Zone in Fujairah, Umm Al Quwain and Ras al Khaimah

	Fujairah Free Zone	Ahmed Bin Radhid Free Zone	Ras al Khaimah Free Zone
Location	Fujairah	Umm Al Quwain	Ras Al Khaimah
Established	1987	1988	2000
Kms from Dubai International Airport	120	55	100
Size of Zone	1.5 million sq.mtrs.	118.000 million sq. mtrs.	1.88 million sq. mtrs.
Lease Period	15 yrs (renewable)	15 yrs (renewable)	5-15 yrs
Ownership	100 per cent	100 per cent	100 per cent
Company Formation Period	3-4 days	3-4 days	3-4 days
Companies Registered	125	35	5
Types of companies which can be formed	Branch of a Foreign Company, Branch of a UAE Company, Free Zone Establishment (FZE), Free Zone Company (FZCO)	Branch of a Foreign Company, Branch of a UAE Company	Branch of a Foreign Company, Branch of a UAE Company, Free Zone Establishment (FZE), Free Zone Company (FZCO)
Activities allowed	Not Specified	Not Specified	Maximum 7 similar product lines under commercial licence
Facilities offered	Warehouse/Factory Units Office Units, Business Club, Plot of Land	Office Units, Land	Office Units, Plot of Land
Types of Licences Issued	Trade & General, Trading Warehousing, Manufacturing	Special Industrial, General Trading Service	Industrial Commercial, Commercial General Trading, Consulting and Service

Concluding Remarks

The increased oil revenues have given an unprecedented fillip to the economic development in the UAE and other Gulf countries. The historical ties and geographical proximity of India with this region have put it in a relatively advantageous position to become a major economic partner in terms of joint ventures as well as supply of a wide variety of manpower. This included sizable, diverse and talented class/groups of entrepreneurs whose contributions to the development of the Gulf countries are of seminal importance. The success of these entrepreneurs is as much predicated upon the existence of the prior generation of the Indian traders and their institutional networks as upon the highly conducive investment climate in the Gulf in general and UAE in particular.

Endnotes

1. Markovits, Claude. 2000. *The Global World of Indian Merchants, 1950-1947: Traders of Sind from Bukhara to Panama,* Cambridge University Press, p. 10.

   Gopal, Surendra. 1998. 'Indian Diaspora in West, Central Asia and Russia in Medieval Times', *Journal of Indian Ocean Studies,* vol 5, no.2, pp. 116-28.

2. Das Gupta, Ashin.1985. 'Gujrati Merchants and the Red Sea Trade, 1700-1726' in Blair B. Kling and M.N. Pearson.eds. *The Age of Partnership,* Honolulu, pp. 123-158.

   Chaudhri, K.N. 1986. *Trade and Civilization in the Indian Ocean: An Economic History from the Rise of Islam to 1950,* Cambridge: Cambridge University Press.

3. Markovits, Claude. *Op.Cit.*

4. Al-Sayegh, Fatma. 1998. 'Merchants' Role in a Changing Society: The Case of Dubai, 1900-90', *Middle Eastern Studies,* vol 34, no. 1, pp. 87-102.

   Allen, Jr., Calvin. 1981. 'The Indian Merchant Community of Masqat', *Bulletin of the School of Oriental and African Studies,* vol. 44, no. 1, pp. 39-51.

   Jain, Prakash C. 2003. 'Culture and Economy in an "Incipient" Diaspora: Indians in the Persian Gulf Region', in Bhikhu Parekh, Gurharpal Singh and S. Vertovec.eds. *Culture and Economy in the Indian Diaspora,* London: Routledge, pp. 102-124.

5. Markovits, Claude. *Op.Cit.*

6. *Ibid.* p.280.

7. *Ibid.* p.287.

8. Franklin, Robert Lee. 1985. *The Indian Community in Bahrain: Labor Migration in a Plural Society,* Ph.D. Thesis, Harvard University. Ann Arbor, MI: University Microfilm International, p.404.

9. Kour, Z.H. 1981. *The History of Aden, 1839-72*, London: Frank Cass, p.26.
10. *Ibid.* pp. 50-51.
11. Gavin, R.J. 1975. *Aden under British Rule, 1939-1967*, London: C. Hurst and Co., pp. 371, 117.
12. Franklin, Robert Lee. *Op.Cit.*, p.378.
13. *Ibid.* p.381.
14. *Ibid.* p.342.
15. *Ibid.* p.343.
16. Lorimer, J.G. 1970. *Gazetteer of the Persian Gulf, Oman and Central Arabia, I Historical Part-2*, Calcutta: Government Printing. p.2379.
17. Ibid. p. 2378.
18. See Buxani, Ram 2003. *Taking the High Road*, Dubai: Motivate Publishers.

13

People of Indian Origin (PIOs) in Sri Lanka and their Contribution to Sri Lanka

L. Vijayanathan

Introduction

The PIOs in Sri Lanka are the progenies of the Indians arrived in the Island during and after 1830 to pre as well as post Independent period of the British colonial rule. The Indians have been a constant and continuous contributor to the largest foreign exchange earning of Sri Lanka, the coffee and tea, since their arrival and more so after the independence of Sri Lanka. Sri Lanka's largest foreign exchange earnings came from the tea plantations up to recent times. The largest section of the PIOs have been and still involved in the plantation economy and being part of the country's foreign exchange. The political leaderships have played a significant role for their identity and social dignity. The Trade Unions have strived hard for their citizenship rights and social welfare. The PIOs have played a significant role in the mainstream political process of the country also ensuring stability. This paper attempts to capture the significant contribution made by the PIO community to Sri Lanka. Since the Indians out there in Sri Lanka dates back to many hundred years, it will be difficult to capture the history that long. Therefore, this paper attempts to bring economic, political and social role of the PIOs since late pre and post independence period capturing the salient points. It should be noted that Sri Lanka is perhaps one of the few countries with a significant population of Indian origins present more for the reason of its close geographic proximity and cultural resembles of its own population in the southern peninsular India. Further, what makes the issue of PIOs significant as well as intricate, is the presence of indigenous Tamil population dating back to a history of more than 2000 years and having an ethno political question unresolved. With this contentious issue in mind an attempt is made to capture the economic, socio and political contributions of PIOs in Sri Lanka. Here the role of India is also taken into account at some point or the other. There has not been any significant documentation done on the contributions of the Indian origins in Sri Lanka nor has there been any attempt to highlight the economic strengths of the PIOs. Therefore, faced with the constraints on availability of background information and statistics, an attempt is made to describe broader sectors and issues where PIOs play a key role.

Defining the PIOs

India has a large section of its former and present citizens outside the country throughout the world. They are termed as Persons of Indian Origin (PIO). They constitute more than 22 million people (an estimated figure). The PIOs become important in the current global economic, political and socio-cultural dimensions to India and as well as the countries where the PIOs are living. As the importance of boundaries is shrinking due to the global process, the importance of economic integration taking unprecedented stance, the importance of PIOs to India is becoming vital for emerging economic and global power block. This becomes evident in the context of PIOs contribution to their country of residence and their economic and political strengths that contributes to India a reasonable space in its global economic and political agenda. Given the far history of India and its people, tracing the Indians outside India becomes difficult. Many research papers by prominent scholars have contributed detailing about the PIOs or the Indian Diaspora giving a time line indicating the period of outward migration. For the readers, this paper attempts to narrow down on the PIOs outward migration to and since 1830s. The discussion in this paper, therefore, revolves around the Indian origins who left the country since the 1830s and are citizens of the country of residence.

PIOs in Sri Lanka

It would be useful to briefly outline the history of the PIOs in Sri Lanka. The composition of the Indian origins in Sri Lanka reveals that majority of the Indians in Sri Lanka are ethnic Tamils. Sri Lanka census identifies four major ethnic groups; Sinhalese, Sri Lankan Tamils, Moors and Indian Origin Tamils. There are small minorities like Malays and Burgers, which are estimated to be 0.25 per cent and other mini minorities who are generally PIOs (Malayalies, Sindhies, Gujaratis,). Going by the explanation of the PIOs given earlier in this paper, the PIOs in Sri Lanka form the section of the population that arrived from India after 1830s. Though there has been number of writings on the history of the Indians in Sri Lanka, for the sake of first time readers, if any, a brief outline of past and present status of the PIOs in Sri Lanka is given here.

After abolition of the slavery in the British colonies elsewhere in the world in 1833, the labour force in those British colonies was hesitant to work in the coffee plantations[1]. This resulted in the expansion of the coffee plantations in Sri Lanka by the British colonial masters since there was an increase in demand for Coffee. However, the peasantry Sinhalese farmers were not prepared to work in difficult conditions in preparing the land for coffee plantations. The option, therefore, was to look elsewhere for cheap labour. The conditions in India, which was also under the British rule, attracted a large section of poor to work in Sri Lanka.

Governor Barnes was the first English planter who brought Indian labourers to Sri Lanka. He used the term *coolies*. They came to work in Barne's own garden[2]. However, Col. H.C. Byrde brought in the first group of *coolies*[3]. The North-eastern region comprised of the West Bengal, Orissa and Bihar and Southern region comprised the then Madras Presidency. The migration was facilitated from the ports of Calcutta and Madras. The labour force, from South India, was brought into Sri Lanka through the ports in Tamil Nadu. While the socially lower class (low caste) who were under extreme poverty was the main source of the labour supply, the somewhat higher caste people were facilitating the organisation of the transportation of the labour (from south India) force. The organisers were also on the move with the labours and later they settled in the plantations. The large scale demand for labour forced the planters to devise different schemes for the importation of labour from India.

Besides the plantation labour force, there were free riders who came to the country for trading. As a result of the expansion of the Sri Lankan economy, there were ample opportunities for trading. The trading groups were Nattukotai Chettiars from Tamil Nadu, Sindhies, Gujaraties and Parsis from North India came to Sri Lanka. There were some working class with special skills like artisans[4]. The traders brought in consumer goods and took away similar items for sales across the seas. Some started to settle in Sri Lanka since there were good environment for business. These businessmen were not limited to ethnic Tamils but also others from different parts of India.

General Overview of PIOs

Large section of the PIOs settled into isolated settlements in the British plantation system. This is unchanged even up to today. The areas of PIO settlements and nearby exhibit a plural society. There were cultural and economic disparities between the PIOs and local Sinhala settlements. This provided for distinction between the PIOs and other communities. PIOs are living in contiguous as well as non contiguous territories. A province and district can be taken as a closed area for easy reference (see map). The majority are ethnic Tamils (say around 80 per cent). And out of which around 80 per cent are plantation workforce. These are estimated figures and do not have real authentication from state agencies. They live in Central, Uva, Sabaragamuwa and parts of Southern Provinces.

The Indian origin Tamils have been separately identified as a minority group in all official records of the government. They differ from the Sri Lankan Tamils, who are mostly settled in north and eastern parts of the country, in economic and to some extent in socio cultural practices. The emigration of Indians to Sri Lanka started in 1834. Till 1938, 1,529,000 Indians (mainly Tamils but there were others like Malayalies, Telugu speaking) had immigrated to Ceylon to work as labourers on the tea plantations[5]. In 1987, their number was 1,023,000 and they constituted 6.28 per cent of Country's population.

PIOs, according to government, account for around 870,000, which is around 5.1 per cent[6] of the total population of Sri Lanka and out of which around two third live in the plantations (Department of Census and Statistics –Census of Population and Housing 2001)[7]. However, the total percentage of the Upcountry Tamil Population widely known in non-published papers is 7.5 per cent (an estimated figure, see also table). Sri Lanka's population in the year 1981 was 14,846,750 out of which the Indian Tamil population was 818,656. It is pertinent to see that the population of Indian Tamil origin is 855,891[8] (Statistical Abstract 2002) in the year 2001.

The latest census, however, indicates that they are around 5.1 per cent. The discrepancies are due to non identifications of some section of the PIOs living in urban areas as 'Indian Origins'. The majority of the persons of Indian origin are still concentrated in the central upland districts of the tea-growing area. Those Indian origins are involved in trade and commerce and dispersed in central as well as urban areas like western province. The other ethnic communities are mostly concentrated in the Colombo capital city. The Indian origin community involved in trade and commerce formed around 7 percent of the Colombo city's population in 1971[9]. A section of the PIOs arrived from time to time since and before independence (1948) for trading and have settled in urban areas. They are ethnically, Tamils, Muslims (boras), Sindhies, Gujaraties, Bengalis, Malayalies and so on. It is noticeably arguable fact that Indian origins in Sri Lanka have had strong cultural links with their ancestral lands and have improved in economic and social life considerably, for example, Sindhies, Gujarathis, Punjabis and Malayalies.

Table 1 : Population by ethnic group ('000)

Ethnic group	1946	1953	1963	1971	1981	2001 +
Total	6,657.3	6,087.9	10,582.0	12,689.9	14,846.8	
Low country Sinhalese	2902.5	3469.5	4470.3	5,425.8	10979.4*	13815.5
Kandyan Sinhalese	1,718.0	2,147.2	3042.6	3,705.5	-	
Sri Lankan Tamils	733.7	884.7	1164.7	1424.0	1886.9	730.2
Indian Tamils	780.6	974.1	1123.0	1174.9	818.7	855.9
Sri Lankan moors	373.6	464.0	626.8	828.3	1,046.9	1,351
Indian moors	35.6	47.5	55.4	27.4	**	**
Europeans	5.4	6.5	**	**	**	**
Burghers and Euro Asians	41.9	46.0	45.9	45.4	39.4	34,6
Malays	22.5	25.4	33.4	43.5	47.0	47.6
Veddahs	2.4	0.8	0.4	**	**	**
Others	41.4	32.2	19.5	15.5	28.4	29.5

Source- *Dept of Statistics and Census*

+ Excluding the districts in north and east

* Low country and Kandyan Sinhalese have been combined

** Included in others category

Sri Lanka – An Introduction

Sri Lanka is an Island with a land area of 65,610 square Kms. It is officially the Democratic Socialist Republic of Sri Lanka. In Sinhala language it is: ශ්‍රී ලංකා and in Tamil: இலங்கை. It was known as Ceylon before 1972 and as Taprobane in ancient times. It is an island country in South Asia, located in the southern tip of Indian sub continent separated by about 31 kilometres. It is home to around twenty two million people.

After over two thousand years of rule by local kingdoms, parts of Sri Lanka were colonized by Portugal and the Netherlands beginning in the 16th century, before control of the entire country was ceded to the British Empire in 1815. During World War II, Sri Lanka served as an important base for Allied forces in the fight against the Japanese Empire. A nationalist political movement arose in the country in the early 20th century with the aim of obtaining political independence, which was eventually granted by the British after peaceful negotiations in 1948.

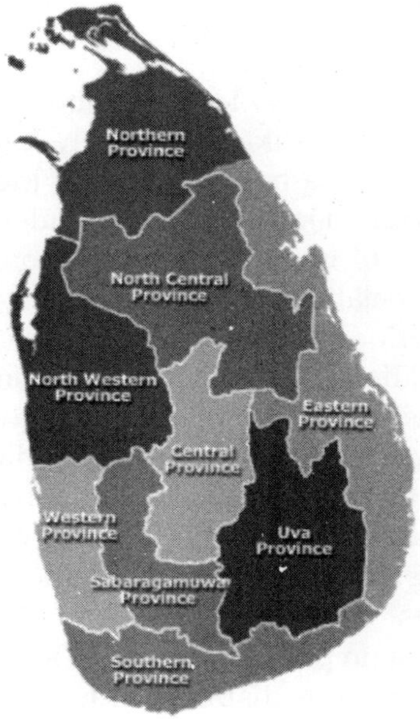

Sri Lanka- Provinces

Post independence Sri Lanka faced sustaining conflict between the ethnic majority Sinhalese and minority Sri Lankan Tamils. The conflict took a violent turn (into war like situation) during from early 1980s that lasted until May 2009 with the demise of LTTE armed movement along with its leader Velupillai Prabhakaran[10]. The violent conflict for most of the period, indicated above, was confined to the north eastern part of the country but had spill over effects that also impacted on the socio-economic growth and political significance of the PIO community.

Sri Lankan economy was dominated by the Plantation system of agriculture for many decades during pre and post independence eras. It was after the SAFTA (South Asian Free Trade Agreement) and concessions that Sri Lanka received for garment industries, Tea lost its first place as largest foreign exchange earner. Though it is in the third place yet it has the highest labour force, making it significant not only for the economy but also for the political economy of the country.

India's Influence

Sri Lanka is one of the close neighbourhoods for India in the southern tip. Sri Lanka is the only neighbour towards south to India. Sri Lanka has been one of India's friendly and confident neighbours. During the post independent era there were some periods of turmoil in the relationship between the two countries especially during 1980s. The main reasons for such a turmoil period would be Sri Lanka's perceived threat in midst of the national question (ethnic conflict) and India's unsolicited involvement in conflict. There have been shifts and changes in the pattern of relationship marked by mutual differences, irritants, co-operation and friendship. In this framework, there has been simultaneity of divergence and convergence of views and perceived common interests between the two countries. India- Sri Lanka relations can be, thus, divided into four main phases[11] namely Decades of differences (1947-63), Resolving the disputes (1964-82), troubled years (1983-90) and Restoring friendship (since 1991). India has also evinced a greater interest in the welfare of the PIOs in Sri Lanka as well. Unlike other countries, India's close involvement in the affairs of Sri Lanka was perceived to be warranted in many cases due to political turmoil, the citizenship issue of PIOs, and Sri Lanka's external policies. The issue of citizenship was on the agenda until it was fully resolved in the year 1988 with then President Ranasinghe Premadasa accepting to grant citizenship to all Indian origins. Despite the intricacies and political problems that dominated and had an impact on

Sri Lanka's growth, the PIOs contribution to the Island nation's tea economy, trading and investment and promoting political stability and peace was high.

Economic Contribution

Tea Industry in Sri Lanka

Sri Lanka's dominant foreign exchange earner for decades was the tea crop. Sri Lankan Tea has a special place in the world tea markets and Colombo is the largest tea auction in the world. Sri Lanka is the world's fourth largest producer of tea and the industry is one of the country's main sources of foreign exchange and a significant source of income for labourers, with tea accounting for 15 per cent of the GDP[12], generating roughly $700 million annually. Sri Lanka was the world's leading exporter of tea (rather than producer) with 23 per cent of the total world export in 1995 but has since been surpassed by Kenya. The tea sector employs, directly or indirectly over 1 million people in Sri Lanka and in 1995 directly employed 215,338 on tea plantations (central bank report). The central highlands of the country, low temperature climate throughout the year, annual rainfall and the level of humidity are more favourable geographical factors for production in high quality tea. The secret behind the success of the tea industry is the Indian immigrant labour.

The majority of the PIOs live on their earning from the plantation industry that covers tea and rubber. Tea contributed 6.8 per cent to the GDP, 51 per cent of export earnings and shared 37 per cent of the World Export in 1965[13]. The contribution from the PIOs was significantly higher. For several decades the Industry fetched the highest foreign revenue until mid 1980s when the garment industry with GSP Concessions from EU made its road to the higher foreign revenue. This also coincided with falling of tea prices in the world market, Iraq war in early 1990s and economic recessions. See table for details of tea production and exports since 1989.

Table 2 : Statistics of Tea Production (1989-2006)

Year	Production (million)	Exports (Rs billion)	Cost of Production	Auction price	FOB price (Rs/kg)
1989	207	204			66.91
1990	213	216		70.97	91.78
1991	241	212		58.27	84.12
1992	179	182	72.26	61.75	81.97
1993	232	218	75.81	69.27	91.16
1994	242	230	73.83	65.12	91.32
1995	246	241	79.14	72.21	102.31
*1996	258	244	100.71	134.35	139.56
2000	305	531	110.64	135.53	184.73
2003	303	659	135.58	149.05	221.01
2004	308	748	158.25	180.74	249.38
2005	317	814	168.85	185.84	263.81
2006	310	916	188.4	198.87	279.97
2008	304	1,135	237.1	279.01	364.28

Importance of PIO Women in the Tea Plantation

The PIOs involve in the tea industry from an early stage. A woman will be registered for regular work at the age of 16. It is a general practice that a woman/ girl, dropped out of school, starts working along with her mother who is a serving worker. The registration is automatically done by presenting herself to the Field Officer with the approval of the Assistant Superintendent (in local term *Sinna Durai*). From the age of 16 she works till her 60 in the tea field plucking tea. Tea plucking becomes part and parcel of her life. Within a short span of time her skills of tea plucking becomes evident with the quantity of the harvest and the quality. The practice makes perfection. At an average, a women makes a harvest of anywhere between 20-25 kgs depending upon the season. The estate management after deliberations with the Trade unions fixed a minimum quantity of harvest and this was 18 kgs (Collective Agreement 2002). A woman worker, at an average, works for 280 to 300 days in the tea fields. Going by this, a woman's average contribution to the estate would be Rs 1,674,000 (2008 figure of Auction price per Kg X18X300). Though this is a crude and not an accurate estimate in terms of real figures, it is shown here to get the value of an average woman who works throughout the year in a tea estate. When it comes to the FOB price, this figure goes further up. The output of the tea is not only dependent on the contribution of a tea plucker, it involves preparation of tea fields, planting, pruning, and then manufacturing process in the factory. All these are done by the PIOs or termed as estate laborers. The management lay of the plantation is with the planters who are generally ethnic Sinhalese. This paper does not describe the skills of PIOs in the tea plantation that helps in increasing productivity and the returns the management receives from the tea industry. However, it is just an attempt to highlight the contribution of the PIOs to the tea industry that is 3rd largest foreign exchange earner in the country.

Business Outside the Tea Plantations

It is also significant to note that the country's largest labor force still lies with the tea industry. This is one of the highest sources of employment in the country. There has been increase in the population of the PIOs, which continue to have an impact on the resource base and employment availability in the tea sector. As in the other countries where PIOs are present, in Sri Lanka too there has been heavy inclination of the PIOs to get their children educated. Education was at high priority for all the PIOs. The political leadership too gave importance to this. It is also triggered by the fact that the tea plantation areas remain largely depended upon the tea economy and the land available for other production opportunities remain scarce and capital investment for furthering in to other economic production has not been forthcoming. The development programmes were not focussed to improve the opportunities for economic production and market expansion of other production related industries in the tea plantation areas that would give the youth a wide range of choices for their employment. Though there is vast potential for development of other industries given the natural resource base, the investment by successive governments and private sector has not been forthcoming. Therefore, formal education was of high priority and Education has been one of the central focuses by the political leadership in the tea plantation areas in the past decades. The sizable donor capital by Swedish government in the area has had positive impacts on the primary and secondary level education. Though this did not meet the emerging job market, there was outward migration of youth from the Tea plantation areas to urban cities in search of better employment opportunities. This outward migration commenced as early as mid 1960s. There were by this time number of commercial establishments in Colombo and other urban areas owned and run by PIOs. Finding jobs in these areas was easy and the number of those who came in search of such opportunities increased every year. The earnings of these youth outside the plantation system have increased, increasing desire of others of their age to come out of the plantation system. The contribution of the youth to the urban economy too increased.

PIOs were of no Big Burden to the State

The plantation system, which was highest in terms of source of employment, the employees, however, was no big burden for the Sri Lankan state. The plantation workers were taken care by the system itself. From the British planters to the local planters employed by the government after 1972 to 1993. In 1993, the plantations were privatised under 22 Regional Plantation Companies. The welfare and social development yet was with the private companies and supported by the bilateral donor countries. There were no state run health centres, schools until the workers were empowered with voting. This indicated the reduced expenditure for the state to maintain the large workforce. Further, the workers were not keen in remitting the earnings back to their country of origin, though the geographical proximity encouraged doing so. Only the supervisory category and businessmen transferred a portion of their earnings to the mother country. This became impossible by legal means after closing the economy. Though the economy was liberalised in 1978, remitting of earnings back to India was almost impossible. Therefore, the earnings and savings, whatever, were reinvested in the country itself. Those managed to save, expanded their wealth by purchasing assets in and around the plantations establishing business and trading. This further provided for expansion of the economy in the areas of plantations. It also led to employment opportunities in and around plantations.

The PIO youth found a special place for their honesty and hard work in cities and across all communities. The less dependency to some extent solved the unemployment problems in the tea estates but also created less availability of labour in some other estates constraining the tea production itself. Today there is a dilemma in some major tea plantations for labour to work in the tea plantations. The technical skills of tea plucking, which transcends to generations with a female PIO are not matched by any other community even with proper training. Such technical skills are now being recognised giving due dignity to the PIOs who have worked for the betterment of the tea plantation for generation. Special programmes are under way to transform the tea industry into a modern workforce with social recognition and dignity so that the industry sustains with improvement in the life of PIOs as well. Though this is the case in some selected Tea Plantations, large number of plantation companies is yet to come up with such programmes.

PIOs in Other Sectors

PIOs have been dominating the consumer markets in urban areas like Colombo and Kandy. They are ethnically Tamils and Muslims who have migrated from India from time to time during and immediate period after British rule. They have been involved in petty trade to large scale wholesale business establishments in consumer goods, food items and hardware markets. The PIOs play a key and dominant role in the Colombo markets on food items like rice, pulses, sugar and other food items.

There are major industries owned and run by PIOs in Colombo with very large investment and labour force. These industries not only provide for the GDP but also employment to all ethnic communities in the country. Some of the key establishments are Eswaran Brothers, Carsons Pvt Ltd, St. Anhtony's, Print Care, Express News Papers Pvt Ltd. These companies have increased since independence. In the recent times investment from India has also flown into various sectors that include, transport, energy, petroleum, and consumer perishables and durable goods. The dominance of Indian industries and market goods has increased many folds. Though the investors cannot be classified as PIOs, the local PIO communities' network has helped greatly to bring in such investments and establish business opportunities in the Island nation.

The PIOs have formed into a Council which is a global network and known as Global Organisation for Indian Origins. Networking and enhancing the capacities of the PIOs for economic growth as well as facilitating and helping PIOs across the world in investment is the main goal of this organisation. It has been functioning since 2000.

Politics of PIOs and their Contribution

During post independent era, the PIOs were subjected to several discussions with India. The subject surrounded; the sending back of the PIOs to India. The government and the Sinhalese perceived PIOs as a great threat in employment opportunities for Sri Lankans and also a burden for social and economic growth. In the year 1939, 6400 PIO workers in the harbour were dismissed over night. This created a controversy and prominent PIOs took the issue with India. Pundit Jawaharlal Nehru made visits to Sri Lanka on the advice of Mahatma Gandhiji. Several rounds of discussions paved way for bilateral agreements. From then onward the issue of PIOs sustained in the bilateral discussions of India and Sri Lanka. More prominent among them was the Srima-Shastry (1964) Agreement, which was implemented partially. This agreement stated that 300,000 PIOs and their natural increase will be given citizenship and another 510,000 and their natural increase will be repatriated to India. The agreement was discontinued with problems in repatriation due to discontinuation of ferry services in the year 1983 due to escalation of the ethnic conflict.

The politics of PIOs surrounded over the issue of repatriation and citizenship. The PIOs have since been playing a key role in the politics of Sri Lanka even before independence. Trade Unions form an integral part of the life of PIOs in the plantation sector. One of the significant contributions towards trade union action in association with others was initiated by a prominent Indian journalist called Natesa Aiyer. A south Indian Brahmin himself was from Tanjore who worked as a Journalist and later turned trade unionist. His first association was with the labourers working in the harbour. Natesa Aiyer later initiated the trade unionism in the plantations for the first time in the year 1931(Jayawardane, 1986, Thondaman, 1986 and Nadesan, 1993). The trade union was called All Ceylon Estate Labour Federation.

The PIOs, however, faced the disenfranchisement after the independence in 1948. The main reason behind this move was the presence of large number of PIOs in the central Kandyan constituency and that the perceived fear that non Indians will be defeated and lose the chance of being represented in the parliament. The struggle for citizenship ran into several decades. The veteran trade unionist and founder of Ceylon Workers Congress (CWC) Sawmiyamoorthy Thondaman was mainly instrumental in getting the citizenship rights to the PIOs.

During the later part of the 1980s after fully winning the franchise the PIOs became an important section in the politics of Sri Lanka. The electoral politics put PIOs in the central focus making them 'king makers'. During this period several attempts were on the way to find a lasting solution to the national question. All the Tamil parties formed a greater alliance in mid 1970s in which the PIO Tamil community was invited to have the co- chairmanship. The PIOs showed their solidarity with rest of the Tamils in the north and east and joined the movement. The Tamil alliance proposed a four point charter in which the fourth one was the universal franchise to all PIOs. However, when the Alliance proposed a secession formula, the PIO leadership opted out proving the importance of sovereignty and united Sri Lanka. This was the first solidarity towards the country of residence's national interest and safeguarding the sovereignty. It was always a consistent policy of the PIOs that Sri Lanka remains an undivided country at the same time recognising the aspirations of the Tamils of north and east. This strong commitment for safeguarding the sovereignty of the country was recognised by the leaders of the country.

Emerging as a strong block in late 1980s and until early 2000, PIOs in politics played a key role in electing the party to form the government. There were policy level changes in the politics of the PIOs in order to suite the day. However, the peace and stability was of primary concern and this was recognised well by the leadership of other political parties. Therefore, it will be prudent to say that PIOs played an important role in peace and harmony in the country at a time of turmoil, which had a secessionist movement fighting for a separate state over 3 decades.

It should be mentioned here that PIOs have shown great restraint when it comes to responding to violence against them. Since 1958 with commencement of Sinhala only policy, the total minority population was affected. The rebellion action by the Tamils of north and east origin led to backlashes in other areas. PIOs from the time of their arrival have been living within the majority community dominated areas. Therefore, whenever the war got hastened the political tension in the other parts of the country including where PIOs were living in majority, were affected. Search operations and detaining the PIO youth were common during later part of

1998 and early 2000 and also after 2004. The tension that developed within areas and the violence against the PIOs took place from time to time. There have been attempts by the separatist's movements to capitalise on such violence to spread their ideology. However, with great restrains, PIOs have managed to avoid such actions. The political leadership of Sawmiyamoorthy Thondaman and later Arumugam Thondaman have been successful in preventing such catastrophe happening in the tea plantation areas.

Sri Lanka, in an attempt to find the solution to the ethnic conflict, made amendments to the constitution, which was the 13th amendment. India played a decisive role in making the 13th amendment. The 13th amendment saw the establishment of the Provincial Council Administration in 8 Provinces in Sri Lanka. The PIOs gave their fullest political support to the 13th amendment. India had maintained that any attempt to fully resolve the national question shall be on the basis of the 13th amendment and or the devolution of power shall be not less than that was accorded under the 13th amendment. With the formation of the Provincial Administration, the importance of PIOs was seen in at-least two major provinces namely the Central and Uva. The Central Province consists of at least more than 40 per cent of the PIOs. The political parties of the PIOs became important constituents in the formation of government in these provinces and contributed to meaningful administration in the two provinces.

At the national level, the PIOs have been represented in parliament since independence. More prominent amongst them were leader of the Ceylon Workers Congress (CWC) Sawmiyamoorthy Thondaman. The PIOs have been in the cabinet and held important portfolios. After 1977, in almost all governments, PIOs were recognised to hold important portfolios. One significant portfolio held by Thondaman lead to massive development in the livestock industry and dairy farming.

In the present government, there are 9 PIO parliamentarians with leader of CWC[14] Arumugam

Thondaman and leader of UWF[15]. P. Chandrasekaran holding cabinet rank and 7 others as junior ministers. Some important portfolios among them were Education, Law, Constitutional affairs (all junior ministries). It can be observed that some key Ministries are held by PIOs and that this contributes to the national development of the country.

During the time of the peace process facilitated by the Norwegian government, several rounds of consultations were held by different organisations. PIOs also organised several workshops and technical seminars on conflict and peace building and provided useful inputs to the national process of the All Party Representative Committee, in conflict resolution through its agencies and civil society organisations. The All Party Representative Committee (APRC) was represented by the PIOs at the political level. The technical and political committee discussions included the administrative and political problems of the PIOs, which were duly highlighted by the trade unions and also civil society organisations of PIOs. Therefore, participation of PIOs was seen important and useful in all national level attempts to solve the ethnic problem. The involvement of the PIOs was widely accepted as positive for a sustainable long lasting solution. In the present day with the actual war coming to an end and a new dimension to the national question emerging, active participation of the PIOs is envisaged by both the government political parties and the opposition. This gives the importance of the PIOs in national politics of the country.

Conclusion

PIOs in Sri Lanka have been playing a significant role in the country's economic growth and political stability. The majority of the PIOs are ethnic Tamils migrated from South India during and after 1830s. They have settled and are productive labour force for Tea and rubber plantations for decades. Tea has been the country's highest foreign exchange earner until late 1980s. At present it is the third largest foreign exchange earner next only to foreign employment and garment industries. The economic contribution by the tea plantations have been studied widely though exclusive contributions made by the PIOs have been little documented and highlighted. Besides the plantation system, PIOs are conspicuous in the other industries that provide significant contribution to the national gross domestic product and provide employment to all communities in the country. The contribution by PIOs outside the plantation system has not been calculated and their economic value is less measured. There is a great need for such documentation, which can be taken up by research agencies or interested academic institutions.

PIOs have played a key role in national and regional politics in Sri Lanka. They have contributed for stable governments when at times the governments in power were at crisis. During difficult periods when the governments have faced turmoil and instability, the political parties of the PIOs have come forward to support governments, which helped greatly for maintaining law and order as well as political stability. Unlike other countries where large numbers of PIOs have settled, the situation in Sri Lanka is complex due to the presence of Sri Lankan Tamils who have a longer history in the Island nation speaking the same language. The Sri Lankan Tamils were fighting for their political rights and a section of youth engaged in a sustained war against the Sri Lankan state. These complexities have however had negative impact of the PIOs. One major negative is the increasing loss of identity and also for a long period suffered the backlash of the ethnic conflict. Even with these constraints the PIOs have shown great restraint and helped safeguard country's sovereignty, peace and stability of the country.

It is important that serious attempts are made to make a full appraisal of the PIO contribution taking all sectors of their involvement. It also will help to assess the strengths of the Indian Diaspora in the Island nation that could be helpful for expanding of the Indian interest be it economic or politics in Sri Lanka.

Endnotes

1. Nadesan. S. 1993. *History of Up Country Tamil People in Sri Lanka,* Hatton: Nandalala Publications.
2. Sabaratnam. T. 1990. *Out of Bondage- An autobiography of Thondaman,* Colombo: Ceylon Workers Congress.
3. Coolies is a term used by the English planters to refer the Indian labourers.
4. Sinnathanmby. M & Vijesundaram. S. 2004. 'Economic Dimensions for Non- Territorial Communities' in Devaraj. P. eds. *Rights & Power sharing Mechanism for Non Territorial Minority Communities in Sri Lanka,* Colombo: Friedrich Ebert Stiftung.
5. Sabaratnam. T. 1990. *Out of Bondage- An Autobiography of Thondaman,* Colombo: Ceylon Workers Congress.
6. Government Census 2001. Dept of Census and Statistics
7. *Ibid.*
8. *Ibid.* Excluding the population of north and east
9. Sinnathanmby. M and Vijesundaram. S. 2004. 'Economic Dimensions for Non- Territorial Communities' in Devaraj. P. eds. *Rights & Power sharing Mechanism for Non Territorial Minority Communities in Sri Lanka,* Colombo: Friedrich Ebert Stiftung.
10. Vellupillai Prabhakaran was a leader of the Liberation Tigers of Tamil Ealam who fought for a separate state for Tamil in the north and east of Sri Lanka since 1970s. He was defeated by the present government and killed in May 2009.
11. Sahadevan. P. 1995. *India and Overseas Indians, the Case of Sri Lanka,* Delhi: Kalinga Publications.
12. Central Bank, *Annual Report*.
13. Chandrabose.2009. *Wage, Employment and Livelihood of the Plantation Workers: A Study on Selected Tea Estates in Sri Lanka'*, sponsored by ADB/DEMP of OUSL 2009 (unpublished).
14. Ceylon Workers Congress (CWC) is the largest and one of the oldest Trade Union in the Plantations. CWC involved in mainstream politics of the country since 1977.
15. Upcountry Workers Front (UWF) was formed by P

Chandrasekar in the year 1987 as a break away group from CWC. It was formed with overwhelming support by youth at that time as an alternative to the main CWC.

14

Indian Diaspora's Contribution to Malaysia

Pankaj Jha

Introduction

The participation of Malaysian Indian Diaspora during most of the Pravasi Bharatiya Divas functions held in January every year during all these years have shown that Indian Diaspora has been thriving and prospering in its adopted country. The diaspora is willing to reinvigorate ties with its home country and help in forging better relations with its adopted country. In fact, the Indian Diaspora delegation from Malaysia has been one of the largest in all these years. Though there have been demands for more facilities and opportunities for the ethnic minorities like Indians in Malaysia but in the overall analysis the situation of the Indian diaspora is comparatively better than a number of countries in Southeast Asia. The active political participation of the Indian Diaspora in the 12th general elections in Malaysia in March 2008 has depicted a different picture and the possibility of emergence of two party system is foreseen in the future. Studies were undertaken to fathom the status of the Indian Diaspora in Malaysia as well as a number of policy briefs and policy documents were published to showcase the role of Malaysian Indians in Malaysia. With a number of studies including that of Edmund Terence Gomez[1], Harold Crouch[2], V Suryanarayan[3], Tridib Chakraborty[4], Lim Hong Hai[5], T G

Ramamurthy[6] etc. have shown that the equity participation of Malaysian Indians is being low at 3 per cent of the national income, shows that Indians have yet to achieve their true potential in Malaysian economic growth. There are a number of success stories also like Ananda Krishnan (one of the richest Malaysian Indian), Tony Fernandes, CEO of Air Asia etc. and in comparison, the proportion of those successful Diaspora in Malaysia is better than majority of Malays. The inter play between majority ethnic community and minority have an inherent element of consociational bargaining and compromise also.

Indians constitute more than seven percent of the population with Tamilians in the lead followed by Telugu, Malayalam and Punjabi speaking people. Indian comprises only 7.7 per cent of the total Malaysian population or 1,680,132 (Malaysian Census, 2001). Other sources estimated that about there are 40,000 (including 3000 professionals) NRI and PIO community is about 2 million. The close correspondence between the ethnic and occupational divisions of the Indian community was inevitably reflected in the community's geographical distribution in Malaya. The South Indian Tamils are concentrated mainly in Perak, Selangor, and Negeri Sembilan, on the rubber estates and railways, though a significant proportion found employment on the docks in Penang. The Telegus were mainly on the rubber estates of Lower Perak and parts of Selangor, while the Malayalees were located predominantly in Lower Perak, Kuala Lumpur, parts of Negeri Sembilan, and Johore Bahru. The business communities, the Gujratis, Sindhis, Chettiars, and South Indian Muslims, were concentrated in the urban areas, principally Kuala Lumpur, Penang, Ipoh, and Singapore. According to latest census, five States with a high density of Indians are Selangor (14.6 per cent - 585,368); Perak (13 per cent- 262,121); KL (11.4 per cent - 146,621); Penang (10.6 per cent - 133,899) & Negeri Sembilan (16 per cent -132,754). Indians are the second most urbanized community in Malaysia[7].

Table 1: Malaysian Population Growth-Ethnic Composition (Units in '000)

	2001	2002	2003	2004	2005	2006	2007	2008	2009
Population by Ethnic Group									
Malaysian Citizens	22,492	22,891	23,276	23,628	23,985	24,345	24,702	25,056	25,409
Bumiputera	14,656	14,956	15,248	15,517	15,791	16,071	16,350	16,630	16,912
Malay	12,038	12,285	12,525	12,746	12,972	13,203	13,434	13,667	13,902
Other Bumiputera	2,618	2,671	2,722	2,770	2,819	2,868	2,915	2,963	3,010
Chinese	5,837	5,907	5,974	6,034	6,093	6,150	6,204	6,256	6,305
Indian	1,723	1,748	1,773	1,794	1,816	1,838	1,859	1,880	1,901
Others	277	279	281	283	285	287	288	290	292
Non-Malaysian Citizens	1,460	1,688	1,967	2,109	2,462	2,523	2,530	2,826	2,664

Source: Malaysian Economy in Figures 2009 at http://www.epu.gov. my/c/document_library/get_file?p_l_id=29580&folderId=29570&name=DLFE-1612.pdf

If we take into account the population increase over the period of nine years from 2001 to 2009 (as shown in Table 1), the following trends are visible in terms of growth of ethnic population. While Malay population has grown by 15.48 per cent, Chinese population has grown by 8.01 per cent while Indians have registered a growth of 10.33 per cent from 2001 to 2009. Though in terms of population these trends might be minuscule but Indian population have been growing much faster than the Chinese in Malaysia.

The struggle for social and economic space has led to configuration of bargaining between different ethnic groups. In most of the countries there is a tendency for the majority ethnic group to conceptualise the nation state in the image of its own culture, with minorities holding the function of 'essentialising' the majority. One of the aspects of majority nationalism is marginalising minorities through migration into minority areas. Another issue, fuelled by majority chauvinism, is projection of 'ethno nationalism'. In many cases ethno nationalism has resulted in secessionist movements and subsequently formation of separate nation state. But most ethnic minorities cannot reach the point of secession due to demographic composition. In the case of Malaysia ethno centric bargaining has started taking shape in Malaysian politics. One of the major causal reasons for this is state policies, which underpin relations between majorities and ethnic minorities. These state policies often hinder the assimilation of ethnic minorities into a nation state[8]. In one of the studies that was done to determine the origin and persistence of ethnic boundaries, it was suggested that the incorporation of ethnic populations and the organisation of inter-ethnic relations are generally related to factors affecting the competition for environmental resources: this appears to be the case in multi ethnic Malaysia[9].

In such a context, it is imperative to analyse the migration of Indian diaspora in Malaysia and what have been the contribution to Malaysian nation building during integration with the larger Malaysian society and political system. The paper would also address the issue of the contribution of the Indian diaspora in the socio-political milieu of its host country.

Historical Background

The British constructed the concept of Indian identity as a corollary to the articulation of a Malay /Malayan identity and Malayan aspirations. This was consistent with their 'divide and rule' policy; their treatment of immigrant workers as transients; and was manifested in the population census report's that identified, differentiated and classified the diverse groups on the basis of ethnicity and place of origin. Identity was also reinforced through the education system. While English was the medium of instruction in schools in urban areas (attended primarily by children from urban, middle class backgrounds), education for working class children was provided in the vernacular and at the primary school level. Thus, plantation workers were educated in Tamil medium schools only, which effectively ensured that they remained trapped in the plantation system without any avenue for upward educational and occupational mobility. This was despite the fact that by 1957 almost 65 per cent of the Indian population was locally born, a proportion that was bound to increase as immigration had surely ceased[10].

In the past Indian society in Malaya was divided along various lines. Linguistic and regional affiliations existed, but there were also religious divisions (e.g. Hindu, Muslim and Sikh) and the divisions caused by caste differences. Nevertheless, while the Indian population represented some of the pluralism of the subcontinent, the character of the migration process, with its emphasis on recruitment from South India, gave this population a degree of homogeneity and cohesion. Approximately 80 per cent of Indians were Tamil and about 10 per cent were Malayalam, Kannada or Telegu speaking people. Moreover about 70 per cent were Hindu, though the Hindu faith did not provide cohesion in the belief structure and cultural/religious practices. Furthermore, the majority of Indians were from the labouring class, employed either on the plantations or in the construction and maintenance of public works and government undertakings (e.g. the railways) in urban areas. This provided them with a sort of unity based on economic activity or employment. Linguistic, religious and economic identity thus played an important role in shaping political activity and the construction of common identity among the Indians in Malaya[11].

When the economic conditions improved, labourers realized that they are not getting their fair share of the new prosperity and they become better organized and more militant. Vernacular newspapers, cultural associations and social action organizations mushroomed among the different ethnic groups. Compared to the labour leadership, the political leadership of the Indian community was more ideologically oriented. The influence of political events on the Indian subcontinent and the communities' ascribed role in Malaya make it highly conscious of safeguarding its cultural identity. The political leadership originated in groups of professionals –lawyers, doctors and teachers and businessmen in the larger urban centres was predominantly north Indian. It established links with the regional middle class groups on the basis of Indian nationalist identity, forming the Malaysian Indian Congress (MIC) in 1946. Early leaders of the organisation included John A. Thivy, Budh Singh, K. Ramanathan and K.L. Devaser. At the initial stage, the national level leadership of the Indian community had little in common with the labour leadership and, consequently, there was little interaction between the two. The national leaders were also in a situation similar to plantation owners and being employers of Indian labour themselves, they were opposed to the radicalisation of Indian labour[12].

Two factors further weakened the influence of this group. The first was the conflict over the reorientation of loyalty to Malaya rather than India, and the second stemmed from the ethnic and linguistic differences between the northerners and the southerners. During the early years of the emergency, the MIC leadership became moribund. It revived gradually in the 1950s under V.T Sambanthan's direction, when a division between the two groups emerged that culminated in the removal of the former, and the supremacy of the latter group. The change in leadership coincided with the redefinition of Indian identity as 'South Indian'. This resulted in an increased use of Tamil, the popularisation of traditional cultural practices, and an increased emphasis on Hinduism in its popular South Indian forms. As the MIC began to cater for the larger South Indian community, its base was broadened and India became a point of cultural and spiritual contact rather than a political link. In 1954, the MIC was incorporated into political alliance with the other two ethnic parties in the country, UMNO and the Malaysian Chinese Association (MCA) ,which forged an alliance in 1952 to contest the 1955 Federal elections under the banner of the Alliance, a United front(Barisan Nasional)[13].The assimilation has provided a platform for ethnic Indians to project themselves in political sphere.

Placing Ethnic Indians in Malaysian Politics

In the current scenario with the changing socio economic structure both at international and national level, there is a need to redefine Diaspora. The new definition of Diaspora should take into account the current political environments and that encompasses all peoples who find themselves in diasporic situations. As borders have become porous and increasing numbers of people have moved into the Diaspora, ways of understanding the diasporic condition –includes questions of who is diasporic and the nature of the diasporic populations' relationship to the wider society – need to shift in order to take into account critical factors of globalization, new understandings of citizenship, the changed international environment, and the unique challenge of the national integration[14]. Malaysia has also been undergoing such a predicament with two of its ethnic minorities - Chinese and Indians. While Chinese have achieved necessary economic clout to safeguard their interests but Indians have been striving to get their due in the predominantly Malay dominated society.

Since its founding in 1963, the federation of Malaysia was established incorporating the British Territories of Sarawak, Sabah and Singapore. Malaysia political system has had to deal with the realities of forging a nation out of peninsular Malaysia, Chinese dominated Singapore, and Sabah and Sarawak on the island of Borneo. As in Indonesia, the majority of the Muslim population in Malaysia is very moderate and embracing of pluralism. The country is ruled by that national front, a coalition of three main parties (UMNO, the Malaysian Chinese Association, and the Malaysian Indian Congress) that represent the three major ethnic groups in the country: Malays, Chinese, and Indians. During the 1959 negotiations that the creation of Malaysia, the leaders of the three ethnic communities raised an understanding that in return for citizenship and full legal and economic rights for the Chinese and Indians, the Malays would dominate the civil service and political leadership. Ostensibly barred from the public sector the more urbanised ethnic Chinese community went on to dominate Malaysia's private sector, causing a widening socio economic gap among the ethnic communities. The growing economic disparities have been their cause of concern and so subsequently the New Economic Policy (NEP) was initiated in 1970s[15].

The new economic policy had two goals: to reduce and eradicate poverty regardless of race and to eliminate the identification of race with the economic function so that no ethnic group to be identified with the specific occupation. To achieve the first goal, the government concentrated on developing the countryside where majority of Malays lived. To achieve the second goal, the government adopted in radical affirmative action program so that jobs and higher education opportunities reflected the racial composition of the country. In addition to affirmative action, the replacement of the English with Malay as the official language and language of instruction by and 1982 greatly favoured Malays at the expense of the minority communities. Reservations were allowed in higher education and even in the share of corporate equity. To achieve this, the government discriminated against ethnic minorities and foreign owned firms[16].

Even after the expiration of NEP, the government unveiled its national development policy that contained most of the NEP's policies and goals, though without specific equity targets and timetables, which in effect renewed the NEP for an additional 10 years. Subsequently, in April 2001 the government released a new plan, the National Vision 2020 policy, which is committed to many of the NEP's original goals. Former Prime Minister Mahathir acknowledged that continued implementation of affirmative action, which was opposed to it has seized in 1990, had contributed to "crutch mentality", specifically among business people. Mahathir even acknowledged that his concerted attempt to develop a new breed of privately owned Malay conglomerates through selective patronage and much protection had failed miserably, and that the only way to promote entrepreneurship was to expose businessmen to competition. While the then prime Minister Abdullah Badawi has concurred with Mahathir, he has qualified his stand by arguing that affirmative action remains relevant because the income disparity between Malays and non Malays has persisted. Abdullah went on to argue that the reason Malaysians were unhappy with this policy was not because they opposed affirmative action, but that they were dissatisfied with its pattern of implementation[17]. During all these years MIC acted as a partner of the government and was able to get one cabinet minister post and two deputy ministers' posts in the cabinet but with the landslide victory of UMNO in 2004 elections and the infiltration of radical islamist tones in UMNO, the role of minority parties have been marginalised. Though MIC has been able to raise the issue of ethnic Indians but the results achieved in terms of employment, education and business opportunities was far from satisfactory. The elections in 2008 led to complete washout for MIC with even the legendary leaders like Sami Vellu losing their parliamentary seat. This clearly showed that ethnic Indians electorate have started to play a major role in Malaysian politics. The role played by ethnic Indians and their grievances were addressed by the current Prime Minster Najib Tun Razak who has been very forthcoming in terms of criticism of the New Economic Policy and has diluted the reserved equity percentage for the ethnic Malays in capital market. Also plans are anvil for the dilution of the New Economic Policy. Najib Tun Razak has instituted One Malaysia policy[18] for integrating all ethnic groups in Malaysian society and equal opportunities for all.

Usually it is not prudent to analyse one election results as the main point for an argument but in the case of Malaysia, the recent elections which are held in March 2008, is rather an interesting phenomena. The rise of opposition and the consolidation of both Malays and ethnic minority voters showed that the political dynamics dominated by BN is undergoing the erosion. Ethnic Indians were instrumental in bringing about a change in the religious and ethnic outlook of the country through demonstrations in November 2007 and the effects of the change are visible both in political stage as well as socio economic milieu. In the socio-economic context, in terms of income, ethnic Indians are slightly better off than Malays.

Indian Diaspora in Malaysia: A Socio-Economic Contribution

With the development in the urban centres and the shutting down of plantation areas, there has been a phased migration of Indian labourers from rural areas to urban centres. As is visible in Table 2, the migration accelerated after

1990s with better economic opportunities as well as the second generation becoming more conscious about education and employment opportunities.

Table 2: Distribution of Indians in Rural and Urban Areas of Peninsular Malaysia

Year	Urban Areas		Rural Areas		Total
	Number	Percentage	Number	Percentage	
1970	323,435	34.7%	609,194	65.3%	932,629
1980	448,397	41.0%	644,715	59.0%	1093112
1991	837,659	63.8%	475,929	36.2%	1313588
2000	1338510	79.7%	341,622	20.3%	1680132

Source: Ensuring Effective Targeting of Ethnic Minorities, The case of Low Income Malaysian Indians at http://www.cpps.org.my/resoruce_centre/low_Income_Malaysian_Indians.pdf (Accessed on 30 May 2008)

Table 3 : Income Distribution among Ethnic Minorities-Relative Income Trends

	1957/58	1967/68	1970	1984	1990	1995
All Groups**	199	217	264	1095	1167	2007
Malay	144(100)	130(100)	172(100)	852(100)	940(100)	1600(100)
Chinese	272(189)	321(247)	394(229)	1502(176)	1631(170)	2895(181)
Indians	217(151)	253(195)	304(175)	1094(128)	1209(128)	2153(135)

Note: Figures in parentheses indicate group incomes relative to Malay incomes. All other figures are in Ringgit.

** Includes minorities and non-citizens

Source: Prema-Chandra Athukorala and Jayant Menon, Export-led Industrialisation, Employment and Equity: The Malaysian Case, http://rspas.anu.edu.au/economics/publish/papers/wp1996/965.pdf

One of the major reasons for the migration of Indians to urban centres has been the income opportunities and as is visible in Table 3, the difference between high income ethnic community and low income communities like Indians and Malay becoming more apparent, the shift to urban centres was called for. Even though in terms of relative income the difference between Malay income and Indian income has become narrower, a reconfiguration of opportunities and reworking of growth options for all ethnic communities is most required arrangement.

As is visible in Table 3 in due course of time the differences between incomes of different ethnic groups have become narrower with Indians forming the second rung of society in terms of income. Even Chinese have seen a marginal drop in their income but compared to Malays and Indians they are still at the top of the income configuration. The reason could be the business acumen of the Chinese while this has been offset by the priority accorded to Malays through the New Economic Policy. But the disparities in income have waned away to a large extent. While addressing the Parliament in 2007, the then Prime Minster Abdullah Badawi stated that in 2007, the average household income of the *Bumiputera* rose by 5.2 per cent to RM3, 156 a month, whereas the average income of ethnic Chinese households rose by 3.0 per cent a year to RM4,853 while that of ethnic Indian households rose by 3.2 per cent to RM3,799[19] (see Table 4) .

Table 4 : Mean Income of Ethnic Groups in Malaysia (2004-2007)

Malaysia/Ethnic Group and Strata	Mean Income (in current Prices, RM)		Growth Rate (% p.a)
	2004	2007	
Bumiputera	2711	3156	5.2
Chinese	4437	453	3.0
Indian	3456	3799	3.2
Others	2312	3651	15.5
Malaysia	3249	3686	4.3
Urban	3956	4356	3.3
Rural	1875	2283	6.8

Source: Mid Term Review of the Ninth Malaysia Plan,2006-2010,p.58

If one takes into account the percentage of ethnic groups

in different income levels, the trends show that Indians still form the second rung of the income distribution but the marginal better off position has been consolidating and there is a gradual improvement in comparison to the Chinese population(as shown in Table 5).

Table 5 : Income Distribution among Ethnic Communities

Ethnic Group	Top	Middle	Bottom	Total
Bumiputera	1,995,500(13%)	5,986,500(39%)	7,368,000(48%)	15,350,000
Chinese	2,040,000(34%)	2,700,000(45%)	1,260,000(21%)	6,000,000
Indians	360,000(20%)	900,000(50%)	540,000(30%)	1,800,000
Total (Percentage of total population)	4,395,000(18.9%)	9,586,500(41.4%)	9,168,000(39.6%)	23,150,000

Source: http://www.cpps.org.my/resource_centre/low_Income_Malaysian_Indians.pdf. Accessed on 30 May 2008.

On the other extreme, another set of social indicators show that the community is in distress. Indians have the lowest life expectancy amongst all major races and they comprised the largest group of suicide victims recorded annually nationwide. There were 21.1 suicides per 100,000 Indians, 8.6 per 100,000 Chinese and 2.6 per 100,000 Malays[20]. Though they form only 7.5 per cent of the population, a higher proportion of Indians were arrested for serious crime or gang related activities. Of the 703 suspected criminals held at the Simpang Renggam Rehabilitation Centre in 2005 (as of March) under preventive detention laws, 377 or 54 per cent were Indians. Studies in developed countries have shown a link between crime and inequality and indicated that groups or gangs engaging in unlawful activities are more likely to form in situations where the chances of achieving success legitimately are small. In many countries it has been found that the crime rate has climbed steeply in an environment of greater affluence combined with growing inequality and a winner/loser culture. Statistics also indicate that the Indian community is to a certain extent falling behind the other communities[21] in terms of social engineering and better understanding.

More than 30 per cent of Indians do not own a house, compared to the national average of 25.2 per cent for Malays and 17.6 per cent for Chinese. Indians collectively own only 1.5 per cent of shares in limited companies; this figure has remained stagnant for years. Official poverty levels among Indians have remained at 1.9 per cent from 1999 to 2002, while it has decreased from 10.2 per cent to 7.3 for *Bumiputera* and from 2.6 per cent to 1.5 per cent for the Chinese.[22] But the initiatives that have been taken by the Najib government are likely to erase these social disparities. Even in terms of employment ethnic Indian diaspora is getting more attracted to technical and professional occupation rather than looking for government jobs.

Employment

The strength of ethnic minorities namely that of Chinese and Indians in the government has been dismally low and this has been due to the preference given to Malays in government jobs because of the NEP and also the utility of Malay language in working of government. With regard to awareness about the Malay language there is rather disinterest among the ethnic Indians as they still have Tamil as the major indicator for socio-political interactions. The ethnic identity has never diluted in the minds of the ethnic Indians. Even if we analyse the trends and the representation of the ethnic groups in government then one can see Malays despite having the population of barely 60 per cent of total population comprises of about 77 per cent of Malaysian bureaucracy while Chinese and Indians comprise about 9 per cent and 5 per cent (see Table 6). The percentage of Chinese is less due to the preponderance of interest towards business but Indians have a reducing strength in the Malaysian bureaucracy. This shows that Indians have become more attracted towards professional occupations more so which are in the field of medicine and law.

Table 6 : Representation by Race in the Malaysian Bureaucracy: 2005

Ethnic group	Top Mgmt. group		Mgmt. and Professional Group		Support group		Total	
	No.	Percent	No.	Percent	No.	Percent	No.	Percent
Malay	1370	83.95	155, 871	81.65	535, 495	75.77	692, 736	77.03
Chinese	151	9.25	17, 896	9.37	66, 248	9.37	84, 295	9.37
Indian	83	5.08	9777	5.12	36, 194	5.12	46, 054	5.12
Other Bumiputera	23	1.41	6156	3.22	63, 649	9.01	69, 828	7.77
Others	5	0.31	1203	0.63	5129	0.73	6337	0.70
Total	1632	100	190, 903	100	706, 715	100	899, 250	100

Source: Hong Hai Lim, Improving Administrative Performance in Malaysia: the more difficult next steps in reform, p.42. at http://*www.policyandsociety.org/archive/vol26no2/vol26_no2_**lim**.pdf* . Also see Oriental Daily News, December 8, 2005. This data does not include the personnel in police and armed forces.

A highly unrepresentative bureaucracy, therefore, has serious implications for equity in administration and consequently for trust in the bureaucracy, government legitimacy and national unity (i.e., race relations) in the country. After reports of blatant bias by Malay police in handling an outbreak of interracial violence in 2001(i.e., in Kampung Medan), then Prime Minister Mahathir has reportedly acknowledged the need for a "sufficiently representative" bureaucracy for promoting national unity:

> The government wants an increase in non Bumiputera representation in the civil service to promote national unity. The then Prime minister Datuk Seri Dr. Mahathir Mohamad said that there was a need to ensure all races were sufficiently represented in all levels in the service. "We are a bit worried that there are not too many non Malays-that is Chinese and Indians-in the government service."...... Fair representation of the races should not only be restricted to government service. It should be reflected in the private sector as well. The present high level of Malay preference and overrepresentation in the bureaucracy needs to be reduced, but some degree of

Malay preference and overrepresentation is still needed in the interest of overall interracial equity[23].

The similar arrangement should also be tried out in private sector.Though various plan documents have recognized the need to make the civil service more representative of the population, it is still made up predominantly of members from one ethnic group. In fact, there has been a drastic drop in the number of non-Malay civil servants in the last two decades as the older batches retire. While Chinese accounted for 29.7 per cent and Indians 9.8 per cent of civil servants in the 1980s, their numbers fell to 8.2 per cent and 5.2 per cent respectively in 2003. A civil service that is not reflective of the population is likely to distort the implementation of government policies. Without adequate representation of all ethnic groups – especially in the key implementing agencies such as information, social welfare, women development, National Population and Family Planning Board, education, healthcare, youth and sports, and entrepreneur development – certain vulnerable sections of the non-*Bumiputera* population will have limited access to public goods and services[24]. In terms of occupation also even if we take the data pertaining got 2005 and 2007(as shown in Table 7), it shows that Indians have been predominantly been doctors and lawyers in the Malaysian society while a sizeable percentage are also dentists and veterinary surgeons.

Table 7 : Employment Pattern of Ethnic Communities in Malaysia

Profession	2005(%)			2007(%)		
	Bumiputera	Chinese	Indian	Bumiputera	Chinese	Indian
Accountant	21.5	73.0	4.9	23.5	71.4	4.9
Architect	45.3	53.1	1.4	46.2	52.1	1.5
Doctor	38.1	31.2	27.4	43.8	28.2	20.2
Dentist	44.4	35.3	18.4	46.5	34.5	16.9
Engineer	46.0	47.6	5.4	46.2	46.0	5.3
Lawyer	38.0	37.1	24.1	39.0	36.5	23.5
Surveyor	48.2	47.0	3.2	50.5	44.7	3.2
Veterinary Surgeon	39.0	32.2	24.8	43.3	34.1	22.5

Source: Mid Term Review of the Ninth Malaysia Plan, 2006-2010, p.60

So Indians have been dominating the technical and professional field in Malaysia and have been contributing substantially to the well-being of the Malaysian society. This also depends on the role of education among the ethnic Indians living in Malaysia.

Education

Under the Eighth Malaysian Plan 2001-5, RM 6.6 billion has been allocated for primary education. Equality, democracy and justice requires Chinese and Tamil primary schools to respectively receive RM 1.4 billion and RM 240 million under the 2000-5 Eighth Malaysian Plan based on the number of pupils enrolled, which is estimated at 21 per cent and 3.6 per cent respectively for Chinese and Tamil primary schools. An equitable distribution of the allocation would mean the national primary schools would get RM 5 billion or 75 per cent, Chinese primary schools RM 1.4 billion or 21 per cent and Tamil primary schools RM 240 million or 3.6 per cent. The government has acknowledged the role and contribution made by mother-tongue as shown by the policies in the development allocation for fully and partially aided in 1,287 Chinese and 576 Tamil primary schools. Despite the crying need for new Chinese primary schools, the government has refused to build them in urban areas or provide much needed funding for existing ones. There are some 60,000 non-Chinese students in the Chinese primary schools in the country, which should have meant the building of some 60 new Chinese primary schools just to cater to this demand - but Chinese primary school enrolment have doubled from 310,000 students in 1957 to over 620,000 students in 2,000, yet the number of Chinese primary schools in the past 43 years has seen a decline of 49 schools.

Under the Seventh Malaysia Plan 1995-2000, national primary schools with 75 per cent of the total primary school enrolment received 96.5 per cent of the allocations, while Chinese primary schools with 21 per cent of the total primary school enrolment was allocated 2.4 per cent while Tamil primary schools with 3.6 per cent of the enrolment allocated one per cent of the total development funds for primary schools for the five-year period. Government is trying to allocate more funds for development of primary schools and allocation is likely to be made on the basis of enrolment, i.e. 75 per cent to national primary schools, 21 per cent to Chinese primary schools and 3.6 per cent to Tamil primary schools[25]. Even with regard to tertiary education the registration of the Indian students in tertiary education has been increasing in all these years. In fact, many of them have emigrated to Australia and US for better quality education and a number of them have been getting education in educational institutions in southern parts of India.

Cultural Participation of Indians in Malaysian Society

Even though there are many ethnic groups of Indians using various mother tongues (such as Telugu, Malayalam, Hindi etc.) but the majority of Indians are Tamils and therefore Tamil Language is widely used among the Indians in Malaysia. Each sub-ethnic group among Indians practices various ways to nurture, preserve and maintain their cultural heritage through their mother tongue. Among the practices are to speak one's mother tongue to communicate among family and friends, practicing rituals and ceremonies in their own language, use of own language for printed materials and records, forming organizations, society and clubs to conduct activities, cultural events and to preserve identity[26]. Tamil News Channel and Newspapers have helped in preserving the cultural affiliations of the Indian Diaspora. More or less the cultural umbilical cord of the ethnic Malaysian has contributed to diversifying the cultural depth and diversity of the Malaysian society. The Tamil films are immensely popular in Malaysia. Also, festivals like Deepawali are public holidays while Thaipusam festival has been the calendar event for the Malaysia tourism. Also, Tamil has been recognised as an official language of Malaysia. There are a number of cultural organisations in Malaysia, which profess different cultures and have been hosting cultural programmes under their aegis. The Sikhs in Malaysia celebrate birthdays and martyrdom days of Sikh Gurus as well as Baisakhi and Lohri.

Conclusion

In the overall perspective, ethnic Indians in Malaysia are not that deprived community but as compared to the other ethnic communities, the economic opportunities are slightly less. However, the options for ascending the economic ladder are emerging. Though there have been irritants like deprivation in terms of religious rights but proactive role of Indian Diaspora in Malaysia has improved situation for the ethnic community. This applies not only to the ethnic Indians but also to ethnic Chinese. Few blogs have stated that Malaysian Indians comprise the most affluent families in certain pockets and also a sizeable number of Indian Diaspora is doctors and lawyers and a large number of doctors are veterinary specialists. Indians have contributed largely to the socio-economic development of Malaysia and it should not be taken as the contribution in national income only. In fact Indian diaspora has facilitated better relations between Malaysia and India. The Indians have contributed to making a diversified Malaysia more harmonious and tolerant. In fact, the rising standards of living of Malaysian Indians as well as empowerment of ethnic community have given a new dimension to growth and prosperity for the country. Indian diaspora is gaining ground but it needs a lot more to reach its true potential.

Endnotes

1. Gomez, Edmund Terence. 2007. *Politics in Malaysia: The Malay Dimension,* London: Routledge.
2. Crouch , Harold. 1996. *Government and Society in Malaysia,* Ithaca, NY: Cornell University Press.
3. Suryanarayan, V. 2008. 'Malaysian Indian Society in Ferment', Paper no. 2880, 14 Oct. http://www.southasiaanalysis.org / papers29paper2880.html. Accessed on 23 December 2009.
4. Chakraborty, Tridib. 2009. 'Ethnic unrest in South East Asia : Role of Religions', International Conference on Interface between East and West: Multiculturalism and Identity: What Can Sociology and Religious Studies Contribute to the Making

of a Better Society, Department of Sociology, Jadavpur University (JU), Kolkata & Department of Literature, History of Ideas and Religion (LIR),University of Gothenburg, Sweden in collaboration with NSS, JU and IFSSR, Kolkata on June 10 - 12, 2009.

5. Hai, Lim Hong. 2002. ' Electoral Politics in Malaysia:'Managing' Elections in a Plural Society' in Aurel Croissant . eds. *Electoral politics in Southeast & East Asia*, Singapore: Friedrich-Ebert-Stiftung, Office for Regional Co-operation in Southeast Asia.
6. Ramamurthy, T. G. 1989. 'Ethnic Indians in Malaysia', *Economic and Political Weekly*, vol. 24, no.39. Sep. 30. pp. 2192-2194.
7. Country Brief Malaysia, http://www.moia.gov.in/pdf/Malaysia.pdf. Accessed on 11 Jan. 2010.
8. Mackeras, Colin. 2003. eds. *Ethnicity in Asia*, Curzon: Routledge, pp.2-13.
9. *Ibid*, pp.12-13.
10. Lal, Brij V. et al. 2006. *The Encyclopedia of the Indian Diaspora*, London: Oxford University Press, p.166.
11. *Ibid*. p.163.
12. *Ibid*. p.165.
13. *Ibid*.
14. McGown, Rima Berns. 2007-08. 'Redefining 'diaspora':The Challenge of connection and inclusion', *International Journal*, p.3.
15. New Economic Policy (NEP), which was adopted in 1970, was meant to favour Malay Muslims in terms of economic opportunities, employment, share in corporate equity, reservation in schools and colleges as well as professional institutions. See, Abuza, Zachary. 2003. *Militant Islam in Southeast Asia: Crucible of Terror*, Boulder, London: Lynee Rienner Publishers, pp. 49-50. Also see, Beng, Ooi Kee. 2006. *Era of Transition: Malaysia after Mahathir*, Singapore: Institute of Southeast Asian Studies (ISEAS), p.53.For more details see, Barlow Colin and Francis Loh Kok Wah. eds. 2003. *Malaysian Economics and Politics in the New Century*, Cheltenham, UK: Edward Elgar.
16. Abuza, Zachary *Op.Cit.*, p.50.

17. Gomez, Edmund Terence. *Op.Cit.*, p.4.

18. One Malaysia is an on-going campaign announced by Prime Minister Najib Razak on September 16, 2008, calling for the cabinet, government agencies, and civil servants to more strongly emphasize ethnic harmony, national unity, and efficient governance. The eight values of One Malaysia as articulated by Najib Razak are perseverance, a culture of excellence, acceptance, loyalty, education, humility, integrity, and meritocracy.On September 17, 2008, Najib launched www.1Malaysia.com.my in an effort to communicate with the citizens of Malaysia more efficiently and support the broader 1Malaysia campaign, He has used the site to highlight his political and policy initiatives and to provide a forum for Malaysians to discuss government matters. One Malaysia is also making extensive use of social media tools such as Facebook and Twitter. While Najib claims One Malaysia is an effort to foster Malaysian unity, the One Malaysia concept has become subject to a broad range of interpretations and discussion, both by those in favor of and opposed to particular government policies, and involving different elements of Malaysia's major ethnic groups. Further details at http://en.wikipedia.org/wiki/Najib_Tun_Razak. Accessed on 12 Jan. 2010.

19. Speech by Abdullah Badawi while introducing the Motion to Table the Mid-Term Review Of The Ninth Malaysia Plan in the Dewan Rakyat Malaysia, 26 June 2008, p. 26 at http://www.epu.gov.my/html/themes/epu/html/mtr-rm9/MTR-RMK9-ucapan.pdf. Accessed on 11 Jan. 2010.

20. The Case of Low Income Malaysian Indians, Ensuring Effective Targeting Of Ethnic Minorities: The Case Of Low Income Malaysian Indians,Centre for Public Policy Studies at http://www.ewrf.org.my/pdf/ASLI_Report.pdf. Accessed on 26 Feb. 2009.

21. *Ibid.*

22. *Ibid.*

23. Hong Hai Lim, Improving Administrative Performance in Malaysia: the more difficult next steps in reform, p.42. at http://www.policyandsociety.org/archive/vol26no2/vol26_no2_lim.pdf. Accessed on 23 July 2008. Also see *New Straits Times*, May

20, 2001.

24. The Case of Low Income Malaysian Indians, Ensuring Effective Targeting Of Ethnic Minorities: The Case Of Low Income Malaysian Indians,Centre for Public Policy Studies at http://www.ewrf.org.my/pdf/ASLI_Report.pdf. Accessed 26 Feb. 2009.

25. Lim Guan Eng, DAP Secretary-General,Media Statement, 'Emergency motion-Poor Condition Of Chinese and Tamil Primary Schools and Need For Adequate Development Allocation' at http://www.dapmalaysia.org/all-archive/English/2005/Sept05/lge/lge195.htm. Accessed on 25 Oct. 2008.

26. Manimaran Subramanium, Nurturing of Languages is Nurturing Culture: Malaysian Indians, Paper Presented at the PIO Diaspora Language Conference on Nurturing PIO Languages for Unity held at Mauritius on November 20-25, 2006.

15

Indo-Fijians and their Success Story in Fiji

Amba Pandey

Introduction

Fiji, the paradise like island nation placed in the blue vast of the Pacific, is more than eleven thousand five hundred kilometers away from India. However, the 18th and 19th centuries saw massive scale of migration from the colonial India to Fiji under the slavery like system of Indenture. Even in the days when crossing the seas was considered a taboo and the people doing so were declared outcaste, the Indians dared to migrate to evade the tyrannical times and improve their socio-economic conditions. However, the new system did not actually give them respite from the hardship of life as the life in Fiji proved tougher. On paper, the terms of indenture appeared more than satisfactory but in practice, things turned out to be different. They still had to deal with the realities of low wages, discrimination and hard work. Nevertheless, during the 20th century the Indian population in Fiji drastically increased as Indians became settled citizens of Fiji. They contributed substantially to economic and material progress of Fiji and emerged as an important political force. There were around 60,000 Indians in Fiji when the Indenture system ended in 1920 and a majority of them decided to stay on. Over the years the Indian community diversified and grew and got settled on leased lands, working mainly in the sugar industry as growers and mill workers. By mid 1940s their population outnumbered the indigenous Fijians giving rise to the fear of the so-called Indian domination.[1] The journey of their progress was full of pain and frustrations but they remained loyal to their culture and religion modifying the socio-cultural and religious traditions of India to suit their needs and conditions.

Strategically located, economically developed and home to the most important regional institutions, Fiji, is the most important of the Pacific Island countries. Before the arrival of Indians, Fiji was a hierarchical tribal structure with a diverse political and social entity. The Fijian life from birth to death was controlled by customs, which formed the backbone of the religion, warfare and everyday life. A chief's power depended on his ability to hold his people together; he enjoyed absolute power and supreme authority in his own *Yayusa*.[2] There were regional differences as well, particularly between eastern and western regions. The Fijians were a martial people and the Fijian society was plagued by inter tribal hostilities and incessant warfare. The early missionaries who arrived in Fiji paint a picture of a tribally violent society.[3] However, it underwent a drastic transformation after the 'White Contact' particularly after becoming the British colony. In the words of Bhagwan Singh, "the introduction of Christianity to Fiji was a turning point in the history of the Fijians, it was a major force in changing the face of the Fijian society very substantially, it tempered down the violence prevalent in old Fiji making them adopt a more docile approach towards life. In more concrete terms Christianity played a pivotal role in bringing modern western education to the islands thereby preparing them for the modern world and forces of external civilization. With the advent of Christianity, for good or for bad Fiji would never be the same again."[4]

The vulnerability of the race ridden Fijian society led Indo Fijians to alternative means of livelihood and hard work for ensuring a better future for their children by focusing on their education. With hard work and education, came prosperity and Indians achieved dominance in commerce, trade and took over most of the white collared jobs. Their success story is a glorious saga in the history of Indian Diaspora. At the same time their success also aided and abetted Fiji in its development and emergence as a modern state. Be it the multiracial social setup or the experimental political and electoral arrangement or the economic accomplishments, in every aspect of Fiji and Fijian life, the contribution of Indo-Fijians cannot be overlooked if History is to be given a fair treatment. However, the ethnic Fijians not only refuse to acknowledge the contribution of the Indo-Fijians but also carry a kind resentment at the visible economic prosperity of the urban, educated, Indian professionals and businessmen, while they themselves are still rooted in the rural lifestyle and feel marginalized in terms of economic power. The colonial Native Policy locked Fijians into a rigid subsistence sector and marginalized them from mainstream commerce and education and by the time of independence Fijians were lagging far behind. This was a direct cause of grievances, which later found expressions in ethno-nationalist agitation and mobilization at the political, social and every other level. What has to be remembered is that in the case of Fiji the socio-economic, cultural, political and socio-psychological issues are so closely interlinked that it is difficult to see them separately. For example, Indians were taken to Fiji to contribute in the development. As the time passed they became prosperous and assertive. They realized that to protect their economic rights it was important to be politically strong. On their part Fijians, who were resentful and suspicious of the Indians and their economic prosperity resisted any type of political sharing and in this turmoil the boogey of land grab was used as a tool for political mobilisation.

Construction of the Indo-Fijian Identity

According to Steven Ratuva the construction of the Indo-Fijian identity is based on the view that, first, Indo-Fijian culture has rich primordial roots in the great Indus civilization as compared to the culture of the Fijians, and secondly, on the assumption that India "was" admittedly the "grandmother" but now Fiji is the "motherland".[5] When Indians decided to make Fiji their home, there arose a whole lot of issues to be addressed. It was not only about survival but also about their existence and identity. Migration, as we know is not a one-time event but an ongoing process. It involves not only leaving a homeland and crossing territorial borders but also continuously crossing social, psychic and symbolic borders that define identity, relations, membership, belonging and worldview of realities of everyday life.[6] In this process, sub-cultures are evolved with distinct identity of their own, drawing their roots form the parent culture or following the same cultural pattern. Likewise, Indo-Fijians too after going through varied social-economic experiences developed a distinct cultural identity. In the words of Adrian C. Mayer, "In some ways social conditions of the indenture period can be seen as 'breakdown' of those of the parent society. But after indenture the immigrants did not rebuilt their old society. Instead they were forced to build an entirely new one-the Fiji Indian-which was a response to conditions in Fiji, even though many of its ways were still Indian.[7] There was also a growing feeling among the Indo-Fijians to assert the uniqueness of their identity, which although originates basically from the mother country but is perhaps different.

As a matter of fact, the system of recruitment, the indentured system and the Indian settlement after that itself had brought many changes in the social structure of the Indians. The caste had ceased to be the backbone of the social structure. In the words of John Durham Kelly "perhaps the most important social change in Fiji Indian history was loss of caste".[8] However other kind of social institutions did develop. Several scholars like Mayer, Schwartz, Gillion etc. have emphasized on the development of non-caste relationship among the Indian workers in Fiji after the indenture period. Social relationships were formed on the basis of common experience residential propinquity and association at work. Different subgroups emerged which were loosely based on immigration history, geographic area of origin in India, and religion. Some of these sub communities were North Indians,

South Indian, Muslim community, the Punjabis and the Gujaratis. In the words of Brij V. Lal, "amidst all the disruption and dislocation new relationship were being formed, now more important then the bond of *Jahaji Bhai*, shipmates, a bond which rather time nor circumstance would be able to erase. It became the foundation of a new enduring and intimate familial relationship. The *Jahajis* treated each other like blood kin, with all the obligations and responsibilities that such relationship entailed".[9]

Meanwhile religion had become the center stage of Indian life. It played a very important role in preserving the Indian culture over seas. It was the primary strength for emotional and moral support and solidarity. From the very beginning Indians were determined to preserve their religion. The pride of Indians towards their culture and religion was so high that Christianity failed to impress the Indians completely. The organizational support of the Sanatan Dharma Sabha and Arya Samaj also helped Indians to reconstitute their ancestral faith and culture.[10] Sanatani Hinduism, Arya Samaj, and Islam were revived after the arrival of Pandit Totaram Sanadhya. The reformist was organized in 1902 at Sambula and began a school for its members. Since then it has taken lead in the Indian education in Fiji. Muslims built a mosque at Narua in around 1900 and other at Naursori soon afterwards. Mirza khan, a mullah who arrived in Fiji in 1898, played important role in the religious education of Muslim Indians.[11] By early years of 20th century formal Hindu organization such as Sanatan Dharma and the Arya Samaj were established, which started a more systematic way of organizing the socio-religious activities.[12] The responsibility of Indian education was mainly left to the socio-religious organizations like Arya Samaj and Sanatan Pratinidhi Sabha.

Another important issue towards identity formation among the Indo-Fijians was the Fiji Hindi. The language of Indo Fijians is one of the chief consequences of the Indian indenture system in Fiji. As we already know most of the Girmitiyas belonged to the backward regions of north India and spoke local dialects like Bhojpuri, Awadhi, and Brij etc.

The new lingua franca, which Gillion called "Fiji Bat",[13] became the language of the Indo-Fijians after the first generation of the *Girmitiyas*. They spoke their own languages along with the new dialect. In the course of time, the new language also adopted from Tamil and English and became in the words of Siegle "A form of Hindustani hardly recognized by the newcomer from India"[14]. Despite its links with the regional dialects and languages spoken in India at the time of indenture, Fiji Hindi has developed its own distinctive character. Even today Fiji Hindi is the main spoken language of Indo-Fijians but the language still lacks standardization and codification of grammar. It is, however, very popular among the youth too. And in spite of the English education and western influence it remains to be the main spoken language of the youth. Although they study "Shudh" Hindi with Devnagari script in schools, they tend to forget the language due to its non-use and have started using Roman script instead of Devnagari for Fiji Baat. Thus, one can see that socio- cultural formation of the Indo- Fijian society although originates basically from India but has developed its own unique features distinct from the Indian society.

Emergence as an Economic Force

As already discussed, Fiji is one of the most developed of the Pacific Island Economies and Indians have played a major role in that. Whether it is their contribution in, what JD Kelly calls, the first economy i.e., resource-oriented primary enterprises, such as, sugarcane growing, copra production, and gold mining as well as the Second economies like the Indian-owned businesses. While Fiji's economy has diversified in recent decades as a whole it is still dominated by its primary industry[15] and sugar industry has remained the backbone of the Fijian economy. The Indians have built the sugar industry of Fiji, and nearly 80 per cent of the tax revenue of Fiji is generated by the Fijians of Indian origin. Sugarcane was the main crop planted every year between hot and wet months of March and April. The major occupation of Indians was agriculture but there were some non-agricultural occupations also like storekeeping. It was mainly dominated by the Gujarati community and that too particularly by women. In the course of time, the storekeepers also started the work of money lending and became objects of hatred among the Indian community. Prof. Brij Lal has discussed the indenture life in his autobiographical piece *Mr. Tulsi's Store* that states how the store also became a centre for casual and social gatherings.[16] Both the Gujaratis and rest of the Indians have together developed the 'second economy' that established the Fiji Indians' place in Fiji. The arrangements turned first economy wages into second economy capital. While Fiji's economy is still heavily dependent on multinational corporations and European, Japanese owned businesses, the local economy has unquestionably been strengthened by the rise of the local Fiji Indian bourgeoisie and its enterprises.

The issue of land has remained a major problem in the Fiji's political and economic scenario. Conflict over land goes back to the colonial era, in the indigenous land ownership and management system. To protect the rights of the indigenous community a highly rigid ownership system was evolved by the British colonial regime in which initially the British and later the Indians were debarred from owning land and vested ownership primarily in the Matangali[17]. The peasant movement organized by the Indian agricultural class led several reforms such as in 1916 and 1940 when NLTB (Native Land Trust Board) were established to protect the community ownership of land to the Fijians and a systematic lease system for Indians. NLTB is the central authority for all communally owned units of land and it maintains an inventory of assets. It had the sole control over custom held land and this facilitated dealings between the major agriculturists of the time – the CSR and Indian Fijian growers – and the indigenous owners. Other than these the NLTBs main act is to collect rent. In 1976, a new act called the Agricultural Land Lord and Tenant Act (ALTA) was passed. It not only retained the powers of NLTB but also aimed at providing institutional and legal structure to the management of leases. Two main features of the ALTA that have today become important issues are the time length of the leases and the rental amount. It will be worth noting here that when the Indians took over the leases, the lands were crowded with huge trees and dumps of thick bushes. What should be taken note of here is that in all these reforms Indians acted as pressure groups for their implementation. After acquiring these lands Indians would work hard to make them usable. The company, sometime with aid and bullocks, also helped them. The Labour government when in power tried to bring the unused land under cultivation and realized that a definite leasing policy was needed to reform the system and do away with the corruption in the system.[18] A desire to enter into sugarcane production is also one of the reasons for the nonrenewable of leases by the Fijians. Another reason for the non-renewal of lease that the Fijians think that they have not received any direct benefit from the subsidy received from the European Union, which is true to some extent.[19]

Thus, one can say that much of the conflict on land is due to the difference in the opinions of the two communities. In the recent years, this conflict has been exalted due to the incomplete information and misinformation. Trust cannot be legislated. It can develop only when there is an effective communication, a shared understanding of the problem.[20] One point of view suggests a complete de-bureaucratization of the land in Fiji by removing a body like NLTB and make use of the land through market mechanism utilization. But it seems unlikely because the chiefs who serve the board and the council of chiefs have vested interest in protecting the status quo. Recognizing this fact, it is advisable to find alternative institutional arrangement. Each of two options under ALTA or NLTA has limitations. According to M. Reddy and others, a rental system based on the actual market value of land, which is equivalent to the present value of expected annual net returns to land, encourages the most efficient use of resources, provided the duration of the tenure is long term.[21]

The issue of Fijian land has always dominated the politics of Fiji also. The practical problems faced by both Fijians and Indians in the process of leasing out land and evolving a workable method for it was just one side of the coin. The other was the politicization of the issue and its use as a tool against the Indians. It was made an instrument to mobilize the ethnic Fijians against the Indians, during almost all the elections and also during the rule of both the Indian dominated governments in 1988 and 2000. Massive demonstrations were held under the Taukei banner against the government over the issue of land. In fact, the governments had done absolutely nothing to threaten any aspect of Fijians land. But it became an anticipatory issue, meaning that it was expected by the Fijians that sooner or later these governments would tamper with the Fijian land Tenure and operations of NLTB.[22] Thus, it can be said that the ruling elite, to maintain Fijian support base, used the "bogey of Indian land grab".[23] The coalition government of 1988, treaded cautiously over the issue of land. In its inaugural policy statement it said, "There will be no change in this recognition (of Fijian ownership rights) nor will the coalition government attempt to change the existing land laws without the full consolation of great Council of Chiefs.[24] However, the government did talk about opening up of the large areas of unused land and for granting secure leases on crown land. But the effort of the coalition to reforms the NLTB and its corrupt bureaucracy went against the ruling chiefly class, particularly from Eastern side, which dominated the NLTB. The common Fijians and the western Fijians perhaps supported this call. But an effort, for reforms, for the sake of efficiency and responsiveness was given a colour of racial conflict. In the words of Brij Lal, "But where the coalition felt afoul of the Fijian establishment was in its grass roots Fijians supported call for reforms in the bloated bureaucracy of the Native Land Trust board, a pillar of chiefly establishment, staffed by many Fijians of eastern provinces".[25]

Another aspect of the Fijian economy where Indo-Fijians have played a significant role is towards migration and remittances. Traditionally a non-remittance country Fiji is now becoming a remittance economy in the Pacific with thousands of citizens heading to work overseas. The volume of remittances in Fiji has increased since 2000. One distictive feature of the international migration in the Pacific is that migrants have typically tended to be settlers. However, temporary migrations are a growing trend in the recent times. According to Kate Hannan the "growth in remittances is a bright spot on Fiji's economic landscape".[26] Since the coups, emigration from Fiji has exhibited two main characteristics. The first is the dramatic increase in emigration since the coups of 1987, the bulk of the emigrants – about 90 per cent – have been Indo-Fijians. In more recent years, educated and skilled indigenous Fijians and other ethnic minority members of the middle class have begun leaving Fiji, but their numbers, while growing, are still small. The cost of emigration to Fiji, however, is well known. Fiji is estimated to lose, on average, $F44.5 million annually due to emigration, mainly through loss of skill, re-training new appointees, and delayed appointments.[27]

According to Manoranjan Mohanty, between 1987 and 1996, 5,100 Indo-Fijian professionals emigrated, of whom 21 per cent were architects, engineers, and related technicians, 15 per cent accountants, 31 per cent teachers, 12 per cent medical, dental, veterinary, and related workers, and 21 per cent other professionals. The impact of their loss on Fiji is visible and acutely felt, particularly in health and education. Once reasonably self-sufficient in medical personnel, Fiji now imports doctors from overseas. And there is a growing shortage of science and mathematics teachers as well. Continuing political turbulence in Fiji – roadblocks, urban crime, talk of another coup – will encourage more migration in the future[28]. Thus, the Indians worked hard to achieve economic prosperity and social status. Although initially they were focused more on their economic well-being but slowly they realized that to get maximum economic benefits also it was important to have political power and a say in the political process, which in turn proved beneficial for the socio-economic growth and development of the country.

Rise and Growth of Political Participation

As the Indian population increased and began to settle down in Fiji, its leaders started aspiring for a greater role in the politics of the country. In spite of the fact that the Indian community by and large accepted the supremacy of Fijian interest, the future uncertainties perhaps led them to assert themselves politically. In the early years of indenture the Indians kept aloof from the political events of Fiji as the rigorous life left them with little time and energy to get involved in political activities. They also lacked awareness towards political rights as at the time of their migration they hardly enjoyed any political rights in India. However, the birth of Indian politics in Fiji started with small gatherings and Ram Mandalis and had nothing to do with the government or opposition to it. Rather it was an attempt to seek redress from what was found irksome in the indenture system. These gatherings were held on Saturdays and Sundays where Ramayana was read and communal matters discussed, afterwards newspapers were circulated and collections taken up. In this way Indians maintained contact not only with each other but also with India and events there. However, they did not intend to plan uprisings or ferment discontent in the country.[29]

The initial trade union strikes and peasant movements started in 1920s. The grievances were general but the strike took a violent turn resulting in confrontations between police and the strikers. However, in spite of some minor gains these strikes came to an end without any substantial gains. But it did herald the beginning of political organization among Indians and the Indians hence onwards came to be received as a monolithic group.[30] Some of the early Indian leaders under whom these strikes were organized were Dr. Manilal and Sadhu Bashist Muni. These strikes, brought forward two major things as Dr. Brij V. Lal puts it, "first the defeated Indo-Fijian realized that to protect their economic interest, they would have to become politically assertive, secondly it exacerbated the social tensions as the government had employed Fijian constables against the strikers".[31] Hence these strikes acted as major stepping-stones towards the growth of political awareness among Indians and helped Indians to emerge as a cohesive force.

However, the real political struggle of Indians was towards the establishment of democratic system in Fiji. The constitution of 1904 presented a new challenge as it denied Indians the right to vote. Indians were given no representation in the Legislative Council while the European community got six seats and ethnic Fijians indirectly chose two chiefs. Hence, there arose the necessity to fight for political rights. Leaders started emerging from within the community who were completely devoted to political causes. In 1909 Indians in India were given the right to vote for electing their representatives to the Viceroy's Council, thereby giving a boost to the ongoing struggle for representation to Indians in Fiji.[32] The first tentative move towards the struggle for representation came in 1910, when the Indian community gave a petition to the government, which the government completely ignored. However, by that time Indians already had right to franchise at municipal level in some districts but in 1915 it was made limited only to those who could read and write English and an education test was prescribed for that.[33] The legislation was highly discriminatory as most of the Indians at that time were illiterate in English. However, as Stephanie Lawson puts it, "it had at least one important positive result. It provided an essential stimulus to Indian political consciousness and activity, as oppressive measures frequently do".[34] In 1916, the government decided to allow representation to the Indians in the legislative council.[35] But instead of appointing a candidate of Indian choice someone else was appointed.

The government of India on its part too was concerned about the political status awarded to Indians in these colonies along with their social and economic conditions. The issue of Indian enfranchisement was also closely linked to the abolition of the indentured system. When in 1920 the indenture system was finally abolished the colonial government still needed cheap labour. For this free immigrations were encouraged so living conditions were improved to attract the immigrants. The legislative council passed several resolutions related to the living conditions of the labours such as housing and medical, education and religious facilities. As Stephani Laweson sees it

Procuring franchise rights to the Indians was also a part of this preparation. Anyhow, the Indian community was given the right to elect two members to the legislative council. However, the issue of extending franchise rights to Indians was opposed, not only by Europeans, but also by ethnic Fijians.

But the Indian leaders kept insisting on the demand of common electorate. The government, however, remained opposed to any such possibility. It also faced strong opposition from the European and ethnic Fijian communities. They saw it as an attempt by the Indians to eventual political domination. The principle of common roll and "one man, one vote, one value", also went against the doctrine of "the Paramountcy of Fijian interests" established by the British to protect the social, economic and political rights of the ethnic Fijian people. Unfortunately, however, the Indians themselves were united on the issue, as there was a clear divide between Hindu and Muslims, Sanatanis and Arya Samajis. The Muslims from the very beginning under the leadership of Muslim League was keen to "take every precaution in safe guarding the interests of the Muslim minority community when political privileges are extended to the Indians of Fiji".[36] However, the Indian members of Legislative council continued their demand for the common roll. But democracy in a majoritarian form including the principle of one man, one vote, and one value was totally unacceptable to the European and Fijian community and had no supports in the colonial government of Fiji. During the World War II also the Indian demand for a greater political role and a common electoral roll continued putting a big question mark on the Indian loyalty towards the British. The developments in India during the national movement also had a great impact on the Indians in Fiji.

The decade of 1960s in Fiji also saw the formation of political parties for the first time in Fiji. Thus, one can see and as Stephanie Lawson points out that the party system, which emerged in 1966, gave institutional expression to the notion engendered throughout the colonial period that interest of Fiji Indians were essentially in opposition to those of the other racial communities and, most particularly to those of Fijians.[37] National Federation Party (NFP) emerged as the Indian Dominated party. Despite attempts to appeal to Fijians and to general voters, the NFP was never able to attract substantial level of support from the non-Indian sections of the electorate. A new constitution was adopted in 1965 but the system of communal rolls did not only continue but the idea of "two nations" even got reinforced.[38] The doctrine of "Paramountacy of Fijian interests" continued to dominate the Fijian politics and constitutional developments. Thus, the constitutional reforms failed to satisfy the Indo-Fijians and their quest for political equality continued.

Fiji got independence in 1970 and a new constitution came in force but the system of communal representation continued. The constitution gave any three nominees of 'Council of Chiefs', effective veto over any legislative attempt to interfere with core Fijian interests such as land, customs and way of life. The second General Elections were held in Fiji in 1977 in which NFP won the majority of seats. A clear-cut rift within the ranks of NFP and even after 4 days of the declaration of the results, NFP failed to put forward the name of the prime ministerial candidate. The emergence of the Labour, hence, was a natural corollary to situation when long rule of Alliance had made it arrogant towards the problems of common people. NFP, on its part, failed to take up the issues with the government or to put a unified front against the government. Being a multiracial party, they decided that an ethnic Fijian should lead the party. The issues taken up during the election campaign for 1987 elections were broad based and multiracial such as, corruption, wages, working condition, distribution of Fijian land among Matangalis, role of chiefs in the modern Fijian politics etc. However, Labour party also when in power failed to bring about any change in the existing scenario. It was only in the 1997 constitution that the numbers of communal seats were reduced and the open seats rose up to 25, which can be considered as a victory for the Indo Fijian Demand.

As a matter of fact, ethnic division had always dominated the politics of Fiji and had its root deeply embedded in the history. At the time of independence also the British failed to create a sustainable power sharing arrangement between Fijians and Indo Fijians. The so-called democratic political system, which was set up by the colonial masters, was discriminatory in it self and helped to institutionalize the supremacy of indigenous Fijians. During the colonial period, the Fijians never considered themselves colonized but believed that the British were their protectors and benefactors. As in the other colonies, Britain had ruled Fiji through dividing the people into various groups in not only political sphere but beyond it, into social, religious, educational, and others. The attempts to reconstruct a multi ethnic society was also thwarted by native politicians and interested groups. The Indians, also harbour a sense of injustice after the coups. There is a sense of personal insecurity among them. The rhetoric of Fijian paramountcy has made many younger generation Fijians believe that they are special citizens of the country, on the other hand, the Indians lament about the special privileges given to the Fijians, while the Indians pay the major taxes. The politicization of race, therefore, has aggravated the sense of insecurity amongst the Indo Fijians; it was their fight for survival, fight for a life, for respect and dignity, which led them to the path of success. It was their unwillingness to accept a subservient role that sharpened the already existing ethnic divides. The overthrow of Indian dominated governments in past coups, have sharpened the problem of ethnic divide in Fiji. Today, the question of power sharing and land remains the main economic and social problems. Thus, one can see that the emergence of Indians as a political force in Fiji was not an easy journey. It was full of struggle, difficulties and hardships. The 1997, Constitution Review Commission (CRC) participated by the Indo Fijian scholar produced a voluminous proposal for constitutional reform, *The Fiji Islands: Towards a United Future,* which recommended that Fiji move "gradually but decisively" away from communalism towards a free, open and multi-ethnic political system. Acknowledging that political parties in many ethnically-divided societies tend to be based around particular ethnic groups, the Commission's stated objective was "to find ways of encouraging all, or a sufficient number, of them to come together for the purpose of governing the country in a way that gives all communities an opportunity to take part"[39].

Conclusion

The journey of the Indo-Fijians towards social political and econoic development got intertwined with the development of Fiji, which led to its emergence as the most important Island nation of the South Pacific. As far as juxtaposing the Indo Fijians in the Fiji's history is concerned, the history books of the country completely ignore their contribution. There is almost no acknowledgement of their contributions to Fiji's development. As several of the scholars interpret, it was a deliberate attempt to undermine them. Whatever little literature is available, it is about the sufferings of the *Girmitiyas*. The legacy of the native policies continues to this very day, which undermines the role and contribution of the Indo Fijians right from the *Girmitiya* period to the present. The fact of the matter, however, is that had it not been Indo Fijians, Fiji would not have been known as a democratic republic with a successful multiracial social construct and a relatively better economy as compared to its Pacific counterparts.

Endnotes

1. Gillion, K. L. 1977. *The Fiji Indians: Challenges to European Dominance 1920-1946*, Canberra: Australian National University Press.
2. Singh, Bhagwan and Das P. K. 1995. *Fiji: The Changing Face*, Delhi: Har Anand Publications, p. 12.
3. See for example, Calvert, James. eds. 1985. *Fiji and the Fijians, 2, Mission History*, London: G Roue, p.1.
4. Singh, Bhagwan . *Op.Cit.*, p.6.
5. Ratuva, Steven. *The Paradox of Multi-Culturalism: An Assessment of Ethno-Political Conflict in Fiji*, Queensland, p. 16.
6. Berger, Peter and Luckmann Thomas, 1966. *The Social Construction of Reality: A Treatise in the Sociology of Knowledge*, Garden City, New York: Double days company Inc.

7. Mayer, A.C. 1961. *Peasants in the Pacific: A Study of Fiji Indian Rural Society*, London, p.5

8. Kelly, J. D. 1998. 'Fiji Indians and Political Discourse in Fiji: From the Pacific Romance to the Coups,' *Journal of Historical Sociology*, vol.1, March, p. 402.

9. Lal, Brij V. 2001. *Mr Tulsi's Store: A Fijian Journey*, Pandanus Books, p.31.

10. Lal, Brij V. 2000. *Chalo Jahaj*, The Fiji Museum Suva & The Australian National University, p. 57.

11. Lal, Brij V. 1992. *Broken Waves*, University of Hawaii Press, p. 40.

12. For details see Billimoria, Pursottama. 1985. 'The Arya Samaj in Fiji: A movement in Hindu Diaspora' and Kelly. 'A Politics of Virtue', *Religion*, vol. 15, pp. 103-129.

13. Gillion, K. L. 1977. *The Fiji Indians: Challenges to European Dominance 1920-1946*, Canberra: Australian National University Press.

14. Siegel, Jeff . 1998. 'Indian languages in Fiji: Past, Present and Future', *South Asia*, vol.21, (special issue), p. 201.

15. Kelly, John D. 1992. ' Fiji Indians and "Commoditization of Labor"', *American Ethnologist*, vol. 19, no. 1. Feb., p.99.

16. Mayer, A.C. 1961. *Peasants in the Pacific: A Study of Fiji Indian Rural Society*, London: Berkeley University, California Press.

17. Lal, P. and Reddy M. 'Old wine in a new bottle? Proposed sugar industry restructuring and land conflict in Fiji,' *Pacific Economic Bulletin*, vol.18, no. 1, p. 81.

18. Lal, Brij V. 1992. *Op.Cit.*,p. 102.

19. Rakai, M.E.T, Exizbalike I. C. and Williamson I.P., 1995. 'Traditional Land Tenure Issues for LIC in Fiji', *Survey Review*, vol 33, no 258, pp 24-76.

20. Lal, P. and Reddy M. *Op.Cit.*, p. 95.

21. Reddy, M. *Land Tenure Dilemma*, p. 16.

22. Premdas, Ralph R and Jefery S Steeves. 1991. 'Fiji Problems of Ethnic Discrimination and Inequality in the New Constitutional Order', *Round Table*, no. 318, p. 164.

23. Hegan, Stephanie. 1987. 'Race, Politics and the Coup in Fiji',

Bulletin of Concerned Asian Scholars, vol. 19, no. 4 Oct- Dec., p.3.

24. Lal, Brij.V.1998. 'Fiji Indians and the Politics of Exclusion', *Foreign Affair Report*, vol. 38, no. 7 & 8, July-August,p. 104.
25. *Ibid.* p. 104.
26. SSGM Conference Report On 'Globalisation, Governance and the Pacific Islands'.
27. Lal, Brij V. 2003. 'Country Profile', Migration Information Source, April.
28. Manoranjan Mohanty, As quoted in Brij V. Lal, country Profile, Migration Information Source, April 2003 see also, Mohanty, Manoranjan. 2005. 'Globalisation, New Labour Migration and Development in Fiji Islands', paper presented at State, Society and Governance in Melanesia Project Conference on *Globalisation, Governance and the Pacific Islands*, October 25-27, 2005, Australian National University, Canberra.
29. Ahmed Ali," Political Awareness Among Fiji Indians, 1879-1919," *Asian Profile*, vol.6, no.5, Oct. 1978, p. 478-479.
30. Singh, Shubha. 2001. *Fiji: A Precarious Coalition*, New Delhi: Har-Anand Publications Pvt Ltd p. 69.
31. Lal, Brij V.1992. *Op.Cit.*, p. 83.
32. *Ibid*, p. 480.
33. Fiji Legislative Council debates, 9 July 1915, p.90.
34. Lawson, Staphanie. *The Failure of Democratic Politics in Fiji*, p. 125.
35. Letters Patent dated 20 July 1916.
36. Annual Report and Resolutions of the Fiji Muslim League, CSO MP, 167/1929.
37. Staphanie Lawson, *Op.Cit.*, P 179.
38. See Fiji, Legislative Council Debates, 17 Dec 1965, pp. 707-8.
39. Constitution Review Commission 1996, p.308.

Bibliography

Access Economics. 2008. *Migrants Fiscal Impact Model: 2008 Update*, Department of Immigration and Citizenship, Canberra.

Ahe, Molly. 1978. *The Dance in Trinidad and Tobago.* Port of Spain: Golden Heritage, Heritages Culture Ltd., p. 72.

AIC- Department of Foreign Affairs and Trade (DFAT). 2009. 'About the Australia-India Council' http://www.dfat.gov.au/aic/aic_intro.html/accessed 12/4/2009.

Allen, Jr., Calvin. 1981. 'The Indian Merchant Community of Masqat'. *Bulletin of the School of Oriental and African Studies,* vol. 44, no. 1, pp. 39-51.

Al-Sayegh, Fatma. 1998. 'Merchants' Role in a Changing Society: The Case of Dubai, 1900-90'. *Middle Eastern Studies,* vol 34, no. 1, pp. 87-102.

Australia Dancing. 2009. 'Indian Dance in Australia', http://www.australiadancing.org/ subjects/3821.html. Accessed 9 October 2009.

Australia India Business Council .2009. 'What we do' http://www.aibc.org.au/Profile/ What_We_Do accessed 12/4/2009

Australian Bureau of Statistics (ABS). 2008. *Perspectives on Migrants: People Born in China and India.* Canberra: Australian Government.

Australian Bureau of Statistics (ABS)-1. 2009. *Australia Continues to Experience High Population Growth,* Australian Demographic Statistics. Canberra: Australian Government.

Australian Bureau of Statistics (ABS)-2. 2009. *Migration 2007-2008*, Australian Government, Canberra.

Australian Bureau of Statistics (ABS)-3. 2009. *Perspectives on Skilled Migrants*, Australian Government, Canberra, April.

Australian Bureau of Statistics (ABS)-4. 2009. *Australian Social Trends Expanding Links with China and India*, Australian Government, Canberra.

Australian Educational International-1. 2009. *Research Snapshot*, Australian Government, Canberra, June.

Australian Educational International-2. 2009. *International Student Enrolment Data Tables* 7a, 9a, 10a, Australian Government, Canberra.

Bajpai, Gita 2001. 'Colonialism and emigration: The movement of people from north India to Trinidad during 1870s and 1900.' Unpublished paper. Department of History, The University of the West Indies, St. Augustine, Trinidad.

Banham, Cynthia and Gilmore, Heath. 2009. 'Rudd forms Indian Violence Taskforce' *Sydney Morning Herald*, June 3.

Banks, Melissa and Alan Olsen, eds. 2008. *Outcomes of and Impacts of International Education: From International Students to Australian Graduates: The Journey of a Lifetime*, Canberra: IDP Education.

Bettelheim, Judith. 1980. 'Jamaican Jonkonnu and related Caribbean Festivals,' in M.E. Graham and F.W. Knights, eds. *Africa and the Caribbean*. London: John Hopkins Press, pp. 80-100.

Bharat Times. 2009. 'World first maternity concept store launched in Chadstone', September.

Bhatia, Tej. 1988. 'Trinidad Hindi: Its Genesis and Generational Profile', in Richard K. Barz and Jeff Siegel, eds. *Language Transplanted: The Development of Overseas Hindi*. Wiesbaden, Netherlands: Otto Harrassowitz, pp. 178-196.

Birbalsingh, Frank. 2000. *Jahaji: An Anthology of Indo-Caribbean Fiction*. Toronto: TSAR Publications.

Bollywood in Australia. 2009. 'India-Australia Film Relations: A Brief', http://bollywoodinaustralia.com/. Accessed date 9 October 2009.

Bound, Kirsten. 2007. *'India: The Uneven Innovator - The Atlas of Ideas: Mapping the New Geography of Science'*, London: Demos.

Brumby, J. 2009. 'Strengthening Relationships with India', Beyond India, October.

Business 3000 Winners. 2009. Category: Encouragement Award, http://www.b3000.org.au/winners-2009, Accessed 29 October 2009.

Buxani, Ram. 2003. *Taking the High Road*. Dubai: Motivate Publishers.

Castles, S. and Miller, M. J. 1998. *The Age of Migration: International Population Movements in the Modern World*, Second Edition, London: Macmillan.

Chandoo, Ann Marie. 1989. 'East Indian' Influence in the Language of Trinidad with Special Emphasis on Lexicon.' UWI, St. Augustine: Caribbean Studies Project.

Chandrabose. 2009. *Wage, Employment and Livelihood of the Plantation workers: A study on selected tea estates in Sri Lanka'*, sponsored by ADB/DEMP of OUSL 2009 (unpublished).

Chattopadhaya, Hariprasad. 1965. *Indians in Africa: A Socio-Economic Study*. Calcutta: Bookland Pvt. Ltd. pp. 350-364.

Chaudhri, K.N. 1986. *Trade and Civilization in the Indian Ocean: An Economic History from the Rise of Islam to 1950*. Cambridge: Cambridge University Press.

Cohen, Robin. 2001. *Global Diasporas: An introduction*. Oxon: Routledge.

Committee on Prospering in the Global Economy of the 21st Century. 2007. *An Agenda for American Science and Technology Rising Above the Gathering Storm: Energizing and Employing Americans for a Brighter Economic Future*. National

Academy of Sciences, National Academy of Engineering and Institute of Medicine of the National Academies, The National Academies Press, Washington D.C.

Coppin, Addington. 1997. 'Color in an English-Speaking Caribbean Labor Market'. *The Journal of Developing Areas.* vol.31, Spring, pp.399-410.

Das Gupta, Ashin.1985.'Gujrati Merchants and the Red Sea Trade, 1700-1726' in Blair B. Kling and M.N. Pearson. eds. *The Age of Partnership.* Honolulu, pp. 123-158.

Das, Sushi. 2009. 'Students rate Australia safest', *The Age,* 13 October.

Day, Natalie and Stilgoe, Jack. 2009. *Knowledge Nomads: Why Science Needs Migration,* London: Demos.

Department of Foreign Affairs (DFAT). 2009. *'India Fact Sheets'*, Australian Government, Canberra.

Department of Immigration and Citizenship (DIAC)-1. 2009. *'Abolition of White Australia Policy'*, Fact Sheet – 8, Australian Government, Canberra, http://www.immi.gov.au/media/fact-sheets/08abolition.htm. Accessed 6 November 2009.

Department of Immigration and Citizenship (DIAC)-2. 2009. *'Settlement Database Top 20 Countries by Migration Stream'*, Tailored settlement reports, Australian Government, Canberra, data extracted on 9 October 2009.

Department of Immigration and Multicultural Affairs (DIMA). 2000. Multicultural Australia: The India-born Community, Australian Government, Canberra.

Desai, R. 1963. *Indian Immigrants in Britain,* London: Oxford University Press.

Dubey Ajay. 2003. ed. *Indian diaspora: Global Identity.* New Delhi: Kalinga.

Dubey, Ajay. 2003. 'Indian Diaspora in the Francophone Africa', *Africa Quarterly,* vol 43, no.1, pp. 86-91.

Dubey, Ajay ed. 2003. *Indian Diaspora.* New Delhi: Kalinga Publications.

Dutt, R. C. 1969. *The economic history of India in the Victorian age, Vol. II.* New York: August M. Kelley Publishers.

Faria, Ana I. 2001. The future of Indian ethnicity in Australia: An educational and cultural perspective, *International Education Journal,* Educational Research Conference 2001 Special Issue, vol. 2, no. 4, pp. 134-143.

Favell, A. 1998. *Philosophies of integration: Immigration and the idea of citizenship in France and Britain.* London: Macmillan.

Favell, A. 1999. *Integration policy and integration research in Europe: a review and critique,* Report prepared for the Carnegie Endowment Comparative Citizenship Project.

Franklin, Robert Lee. 1985. *The Indian Community in Bahrain: Labor Migration in a Plural Society,* Ph.D. Thesis, Harvard University, University Microfilm International, Ann Arbor, MI.

Frederick Noronha. 1999. 'News Feature Goa: Goans in Mozambique', http://www.goacom.org/news/news99/sep/msg00013.html. Accessed on 23 June 2007.

Fuente, Angel dl and Ciccone Antonio. 2003. *'Human Capital in a Global and Knowledge-Based Economy: Assessment at EU Country level',* Part 2, Employment and Social Affairs, Employment and European Social Fund, European Commission, Directorate-General for Employment and Social Affairs, Brussels, April.

G'day India-1. 2009. 'Indian Consortium Invests $63 million in Australia', vol. 3, no. 30.

G'day India-2. 2009. 'Australia in panic as Indian students back out', vol. 3, no. 28.

G'day India-3. 2009. 'State Premier writes to Indian students', vol. 3, no. 29.

Gafar, John. 1998.'Growth, Inequality and Poverty in Selected Caribbean and Latin American Countries, with

Emphasis on Guyana'. *Journal of Latin American Studies*, vol. 30, pp. 591-697.

Gavin, R. J. 1975. *Aden Under British Rule, 1939-1967.* London: C. Hurst and Co.

Gibbons, Rawle A. 1979. *A Traditional Enactments of Trinidad: Towards a Third Theatre*. St. Augustine, University of the West Indies: M.Phil. Thesis.

Gillard, Julia. 2009. 'Australia India Institute to strengthen international ties', http://www/dewr.gov.au/Ministers/Gillard/MediaReleases /Pages/Article 090807_12. Accessed 9 October 2009.

Girdhari, Gary. 2007. 'Indo-Caribbean Writers" http://www.guyanajournal.com/icw.html. Accessed on 28 May.

Gopal, Surendra. 1998. 'Indian Diaspora in West, Central Asia and Russia in Medieval Times'. *Journal of Indian Ocean Studies*, vol 5, no.2, pp. 116-28.

Gosine, Mahin and Dhanpaul Narine, eds. 1999. *Sojourners to Settlers: Indian Immigrants in The Caribbean and the Americas.* New York: Windsor Press.

Gosine, Mahin, Dipak Malik and Kumar Mahabir. 1995. *The Legacy of Indian Indenture: 150 Years of Indians in Trinidad.* New York: Windsor Press.

Government of India, 2001. *Report of the High Level Committee on the Indian Diaspora*, New Delhi: Indian Council of World Affairs.

Government of India. 2001. *High Level Committee Report on the Indian Diaspora*. Indian Council of World Affairs, New Delhi.

Government of India. 2001. Report of High Level Committee on Indian Diaspora. www.indiandiaspora.nic.in

Grant, K.J. 1923. *My Missionary Memories*. Halifax, Nova Scotia, p.69.

Hawthorne, Lesleyanne -2. 2007. Outcomes: Language, employment and further study, Canberra, Australia Educational International, Australian Government, Canberra.

Hawthorne, Lesleyanne-1. 2007. 'Labour market outcomes for migrant professionals: Canada and Australia comparison', Citizen and Canada, Government of Canada, Ottawa.

High Commission of India in Australia (The). 2009. 'Indian Community in Australia', http://www.hcindia-au.org/indian_in_australia.html. Accessed 5 November 2009.

'Hinduism in Madagascar', http://en.wikipedia.org/wiki/Hinduism_in_Madagascar. Accessed on 30 May 2007.

High Commissioner of India. 2003. *From Indentureship to Entrepreneurship: East Indians and the Socio-Economic Transition in the Caribbean*. Port of Spain: High Commission of India.

Huxley, John. 2008. 'Bollywood film makers turn sport into art', *The Age*, 9 January.

IDP international, 2009. 'Australia still number one for safety survey', presentation to international education conference, 12 October, http://www.aiec.idp.com/medi_releases.aspx. Accessed 29 October 2009.

Indian Voice. 2009. 'Can a mono-cultural police force gain the trust of a multicultural community? July.

Indo-Caribbean Cultural Council. 2006. *Divali: The Spendour of Divali*. San Juan, Trinidad, vol. 8, no. 2.

Indo-Caribbean Cultural Council. 2006. *Indian Arrival Day: Indian Indentureship on Cocoa, Coconut and Rubber Plantations in Trinidad (1845 – 1917)*. San Juan, Trinidad, vol. 8, No. 2.

Isaacman, Allen and Isaacman, Barbara. 1983. *Mozambique: From Colonialism to Revolution, 1900-1982*. United States: West View Press.

Jabbal, Preeti. 2009. 'Making it in a man's world' News Makers in Oz media' Interview with Sushi Das of The Age, *Indian Link*, September.

Jain, Prakash C. 1989. 'Emigration and Settlement of Indians Abroad', *Sociological Bulletin*, vol.38, no.1.

Jain, Prakash C. 2003. 'Culture and Economy in an "Incipient" Diaspora: Indians in the Persian Gulf Region', in

Bhikhu Parekh, Gurharpal Singh and S. Vertovec. eds. *Culture and Economy in the Indian Diaspora*. London: Routledge, pp. 102-124.

Jain, Prakash C. 2004. 'Indians in the United Arab Emirates'. *Gulf Studies Programme*, Centre for West Asian and African Studies, School of International Studies, Jawaharlal Nehru University, New Delhi.

Jain, Prakash C.ed. 2007. *Indian Diaspora in West Asia: A Reader*. New Delhi: Manohar Publishers & Distributors.

Jain, Ravindra K.2003. 'A Civilisation Theory of Indian Diaspora and its Global Implications' in Dubey. ed. New Delhi: Kalinga Publication.

Jain, Surinder. 2009. 'Evolving History of Indian Arrival in Australia: Indian arrival in Australia', http://indians.australians.com/indian-arrival-in-australia.htm. Accessed 21 September 2009.

Jayawardena, K. 1986. *Ethnic and Class Conflict in Sri Lanka*. Colombo: Centre for Social Analysis.

Juliet, Chectam. 1972. *Social Work with Immigrants*. London: Routledge and Kegan Paul ltd.

Kader. B.A. 2002. 'Genesis of the Plantation Trade Unions', *Voice of the voiceless*, Vol. 22.

Kanitkar, H. 1972. 'An Indian Elite in Britain', *New Community*, vol.1, p.378-83.

Karnik, Sharmila S. 1998. 'Goans in Mozambique', *Africa Quarterly*, vol.38, no.3, pp. 95-118.

Karnik, Sharmila. 2000. 'Advent of Portuguese in Mozambique', *Africa Quarterly*, vol. 40, no. 2, pp. 117-135.

Kour, Z.H. 1981. *The History of Aden, 1839-72*. London: Frank Cass.

Krueger, Alan B and Lindahl, Mikael. 2001. 'Education for Growth: Why and for Whom?', *Journal of Economic Literature*, vol. 39, no. 4, pp. 1101-36.

Lal, Brij V., Peter Reeves, Rajesh Rai. 2007. eds. *The*

Encyclopedia of the Indian Diaspora. Singapore, Kuala Lampur. Paris: Editions Diddier Millet in Association with National University of Singapore.

Lal, Brij V.et. al. 2006. *The Encyclopedia of Indian Diaspora.* Singapore: Editions Didier Millet.

Lal, Vinay. 1996. 'Reflections on the Indian Diaspora in the Caribbean and Elsewhere'. *New Quest,* May-June.

Leadbeater, Charles and Wilsdon, James. 2007. *The Atlas of Ideas: How Asian Innovation can Benefit us All,* London: Demos.

Leguen, M. 1979. *Histoire de Ile de la Reunion.* Editions de L'Harmattan: Paris.

Lorimer, J.G.1970. *Gazetteer of the Persian Gulf, Oman and Central Arabia, I Historical Part-2,* Calcutta: Government Printing, Calcutta.

Mahabir, Kumar. 1984. "The influence of the tassa in the making of the steelband: The East Indian contribution to the Trinidad Carnival." Trinidad: Phagwa East Indian Cultural Promotions Brochure, pp. 12-22.

Mahabir, Kumar. 1985. *The Still Cry: Personal Accounts of East Indians in Trinidad and Tobago during Indentureship (1845-1917).* New York: Calaloux Publications, p. 152.

Mahabir, Kumar. 1991. *Medicinal and Edible Plants used by East Indians of Trinidad and Tobago.* San Juan, Trinidad: Chakra Publishing House.

Mahabir, Kumar. 1991. *Caribbean East Indian Recipes.* San Juan, Trinidad: Chakra Publishing House.

Mahabir, Kumar. 2005. *Caribbean Indian Folktales.* San Juan, Trinidad: Chakra Publishing House.

Mahase, Radica. 1996. "The Potential of Hindi as a Language of Study in the Curriculum in Trinidad." UWI, St. Augustine: Caribbean Studies Project.

Mahavir, Vasant. 1993. 'Community of Non-resident Indians and People of Indian Origin in the Netherlands', in *Global Indian Diaspora: Yesterday, Today and Tomorrow,* Jagat K.

Motwani et al., eds. New York: Global Organisation of People of Indian Origin.

Mangru, Basdeo. 1999. *Indians in Guyana: A Concise History from their Arrival to the Present*. Chicago, Illinois: Adams Press.

Manpower. 2008. *'India's Borderless Workforce: A Manpower White Paper'*, Developed in Collaboration with Laveeesh Bhandari and Payal Malik, Indicus Analytics, New Delhi.

Mansingh, Laxmi and Ajai Mansingh. 1999. *Home Away From Home: 150 Years of Indian Presence in Jamaica 1845-1995*. Kingston, Jamaica: Ian Randle Publishers.

Markovits, Claude. 2000. *The Global world of Indian Merchants, 1950-1947: Traders of Sind from Bukhara to Panama*. Cambridge: Cambridge University Press.

Mohanty, Sasmita. 2007. 'Indian Diaspora in Mozambique and Madagascar: A Comparative Analysis'. Unpublished M. Phil Dissertation Submitted to Jawaharlal Nehru University, New Delhi.

Mohideen. M.S.A.H.1995. '100 Years of Trade Unionism in Sri Lankan and its Impact on the Plantations' in *Trade Union Centenary in Sri Lanka*, Mt. Lavania: Worker Educators' Association of Sri Lanka.

Motwani, Jagat K. Mahin Gosine and Jyoti Barot-Motwani, eds. 1993. *Global Indian Diaspora: Yesterday, Today and Tomorrow*. New York: Global Organisation of People of Indian Origin.

'Mozambique: Ministry of Overseas Indian Affairs', http://www.indiandiaspora.nic.in/. Accessed on 24 May 2006.

Nadesan. S. 1993. *History of Up Country Tamil People in Sri Lanka*. Hatton: Nandalala Publications.

Newsday.1998. Ahamad , Riyaz. 'Chairman's Message', 12 July, p. 2.

Niranjana, Tejaswini. 2006. *Mobilizing India: Women, Music and Migration Between India and Trinidad*. Durham, NC: Duke University Press.

OECD. 2009. 'International Migration Database: OECD Stat Extracts', Organisation for Economic Co-operation and Development, Paris, http://stats.oecd.org/index.aspx?lang=eng. Accessed 30 October 2009.

OECD-1. 2008. '*Science, Technology and Industry Outlook*', Organisation for Economic Co-operation and Development, Paris

OECD-2. 2008. '*The Global Competition For Talent: Mobility of the Highly Skilled*', Organisation for Economic Co-operation and Development, Paris.

Olsen, Reed Neil and Addington Coppin. 2001. 'The Determinants of Gender Differentials in Income in Trinidad and Tobago'. *The Journal of Development Studies*. vol.37, no.5, June, pp.31-56.

Pala, Adavjee Anilkumar. 2003. 'Indian Community in Madagascar', *Africa Quarterly*, vol. 43, no. 1, p. 99.

Pariag, Florence. 2004. *East Indians in the Caribbean*. Kingston, Jamaica: Arawak Publications.

Parke, Melissa. 2009. 'More to relation with Indian than curry and cricket', *Daily Telegraph*, 18 August, http://www.daily telegraph.com.au/news/breaking-news/more-to-relationship-with-india-than-cricket-and-curry/story-e6freuyi-1225763324890. Accessed 12 October 2009.

Persaud, Harry, ed. *Indian Frontiers – With Special Reference to Guyana*. Toronto, Canada. Vol. 1, No 1.

Pillai, P. 1999 'The Malaysian state's response to Migration', *Sojourn*, vol.14, no.1, pp.178-97.

Pillai, Suresh Kumar. 2003. *Indentured Indians*. New Delhi: Siewdass Sadhu Cultural Center.

Prakash, Jeevan. 2005. *An Autobiography of an Indian Labourer Munshi Rahaman Khan (1874-1972)*. Delhi: Shipra Publications.

Productivity Commission. 2002. '*Skill and Australia's Productivity Surge*', Australian Government, Canberra.

Ramharack, Baytoram. 2001. *Centenary Celebration of the Arrival of Indians to British Guiana (1838 – 1938): The British Guiana East Indian Association.* San Juan, Trinidad: Chakra Publishing House.

Ramharack, Baytoram. 2005. *Against the Grain: Balram Singh Rai and the Politics of Guyana.* . San Juan, Trinidad: Chakra Publishing House.

Ramnarine, Tina K. 2001. *Creating Their Own Space: The Development of Indian-Caribbean Musical Tradition.* Jamaica: University of the West Indies Press.

Ramnath, Harry. 1980. *India Came West.* Marabella: Self-published.

Rampersad, Kris. 2003. *Finding a Place: Indo-Trinidadian Literature.* Kingston, Jamaica:Ian Randle Publishers.

Ranahan, Demerris C. 1981. *Contributions of Women in Medicine.* USA, Dillion Press.

Rath, J. 1999. 'The Netherlands. A Dutch treat for antisocial families and immigrant ethnic minorities', in M. Cole and G. Dale .eds. *The European Union and Migrant Labour,* Oxford: Berg Publishers, pp. 147-170.

Rath, J. 2001. 'Research on Immigrant Ethnic Minorities in the Netherlands' in Ratcliffe.ed. *The politics of social science research. Race, ethnicity and social change.* New York: Palgrave.

Report of High Level Committee on Indian Diaspora, 2001. *'The Indian Diaspora'*, Ministry of External Affairs, Government of India, New Delhi.

Reuters India. 2009. 'Indian students protest in Australia against attacks', 7 June, http://in.reuters.com/article/topNews/idINIndia-40139420090607. Accessed 2 November 2009.

Robinson, Vughan. 1990. "Boom and Gloom: The Success and Failure of South Asians in Britain", in Colin Clarke et al.eds., *South Asians Overseas,* Cambridge: Cambridge University Press.

Sabaratnam. T. 1990. *Out of Bondage- An autobiography of Thondaman*. Colombo: Ceylon Workers Congress.

Sahadevan. P. 1995. *India and overseas Indians, the case of Sri Lanka*. Delhi: Kalinga Publications.

Samaroo Siewah and Sattie Arjoonsingh, eds. 1996. *Basdeo Panday: The Making of a Prime Minister - Selected Speeches (1976-1996)*. San Juan, Trinidad: Chakra Publishing House.

Samaroo, Brinsley, Kusha Haracksingh, Ken Ramchand, Gérard Besson and Dianne Quentrall-Thomas, eds. 1995. *In Celebration of 150 Years of the Indian Contribution to Trinidad and Tobago*. Port of Spain, Trinidad: Historical Publications Limited.

Seecharan, Clem. 1997. *Tiger in the Stars: The Anatomy of the Indian Achievement in British Guiana 1919-29*. London: MacMillan Education Ltd.

Seesaran, Rosabelle E.B. 2002. *From Caste to Class: The Social Mobility of the Indo – Trinidadian Community 1870-1917*. Penal, Trinidad: Rosaac Publishing House.

Singh, Gurmukh. 2009. 'I am in the race to become Governor: Indian American Woman', G'day India, vol. 3, no. 28.

Sinnathanmby. M and Vijesundaram. S .2004. 'Economic Dimensions for Non- Territorial Communities' in Devaraj. P. eds. *Rights & Power sharing Mechanism for Non Territorial Minority Communities in Sri Lanka*. Colombo: Friedrich Ebert Stiftung.

Sookdeo, Neil A. 2000. *Freedom, Festivals and Caste in Trinidad after Slavery: A Society in Transition*. USA: Xlibris Corporation.

Sookdeo, Sandra. 1994. *Indian Dance in the Caribbean*. San Juan, Trinidad: Chakra Publishing House.

Speech opening the exhibit on the 'Art, Culture and Social Reality' at the Wits Spring Festival,University of Witwatersrand, 1991, http://www.anc.org.za/un/reddy/culture.html. Accessed on September 2008.

Steele, Peter. 2008. 'Miles and More: Highly Skilled Migration, Global Innovation Culture and the question of Regional Embeddedness' in Ajaya K Sahoo and K Laxmi Narayan, eds, *Indian Diaspora Trends and Issues*, New Delhi: Serials Publications.

Thaniyayagam, Xavier S. 1968. *Tamil Migrations to Guadeloupe and Martinique, 1853 to1883*. Paper presented at Second International Conference Seminar of Tamil Studies. Madras.

Thompson Virgina and Richard Adloff. 1965. *The Malagasy Republic*. Stanford, California : Stanford University Press.

Thondaman. S. 1994. Tea and Politics, My life and times Vol 1, An autobiography, Colombo: Navarang and Vijitha Yapa Publications.

Thondaman.S .1987. *My life and times Vol 1, An autobiography*. Colombo: Ceylon Workers Congress.

Tiffins. 2009. 'About us', http://www.tiffins.com.au. Accessed 16 October 2009.

Tinker, Hugh 1990. 'Indians in Southeast Asia: Imperial Auxiliaries', in Colin Clarke et al. eds., *South Asians Overseas: Migration and Ethnicity*, Cambridge: Cambridge University Press.

Tinker, Hugh. 1974. *A New System of Slavery. The Export of Indian Labours Overseas, 1830-1920*, London: Oxford University Press.

Tinker, Hugh. 1977. *Banyan Tree: Overseas Emigrants from India, Pakistan and Bangladesh*. London: Oxford University Press.

Tsukamoto, K. 2009. 'The interconnections between Australia's international education industry and its skilled migration programs' in J Fegan and M H Field, eds, *Education Across Borders: Politics, Policy and Legislative Action*, Dordrecht: Springer.

Vamadevan. M. 1987. *Socio-Economic conditions of Sri Lankan Repatriates in Tamil Nadu*, A research report, Trichirapalli: NORAD.

VenuGopal, R. 2009. 'Danny-guide for international students', *Bharat Times*, October.

Vertovec, S. 1999 'Conceiving and researching transnationalism', *Ethnic and Racial Studies* , vol.22, no.2. 445-62.

Vijayanathan. L .2005. *Development Dilemmas of Indian Origin Tamils in Sri Lanka: Politics and Violence in Relation to Human Security*. Foundation for Community Transformation, Colombo.

Voight-Graf, Carmen. 2005. 'The construction of transnational spaces by Indian migrants in Australia', *Journal of Ethnic and Migration Studies,* vol. 31, no. 2, pp. 365-384.

Wink, A. 1990. *Al Hind: The Making of Indo-Islamic World,* vol.1, *Early Medieval India and the Expansion of Islam,* 7-11th Centuries, Leiden: University of Leiden Press.

www.axess.se/english/archive/2004/no2/currentissue/theme-indiawork

www.cqoj.typepad.com/chest/2005/02/english_version.html

www.freebase.com/view/en/indians_in_guadeloupe

www.indiawijzer.nl/business-and-india/articles/presentation-pk.htm

Xavier, Constantino Hermanns. 2006. 'A Little Goa in Southern Africa', Unpublished Seminar Paper presented in CIPOD, School of International Studies, Jawaharlal Nehru University, New Delhi.

Yellow Pages-1. 2009. 'Restaurants Indian - all states', http://www.yellowpages.com.au/. Accessed 2 November 2009.

Yellow Pages-2. 2009. 'Yoga - all states', http://www.yellowpages.com.au/. Accessed 2 November 2009.

York University. 1988. *East Indians in the Caribbean 150th Anniversary, 1838-1988*. Toronto: York Indo-Caribbean Studies Conference.

York University. 1990. *3rd Annual Indo- Caribbean Heritage Day*. Ontario: Ontario Society for Studies in Indo-Caribbean Culture.